The 9/11 Mystery Plane

and the Vanishing of America

Mark H. Gaffney

Foreword by Dr. David Ray Griffin

Published by:
Trine Day LLC
PO Box 577
Walterville, OR 97489
1-800-556-2012
www.TrineDay.com

Library of Congress Control Number: 2008907274

Gaffney, Mark H.
The 9/11 Mystery Plane and the Vanishing of America / Mark H. Gaffney—1st ed.
p. cm. (acid-free paper)
Includes references and index.
(ISBN-13) 978-0-9799886-0-8 (ISBN-10) 0-9799886-0-8
1. September 11 Terrorist Attacks, 2001 2. War on Terrorism, 2001 3. Terrorism investigation—United States 4. Conspiracies—United States—History—21st Century 5. United States—Politics and Government—2001. 1. Title
HV6432.7.G   937.931—dc22

FIRST EDITION
10 9 8 7 6 5 4 3 2

Printed in the USA
Distribution to the Trade by:
Independent Publishers Group (IPG)
814 North Franklin Street
Chicago, Illinois 60610
312.337.0747
www.ipgbook.com

— Publisher's Foreword —

What a world we live in! How much of it is of our own making? Are there possibly deep currents of a corruption that channel managed confrontations towards a contrived reality misusing our fears, our prejudices, our ignorance and, insidiously, even our hopes, as shackles of manipulation, and subjugation?

We all, on that fateful Tuesday, watched in shock and horror as the images of tragedy kept flashing into our brains over and over and over and over again. For days the replays were constant, new views, different angles, if not on TV, then in our heads: Airliners enveloped by explosions smashing sleekly into skyscapers. Planes loaded with people ripping mightily into a busy workplace.

Traumatic — leaving a grieving nation in shock and ... easy to mislead.

Much angst, blood and treasure have been spent and our collective weals and freedoms have since morphed into an endless war-footing, *demanding* a limitation of personal liberties, the application by the state of torture, the stultification of habeas corpus, and a dictatorial executive. A country lost, where we the people, are given false witness, and then asked to supply the funds for battle, the fodder for the cannons and moral support for endless war.

With this book, Mark Gaffney chronicles, as he puts it, "... an unraveling, the likes of which we have never seen in our history," about how "... the official story about that terrible day [the day that changed everything] is disintegrating." Need we say more ...

Mark brings together the research and hard documentation that leaves one facing questions that most of us would rather not think about, let alone deal with. But engage we must, for if we the people shall ever hope to direct our own destiny ... there is business that needs to be taken care of.

So do read on, and please mark my words: never believe everything you read, but do take what you discover and think for yourself. Don't simply be told what to think, believe or do. Investigate, spend some time (it won't take long), if not for yourself, for your country, for your children, for ... our world. Let us join with others in conversation, discourse and investigation; as history has shown, we the people can make a difference. To effect lasting change we need to gather understanding about the webs of perfidy, deceit and bamboozlement surrounding us. This book is a good beginning ... the end is in all of our hands.

Onward to the utmost of futures!

Peace,

Kris Millegan
Publisher
September 22, 2008

This book is dedicated to the many victims of 9/11, both at home and abroad. Their number is not limited to the nearly 3,000 who perished on the day of the "attack," but include more than 4,000 dead American soldiers (as of this writing) and numberless dead Iraqis and Afghanis.

— Acknowledgments —

This book would never have happened without the magnificent contributions of numerous individuals. However, among the many, several were especially generous with their time, ideas, and information. I am particularly indebted to Bob ("Pinnacle"), an indefatigable investigator who was one of the first to recognize the importance of the mystery plane. John Farmer not only contributed his expertise but also generated cool graphic images for the discussion of the 9/11 radar data. Indeed, chapter four was only possible thanks to his invaluable assistance. My thanks also to Robin Hordon and Colin Scoggins, who provided professional expertise about the FAA. Others who gave feedback or provided assistance include Marco Bollettino, Chris Bornag, Linda Brookhart, David Ray Griffin, Eric Douglas, Daniele Ganser, Jim Hoffman, Rebecca McNerney, Ken Jenkins, Ian Henshall, Frank Legge, Kevin Ryan, Steven Jones, Gary Nichols, Joel Meyerowitz, Rowland Morgan, Barbara Honegger, Matt H. (BoneZ), Ron Hamburger, Bob Bowman, Jack Yolam, Bill and Kathy Christison, Paul Balles, Louis "Butch" Nagel (who regularly threw hundred-dollar bills in my direction), my webmaster Kirk Oakes, my neighbor Ed Atkin (my reader), and (last but not least) my old friend Garry Lambrev. I sincerely apologize to anyone I may have inadvertently forgotten. I am solely responsible for any errors that mar the book.

— Table of Contents —

Author's Preface to the Second Printing

To the extent that writing explores the unknown, the process of writing often takes on a life of its own, with unexpected twists and turns, and little regard for human timetables. This includes the realities of the publishing world.

In July-August 2008, as the publication deadline drew near for *The 9/11 Mystery Plane*, Freedom of Information Act (FOIA) requests filed, long before, by my colleague Bob Pinnacle finally bore fruit in a flurry of just-released FAA documents. This new evidence finally confirmed that two US Air Force E-4B command and control planes did indeed take off from Andrews Air Force Base on the morning of September 11, 2001. Also known as the "doomsday plane", the E-4B is the world's most advanced electronics platform. The first E-4B (call sign: SWORD 31, or: WORD 31) lifted off the runway at Andrews at 9:26 AM (eastern time), about twelve minutes before the Pentagon strike. The second E-4B (call sign: VENUS 77) lifted off at 9:44 AM, six minutes after the Pentagon strike.

This information came into our hands just days before *The 9/11 Mystery Plane* went to press.

At the time, I thought we were fortunate to go with what we had. However, 20-20 hindsight can be brutal, like a slap in the face. Looking back, it's clear I needed more time to sift through the disparate and at times contradictory evidence discussed in chapter four. Revisiting this portion of the book now is a painful experience for me, and I must caution the reader to view it not as the last word, but as a moment in a continuing investigation. I will now add a brief summary of what we subsequently learned.

In September 2008, several weeks after the book went to press, my colleague John Farmer visited Washington and retraced my steps at the White House. In the process of double-checking my research on site, Farmer found something I had missed; and as a result of his discovery we now believe that Linda Brookhart, who captured the photo on the front-cover of the book, was facing generally north when she snapped the shot of the doomsday plane, not southeast as I stated in the first printing. The photo was a key piece of evidence, and I regret to say that my interpretive error led me into a blind alley of speculations.

I had experienced no difficulty locating the building in the Brookhart photo during my earlier trip to Washington. The building has a unique corner facade, and I found it after a ten-minute foot search through the streets of Washington: a triangular shaped structure just one block north-west of the White House, on the corner of Pennsylvania Avenue and 18th Street. At the time, I concluded that when Ms. Brookhart snapped the shot she was standing on this corner looking back down Pennsylvania Avenue (southeast toward the White House). This appeared to be consistent with press reports, and would have placed the E-4B almost directly above the presidential mansion.

However, during his own subsequent visit to Washington Farmer discovered that the building actually has two identical corners! The other corner facade is at the south end of the building. Farmer concluded that Linda Brookhart probably had been standing near this other facade, facing north along 18th Street when she snapped the picture; because this orientation just happens to jibe perfectly with the known flight path of the second E-4B (VENUS 77), that morning. The 9/11 radar data shows that VENUS 77 passed over downtown Washington about two miles north of the White House at 9:47 AM, on a northwest heading.

In the end, I had to agree with Farmer.

Deciphering the Brookhart photo did not resolve all issues, however. VENUS 77 does not explain ABC news anchor Peter Jennings' report, that morning, of a plane over the White House. The problem is that when Jennings aired his report on national television at 9:41 AM, VENUS 77 was still sitting on the tarmac at Andrews AFB——it had not yet even departed. The ABC report of a plane over the White House has never been explained. It remains one of the bona fide 9/11 mysteries.

The same can be said of Department of Energy analyst Rebecca Mc-Nerney's testimony. McNerney told me that sometime after the Pentagon strike she observed a large military aircraft flying very low, eastward up the Mall toward the Capitol. Although she identified the aircraft as an E-4B, her account is unsupported: There is no radar track of a plane flying up the Mall to the Capitol.

Senior NBC correspondent Bob Kur's eyewitness testimony is also hard to explain. On the morning of September 11, 2001, Kur was at the White House, and at 9:54 A.M. he told Katie Couric on national television that a large white plane had been seen circling near the presidential mansion. Kur's on-air dialogue with Couric was interrupted in dramatic fashion by the sudden collapse of World Trade Center Two.

Although Bob Kur declined to be interviewed for THE 9/11 MYSTERY PLANE, when I caught up with him again in November 2010 he agreed to respond to questions. I shared the 9/11 radar data with him, at that time, including the known flight path of VENUS 77. I was surprised by Kur's response: "It seems inconsistent with other information you have ... but to me ... right there near 1600 Pa. Ave., it [i.e., the white plane] seemed *very close ... very unusually close and low.*"

I followed up with another round of questions. I wanted to tease out as many details as possible. When I asked Kur "Where in the sky did you observe the plane?" he replied, "I recall my back being toward the White House ... in or very near the park [i.e. Lafayette Park] ... looking up and seeing the plane to my right in the sky."

Kur was unable to remember which way the plane was moving, but he insisted he had seen a jumbo jet, meaning, a Boeing 747. This was the correct answer——an E-4B is a modified Boeing 747. Yet I was surprised, nonetheless, because, as noted, VENUS 77 never approached closer than two miles from the White House. From where Kur stood the craft would have been small in the sky, about the size of the white plane in the Brookhart photo. So, how did he manage to identify the E-4B from this distance? And why did Kur describe it as "very unusually close"? We do not know.

Nor have we resolved the big question: Why two US Air Force command and control planes were flying around in the skies over Washington during the 9/11 terrorist attacks. Although one and perhaps both of the E-4Bs had been participating in Global Guardian, an annual war game military exercise, this does not explain why VENUS 77 flew over downtown Washington, through the most restrictive airspace on the planet. Nor does it explain SWORD 31's close fly-by of the incoming aircraft that struck the Pentagon (presumably American Airlines 77). On October 11, 2008, a former intelligence officer named Miles Kara informed me that SWORD 31 and American Airlines Flight 77 had passed in opposite directions over northern Virginia, "like ships in the night." In his email, Kara, who prepared the radar analysis for the 9/11 Commission, referred to this strange fly-by as "the compelling 'snapshot' of the day"; a curious phraseology, to say the least.

For more than a year after the release of the first printing, I administered a web site (The911mysteryplane.com) where I posted updates on the issues raised in the book. By late 2009 the site was attracting a lot of attention. It had begun to receive a lot of "hits" on the Internet. However, in February 2010, the site was attacked and taken down by unknown hackers or spooks, which, in my opinion, suggests that my E-4B research was on the right track.

The Lies of the Mighty

by David Ray Griffin

What if Americans had concrete evidence that our top officials in the Pentagon, both civilian and military, had lied about 9/11? How would we react?

That would depend, surely, on the nature of the lie. Some lies we would dismiss as of little consequence. We could understand, for example, if Pentagon officials had lied simply to cover up some mistake they had made. Such lies, most of us probably assume, are told all the time.

But what if the lie were such that we could understand it only as an attempt to cover up something far worse — something which might mean that our entire foreign policy, and much of our domestic policy, since 9/11 had been based on a lie about what really happened on that fateful day?

This book by Mark Gaffney is about an episode that provides concrete evidence of such a lie.

The episode involved a large white airplane flying over the White House at the time of the attack on the Pentagon. This "mystery plane" was reported that day by CNN, ABC, and NBC, but then largely forgotten. The *9/11 Commission Report* did not mention it.

In 2006, however, an independent researcher in the greater Los Angeles area notified his congressman, Adam Schiff, about this plane, asking him to write to the U.S. Air Force about it. Schiff did so and received a letter, dated November 8, 2006, saying, "Air Force officials have no knowledge of the aircraft in question."

Almost a year later, on September 12, 2007, television journalist John King, who had given the CNN report about the plane on 9/11, presented a new report on *Anderson Cooper 360°* that showed that reply by the Air Force to be a lie. He gave irrefutable proof, by means of film and testimony from a retired Air Force officer, that the plane was a U.S. Air Force plane with the most advanced electronic capabilities.

Why did this revelation provide evidence that the official story about 9/11 was false? Because part of that story was that the attack on the Pentagon, said to have been a strike by American Flight 77, was a complete surprise. One official said, "The Pentagon was simply not aware that this aircraft was coming our way."

That was the reason given for not evacuating the Pentagon. This was a serious issue, because 125 people in the Pentagon were killed, and 92 of these were on the first floor. Therefore, if an evacuation order had been issued even a minute or so before the attack, most of those people probably would have escaped death. Pentagon officials were excused from culpability for those deaths on the assumption that the attack was a surprise — that they had no idea that an aircraft was bearing down on the Pentagon.

The revelation of the Air Force plane, with its extraordinary capacities, flying over the White House, just a few miles away, undermines this claim. According to the official report put out by the National Transportation Safety Board, the attacking airplane executed a 330-degree downward spiral before striking the Pentagon, and this spiral took 3 minutes and 2 seconds. Even if this plane did not have the means to prevent the attack, it certainly would have had time to tell officials in the Pentagon to evacuate the building.

Besides showing the claim that the attack was a surprise to be a lie, the revelation of the plane's presence over the White House provided the occasion for military officials to tell another lie. Having already lied to Congressman Schiff, Pentagon officials repeated the lie to CNN. As John King said, "Ask the Pentagon, and it insists this is not a military aircraft." For Pentagon officials to continue to lie about this, in the face of indisputable evidence to the contrary, suggests that they are covering up something that dare not be revealed and are, in fact, telling news agencies to back off and quit reporting about the episode. The news agencies have obliged.

But the story is now out. A mainstream television show has revealed, for all the world to see, the fact that Pentagon officials have constantly lied about the plane flying over the White House on the morning of 9/11. And this lie clearly suggests that the entire official story about the Pentagon attack is a lie.

Mark Gaffney has been a central figure in the exposure of this lie. In April 2007, he published an online essay entitled "The 9/11 Mystery Plane," which appears to have influenced John King's presentation. Although King did not mention Gaffney's article, he did show a photograph of the white plane that was included in that article. He also, in identifying the white plane, listed the same three points and in the same order.

Gaffney had written:

> Notice … the U.S. flag painted on the vertical stabilizer (i.e., the tail), and the blue stripe and insignia on the fuselage. The clincher, however, is the "bump" directly behind the bulging 747 cockpit.

According to King's CNN narrative:

> This comparison of the CNN video and an official Air Force photo … Note the flag on the tail, the stripe around the fuselage, and the telltale bubble just behind the 747 cockpit area.

Having been instrumental in getting the covered-up white plane episode exposed, Gaffney has now written a fascinating and informative study to alert the wider public to its reality. And its implications.

For further discussion see Chapter 21 of my *9/11 Contradictions: An Open Letter to Congress and the Press* (Northampton: Olive Branch, 2008).

— The First Official Timeline —

**NORTH AMERICAN
AEROSPACE DEFENSE COMMAND**

Directorate of Public Affairs, Headquarters, North American Aerospace Defense Command & US Space Command, 250 S. Peterson Blvd, Suite 116, Peterson AFB, Colorado Springs, Colo. 80914-3190 Phone (719) 554-6889 DSN 692-6889 NORAD and US Space Command website address: http://www.peterson.af.mil/norad or http://www.peterson.af.mil/usspacecom

18 September, 2001

Contact: (719) 554-6889

NORAD'S Response Times

PETERSON AFB, Colo. --The following timelines show NORAD's response to the airliner hijackings on September 11, 2001.

* All times are Eastern Daylight Time; NEADS = North East Air Defense Sector, NORAD
** Scramble = Order to get an aircraft airborne as soon as possible
***Estimated = loss of radar contact
**** Flight times are calculated at 9 miles per minute or .9 Mach
***** The FAA and NEADS established a line of open communication discussing AA Flt 77 and UA Flt 93

American Airlines Flight 11 – Boston enroute to Los Angeles
FAA Notification to NEADS0840*
Fighter Scramble Order *(Otis Air National Guard Base, Falmouth, Mass. Two F-15s)*0846**
Fighters Airborne 0852
Airline Impact Time (World Trade Center 1)0846 *(estimated)***
Fighter Time/Distance from Airline Impact LocationAircraft not airborne/153 miles

United Airlines Flight 175 – Boston enroute to Los Angeles
FAA Notification to NEADS0843
Fighter Scramble Order *(Otis ANGB, Falmouth, Mass. Same 2 F-15s as Flight 11)*0846
Fighters Airborne 0852
Airline Impact Time (World Trade Center 2)0902 *(estimated)*
Fighter Time/Distance from Airline Impact Locationapprox 8 min****/71 miles

American Flight 77 –Dulles enroute to Los Angeles
FAA Notification to NEADS0924
Fighter Scramble Order *(Langley AFB, Hampton, Va. 2 F-16s)*0924
Fighters Airborne 0930
Airline Impact Time (Pentagon)0937 *(estimated)*
Fighter Time/Distance from Airline Impact Locationapprox 12 min/105 miles

United Flight 93 – Newark to San Francisco
FAA Notification to NEADSN/A *****
Fighter Scramble Order *(Langley F-16s already airborne for AA Flt 77)*
Fighters Airborne (*Langley F-16 CAP remains in place to protect DC)*
Airline Impact Time (Pennsylvania)1003 *(estimated)*
Fighter Time/Distance from Airline Impact Locationapprox 11 min/100 miles

(from DC F-16 CAP)

-30-

This is the first official timeline offered by the U.S. government about NORAD's response.

— The Second Official Timeline, p.1 —

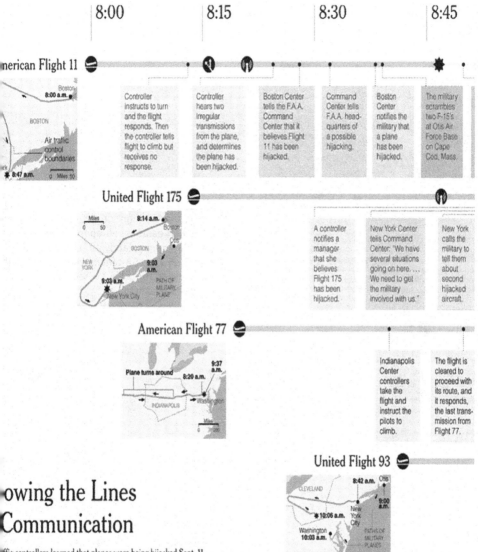

	8:00	8:15	8:30	8:45

nerican Flight 11

Boston
8:00 a.m.

BOSTON

Air traffic
control
boundaries

8:47 a.m. | 0 Miles 50

Controller instructs to turn and the flight responds. Then the controller tells flight to climb but receives no response.

Controller hears two irregular transmissions from the plane, and determines the plane has been hijacked.

Boston Center tells the F.A.A. Command Center that it believes Flight 11 has been hijacked.

Command Center tells F.A.A. headquarters of a possible hijacking.

Boston Center notifies the military that a plane has been hijacked.

The military scrambles two F-15's at Otis Air Force Base on Cape Cod, Mass.

United Flight 175

Miles 0 50
8:14 a.m.
Boston

BOSTON

NEW YORK
9:03 a.m.
9:03 a.m.
PATH OF MILITARY PLANE
New York City

A controller notifies a manager that she believes Flight 175 has been hijacked.

New York Center tells Command Center: "We have several situations going on here. ... We need to get the military involved with us."

New York calls the military to tell them about second hijacked aircraft.

American Flight 77

Plane turns around
9:37 a.m.
8:20 a.m.
INDIANAPOLIS
Washington
Miles 0 200

Indianapolis Center controllers take the flight and instruct the pilots to climb.

The flight is cleared to proceed with its route, and it responds, the last transmission from Flight 77.

United Flight 93

CLEVELAND
8:42 a.m. Otis
9:00 a.m.
New York City
10:06 a.m.
Washington
10:03 a.m.
PATHS OF MILITARY PLANES
Langley 9:32 a.m. | Miles 0 150

owing the Lines
Communication

ffic controllers learned that planes were being hijacked Sept. 11,
y faced major communication obstacles. The protocols in place for
o a hijacking assumed that the Federal Aviation Administration and
vould more easily identify the aircraft, have more time to track them
he hijackers would not intend to crash them.

ons of local F.A.A. controllers — 🔵 Takeoff

ts to higher F.A.A. centers — 🟤 Transponder turned off or code changed

ary alerted — 🔵 Deviation from flight plan

ary action — ✴ Crash

atements of the Sept. 11 commission

President and Vice President

The 9/11 Commission's timeline — here codified by the mainstream media — deviates from the Pentagon's September 18, 2001 timeline in some important respects. The Pentagon admitted that it received notification from the FAA about Flight 175 at 8:43 A.M., and about Flight 77 at 9:24 A.M. However, the 9/11 Commission denied this and asserted that the FAA failed to inform the military that either of these planes had been hijacked until after they had crashed.

— The Second Official Timeline, p.2 —

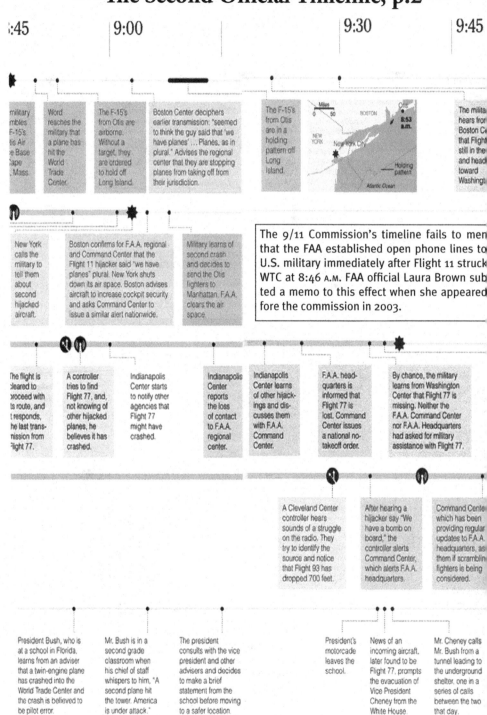

:45   9:00   9:30   9:45

military mbles F-15's is Air e Base ape Mass.

Word reaches the military that a plane has hit the World Trade Center.

The F-15's from Otis are airborne. Without a target, they are ordered to hold off Long Island.

Boston Center deciphers earlier transmission: "seemed to think the guy said that 'we have planes'... Planes, as in plural." Advises the regional center that they are stopping planes from taking off from their jurisdiction.

The F-15's from Otis are in a holding pattern off Long Island.

The milita hears fron Boston Ce that Flight still in the and head toward Washingto

New York calls the military to tell them about second hijacked aircraft.

Boston confirms for F.A.A. regional and Command Center that the Flight 11 hijacker said "we have planes" plural. New York shuts down its air space. Boston advises aircraft to increase cockpit security and asks Command Center to issue a similar alert nationwide.

Military learns of second crash and decides to send the Otis fighters to Manhattan. F.A.A. clears the air space.

The 9/11 Commission's timeline fails to men that the FAA established open phone lines to U.S. military immediately after Flight 11 struck WTC at 8:46 A.M. FAA official Laura Brown sub ted a memo to this effect when she appeared fore the commission in 2003.

The flight is cleared to proceed with ts route, and t responds, he last trans- mission from Flight 77.

A controller tries to find Flight 77, and, not knowing of other hijacked planes, he believes it has crashed.

Indianapolis Center starts to notify other agencies that Flight 77 might have crashed.

Indianapolis Center reports the loss of contact to F.A.A. regional center.

Indianapolis Center learns of other hijack- ings and dis- cusses them with F.A.A. Command Center.

F.A.A. head- quarters is informed that Flight 77 is lost. Command Center issues a national no- takeoff order.

By chance, the military learns from Washington Center that Flight 77 is missing. Neither the F.A.A. Command Center nor F.A.A. Headquarters had asked for military assistance with Flight 77.

A Cleveland Center controller hears sounds of a struggle on the radio. They try to identify the source and notice that Flight 93 has dropped 700 feet.

After hearing a hijacker say "We have a bomb on board," the controller alerts Command Center, which alerts F.A.A. headquarters.

Command Cente which has been providing regular updates to F.A.A. headquarters, as them if scramblin fighters is being considered.

President Bush, who is at a school in Florida, learns from an adviser that a twin-engine plane has crashed into the World Trade Center and the crash is believed to be pilot error.

Mr. Bush is in a second grade classroom when his chief of staff whispers to him, "A second plane hit the tower. America is under attack."

The president consults with the vice president and other advisers and decides to make a brief statement from the school before moving to a safer location.

President's motorcade leaves the school.

News of an incoming aircraft, later found to be Flight 77, prompts the evacuation of Vice President Cheney from the White House.

Mr. Cheney calls Mr. Bush from a tunnel leading to the underground shelter, one in a series of calls between the two that day.

— The Second Official Timeline, p.3 —

| 10:00 | 10:15 | 10:30 | 10:45 |

Military fighters from Langley Air Force Base, in Virginia, take off and are directed toward Baltimore as an intercept.

The 9/11 Commission's timeline also has VP Cheney arriving at the White House bunker shortly before 10 A.M., a chronology that was flatly contradicted by Norman Mineta, who testified that Cheney was already in the bunker by 9:20 A.M. By the way, Mineta's version of events is supported by the testimony of Karl Rove and Secret Service official Barbara Riggs.
And nowhere is there a mention of a mysterious white plane circling over Washington DC.

...ary learns that fighters are out ...Atlantic Ocean ...e of a confusing ...n. As Flight 77 ...Pentagon, the ...are about 150 ...ay.

...dquar- tells ...mmand ...ter that ...mbling ...ers is ...g ...ussed.

Cleveland Center, unaware the plane has crashed, calls the military. The military is unable to locate the plane on radar.

Command Center gets report of "black smoke" and alerts F.A.A. headquarters, suggesting the plane may have crashed.

The military contacts the F.A.A. and learns that the plane has crashed.

...a ...arts ...lesti- ...he ...o get ...as

The vice president arrives in the conference room and is told a combat air patrol is above Washington. Mr. Cheney says the president has authorized the fighers to shoot down planes if necessary.

The Secret Service, which still thought Flight 93 was headed to Washington, alerts Mr. Cheney. He authorizes the fighters to shoot if necessary.

A lieutenant colonel at the White House relays the order to the National Military Command Center.

The military commander in charge of the Langley and Otis fighters first learns of the authorization to shoot, but the pilots are not told because of confusion over the order.

After consultation with the Secret Service, fighters are launched from Andrews Air Force Base, near Washington, with orders to protect the White House and take out any aircraft that threaten the Capitol.

Steve Duenes, Matthew Ericson, William McNulty, Brett Taylor, Hugh K. Truslow and Archie Tse/The New York Times

... it was Humpty Dumpty himself. "It can't be anybody else!" she said to herself. "I'm as certain of it, as if his name were written all over his face!"

LEWIS CARROLL
Through the Looking-Glass and What Alice Found There

The Great Unraveling

Humpty Dumpty sat on a wall.
Humpty Dumpty had a great fall.
All the king's horses and all the king's men
Couldn't put Humpty together again.

Today, Americans are witness to an unraveling, the likes of which we have never seen in our history. For many months now the official narrative about the September 11, 2001 terrorist attack on America has been coming apart, and I mean: at the seams. As I write, the official story about that terrible day is disintegrating. The trend shows no sign of abating and it even appears to have accelerated. Soon there will be nothing left of the official version of events but a discordant echo and a series of extremely rude aftershocks.

Is our nation prepared for those rude shocks?

Exactly when the unraveling began is a matter of opinion. My own 9/11 research dates to only 2006, so I am a relative newcomer to these issues. Others who have been tracking 9/11 longer than I tell me the official story began to unravel almost from the day of the attack. In any event, there is little doubt that the official version of events suffered a major setback on August 2, 2006, when the *Washington Post* revealed that members of the 9/11 Commission were convinced that government officials, including NORAD generals, had deceived them during the hearings — in essence, had lied to their faces.[1] According to the *Post*, members of the 9/11 Commission vented their frustrations at a special meeting in the summer of 2004. This was just weeks after the release of the *9/11 Commission Report*. The panel even considered referring the matter to the Justice Department for a criminal investigation.

The unraveling accelerated with the release of a follow-up volume, *Without Precedent,* authored by the two men who had co-chaired the commission, Thomas H. Kean and Lee H. Hamilton. The two had come under increasing fire since the release of their final report, for presiding over what many now believe was a failed investigation. Stung by so much criticism, Kean and Hamilton evidently felt the need to defend themselves and their conclusions. The gist of their 2006 book is easily summarized. They write, "We were set up to fail."

The bleeding continued in May 2007 with the stunning announcement that former BYU physicist Steven Jones had found residues of thermate, a high temperature explosive, in the dust of the collapsed World Trade Center.[2] The discovery has the gravest implications for our nation and, no doubt, for this reason the announcement was censored by the U.S. media. In chapter six I will examine this important evidence. As we will learn, the truth about what really happened at the World Trade Center on 9/11 is whispering to us in prophetic fashion, from the dust ...

Another crucial development also received scant attention in the national press. I refer to the October 2007 release of NORAD's 9/11 radar data by the U.S. Air Force. I wager we will look back on its release as one of the turning points in the movement for 9/11 truth. In chapter four I will examine this hard evidence in detail. As I will show, it proves that the official story is a cover-up. With hindsight, it is astonishing that the Pentagon ever allowed this radar data to see the light of day. It slipped out, in my opinion, because the overwhelming majority of people who work in government and the military are honest. Whoever made the decision probably took it as an article of faith that the official story was correct, hence saw no problem releasing the 9/11 radar data in accordance with the Freedom of Information Act. The individual had no clue just how damaging the radar data would turn out to be. A small group within the military/intelligence community no doubt rue the day of its release.

One startling revelation in December 2007 did cause a stir in the press — briefly. The *New York Times* reported that the CIA had destroyed evidence in the form of audiotapes deemed vital to the official 9/11 investigation.[3] The news prompted 9/11 Commission co-chairs Kean and Hamilton to fire off an angry salvo, also published in the *Times,* charging that the CIA had obstructed their investigation.[4] Their blunt accusation was explosive and should have caused every American to sit up and take notice. Unfortunately, the average American probably failed to connect the dots because, as usual, the U.S. media offered nothing in the way of helpful context or analysis. We were fed the usual diet of tidbits and sound bytes: a stream of minutiae. The big picture remained elusive.

I wrote this book, in part, to overcome this vexing problem. I have always been skeptical of the official story about 9/11. In the aftermath of the September 11 attack, I shared the disquiet of many Americans about the Bush administration's rush to war. I could not shake the irksome feeling that somehow I (we) had been set up — that the country was being manipulated. The research for this book was driven by my personal need to understand what *really* happened on 9/11. In the end it was not one or another piece of information, but the totality of evidence, which ultimately persuaded me that 9/11 was an "inside job." In the following pages I will present what I have learned, in the hope that it can assist others to peel away their own layers of denial and glimpse the true picture. Assuming knowledge is power, perhaps in this way we can fortify ourselves to bring about the changes that are desperately needed in our country — before we lose it. But I have digressed. Back to the unraveling story …

The CIA Destroyed Evidence

Starting in 2002, the CIA conducted interrogations of captured al Qaeda operatives, including Abu Zubaydah and Ramzi Binalshibh, at undisclosed CIA prisons. During these interrogations the CIA resorted to "enhanced interrogation techniques" (the CIA's euphemism for torture) to extract information.[5] The methods included "waterboarding," which induces a sensation of drowning in the unlucky individual. Evidently, the CIA decided for its own internal reasons to videotape these early interrogation sessions. However, several years later (in 2005), Jose A. Rodriguez, the CIA's Director of Operations, ordered the tapes to be destroyed. For what reason? Well, according to CIA Director Michael V. Hayden, because the tapes posed "a serious security risk."[6] Hayden went on to clarify his rather cryptic remark for the benefit of the press. He explained that if the tapes had become public, they would have exposed CIA officials "and their families to retaliation from al Qaeda and its sympathizers." The excuse was a dodge — obvious flimflam. But the reporters hung on Hayden's every word as if he were speaking gospel. They certainly did not throw him any hardballs or press him on the matter.

Hayden also claimed that the CIA had followed the letter of the law in 2005, by notifying the appropriate committee heads in Congress *before* destroying the evidence. However, according to the *Times,* this was immediately disputed by the top two members of the House Intelligence Committee. A spokesman for Representative Peter Hoekstra (R-MI), who at the time chaired the oversight committee, said that he was "never briefed or advised" that the tapes even existed, let alone "that they were going to be destroyed."[7]

Kean and Hamilton had a similar gut reaction: outrage. In their January 2008 article in the *New York Times* they state categorically that the CIA never informed them about any taped interrogations, despite their repeated requests for all pertinent information about the captured al Qaeda operatives, who were then in CIA custody. In fact, as damaging as the news about the destruction of evidence surely was, the story laid bare an even more serious problem. One might naturally assume that the official commission charged to investigate the events of 9/11 would have had unfettered access to *all* of the evidence pertinent to the case, including government documents, and especially key witnesses. This goes without saying. Access was vital to the success of the investigation. How else could the commission do its work? Yet, it never happened.

The CIA Stonewalled the Official Panel

In the same article Kean and Hamilton summarize their dealings with the CIA.[8] They describe their private meetings with CIA Director George Tenet and how he denied them access to the captured members of al Qaeda. Notice, this means that the panel never conducted its own interviews. Tenet even denied the co-chairs permission to conduct secondhand interviews with the CIA interrogators, which Kean and Hamilton felt were needed "to better judge the credibility of the witnesses and clarify ambiguities in the reporting."[9] Ultimately, the commission was forced to rely on third-hand intelligence reports prepared by the CIA itself. Many of these reports were poorly written and incomplete summaries[10] that, according to the co-chairs "raised almost as many questions as they answered."[11]

In order to resolve the many uncertainties, the commission prepared a list of questions, which it then submitted to the CIA. The questions covered a range of topics, such as the translations from the Arabic, inconsistencies in the detainees' stories, the context of the questioning, how the interrogators followed up certain lines of questioning, and the assessments of the interrogators themselves. But the CIA's response was less than helpful. According to Kean and Hamilton, "the [CIA] general counsel responded in writing with non-specific replies." This is a bland way of saying that the agency rebuffed the panel. Not satisfied, Kean and Hamilton made yet another attempt to gain access to the captives, but were again denied permission during a face-to-face meeting with Tenet in December 2003.

For this reason the ambiguities and other questions went unresolved, flawing the commission's final report. Yet, as I have indicated, the more serious problem was the panel's lack of access to begin with, a problem which was by no means obvious until this story broke in the mainstream press. In fact, Kean and Hamilton had inserted a caveat in their report (on page 146) conceding this crucial point: that they were denied access to the witnesses. Most readers probably passed over it without understanding its awful significance. I know I did on my first reading.

There was another revelation — no less disturbing. Not even Porter J. Goss, CIA Director at the the time, knew about the destruction of the audio-tapes, which, as noted, had been ordered by Jose A. Rodriguez, the CIA's Director of Operations (as in *covert operations*). According to the *Times*, Goss was angered to learn that he had been kept out of the loop.[12] However, he declined to make a public statement.

What are we to make of this? Why was the CIA chief kept in the dark about the destruction of evidence deemed vital to the 9/11 investigation? This is no less shocking than the destruction of the tapes, because it points to a disconnect in the chain of command. At very least, it means that Goss was not fully briefed about the CIA's handling of the 9/11 interrogations when he was appointed to the Directorship. But why wouldn't he be? Was the CIA's covert branch, long notorious for staging rogue operations, up to its old tricks? Are there loose cannons at Langley, still?

Of one thing there can be no doubt: The *9/11 Commission Report* was packaged and sold to the American people like some trendy product. The mass media have told us countless times that it is the definitive version of the events of September 11. No wonder that in 2008 most Americans probably take this for granted. When something is repeated enough times by the "authorities," people absorb it. The public ends up believing whatever it is told, whether true or not.

We witnessed a similar case during the run-up to the 2003 U.S. invasion of Iraq, when the Bush administration mantra about Saddam Hussain's Weapons of Mass Destruction and his supposed links to al Qaeda were drummed into the brain of every American through mass marketing. Today, of course, we know different. None of it was true. Yet, on the eve of that war a *Washington Post* poll found that 70% of Americans believed that Saddam had WMDs and was responsible for 9/11. The case is a sobering reminder of the power of the corporate media to shape public opinion with — let us call it by its true name — propaganda.

OK. The better part of a decade has passed. Are we Americans prepared to face reality? The 9/11 Commission's lack of direct access to the captured members of al Qaeda can only mean that the official 9/11 investigation was fundamentally compromised from the outset. Given the disclosures I have cited, no other conclusion is possible. In their January 2008 article in the *Times*, Kean and Hamilton do not repudiate their own report, at least not in so many words. But they come close. They insinuate that the CIA's stonewalling calls into question the veracity of key parts of the official story, namely, the plot against America supposedly masterminded by Khalid Shiekh Mohammed and approved by Osama bin Laden.

Until now, the nation has assumed that all of this was soundly based on the testimony of the captured al Qaeda operatives, several of whom supposedly confessed. This is the story as told in the *9/11 Commission Report*. But probe more deeply and one finds the devil lurking in the details. The reality is that, without independent confirmation about what the captives actually confessed to, precisely what was said and by whom, indeed whether they confessed at all, there is absolutely no way for us to know how much of the official story is true and how much was fabricated by the CIA for reasons we can only guess.

There is another problem. If the confessions were extracted by means of torture, then just how reliable can they be? It comes down to whether the CIA is telling the truth. Should we believe them? If the captives did confess as reported, why did the CIA refuse the 9/11 Commission access to the witnesses? Obviously, something is not right. In fact, for all we know, the entire story is a pack of lies. And there is another important question: How did the miscarriage of a lawful process of discovery happen, given that Congress invested the 9/11 Commission with the authority to subpoena evidence?

The Uncensored History ...

Fortunately, in February 2008, along came *The Commission*, a "tell-all" book by Philip Shenon with much to say about the above, and some answers. The book's sub-title, *The Uncensored History of the 9/11 Investigation*, sounds promising, and the author does not fail to deliver. Shenon covered the 9/11 Commission for the *New York Times*, and over the course of the investigation he personally interviewed many of the commissioners and staff. His best-selling book is a well written exposé and our best look yet at what went on behind-the-scenes. Shenon obviously enjoys playing the role of reporter. Although he makes his opinions known in the book, the author fortunately does not overburden us with his own conclusions. Most of the time Shenon describes what happened through the eyes of the commissioners and staff. For this reason his book offers valuable insights about why the investigation failed.

Of course, we already knew large parts of the story. We knew, for example, about National Security Adviser Condoleezza Rice's incompetence, and about the serious conflicts of interest on the commission, particularly in the person of Philip Zelikow, who served as the panel's executive director. In that capacity Zelikow controlled many facets of the investigation, including the scheduling of witnesses and the vital flow of information between the staff and commissioners. Zelikow also edited (and, no doubt, doctored) the final report. In addition to being a long-time confidante of Rice, with whom he coauthored a book, Zelikow served on G.W. Bush's transition team and even drafted a national security strategy paper the Bush administration later used to justify the 2003 war against Iraq.

It is hard to believe that Kean and Hamilton, who claim that their goal was to lead a nonpartisan investigation, would have knowingly hired such a man — a neocon — to manage the panel's day-to-day affairs. According to Shenon, it only happened because Zelikow failed to report the full extent of his ties to the Bush administration when he submitted his resume for the job. If Zelikow had been more forthcoming, he would have been instantly eliminated from consideration. But this hardly excuses Kean and Hamilton for failing to thoroughly vet the candidate. They would have been wise to listen to the families of the victims, who demanded Zelikow's resignation. The families believed that more than enough *was* known about the man, and hindsight proves them correct.

Shenon's most important revelation has sped the unraveling process. The author names CIA Director George Tenet as one of the government officials who the commissioners and staff were convinced had lied during the hearings.[13] Tenet gave testimony on three occasions (in addition to the private meetings with Kean and Hamilton), and in each of these hearings the CIA Director suffered from a faulty memory, frequently responding with "I can't remember." Initially, the commissioners were inclined to be sympathetic, and gave the director the benefit of the doubt. (At the time, Tenet's supporters at the agency reportedly made excuses for their boss: George cannot remember because he is dead-tired, physically exhausted from dealing with the war on terrorism. Or: he has been suffering from sleep deprivation — not getting enough shuteye.[14] Poor old George.) But gradually the tide turned. By Tenet's third appearance it was obvious to everyone he was perjuring himself.

Again, some of his perjury had been known. For instance, it was known that Tenet lied to the 9/11 Commission in April 2004 when he denied his meetings with President Bush in the weeks before the September 11 attack. "I didn't see the president," Tenet told commissioner Tim Roemer. "I was not in briefings with him during this time. He [i.e., Bush] was on vacation; I was here [i.e., in Washington]." Tenet added that he did not even speak with Bush on the telephone during this period.[15] But Tenet's denial was immediately exposed as a lie, because the president had *already* gone on record about the meetings. On August 25, 2001 during a walking tour of his Crawford ranch, Bush casually "let slip" to the press that he had met with Tenet the previous day about "a very important subject."[16]

The CIA was forced to issue a retraction the day after the hearing: Tenet "misspoke."[17] Yet, from Bush's 2001 remarks, it is abundantly clear (with the benefit of hindsight) that the August 24, 2001 meeting at the ranch was less a briefing than a war council. The pow-wow took place on Bush's front porch and by his own estimate lasted about six hours — most of the day. Also in attendance: National Security Adviser Condoleezza Rice, Secretary of Defense Donald Rumsfeld, and Vice Chairman of the Joint Chiefs Richard Myers. This was a little more than two weeks before the attack. Yet, we are supposed to believe that Bush was on vacation, down on the ranch. Is it reasonable to think that Tenet simply forgot about the meeting? No, of course not. It appears that he lied in an attempt to keep it secret.

Tenet's performance before the commission must have been a spectacle to behold, but one would never know this from reading the *9/11 Commission Report*, which gives no hint that the Director of Central Intelligence lied to the panel. Why not? Thomas Kean gave the reason at the commission's first public hearing in New York City, when he said, "Our ... purpose will not be to point fingers." I should add that his comment was not well received. According to Shenon, it prompted a rumble in the audience, and even elicited sneers from the families of the victims who wanted the responsible officials to be held accountable.[18] But not even this reluctance to assign blame adequately explains why the panel took the CIA at its word regarding the interrogations of the al Qaeda captives, since by this time it was common knowledge that Tenet was lying through his teeth. We are left to ponder why Kean and Hamilton failed to insist on some type of independent confirmation.

Of course, when Tenet stiffed the commission, he was merely carrying on a time-honored Langley tradition. For the first 25 years of its existence, the CIA functioned entirely outside the U.S. constitutional framework of government. Like it or not, this is the reality. This state of affairs prevailed until the Watergate era, when the Church hearings in the Senate exposed a laundry list of criminal activities by the CIA, such as domestic spying, the assassination of foreign leaders, the overthrow of governments, not to mention the nasty habit of deceiving Congress. Those dark revelations shocked the nation and led to the creation of House and Senate intelligence committees, to provide the democratic oversight that was sorely lacking.

Anyway, such was the intent. But, as with so many good ideas, things did not turn out as expected. The CIA soon found ways around the oversight process, which is not surprising when you consider that clandestine operations are what the CIA is all about. Today, the Intelligence Committees in both houses are widely viewed as a joke, and despite a chorus of denials from the agency and its admirers, the perception is undoubtedly correct. To his credit, Shenon touches on the issue in his book. The author mentions that one of the commissioners, former Senator Slade Gorton (R-WA), once served on the Senate Intelligence Committee but quit in frustration because of the lack of any serious business. Said Gorton, "I felt it was a useless exercise — I never felt I was being told anything that I hadn't learned in the *Washington Post*."[19]

Does Such an Agency Deserve Our Trust and Respect?

As to why Kean and Hamilton did not make more aggressive use of their authority to subpoena evidence, Shenon's answer is not very satisfying, but it rings true. The co-chairs were overcautious because they wished to avoid a legal showdown that would drag out in the courts.[20] A legal stalemate threatened to delay their investigation beyond the mandated deadline. This, in their view, would have been tantamount to a Bush victory. But it was a huge mistake — their worst.

Had Kean and Hamilton stood tough and issued blanket subpoenas early in the investigation, as their legal counsel advised, the inevitable showdown in the courts might have worked in their favor. Bush and Tenet would have been perceived — correctly — as obstructing the investigation and would have come under increasing pressure and scrutiny. That sort of confrontation would have served the discovery process and the cause of 9/11 truth. Unfortunately, it didn't happen. This helps to explain why the official investigation failed in its stated objective: "to provide the fullest possible account of the events surrounding 9/11."[21]

Although Philip Shenon supports the official narrative, his research was so narrowly focused that his rather casual discounting of "conspiracy theorists" can do no harm to the 9/11 truth movement. (Here, of course, "conspiracy theorist" means anyone who does not agree with the *official* conspiracy theory.) I gave Shenon's book only three stars in my review at Amazon.com, because the author seems genuinely unaware that by 2007 the evidence had shifted decisively in favor of the "conspiracy theorists." There is simply no excuse for Shenon not knowing the facts. In the following pages I will present much of this evidence.

A showdown over 9/11, though long delayed, appears to be developing, and portends — I believe — a coming shift in the terms of the debate: away from the previous discussion about the incompetence of officials and "security failures" to more grave issues. But how this important drama will play out remains unclear. Obviously, a new legally-empowered investigative body is urgently needed. Will it happen? Perhaps, but only if the American people demand it.

Seven years after the terrible events of 9/11, numerous anomalies associated with the collapse of the World Trade Center and the Pentagon crash have yet to be explained, and remain controversial. To this day, there is also considerable uncertainty about the actual chronology of events, i.e., exactly what happened and when. A glance at Paul Thompson's invaluable book, *The Terror Timeline*, shows that the official narrative as presented in the *9/11 Commission Report* is at best a partial record and at worst a fabrication, since what it leaves out often conflicts with the official story it presents.[1] Fortunately, an updated version of Thompson's timeline is readily accessible on the Internet.[2]

Professor David Ray Griffin's books about 9/11 are also an invaluable resource, particularly his most recent, *9/11 Contradictions* (2008) and *Debunking 9/11 Debunking* (2007). Griffin is a careful scholar and has exposed numerous flaws in the official investigation, including cases of deception. His books should be regarded as companion volumes to the *9/11 Commission Report*, and, together with Thompson's website, are indispensable to anyone trying to understand what happened on that historic day.

One thing is certain: The same powerful interests that conspired to subvert the 9/11 Commission will use all of their influence to defeat a new investigation, first by attempting to block its creation, and, failing that, by controlling it. Americans who are committed to 9/11 truth must not allow this to happen. We must steel ourselves to whatever level of struggle is required to expose the truth. To say that the stakes are high would be an understatement. The future of our nation — whether the republic will survive — may hinge on the outcome. Without question, we have entered the most dangerous time in U.S. history. If there is good news it is the irreversible nature of the unraveling process. Once begun, it moves in only one direction. Today, as in the famous nursery rhyme, the official reality, i.e., Humpty Dumpty, is falling apart, and the pieces will never be put back together again.

Endnotes

1. Dan Eggen, "9/11 Panel Suspected Deception by Pentagon," *Washington Post,* August 2, 2006.

2. The Jones paper is posted at http://www.journalof911studies.com/volume/200704/JonesWTC911SciMethod.pdf.

3. Mark Mazzetti, "CIA Destroyed 2 Tapes Showing Interrogations," *New York Times,* December 7, 2007.

4. Thomas H. Kean and Lee H. Hamilton, "Stonewalled by the CIA," *New York Times,* January 2, 2008.

5. "CIA destroyed terrorism suspect videotapes. Director says interrogation tapes were security risk. Critics call move illegal," *NBC News,* December 7, 2007.

6. Mark Mazzetti, op. cit.

7. Ibid.

8. Thomas H. Kean and Lee H. Hamilton, op. cit.

9. *The 9/11 Commission Report. Final Report of the National Commission on Terrorist Attacks Upon the United States,* W.W. Norton & Co., New York, 2004, p.146.

10. Philip Shenon, *The Commission: The Uncensored History of the 9/11 Commission,* Grand Central Publishing, New York, 2008, p. 391.

11. Thomas H. Kean and Lee H. Hamilton, op. cit.

12. Mark Mazzetti, op. cit.

13. Philip Shenon, op. cit., p. 360.

14. Ibid., pp. 258-260.

15. National Commission on Terrorist Attacks Upon the United States. Tenth Public Hearing, Washington, DC, Hart Senate Office Building, Wednesday, April 14, 2004, posted at http://www.9-11commission.gov/archive/hearing10/9-11commission_hearing_2004-04-14.htm.

16. President Gives Tour of Crawford Ranch, Remarks by the President, Prairie Chapel Ranch, Crawford, Texas, August 25, 2001.

17. "Tenet misspoke about not meeting with Bush in August 2001," AP, April 15, 2004.

18. Philip Shenon, op. cit., p. 99.

19. Ibid., p. 229.

20. Ibid., pp. 94 and 201.

21. *The 9/11 Commission Report,* p. xvi.

Members of the 9/11 Commission. Top row: Richard Ben-Veniste - Democrat, attorney, former chief of the Watergate Task Force of the Watergate Special Prosecutor's Office; John F. Lehman - Republican, former Secretary of the Navy; Timothy J. Roemer - Democrat, former U.S. Representative from the 3rd District of Indiana; James R. Thompson - Republican, former Governor of Illinois; Bob Kerrey - Democrat, President of the New School University and former U.S. Senator from Nebraska; Slade Gorton - Republican, former U.S. Senator from Washington. Bottom Row: Fred F. Fielding - Republican, attorney and former White House Counsel; Lee H. Hamilton (Vice Chairman) - Democrat, former U.S. Representative from the 9th District of Indiana; Thomas Kean (Chairman) - Republican, former Governor of New Jersey; Jamie Gorelick - Democrat, former Deputy Attorney General in the Clinton Administration.

THE

9/11

COMMISSION

REPORT

FINAL REPORT OF THE NATIONAL COMMISSION ON
TERRORIST ATTACKS UPON THE UNITED STATES

1

Overview of the Official Story

The official 9/11 narrative did not emerge in its present final form all of a piece. The official story is the product of evolution and underwent two major revisions. The military announced the first revision a week after the attack. The 9/11 Commission unveiled the second in its final report, released in July 2004. Dr. David Ray Griffin has argued persuasively that both revisions were attempts to salvage the official conspiracy theory.

Before we proceed, it might be helpful to review how this process unfolded. We start, of course, with the events themselves and the raw news coverage on the day of the attack, especially the riveting television reports, which exposed NORAD's failure to intercept any of the four allegedly hijacked planes. At first, of course, the nation was understandably in a state of shock, but within days the full magnitude of the U.S. military's failed response began to sink in. On September 13, 2001, General Richard Myers, acting Chairman of the Joint Chiefs of Staff, admitted to the Senate Armed Services Committee that the first Air National Guard fighters had not arrived to defend Washington until well *after* the Pentagon strike, roughly 90 minutes after the first sign of trouble aboard American Airlines Flight 11.[3] During all of that time the nation's capital had been exposed — undefended.

Myers' testimony caused huge problems for the military because NORAD's failure went beyond negligence and looked like a deliberate standdown, which, if true, was treason. Days later, on September 18, 2001, the Pentagon attempted to shield itself from mounting criticism by announcing the first revised timeline, essentially placing the blame for the massive breach of security on the Federal Aviation Administration (FAA).[4] The

Joint Chiefs claimed that the military was unable to respond in a timely manner because the FAA failed to notify NORAD about the hijacked planes until too late. As 9/11 commissioner Bob Kerrey later pointed out, this first major alteration in the story occurred immediately *after* Pentagon generals (probably including Myers) briefed President Bush on September 17, 2001.[5] His point was that the White House obviously had instructed the Joint Chiefs to change their tune.

This first revised timeline stood for almost three years, but suffered from the serious problem of being improbable. Why? In the first place, because there is nothing unusual about the FAA's scrambling of NORAD fighters. The procedure is routine. If a commercial or private aircraft deviates from its scheduled flight-path by as little as two miles, or if there is a loss of radio contact, or if its transponder stops transmitting, FAA air traffic controllers will first attempt to contact the pilot and remedy the problem. Failing this, the standard FAA protocol is to request immediate assistance from NORAD. Furthermore, if there is any doubt, FAA policy is to assume the worst and declare an air emergency, which means an automatic scramble.[6] During one nine-month period in the year 2000 the FAA made sixty-seven such requests, and in every case NORAD responded by scrambling fighters — all without a hitch.[7] This is an average of about two scrambles a week, more than 100 per year. Yet, we are supposed to believe that on 9/11, for no apparent reason, FAA controllers began to behave like a bunch of morons.

Their alleged failure to contact NORAD on 9/11 was doubly strange, even bizarre, since the FAA simultaneously showed remarkable professionalism and skill by grounding approximately 4500 commercial and private aircraft in less than three hours, all without a single mishap. The shutdown started in New York after the second WTC impact (at 9:03 A.M.), and quickly spread. By 9:26 A.M. the ground-stop was nationwide. The FAA shutdown of the entire air traffic system was unprecedented in the annals of U.S. aviation and was all the more impressive given the adverse, i.e., essentially wartime, conditions that prevailed. At least two FAA facilities had to be evacuated that morning in response to perceived threats of terrorism.[8] The commission even admits in its final report that the FAA performed "flawlessly."[9] Yet, we are supposed to believe that on the same morning this same agency fumbled a routine phone hand-off to NORAD four times in succession. This simply does not add up.

As time passed it also became apparent that the Pentagon's revised timeline suffered from an even more serious problem. Assuming the revised story was correct, arguably there was still sufficient time for NO-RAD to scramble fighters and intercept at least two of the "hijacked" planes, namely, Flight 77 (which allegedly hit the Pentagon) and Flight 93 (which allegedly crashed near Shanksville, PA).[10] The time from scramble-to-intercept normally takes about ten minutes.

The 9/11 Commission acknowledges these difficulties in its final report released in July 2004, then attempts to resolve them by introducing a second major revision of the story, which puts the blame even more emphatically on the FAA. According to this most recent official timeline, the FAA was not merely tardy in making the hand-offs, *it failed altogether.* In the case of Flight 77 officials supposedly had less than two minutes of warning about its final approach. The report further asserts that NORAD did not receive notification that Flights 175, 93 and 77 had been hijacked until *after* the planes had crashed. The new timeline effectively absolves the Joint Chiefs of Staff of any negligence.

The Phantom Plane

The latest revision was supposedly based on new evidence that exposed serious discrepancies in the Pentagon's previous testimony before the panel in May 2003. During those early hearings USAF Col. Alan Scott told the commission that F-16 fighters had been scrambled from Langley AFB near Hampton, Virginia, at 9:24 A.M. (and were airborne by 9:30 A.M.) for the purpose of intercepting Flight 77. NORAD Maj. Gen. Larry Arnold also testified at this same hearing. He confirmed this scramble time, but stated that the Langley fighters had been sent to protect Washington from hijacked Flight 93.[11]

The new evidence was in the form of NORAD audio-tapes from 9/11, which the government had withheld for many months, but which thanks to a court order were finally handed over to the 9/11 Commission late in the investigation. When the panel reviewed these NORAD tapes in June 2004, they discovered a previously unknown transmission, which became the basis for a completely new element in the story: the so called "phantom plane scenario," first unveiled in the *9/11 Commission Report.*

The transmission supposedly proves that in the one instance where the FAA *did* alert NORAD, i.e., in the case of hijacked Flight 11, the FAA got it wrong and passed incorrect information, sending NORAD on a wild-goose chase after a nonexistent aircraft. According to the report, someone at the FAA mistakenly notified NORAD at 9:24 A.M. that Flight 11 was still in the air, that is, had *not* crashed into the North Tower, and was head-

3

ing south toward Washington.[12] Based on this false information NORAD scrambled three F-16s from Langley AFB near Hampton, Virginia to intercept southbound Flight 11, now deemed a threat to the nation's capital. The fighters were armed and the intercept was supposed to happen near Baltimore.

Here, the plot thickens, however, because at this point a bizarre screw-up occurred, one that has never been explained. Instead of handing-off the Langley fighters to air traffic controllers in the Washington DC area, local controllers sent the fighters to a military training airspace over the Atlantic known as "Whiskey 386." This explains why the fighters failed to arrive in time to defend against incoming Flight 77, which in the meantime had mysteriously appeared on the radar screens southwest of the capital.[13] Incredibly, a similar scenario had unfolded earlier in the case of the F-15s scrambled from Otis ANGB. Instead of flying directly to Manhattan, the two fighters ended up in holding pattern off Long Island, more than 100 miles from the World Trade Center.[14]

This new disclosure was a major change in the official story and was embarrassing to the Pentagon, because it contradicted earlier testimony of Col. Alan Scott and Generals Richard Myers, Ralph Eberhart and Larry Arnold, none of whom had previously mentioned the phantom plane. Indeed, when Arnold was recalled for his second appearance before the commission in June 2004 he *still* did not have his facts straight, *nearly three years after the event*. Arnold had to be coached by panel members. His inability to recall details that as a NORAD commander he should have known caused shock and outrage on the panel. According to the *Washington Post*, the commission and staffers were convinced that the Pentagon had deliberately deceived them: "[S]uspicion of wrongdoing ran so deep that the ten-member commission, in a secret meeting at the end of its tenure in summer 2004, debated referring the matter to the Justice Department for criminal investigation." John Farmer, one of the commissioners, said, "I was shocked at how different the truth was from the way it was described."[15]

But the outrage never made it into the *9/11 Commission Report*, which mentions nothing about deception. The report merely states that the generals' previous testimony was "incorrect."[16] Although much has been made of this loss of face by the Pentagon, "what is really going on," as David Ray Griffin has pointed out, "is that the military is briefly suffering a little embarrassment, experienced primarily by a few scapegoats [eg., General Arnold], for the sake of the new story, which, if accepted, permanently removes the suspicion of guilt for treason and murder from everyone in the military."[17] Griffin has it right. A close reading of the *9/11 Commission Report* shows that its main objective is to exonerate the Pentagon brass of responsibility for the breach of security on September 11.

This is why the latest Kean/Hmilton about-face discussed in my introduction is so important. The sharp tone of Kean and Hamilton's January 2008 op-ed in the *New York Times* blasting the CIA for obstruction is a radical departure from the bland non-confrontational style of their final report, which pointed no fingers (except in the direction of the FAA) and indeed bent over backward to exonerate the Pentagon and CIA from any culpability. The shift in tone is a red flag, and this should alert us.

We must not be fooled by the bland language of the *9/11 Commission Report*, which deserves to be recognized for what it is: a thoroughly sanitized account. Crucially, the commission failed to subject the NORAD tapes to forensic analysis, which ought to have been a priority, given the disparities in the previous testimony as evidenced by the tapes. The *9/11 Commission Report* fails to provide even one checkable source to substantiate the NORAD tapes as evidence. It is the same problem we encountered in the case of the CIA interrogations. In the absence of independent confirmation, we have no assurance about the NORAD tapes' authenticity, hence, can have no confidence in the "corrected" story.

Perhaps the phantom plane played no part in the earlier timeline because, as Griffin suggests, its part in the story is simply a fabrication. That would certainly explain why the generals failed to mention it in their previous testimony, and why General Arnold was unfamiliar with it as late as June 2004. At issue here is whether the Pentagon and the commission are telling the truth. The added problem, as Griffin has ably shown, is that even if we wish to believe the latest version of the official narrative, this means we must also accept that the Joint Chiefs deliberately deceived the panel and the nation about the previous timeline for nearly three years. Moreover, because the entire chain of command remained silent, it too was complicit in the deception.

While it is usually assumed that if the generals lied it was to conceal their own incompetence, why would they expose themselves to the treasonous charge of implementing a stand-down by *understating* the FAA's degree of negligence on 9/11, as they did in their first revised narrative, if the FAA was in fact even more culpable, as the latest revision holds?[18] This makes no sense and should increase our skepticism about every facet of the official story. Indeed, we are compelled to consider the admittedly sinister alternative explanation that the generals lied to conceal their complicity in the 9/11 attack, perhaps even their role in staging it. This would explain both their previous "incorrect" testimony and their unreserved acceptance of the new timeline. One of the NORAD generals was actually heard to remark, "The real story [i.e., the latest version] is better than the one we told."[19] Given that the latest version had the effect of exonerating the generals, one can appreciate his point of view. But was it "better" for the nation?

There is another serious problem: Assuming the FAA was guilty of gross negligence on 9/11, why was no one ever held accountable? Not a single FAA official was ever prosecuted, dismissed, demoted, or even reprimanded. Why not? Did the Bush administration refrain from disciplining the FAA because this would have begun a legal process of discovery/appeal involving the scrutiny of relevant documents by the courts and the release of real evidence, a process which had to be avoided at all costs? As we know, instead of handing out dismissals and demotions, the Bush administration rewarded a number of officials and officers who held responsible positions on 9/11. CIA Director George Tenet, a prime example, was awarded the Medal of Freedom, the nation's highest honor, despite presiding over the "worst security failure" in U.S. history. The Bush policy of rewarding failure was perverse and violated the most basic principle of good government, which is that people should be held accountable for their actions. This strongly suggests that the Bush White House purchased the cooperation and silence of numerous officials by handing out bribes. Spectacular compensatory awards were also offered to families of the victims. The cash payments reportedly averaged $1.8 million apiece. But to receive the money the families had to sign a waiver forfeiting the right to legal action.[20]

9/11 Live: The NORAD Tapes

The phantom plane story had the effect of letting the U.S. military off the hook. Was it a device contrived for this purpose? Although the *9/11 Commission Report* fails to explain how the phantom plane story originated,[21] in September 2006 Michael Bronner disclosed more details in a much-ballyhooed article in *Vanity Fair* magazine, "9/11 Live: The NORAD Tapes." Bronner is a former producer of *60 Minutes* and also helped produce the film *United 93*.[22] For reasons that have never been explained, the U.S. military blessed Bronner with exclusive access to the same NORAD tapes that the 9/11 Commission obtained only after a lengthy court battle.[23] The tapes became the grist for Bronner's *Vanity Fair* article, which defends the official story presented in the *9/11 Commission Report.* Although Bronner asserts that "the truth is all on tape," there are solid reasons to question his arguments and conclusions.

As part of his research, Bronner interviewed Colin Scoggins, who on September 11, 2001 was the military liaison at the FAA's Boston Air Traffic Center, where much of the action occurred. Scoggins told Bronner the phantom plane story began as a misunderstanding during a teleconference "in the flurry of information zipping back and forth ... [and] ... transmogrified into the idea that a different plane had hit the tower, and that American 11 was still hijacked and still in the air."[24] Although the *9/11 Commission Report* does not mention Scoggins by name, it was he who made the crucial call to NEADS at 9:24 A.M. informing the military that Flight 11 was heading toward Washington.[25] When I conducted my own interview with Scoggins in 2007, he acknowledged that Boston Center had tracked Flight 11 continuously until just north of the World Trade Center, but denied that the FAA ever tracked a phantom plane south of Manhattan. As Flight 11 approached the World Trade Center, it was then nearly out of range of Boston Center's radar coverage. The plane was lost to radar at an altitude of just under 2,000 feet.[26]

In his article, Bronner tagged Scoggins with the responsibility for the mistaken report, but Scoggins told me he merely relayed what he had overheard during an FAA conference call. More details emerged during our interview and subsequent email exchanges. Scoggins thinks someone at FAA headquarters (which is located on Independence Avenue in downtown Washington) dropped a "call sign" during the 9/11 teleconference, meaning that during the discussion about hijacked planes someone failed to mention a flight number, leading to a mix-up.[27] Numerous individuals from various agencies were on the line that morning. Scoggins doesn't know exactly who or how many people were listening. The conference call may well have included staffers from the Pentagon and NORAD, which, if true, would mean that the military overheard the entire conversation with the FAA, and therefore by 9:24 A.M. surely knew about *at least one* of the other hijacked planes in addition to Flight 11. This would contradict the official story that the military was in the dark.

Scoggins doubts this interpretation, but it is certainly possible, because the Pentagon and NORAD were usual participants in FAA conference calls. This was confirmed by the FAA's Deputy in Public Affairs Laura Brown in a May 2003 memo to the 9/11 Commission, in which Brown sought to clarify the FAA's role. Her memo states, "Within minutes after the first aircraft hit the World Trade Center [at 8:46 A.M.], the FAA immediately established several phone bridges that included FAA field facilities, the FAA Command Center, FAA headquarters, DoD [the Department of Defense, i.e., the Pentagon and NORAD], the Secret Service, and other government agencies."[28] Notice, if Brown is correct, the FAA notified the military much earlier than 9:24.

The panel discussed Brown's memo during its hearings. Richard Ben-Veniste, one of the commissioners, even read it into the record.[29] Yet, her memo is conspicuously absent from the *9/11 Commission Report*. Why? The probable answer is that it contradicts the official story that the U.S. military was out of the loop. Anyone who thinks the military was not on the line should review the enormous amount of evidence to the contrary assembled by David Ray Griffin in *Debunking 9/11 Debunking*. Griffin thinks the FAA phone bridge with the military actually started much earlier, indeed, as early as 8:20 A.M., and he is probably correct.[30]

Pushback? Or Obfuscation?

Michael Bronner makes another serious charge in his *Vanity Fair* article. He claims that the operational commander of NORAD's Northeast Sector (NEADS) was unable to deploy his fighters over Manhattan on September 11 because he encountered resistance from the FAA. With both WTC towers in flames, as Bronner tells it, the NEADS mission-crew commander Major Kevin Nasypany was intent on moving his F-15s into position to protect New York. The planes had finally been scrambled (at 8:52 A.M.) from Otis ANGB, on Cape Cod. According to Bronner, however, as they approached the city NEADS received "pushback" from FAA controllers, who were concerned that NORAD's "fast-moving fighters" might collide with commercial passenger planes, hundreds of which were "in the area, still flying normal routes." At this point the FAA ordered the Otis pilots to stand by in a holding pattern off Long Island. Bronner is correct that the FAA had "the final authority over the fighters as long as they [were] in civilian airspace," and he is also correct that the FAA hesitated to allow NORAD fighters over New York City. What he fails to mention is that the FAA was simply doing its job — following long-established rules in the interest of air safety.

The danger was real enough. The airspace around New York is by far the most congested on the planet. Three international airports service the greater metropolitan area. Two of them, JFK and La Guardia, are east of

Manhattan and the third, Newark Airport, is located in New Jersey, west across the Hudson. Flights arrive at these busy airports from all points on the compass and depart to all points on a continuous 24-hour basis. Although none of the associated flight corridors or holding patterns intersect the borough of Manhattan, moving the fighters safely into position meant routing them through some very congested airspace.[31] Moreover, after the second impact at 9:03 A.M., local controllers began shutting down New York City air space, which added further complexity to an already difficult situation. This was no small concern.

Robin Hordon, a pilot and former air traffic controller who worked at the FAA's Boston Center for eleven years, thinks Bronner's article obfuscates the real issue, which is why NEADS did not scramble the Otis fighters much sooner. According to Hordon, the FAA response protocol for hijackings is quite different — and slower — than in the case of air emergencies.[32] He says Flight 11 should have been treated as an air emergency, in which case the scrambled fighters from Otis would have had priority. FAA controllers would have cleared the airspace ahead of the fighters, and they would have arrived in plenty of time to intercept Flight 11. By delaying to "pick up the phone" until after the FAA reverted to the more cumbersome hijack protocol, NEADS insured that its fighters would have a lower priority status, in accord with standard protocols, hence would have to wait their turn to transit through New York City airspace. Hordon believes the initial delay was part of a deliberate strategy to effect a standdown. The FAA was an easy scapegoat.

He may be correct. As we know, the two pilots from Otis who ended up in a holding pen south of Long Island later explained that while they waited for orders, they watched the ominous plume billowing from the WTC, conspicuous from 70 miles away.[33] They only learned about the second strike when they called their commander for an update.[34] The *9/11 Commission Report* fails to clarify this important part of the story. Indeed, a footnote buried in the report even suggests that the pilots from Otis took the initiative themselves.[35] The note informs us that at 9:13 A.M., the pilots "told their Boston Center controller that they needed to establish a combat air patrol (CAP) over New York," which they finally accomplished at 9:25 A.M., much too late to make a difference.[36] In a more recent account, author Lynn Spencer, who is a pilot herself, claims that Nasypany's boss, Col. Robert Marr, the NEADS battle commander, grew so impatient with the delays that he used his authority to override the FAA. He did this by declaring an AFIO, that is, an "Agreement for Fighter Interceptor Operations," a rarely-used provision that allows the military to enter FAA airspace without permission.[37] Of course, by then it was too late to matter.

Given the above, Bronner's charge that the FAA obstructed and delayed NEADS on 9/11 is dubious. All of the evidence suggests that FAA controllers were begging for fighter protection. Colin Scoggins told me he made as many as forty calls to NEADS on the morning of September 11 trying to get fighters in the air. During some of these calls he attempted to persuade NEADS to scramble fighters from bases that were not officially on alert, such as the Pomona base near Atlantic City, which is much closer to New York than the NEADS alert base on Cape Cod (Otis ANGB). Pomona is the home of the Air National Guard's 177th fighter wing, which was in the habit of launching F-16s almost every morning on training flights.[38] The F-16s often practiced bombing runs over a remote stretch of New Jersey pine barrens.

Scoggins knew about these almost daily training flights — his impulse was correct. As we now know, on the morning of September 11, F-16s from the 177th fighter wing were at that very moment taxiing on the runway at Pomona preparing for take off at 9 A.M., and could easily have been rerouted to Manhattan in just minutes.[39] The *9/11 Commission Report* mentions the call by Scoggins, but distorts what actually happened. The report states, "… the [Boston] Center also tried to contact a former alert site in Atlantic City, unaware it had been phased out."[40] This is hogwash. Scoggins was well aware that the Pomona base was not officially on alert, but was rightly undeterred by this formality which under the circumstances was irrelevant. Given that a hijacking was believed to be in progress just a few miles up the coast, the fighters from the Pomona base could and should have been mustered without delay. While it is true they were unarmed, this should not have been a consideration, because a shootdown order is always a last resort in any event. Amazingly, instead of being scrambled the Pomona fighters were ordered to return to the hanger.[41]

The *9/11 Commission Report's* misrepresentation of the call by Scoggins was a case of deception, and the same can be said of Bronner's article, which — we must conclude — was a carefully-crafted piece of disinformation. Unfortunately, ordinary citizens who know nothing about FAA protocols and no-fly zones probably found it persuasive. Although Bronner claims to have heard thirty hours of NORAD tape, according to Scoggins most of those hours were probably "dead time": empty tape. Scoggins thinks Bronner heard only snippets, about ten or eleven of which are mentioned in his article. It is also likely that the information Bronner received from NORAD was cherry-picked ahead of time to convey the desired impressions. Scoggins thinks the snippets represent only a fraction of the 100-300 phone calls made on the morning of 9/11, not to mention FAA recordings and in-house tapes recorded by American and United Airlines. In short, there are excellent reasons to be wary of the picture Bronner paints. Only a comprehensive review of all of the recordings and radar data from 9/11 can reveal what actually happened. And this, I should add, has not been done, even to this day.[42]

Andrews Air Force Base, located just minutes by air from the White House, is another facility that NEADS could have mustered on 9/11. Andrews has a long tradition of servicing and defending the nation's capital. The base is the home of Air Force One and has long been the usual port of entry to and from Washington for U.S. presidents and diplomats. Although it was not one of NORAD's officially designated alert bases on 9/11, at least two combat-ready fighter units were based there, including a DC Air National Guard (DCANG) squadron of the 113th fighter wing. The 113th's mission, as stated on the Andrews website, was to provide "capable and ready response forces for the District of Columbia."[43] On a separate page the DCANG squadron boasted about providing "combat units in the highest possible state of readiness."[44] The 321st Marine Fighter Attack Squadron was also based at Andrews and flew the sophisticated F/A-18 Hornet.[45]

Nor was Andrews the only response-capable facility in the area. The Patuxent Naval Base in Maryland also had fighters. In fact, on September 11 former Secretary of Defense Casper Weinberger told FOX News, "The city [Washington] is ringed with Air Force bases and Navy bases, and the ability to get defensive planes in the air is very, very high."[46] But strangely, not on 9/11. As we know, some of the DCANG fighters were away at the time of the attack, participating in a military exercise in North Carolina, and this delayed their response. During a teleconference that morning convened by counter-terrorism czar Richard A. Clark, General Richard Myers appeared to take credit for rousting these fighters when he explained that F-16 fighters from the DCANG squadron at Andrews had finally been scrambled.[47] Myers failed to mention that it was not the Pentagon who mustered them, but the Secret Service.[48] The DCANG F-16s arrived over Washington even later than the fighters from Langley, too late to matter.

This story about Andrews has a postscript. Soon after the 9/11 attack 9/11 truth investigators discovered that someone had scrubbed the

DCANG webpage from the Internet, including its mission statement about "providing combat units in the highest possible state of readiness."[49] Fortunately, several months before 9/11 the page had been archived, so the key information can still be viewed on line.[50] Several others had already reported the facts in this case, but the story bears frequent repeating because it involves the destruction of important evidence.

Failure to Track Flight 11

In our interview Scoggins also provided details about another important matter that the commission failed to explain. Although the FAA's Boston Center tracked Flight 11 continuously on radar, for some reason NEADS never did locate the aircraft. Scoggins told me he gave them "nav aids," that is, commonly used reference points, even precise latitude and longitude coordinates, in short, all of the necessary information, but to no avail. Lt. Col. Dawne Deskins, who worked at NEADS and was on the receiving end of his call, told FOX News exactly what Scoggins told me: "He [Scoggins] gave me the latitude and longitude of that track ... but there was nothing there."[51] NEADS's failure to locate Flight 11 haunts Scoggins to this day because, he says, the plane was moving at 600 mph and should have been conspicuous on radar. The anomaly has never been explained. (Nor was it a lone case. As we will discover later, there were also *other* radar anomalies on 9/11.) Getting to the bottom of it should have been one of the priorities of the official 9/11 investigation. Yet, incredibly, the *9/11 Commission Report* barely mentions the issue. Instead of doing its job, i.e., digging for the truth, the commission meekly accepted the Pentagon's various excuses, usually without a word of protest.

The generals found various ways to dump on the FAA. Their excuses ranged from General McKinley's simple one-liner, "We are dependent on the FAA"[52] to convoluted statements by General Arnold, including this one: "Everything that we were doing, remember, was being relayed from the FAA. We had no visibility on those aircraft, couldn't see, we had no radars, couldn't talk to our pilots." At times, the generals were evasive, dodging direct questions instead of answering them. When commissioner John F. Lehman asked Arnold, "Why did they [i.e., the Langley fighters] go out to sea?" the NORAD general served up this word salad:

> When we scramble an aircraft, there is a line that is picked up, and the FAA and everyone is on that line. And the aircraft take off and they have a predetermined departure route. And, of course,

it's not over water, because our mission, unlike law enforcement's mission, is to protect things coming towards the United States. And I might even add, in all of our terrorist scenarios that we run, the aircraft, if we were to intercept aircraft, it is usually always from outside the United States coming towards us. So our peacetime procedures, to de-conflict with civil aviation's, so as not have endanger [sic] civil aviation in any particular way.[53]

Arnold's answer was borderline gibberish. (By the way, I triple-checked his syntax just to be sure I got it right.) But if the general meant to dissemble, he succeeded. To be sure, his reply did contain one of the military's favorite lines: NORAD could not protect America because it was configured to "look outward" for foreign threats, rather than inward.[54] General Richard Myers gave the same excuse the following year when he told the commission, "We were looking outward. We did not have the situational awareness inward because we did not have the radar coverage."[55] Here, the general raised an interesting point.

Students of 9/11 have often puzzled over the extended westerly flight paths of Flights 77 and 93, which do seem strange and irrational from the standpoint of terrorists bent on crashing planes into buildings, because these long detours exposed the alleged hijackers to countermeasures. The routes increased the odds that the planes would be intercepted, diminishing the chances for a successful attack. Would real terrorists have done this? Very doubtful. From a different point of view, however, the chosen flight paths make perfect sense. Assuming the 9/11 attack was staged or assisted by insiders, the long detours conveniently took the "hijacked" planes outside the range of NORAD's long-range radar towers situated on the east coast, essentially dumping the issue of radar coverage back into the FAA's lap. Was this done by design, to lay the basis for the cover story, i.e., that NORAD could not see because "we were looking outward"? Although this is speculation, if correct it means the truth is simpler than many of us have supposed.

As it happened, General Myers' statement prompted one of the panel's few finer moments. Commissioner Jamie Gorelick, a former legal counsel to the Department of Defense, evidently had boned up on military doctrine since the previous hearing. She knew the Chairman of the Joint Chiefs was pulling a fast one and, to her credit, Gorelick rose to the occasion. She corrected Myers, pointing out that the NORAD charter says no such thing. In fact, NORAD is charged with "control of the airspace above the domestic U.S." in addition to defending against external threats. At this, Myers responded with an absurdity, citing the Posse Comitatus Act, which prohibits the U.S. military from domestic law enforcement. This surely exasperated Gorelick because she again politely interrupted Myers with another correction, pointing out that the "Posse Comitatus Act says you can't arrest people. It doesn't mean that the military has no authority, obligation or ability to defend the United States from attacks that happen to happen in the domestic United States."[56]

For once, the dialogue looked promising. Unfortunately, it ended right there because Gorelick ran out of her alloted time, and Myers had to leave for another appointment. But the facts did not matter, in any event. There is not a word in the final report about Gorelick's important point, and nothing about her exchange with Myers. Incredibly, the report borrows the very phraseology used by Myers. One passage reads, "America's homeland defenders faced outward ... "[57]

One of the generals' lamest excuses was that NORAD could not track the hijacked planes after the transponders went off because of antiquated radar equipment. During his October 2001 testimony to the Senate Armed Services Committee, General Ralph Eberhart had described NORAD's command-and-control systems as "'70s and '80s technology." He went on: "[NORAD's technology] really hasn't kept pace over the years. So we need to bring those into the 21st century."[58] Later, General Arnold told the commission basically the same thing. "Our resources were extremely limited in many cases," he said, "because we initially could not even see what the FAA could see ..."[59] The statement was untrue, but the panel swallowed it unreservedly.

Michael Bronner echoes the same theme in his *Vanity Fair* article. Indeed, he amplifies it in melodramatic fashion, and because the issue is so important I am going to cite a passage verbatim.

> Radar is the NEADS controllers' most vital piece of equipment, but by 9/11 the scopes were so old, among other factors, that controllers were ultimately unable to find any of the hijacked planes in enough time to react. Known collectively as the Green Eye for the glow the radar rings give off, the scopes looked like something out of *Dr. Strangelove* and were strikingly anachronistic compared with the equipment at civilian air-traffic sites.[60]

Dramatic: but irrelevant. Yes, NEADS was using older hardware on 9/11, but so what? Colin Scoggins confirmed to me that NEADS could see everything the FAA could see, and more.[61] The military radar was adequate, and former FAA air traffic controller Robin Hordon says the same thing. He explained to me that although NEADS was using older scopes on 9/11, the quality of the radar data that was being input had never been higher, as a result of continual upgrades in radar technology, of which NORAD has the world's best.[62]

Another whopper was Bronner's claim that NEADS technicians "were at a loss" because Flight 11 had ceased transmitting a transponder signal. Bronner's point was that NEADS needed the signal to locate the plane. More nonsense. This is what Scoggins was referring to when he mentioned that NEADS could see "everything the FAA saw, *and more.*" Unlike the FAA's radar, NORAD does not need a transponder code to track a plane. If it did, as David Griffin has pointed out, the Soviets could easily have mounted a sneak attack against the United States during the Cold War any time they liked, simply by turning off their military transponders.[63]

But perhaps the most flagrant example of deception in the *Vanity Fair* article is the statement by NEADS commander Major Kevin Nasypany, who told Bronner, "You would see thousands of green blips on your scope. And now you have to pick and choose. Which is the bad guy out there? Which is the hijacked aircraft? And without that information from the FAA, it's a needle in a haystack."[64] Once again, not true. In fact, it is for this very reason that each radar scope at NORAD shows only a small portion of the total area in the region: precisely so that technicians will *not* be overwhelmed by blips. And the FAA is set up the same way. This was confirmed to me by Robin Hordon, who said he was so infuriated by Bronner's deceptions that he could no longer keep silent.[65] After the September 2006 *Vanity Fair* article, Hordon began to speak out about 9/11 and has been doing radio interviews ever since.[66]

NEADS' failure to locate Flight 11 on radar had the serious consequence of slowing down its response time, because Col. Marr, the NEADS battle commander, was reluctant to scramble fighters from Otis ANGB without a target. However, if delay was the object, the outcome was a "success," not a failure of intelligence or military readiness.

Here, I must mention that although Bronner's article supports the official story as revised by the 9/11 Commission, it is of interest that NEADS commander Nasypany himself did not agree. Nasypany told Bronner, "I knew where Flight 93 was. I don't care what [the 9/11 commission says].

15

I mean, I care but I made that assessment to put my fighters over Washington. Ninety-three was on its way in [to Washington] ..."[67] In a later discussion I will return to this point, and we will discover why it is so important.

Major Nasypany was a beneficiary of the Bush administration's war on terrorism. The major was later "punished" for his unit's failed performance on 9/11 with a promotion and pay raise. Of course, there will always be winners and losers in time of war. But where is the wisdom in rewarding failure? I would argue: There is none. It is always a misguided policy, and in this case was symptomatic of an even more serious malady: failed leadership at the highest level of government, the same "leadership" — I should add — that is responsible for the deepening quagmires in Iraq and Afghanistan.

Evidence of a Stand-down

NORAD's multiple failures on September 11, 2001 led Robin Hordon and others to suspect that a stand-down order was in effect. The 9/11 Commission added fuel to this fire by failing to satisfactorily answer key questions, such as the fiasco of the scrambled fighters from Langley AFB. The *9/11 Commission Report* suggests that the lead pilot from Langley misunderstood his orders.[68] Yet, another passage elsewhere in the report states that the pilots were never briefed. As one pilot later explained, "I reverted to the Russian threat," meaning that in the absence of an order he defaulted to "plan B," a backup order.[69] Does this explain the holding pattern over the Atlantic?

Certainly the screw-up was a "red flag" and cried out for further investigation. In a military chain of command, the responsibility for issuing orders rests with ranking officers. Therefore, if orders were never issued, someone had to be responsible, and that individual may have been derelict in his duty. Here, then, was a golden opportunity for the official investigation to discover what really happened. All the panel had to do was interrogate the Langley pilots and trace the orders (or lack of them) back up the food chain. The panel had a mandate to "provide the fullest possible account." It also had the authority to issue any subpoenas that were necessary. So, where are the transcripts of these crucial interviews, which apparently were conducted behind closed doors? The transcripts have never been made public and are nowhere to be found in the *9/11 Commission Report*. Did the commission shield high-ranking officers from scrutiny — and accountability?

Of course, an insider familiar with FAA protocols, NORAD, and the military's rules of engagement would have known how to manipulate the system and get away with it. Were honest radar technicians confused on September 11 by phony blips on their radar screens? Were genuine radar signals secretly scrubbed by hackers participating in war games? Perhaps there was something, after all, to Major Nasypany's complaint about "thousands of green blips." Was this an oblique reference to military exercises? We know that a dozen or more drills were in progress on the morning of 9/11.[70] One effect was to "thin out" the nation's air defenses. Fighters had been dispatched to northern Canada, Iceland, Turkey and also to North Carolina, as noted, which reduced the number of available assets in the event of an emergency. I was shocked to learn that at least one of the exercises involved simulated hijackings. Another included an accidental (non-terrorist) plane crash into a building.[71]

Vigilant Guardian

In a 2002 interview, NORAD General Larry Arnold affirmed that at the start of the September 11 attack his command was in the midst of one such exercise, Vigilant Guardian. The general's first reaction on hearing the news about Flight 11 was "It's part of the exercise!"[72] This speaks volumes. Nor was Arnold alone. His reaction was typical. When NEADS commander Major Nasypany learned about Flight 11, he thought someone had started the exercise early. He told Michael Bronner that he was so surprised he even thought out loud, "The hijack's not supposed to be for another hour."[73] Snippets from the NORAD tapes include the similar surprised replies of other NEADS technicians, including Jeremy Powell, who asked Boston Center, "Is this real-world or exercise?"[74] Bronner writes that Vigilant Guardian involved "a range of scenarios, including a 'traditional' simulated hijack in which politically-motivated perpetrators commandeer an aircraft, land on a Cuba-like island, and seek asylum." But is this more smoke and mirrors?

In 2006, an army sergeant flatly contradicted Bronner with information about Vigilant Guardian. Sergeant Lauro "L.J." Chavez claimed that on September 11, 2001 he was stationed at McDill AFB in Tampa, Florida, home of the Central Command (CENTCOM), the joint headquarters for all U.S. military forces in the Middle East, East Africa, and Central Asia. Chavez said he is a computer expert and at the time ran a team of technicians who serviced all of the office computers at CENTCOM, including those used by (four-star) General Tommy Franks, the ranking officer and regional commander. Due to the nature of his work Chavez held a top secret clearance and enjoyed free access to the most secure parts of the base.

He claimed that on September 10, 2001 he was providing computer support within a secure command post when by chance he happened to see something he was not supposed to.[75] One of the senior officers had left a top-secret document open on the desk beside the computer that Chavez was servicing. As he waited for software to download, Chavez couldn't help but read it. He says the document pertained to Vigilant Guardian and outlined various hijack scenarios that were anything but "traditional." The scenarios included crashing hijacked planes into a nuclear reactor in California, the Sears tower in Chicago, and, yes, also the World Trade Center, Pentagon and White House. But Chavez was even more surprised that the details were classified top secret.

In his experience this was most unusual. Chavez claims that over the course of his army career he participated in a number of war games and military exercises, but not one of them was designated top secret except for this one case on 9/11. Normally, the Pentagon provides at least a modicum of information to the FAA and other public/state agencies about planned military exercises, for reasons that should be obvious and have to do with air safety and commerce. This is especially true when military drills occur in heavily populated areas. If Vigilant Guardian's hijack scenarios on September 11, 2001 were classified as top secret, the question we should be asking is: Why?

I must mention here that after Lauro Chavez went public with the above testimony, he came under intense attack by Internet debunkers who accused him of being an impostor and of faking his military record. I must acknowledge that I have been unable to determine the truth in the matter, despite strenuous efforts to do so. Nonetheless, I have decided to include his testimony in this discussion, with this caveat, because I find his story plausible.

Nor does it stand alone. In fact, similar information had already come to light: In April 2004, just days after National Security Adviser Condoleezza Rice explained to the 9/11 Commission that the White House never anticipated that hijacked planes might be used as weapons, a watchdog group released a NORAD document proving otherwise.[76] The document confirmed that in the period prior to 9/11, the U.S. military did indeed contemplate hijack scenarios involving crashes, i.e., planes used as weapons. Unlike the hijackings on 9/11, most of these proposed scenarios involved planes originating from foreign airports. The hijackings were to occur *before* the planes entered U.S. airspace. Even so, at least one hijack exercise in July 2001 involved departures from Utah and Washington state. In a written statement NORAD acknowledged that the threats of killing hostages or crashing planes had been left up to the scriptwriters who developed the drills. There was no indication whether any of these hijack exercises had been classified top secret.

In this respect the information about Vigilant Guardian released by Lauro Chavez in 2006 was qualitatively different and potentially more ominous. Obviously, the 9/11 Commission should have thoroughly investigated the military exercises that were in progress on 9/11, in order to "provide the fullest possible account" of the events of that day. Instead, as we know, the panel made a decision *not to go there*. The only reference to the drills in the final report is a single passing remark about Vigilant Guardian buried in a footnote.[77] It is yet another powerful indication of a failed investigation.

Stand-down Redux

Lauro Chavez also claims that on the day of the attack he personally witnessed evidence of a stand-down.[78] He says he was in a CENTCOM command post when the word came through about the World Trade Center: All at once there was a buzz of activity. Someone switched on CNN, and they were watching the events on a large screen. The second strike occurred, and suddenly everyone in the room was on his feet. Chavez heard many people say, "Why aren't they scrambling jets?" Colonels and Lt. Colonels crowded around the Air Force liaison officer, wanting to know: "Where are the fighters from NORAD?" According to Chavez the Colonel said, "We received an order to stand-down." This, of course, perplexed everyone. Chavez says he also witnessed unusual security measures the day before the attack: CENTCOM headquarters was being heavily fortified, and access to the base was restricted to personnel with top-secret clearances.

But the most compelling evidence for a stand-down on 9/11 was presented by Secretary of Transportation Norman Mineta during his 2003 testimony before the 9/11 Commission. Mineta told the panel that on 9/11 he arrived at the PEOC (the presidential bunker under the White House) at 9:20 A.M., where he joined Vice President Cheney, who was already present. Incidentally, this time of 9:20 A.M. flatly contradicts the official narrative, which claims that Cheney did not arrive until shortly before 10 A.M..[79] A few minutes later, Mineta overheard a conversation, the significance of which he says he failed to comprehend at the time. At 9:25-26 A.M., a young man came in and warned Cheney about an incoming aircraft. The warning was repeated several times. Initially, the plane was 50 miles out, then 30 miles out. Finally, in Mineta's own words:

> When it got down to "The plane is 10 miles out" the young man also said to the vice president, "Do the orders still stand?" And the vice president turned and whipped his neck around and said, "Of course the orders still stand. Have you heard anything to the contrary?"[80]

In the hearing, Mineta identified this incoming aircraft as the plane that hit the Pentagon, presumably AA Flight 77. He was explicit on this point. He told the commission that, in his opinion, the young man and vice president were referring to a shoot-down order. But, of course, this makes absolutely no sense. Given the context and the fact that the bogey was *not* shot down, the exchange can only refer to a stand-down. Obviously, the technician had been tracking the incoming aircraft on radar, which, of course, means that the presidential command center was equipped with a real-time radar link to the FAA and possibly NORAD. I hasten to add: This is not controversial. Multiple sources have confirmed the radar link, including the *Washington Post*,[81] as well as counter-terrorism czar Richard A. Clarke, who mentions it in his 9/11 memoir.[82]

The link was even confirmed by VP Cheney himself during a September 16, 2001 interview on *Meet the Press*. On live television Cheney told Tim Russert that "the Secret Service has an arrangement with the FAA. They had open lines after the World Trade Center was ..."[83] Here, Cheney stopped abruptly in mid-sentence, as if catching himself before revealing too much. No question, Norman Mineta's testimony challenges the official explanation that the Pentagon was not informed about Flight 77, because if Cheney knew, so did some in the U.S. military. In fact, during the Russert interview Cheney stated that while in the bunker he was in contact with Secretary of Defense Rumsfeld, who was then at the Pentagon.[84] It is astonishing that the U.S. media missed this connection.

Notice, Mineta's testimony also places Cheney at the epicenter of events, and this flatly contradicts the official story that the vice president did not arrive at the command center until much later. Obviously, the official timeline is a fabrication designed to shield Cheney by distancing him from events. Not surprisingly, Mineta's explosive testimony is nowhere to be found in the *9/11 Commission Report*. Fortunately, it was filmed as a part of the hearings and is an indisputable part of the historical record.

It was obvious, in fact, from the first days, long before Mineta testified before the commission, that his presence in the bunker posed a serious problem for Cheney. The White House had little reason to think it could count on Mineta's loyalty. He was a civil servant, after all, not a neocon, the only Democrat in Bush's cabinet. With the benefit of hindsight, it certainly appears that the White House responded to this "threat" by attempting to head off trouble. Late in 2001, the well-known journalist Bob Woodward was summoned by the White House and invited to write a retrospective series of articles about September 11, as seen through the eyes of the president and his staff. Woodward was only too happy to oblige and, as we know, he went on to serve for a time as Bush's court historian.

The result, beginning in January 2002, was a series in the *Washington Post*.[85] His articles present a White House-friendly version of events, and one story recounts the famous episode in the bunker. In Woodward's redacted version, however, Cheney has become the man of the hour who rises to the press of terrible events. The same young man approaches the VP and warns about the incoming airliner. But the timeline has been pushed back. Now it is nearly 10 A.M., and the plane is Flight 93, not Flight 77. The hijacked plane is 80 miles out, not 50. There is also another huge difference. Instead of a stand-down order, it is a shoot-down order. When the young man says, "There is a fighter in the area. Should we engage?" Cheney responds by making the tough call to shoot down the plane. But the young man hesitates.

As narrated by Woodward, the tension in the room mounts and reaches a pitch. The plane is rapidly closing and is now only 60 miles out. The young man repeats the question, and again Cheney gives the command. But the young man *still* hesitates. "Does the order still stand?" he mumbles. Finally, Cheney snaps and says, "Of course it does!"

Woodward's redacted history is more colorful. The problem is that it is a complete fabrication. It does not even agree with the official narrative presented in the *9/11 Commission Report,* because at no time on September 11 did Flight 93 approach anywhere near as close as 60 miles to the White House — nor even 80. This crucial detail exposes the fraud.

One day, the episode in the White House bunker will be among the most cited events in U.S. history. Future generations of Americans will revile Cheney and the rest as traitors who usurped the Constitution and catapulted our nation into war after needless war, while devastating the U.S. economy. Unfortunately, the events of 9/11 have been so obscured that most Americans, including many who strongly oppose the Bush administration, have yet to unmask the official narrative for what it is.

There are countless examples, but let us take the case of *Boston Globe* reporter Charlie Savage, who won a Pulitzer Prize in 2007 for his book *Takeover.*[86] I do not question Savage's ability as a writer. His book is a trenchant analysis of George W. Bush's imperial presidency. The author's critical faculties shine as he details how Dick Cheney and the neocons went about the business of expanding the power of the presidency at the expense of our constitutional framework. As a historian Savage shows a capable hand, that is, *until* he turns to the famous scene in the bunker on 9/11, when suddenly his critical faculties desert him. At a glance it is obvious that Savage learned everything he knows about 9/11 from Bob Woodward and the *Washington Post,* which he apparently views as gospel, or, at any rate, good enough.

Someone needs to inform Savage — he seems unable to make the connection — that it is only a single step from the sub-title of his book, i.e., *the Subversion of American Democracy,* to the cold-blooded murder of 3,000 of our fellow citizens for the purpose of galvanizing the nation behind the imperial president and the neocons' push for world domination. Which, after all, was never a secret.

But what does it say about our political culture that a writer like Savage can get his facts wrong, yet still win a Pulitzer? At very least, I think it tells us that Adolph Hitler made a disturbingly accurate insight into human nature when he wrote in *Mein Kampf,* "The great mass of the people will more easily fall victims to a great lie than to a small one." I think it also tells us that the judgment of history belongs to the future. For the present, this remains our problem — and our challenge.

By the way, Norman Mineta has stood by his testimony.

Flight 77 Never Crossed the Potomac

Colin Scoggins made one other important call on the morning of September 11. At 9:36 A.M., he notified NEADS about an unidentified plane six miles southeast of the White House.[87] At the time Scoggins was not himself tracking the plane on radar. When he placed this call, as before, he was merely relaying information that he believes originated at the FAA's Washington headquarters. According to the *9/11 Commission Report*

(p. 27), this call sparked a frenzy: NEADS responded by immediately redirecting the Langley fighters to Washington. As the reader will learn in subsequent chapters, however, this is a fable. No such response occurred.

The *9/11 Commission Report* also implies that this unidentified plane at 9:36 A.M. was AA Flight 77. Supposedly, the call at 9:36 A.M. was NORAD's first notification of its approach, roughly two minutes (or less) before the crash. Michael Bronner also repeats these assertions in his *Vanity Fair* article about the NORAD tapes. Yet during our interview, Scoggins told me that at the time he had no idea about the identity of the plane. Later, like everyone else, he simply assumed it was Flight 77. Scoggins says he was also under the impression that it passed near the White House. Scoggins is not alone in this. Even today, many Americans probably believe that Flight 77 made a loop over Washington before striking the Pentagon. White House spokesman Ari Fleischer actually gave rise to one of these stories, which were widely reported in the media.[88]

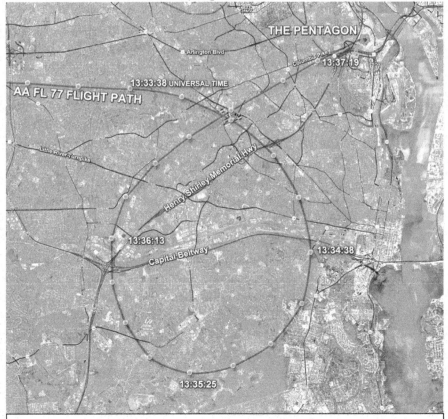

Flight path of American Airlines Flight 77 in its approach to the Pentagon. For practical purposes, Universal Time is equivalent to Greenwich Mean Time, which is four hours ahead of Eastern Daylight Time.   Source: RADES radar data

23

The reality, however, is that at no time on September 11 was Flight 77 six miles southeast of the White House. A glance at a map will show that the Potomac River lies directly south of the presidential mansion. This means that the unidentified plane Scoggins reported at 9:36 A.M. was over Maryland at the time, and this rules out Flight 77. We know this from an abundance of evidence, including eyewitness accounts, radar data, and the National Transportation Safety Board (NTSB) flight path study of Flight 77, which was released in August 2006.[89] Although critics have identified major problems with the NTSB study, these pertain to the final approach of whatever hit the Pentagon, and have nothing to say about its general flight path, which remains uncontroversial.

The bogey generally approached from the west before veering south to complete its now-famous downward spiraling 330-degree loop over Alexandria, during which the aircraft lost roughly 5,000 feet in altitude (dropping from 7,000 feet to about 2,000 feet). The loop took just over three minutes, after which the aircraft made its final approach. I have used the expression "whatever hit the Pentagon" because the identity of this plane has never conclusively been determined. In fact, because of the issues raised about the NTSB study, some skeptics hold that the plane never even hit the Pentagon, but passed over it and simply flew away. They argue that the damage to the building was caused by a missile, or pre-set explosives. While I am open to the likelihood of explosions, because witnesses reported the smell of cordite, I view the fly-over scenario as implausible because it cannot explain the broken light poles in the approach path.

At 8:56 A.M., as Flight 77 completed the westward leg of its flight path on 9/11, its transponder was turned off, and moments later the plane was lost to primary radar. Eight minutes later, a blip suddenly appeared on radar over West Virginia. Most have interpreted this as the reappearance of Flight 77. However, this conclusion remains an assumption, because the aircraft in question was not transmitting a transponder signal at the time. Nor was there any subsequent radio contact with the pilot. For these reasons, the identity of the aircraft that struck the Pentagon was never positively reestablished. It was probably Flight 77, but we cannot be certain, because the U.S. military has never released the serial numbers from the wreckage, which would positively identify the aircraft. Furthermore, the three short video clips of the impact from the Pentagon security cameras which have thus far been released (out of an estimated total of 85) are inconclusive.[90] For these reasons, I will employ a writer's device to convey this uncertainty, and will refer to the aircraft as Flight 77(?).

Of one thing we can be certain. Whatever aircraft Colin Scoggins reported at 9:36 A.M. was not Flight 77. What, then, were FAA controllers seeing in that moment on their radar screens? As the reader is about to discover, there was a mysterious plane in the skies over Washington that morning.

Endnotes

1. Paul Thompson, *The Terror Timeline: Year by Year, Day by Day, Minute by Minute*, Reagan Books, 2004.

2. Go to http://www.cooperativeresearch.org/project.jsp?project=911_project.

3. Senate Armed Services Committee, Chairman, U.S. Senator Carl Levin (D-MI), Hearing On the Nomination of General Richard Myers to be Chairman of The Joint Chiefs of Staff, September 13, 2001. Archived at http://emperors-clothes.com/9-11backups/mycon.htm.

4. Pentagon officials presented a detailed chronology of this revised timeline in testimony before the 911 Commission in May 2003. National Commission on Terrorist Attacks Upon the United States, Public Hearing, May 23, 2003. Transcript posted at http://www.9-11commission.gov/archive/hearing2/9-11Commission_Hearing_2003-05-23.htm. Also see Press Release, Directorate of Public Affairs, NORAD, September 18, 2001. Archived at http://www.public-action.com/911/noradresponse/.

5. National Commission on Terrorist Attacks Upon the United States, Public Hearing, June 17, 2004. Transcript posted at http://www.washingtonpost.com/wp-dyn/articles/A49429-2004Jun17.html.

6. The source here is the FAA's *Aeronautical Information Manual. Official Guide to Basic Flight Information and Air Traffic Control (ATC) Procedures*, posted at www.faa.gov.

7. AP, August 13, 2002.

8. Interview with Colin Scoggins, March 10, 2007; email from Scoggins, March 15, 2007.

9. *The 9/11 Commission Report, Final Report of the National Commission on Terrorist Attacks upon the United States*, WW Norton and Company, New York, 2004, p. 31.

10. The panel even admits this. *The 9/11 Commission Report*, p. 34.

11. National Commission on Terrorist Attacks Upon the United States, Public Hearing, May 23, 2003, loc. cit.

12. *The 9/11 Commission Report*, p. 26.

13. Ibid., p. 27.

14. Ibid., pp. 20 and 24.

15. Dan Eggen, "9/11 Panel Suspected Deception by Pentagon," *Washington Post*, August 2, 2006.

16. This term occurs numerous times. *The 9/11 Commission Report*, p. 34.

17. David Ray Griffin, "9/11 Live or Fabricated: Do the NORAD Tapes Verify The 9/11 Commission Report?" September 4, 2006, posted at http://www.911truth.org/article.php?story=2006091418303369.

18. *The 9/11 Commission Report*, p. 34.

19. Michael Bronner, "9/11 Live: The NORAD Tapes," *Vanity Fair,* August 2006, p. 264. Posted at http://www.vanityfair.com/politics/features/2006/08/norad200608?prin table=true&currentPage=all.

20. Tim Harper, "Families sue U.S., reject 9/11 'bribe,'" *Toronto Star,* December 23, 2003.

21. "We have been unable to identify the source of this mistaken FAA information." *The 9/11 Commission Report,* p. 26

22. Not to be confused with the 2005 Discovery Channel docudrama, *The Flight that Fought Back,* which I will discuss in the next chapter.

23. Subsequently, the transcripts were released and are currently available for download at George Washington University's National Security Archive, along with the National Transportation Safety Board (NTSB) flight path studies for flights 11, 175 and 77. Go to http://www.gwu.edu/~nsarchiv/NSAEBB/NSAEBB165/index.htm.

24. Michael Bronner, op. cit.

25. *The 9/11 Commission Report,* p. 34.

26. Interview with Colin Scoggins, March 10, 2007.

27. Email from Colin Scoggins, April 27, 2007.

28. FAA Communications with NORAD On September 11, 2001, FAA clarification memo to 9/11 Independent Commission, posted at http://www.911truth.org/article. php?story=2004081200421797.

29. National Commission on Terrorist Attacks Upon the United States, Public Hearing, May 23, 2003, loc. cit.

30. David Ray Griffin, *The 9/11 Commission Report: Omissions and Distortions,* Olive Branch Press, Massachusetts, 2005, pp. 186-188.

31. Reynolds Dixon, "The Flying Elephant: Evidence for Involvement of a Third Jet in the WTC Attacks," *Journal of 9/11 Studies,* Vol 1, Scholars for 9/11 Truth, June 2006, posted at http://journalof911studies.com/.

32. Email from Robin Hordon, March 17, 2008.

33. Kevin Dennehy, "I thought it was the end of the world," *Cape Cod Times,* August 21, 2002.

34. "Moments of Crisis, Part I: Terror Hits the Towers," ABC News, September 14, 2002.

35. *The 9/11 Commission Report,* p. 459, note 120.

36. Ibid., p. 24.

37. Lynn Spencer, *Touching History: The Untold Story of the Drama That Unfolded in the Skies over America on 9/11,* Free Press, New York, 2008, p.113.

38. Ibid., p. 34 and 120.

39. M. Kelly, North Jersey Media Group, "Atlantic City F-16 Fighters Were Eight Minutes Away from 9/11 Hijacked Planes," posted at http://www.prisonplanet. com/051203atlanticcityfighters.html.

40. *The 9/11 Commission Report,* p. 20.

41. Lynn Spencer, op. cit., p. 120

42. An independent investigator named John Farmer has been conducting a comprehensive review of the NORAD tapes in conjunction with the RADES radar data released in October 2007 as a result of a FOIA request. I will touch on one of Farmer's discoveries

in chapter 11.

43. The Andrews webpage has been archived. To see it as it looked in September 2001 go to http://emperors-clothes.com/9-11backups/dcmilsep.htm.

44. The original page has been archived. Here's how it looked on April 19, 2001: http://emperor.vwh.net/9-11backups/dcandr2.htm.

45. The Andrews page has been archived. Scroll to the bottom: http://emperors-clothes.com/9-11backups/dcmil.htm.

46. Interview with Casper Weinberger, FOX News, September 11, 2001.

47. Richard A. Clark, *Against All Enemies,* New York, The Free Press, 2004, p.12.

48. General Arnold admitted this in a January 2002 interview. "Conversation with Major General Larry Arnold, Commander, 1st Air Force, Tyndall AFB, Florida," *Code One* magazine, Vol. 17, No. 1, January 2002. Posted at http://www.codeonemagazine.com/archives/2002/articles/jan_02/defense/.

Arnold later restated this during his testimony before the 9/11 Commission. Transcript, National Commission on Terrorist Attacks Upon the United States, Public Hearing, May 23, 2003, loc.cit.

49. Illarion Bykov and Jared Israel were the first to report this, in November 2001. Go to http://emperors-clothes.com/indict/indict-1.htm.

50. Here's how the original page looked on April 19, 2001: http://emperor.vwh.net/9-11backups/dcandr2.htm.

51. Steve Brown, "Air Defenders Learn Lessons from September 11," FOX News, September 8 2002.

52. National Commission on Terrorist Attacks Upon the United States, Public Hearing, Friday, May 23, 2003, loc. cit.

53. Ibid.

54. General Eberhart gave this excuse during a hearing before the Senate Armed Services Committee, chaired by Senator Carl Levin, October 25, 2001. The excuse was later repeated by Generals McKinley and Arnold before the 9/11 Commission. National Commission on Terrorist Attacks Upon the United States, Public Hearing, May 23, 2003, loc. cit.

55. National Commission on Terrorist Attacks Upon the United States, Public Hearing, June 17, 2004, loc. cit.

56. Ibid.

57. *The 9/11 Commission Report,* p. 352.

58. FDCH Transcripts, Senate Armed Services Committee Holds Hearing on Role of Defense Department in Homeland Security, October 25, 2001.

59. National Commission on Terrorist Attacks Upon the United States, Public Hearing, May 23, 2003, loc. cit.

60. Michael Bronner, op. cit.

61. Email from Colin Scoggins, March 15, 2007.

62. Email from Robin Hordon, March 17, 2008.

63. David Ray Griffin, *Debunking 9/11 Debunking,* Olive Branch Press, Northampton, MA, 2007, p. 48.

64. Ibid.

65. Ibid., pp. 46-47.

66. Email from Robin Hordon, March 7, 2008.

67. Michael Bronner, op. cit., p. 285.

68. *The 9/11 Commission Report*, p. 27.

69. Ibid., p. 45.

70. Webster Griffin Tarpley gives the fullest account I have seen in his book *9/11 Synthetic Terrorism: Made in the USA*, Progressive Press, 2006. See the preface and pp. 203-215. The number of drills has continued to climb. At last count it was approaching twenty-five. See Tarpley's presentation at the Vancouver 9/11 Truth Conference, June 22-24, 2007. Tapes are available from www.v911truth.org.

71. John L. Lumpkin, "Agency planned exercise on Sept. 11 built around a plane crashing into a building," *AP News*, August 21, 2002.

72. "Conversation with Major General Larry Arnold, Commander, 1st Air Force, Tyndall AFB, Florida," *Code One*, Vol. 17, No. 1, 1st Quarter 2002.

73. Michael Bronner, op. cit.

74. Ibid.

75. Steve Watson, CENTCOM Sergeant Details Traitorous Stand-down Orders on 9/11. Military whistleblower comes forward with key information," *Infowars*, September 26, 2006.

76. The name of the watchdog group was the Project on Government Oversight. Steven Komarow and Tom Squitieri, "NORAD had drills of jets as Weapons," *USA Today*, April 18, 2004.

77. Vigilant Guardian was a NORAD exercise that supposedly postulated a Soviet bomber attack. *The 9/11 Commission Report*, p. 458, note 116.

78. Steve Watson, op. cit.

79. By the way, Mineta's Cheney timeline is corroborated by multiple sources. For a thorough discussion see David Ray Griffin's latest book, *9/11 Contradictions*, Olive Branch Press, Massachusetts, 2008, pp. 12-21.

80. National Commission on Terrorist Attacks Upon the United States, Public Hearing, Friday, May 23, 2003, loc. cit.

81. Don Phillips, "White House Overflights Breach Strict Security Zone: FAA Warns Pilots, Traffic Controllers," *Washington Post*, September 21, 1998.

82. Richard A. Clark, op. cit., p. 7.

83. "The VP appears on Meet the Press with Tim Russert," September 16, 2001. The interview is posted at http://www.whitehouse.gov/vicepresident/news-speeches/speeches/vp20010916.html.

84. Ibid.

85. Bob Woodward and Dan Balz, "America's Chaotic Road to War: Bush's Global Strategy Began to Take Shape in First Frantic Hours After Attack," *Washington Post*, (first in a series) January 27, 2002, posted at http://www.washingtonpost.com/wp-dyn/articles/A42754-2002Jan26_4.html.

86. Charlie Savage, *Takeover: The Return of the Imperial Presidency and the Subversion of American Democracy*, Little, Brown & Co., New York, 2007.

87. *The 9/11 Commission Report*, p. 27. An audio of this radio transmission was included in a History Channel program, *The 9/11 Conspiracies: Fact or Fiction*, cat. # AAE

- 103790, 2007.

88. "Primary Target: The Pentagon," CBS News, September 21, 2001; *Boston Globe*, November 23, 2001; *Daily Telegraph*, September 16, 2001.

89. One important eyewitness was Chris Stephenson, chief air traffic controller at Washington's Reagan National Airport. At 9:30 A.M. on the morning of 9/11, Stephenson received a call from the Secret Service warning him that an unidentified aircraft was approaching Washington from the west at high speed. Stephenson quickly checked his scope and located the plane on radar about 5 miles west of the city. He then looked out the window and actually saw the aircraft approaching. He watched it turn south and make a 330-degree looping spiral, descending all the while. The plane came back around and passed out of view behind some tall buildings in Crystal City, immediately south of the Pentagon. Stephenson then witnessed a huge fireball. Alan Levin, "Voices from the Air Traffic World," *USA Today*, August 12, 2002.

To view a map of Flight 77's final approach to the pentagon or to download the NTSB's flight path study go to http://www.gwu.edu/~nsarchiv/NSAEBB/NSAEBB165/index.htm. I will discuss the radar data in chapter four.

90. The FBI reportedly confiscated all of the film from the Pentagon security cameras immediately following the Pentagon strike. Presumably all of this important evidence remains in its possession.

2

The White Plane

As the eyes of the nation were focused on the gruesome events at the World Trade Center, the networks interrupted their 9/11 television coverage with a breaking story from Washington. A large plane had just been sighted over the White House. Exactly when it first appeared over the city is uncertain, but the reports aired shortly after the Pentagon strike. Witnesses who saw the plane say it circled over Washington.

ABC anchor Peter Jennings was the first journalist to mention the mysterious plane, which he did on air at 9:41 A.M. We know the time because a digital clock was embedded in the screen during ABC's coverage. Here is what Jennings said: "The White House, of course, is--is--is--has leapt to the forefront of people's concern this morning. And there is a plane circling the White House at the moment. And they're clearing the grounds there.... We've had incidents, as you know, in the past, several years ago where a small aircraft landed in the White House--in the White House garden and the pilot mentally deranged, as I recall at the time, was killed. But the White House is certainly--certainly been very heavily defended. And this plane circling the White House adds to the trauma that people are feeling today, but we have no idea precisely what that means."[1]

CNN's Senior White House correspondent John King was across the street from the White House, in Lafayette Park, when he saw the plane. At about 9:53 A.M., King reported live that "about 10 minutes ago, there was a white jet circling overhead. Now, you generally don't see planes in the area over the White House. That is restricted air space. No reason to believe that this jet was there for any nefarious purposes, but the Secret Service was very concerned, pointing up at the jet in the sky."[2]

Kate Snow, another CNN correspondent, was standing two blocks from the Capitol when she saw the plane. Snow also mentioned it on-air, adding that a security guard told her it was responsible for the decision to evacuate the seat of government.[3] In his 9/11 memoir *Against All En-*

emies, counter-terrorism czar Richard A. Clarke writes that the decision to evacuate the White House was made after the Secret Service issued a warning about the approach of an unidentified aircraft.[4] But Clarke does not specify whether he means Flight 77, or this other mysterious aircraft.

NBC host Katie Couric was covering the unfolding events at the World Trade Center when she interrupted her broadcast at about 9:54 A.M. with a live report from Bob Kur, the network's senior Washington correspondent. Kur was at the White House, and he described the tense evacuation then in progress: "Administrators, cooks, whatever, running at a fairly high speed all of the way out of the building, through the top gates. Then we huddled for a while in Lafayette Park, across the street. And we've been moved, now, from there a block or so away. The offices along Jackson Place which are across the street from the White House and adjacent to Lafayette Park also have been evacuated. And in the most surreal of this morning's scenes here at the White House, *a white plane, a very big jet, was flying an unusual pattern near the White House over Lafayette Park. Very slowly it made one circle* and then, we have not seen it since [my emphasis]. There was a lot of concern about what this plane might be. But, again, it's only speculation. But most people say that since flights have been cleared from U.S. air space, and it was a totally white plane, looked unusual to all of us, that it was a government plane of some kind."[5] At 9:59 A.M. Couric again mentioned Kur's "haunting" report from the White House. In fact, she was in mid-sentence when all attention shifted due to the sudden collapse of the South Tower.

CNN actually photographed the plane over the Capitol. Unfortunately, the aircraft was too far away to identify from the screen shot.[6]

Area P-56

The sighting of a large white plane over the White House on September 11, 2001 was noteworthy. As mentioned by John King and Peter Jennings, the airspace over Washington is very tightly restricted. In fact, it's probably the most restricted airspace on the planet. At the time of the attack, the prohibited zone, known as area P-56, extended in all directions from the Washington Monument.[7] The no-fly zone included the Pentagon and much of the city of Washington, and was closely monitored by FAA radar. Every plane entering this area would have been detected immediately and if not identified should have activated Washington's air defenses. The Secret Service would also have been alerted, because, as I mentioned in the previous chapter, the agency had a direct feed to FAA radar. The core of P-56 is centered around the White House and stretches from the Potomac River to the Capitol. A separate area known as P-56B surrounds the Vice Presidential mansion on the grounds of the Naval Observatory, near Wisconsin Avenue. Other than approved flights, no aircraft are allowed to fly through these areas.

One of Washington's biggest security issues has always been the city's close proximity to Reagan National Airport, which is in Arlington just west of the Potomac River. Reagan's flight corridors follow the Potomac, directly adjoining this prohibited area. After a series of violations in the 1990s, the FAA and Secret Service jointly conducted a security review and arrived at a memorandum of understanding. In 1996 a "P-56 Work Group" was set up to review procedures and make recommendations, some of which were implemented. Nonetheless, occasional over-flights continued to be a problem. In July 1998, a scheduled American Airlines flight accidentally passed directly over the White House en route to Reagan Airport. The event prompted the airport manager to issue a stern warning to his flight controllers to "treat this area as a 'Granite Mountain' to be avoided in every possible way." A similar letter was sent to pilots. Even so, there were occasional incidents in the period before the September 11 attack.

Given all of this, it is not surprising that the sudden appearance of an unidentified low-flying plane over the White House on 9/11 would set off alarms. Let us remember, by this time the World Trade Center was in flames. Hundreds of people had already perished. Multiple hijackings were believed to be in progress. The only planes with legitimate reason to be in the sky over Washington were fighters for the purpose of protecting the nation's capital. Yet, as we know, Washington lay completely undefended. Scrambled F-16 fighters from Langley AFB did not finally establish a combat air patrol over the city until shortly before 10 A.M. — much too late — and subsequently, as we also know, the 911 Commission absolved the Joint Chiefs of all responsibility for this shocking breach of security. The panel put the blame squarely on the FAA, claiming it had failed to notify NORAD about the hijackings.

But what about this mysterious white plane which circled over the president's house? The fact that it penetrated to the core of P-56 raised obvious questions that the 9/11 Commission should have investigated. Incredibly, the panel never even broached the issue. There is no mention of the white plane and its strange fly-over in the *9/11 Commission Report,* not even a passing remark in a footnote. Nor is there any reference to the news stories cited above. Why not?

After a crime, it is standard procedure for police detectives to interrogate witnesses who were at the scene and cross-check their testimony in an attempt to reconstruct what actually happened. Had the members of the 9/11 Commission been serious about their mandate to provide "the fullest possible account"[8] of the horrific events of September 11, 2001, they would have followed this well-established procedure. Certainly the news reports carried by numerous networks and the many eyewitnesses at the White House merited attention. These were obvious starting points for the official investigation. It was not necessary for the panel members to go above and beyond the call of duty. Had they merely done their job, they surely would have discovered the evidence I am about to present. This, in turn, would have prompted further inquiries, and, quite probably, some conclusions different from those in their final report.

After the collapse of the South Tower at 9:59 A.M., the U.S. media appeared to forget about the mysterious white plane. This was not due to a general lack of press coverage about 9/11. During this same period the networks featured numerous follow-up reports. As I have noted, leading newspapers such as the *Washington Post* ran lengthy retrospective articles. However, with the exception of one indirect reference in *Newsweek,* there was no further mention of the strange fly-over. The incident dropped out of history for six years. The U.S. military also ducked the issue. To this day, the U.S. Air Force claims that it has no knowledge of any such plane. Yet, as I will now show, an abundance of hard evidence conclusively refutes this official denial.

The Evidence

Like most Americans, I too was ignorant. I first learned about the mystery plane only in March 2007. Days after posting an Internet article in which I professed skepticism about the official 9/11 conspiracy theory, I received an email from an independent investigator who directed me to some remarkable evidence of which I was unaware. (The individual prefers to remain anonymous because he is currently pursuing several FOIA requests and does not wish to place them in jeopardy. I will refer to him by his Internet screen name: "Pinnacle.")

I was surprised to learn that the evidence had been around for quite some time. It seems that during the evacuation of the White House on September 11, a woman captured an amazing photo of the mysterious plane. Linda Brookhart, at the time Vice President of the Taxpayer Federation of Illinois, was in Washington on 9/11 attending a National Taxpay-

Linda Brookhart's photo of the white plane, taken near the White House.

Source: Linda Brookhart

ers Conference in the old Executive Office Building (located immediately next to the White House) when she and many others were told to vacate the building. Ms. Brookhart later explained to me that after she hurried outside, she was standing in the street talking to a security guard when she just happened to look up and see a plane overhead.[9] Reacting on impulse, she grabbed her Pentax and snapped the excellent quality photo on the front cover of this book (at the top, and shown here in black-and-white). This single photo refutes the Pentagon denials, and, as we are about to discover, it contains enough information to identify the plane. "Pinnacle" actually made the correct identification as early as May 2006, based on this one photo.

A blow-up from Linda Brookhart's photo.

Source: Linda Brookhart

"Pinnacle" also guided me to other evidence. It seems the BBC filmed the mysterious plane as it circled over Washington, and the network aired this footage in a live report in the U.K. at 11:50 A.M. (EDT) on the day of the attack. Unfortunately, the footage is of rather poor quality. However, the Spanish ABC network also captured similar footage, and they too aired a live report. The following excellent still-shot was taken from this video footage. Notice, the caption informs us in Spanish that a third hijacked plane hit the Pentagon. It also gives the initially-reported impact time: 9:43 A.M. The segments are similar and were probably filmed from Lafayette Park, across the street from the White House.

Photo-grab of white plane from Spanish ABC network.

9:43

UN TERCER AVIÓN SE ESTRELLA CONTRA EL PENTAGONO

But the best evidence was yet to come. It seems that a reporter at the White House captured an excellent video clip of the white plane as it made a banking turn. This short segment actually appeared in a two-hour made-for-TV docudrama about Flight 93, which aired on the Discovery Channel in August 2005: *The Flight that Fought Back*. Once alerted to its existence, I had no trouble locating this short segment on the Internet. A 9/11 investigator named Chris Bornag had pulled it from the film and posted it at YouTube as part of a melange from 9/11. The clip has since been removed due to a copyright infringement. However, for many months it was viewable on line by anyone with access to cyberspace. The following still-shot was taken from this footage.

A DVD of the original Discovery Channel movie is still available for purchase at Amazon.com. The crucial segment appears 47 minutes into

Photo-grab of white plane from Discovery Channel program: *The Flight That Fought Back.*

the movie (in scene four). It is not a part of the dramatic production itself, but is a short segment of raw documentary footage embedded in the film. The crucial segment is very brief, only about three- to four-seconds long. This probably helps to explain why this remarkable footage did not attract more attention. At that time I had seen no reference to it in any of the published literature about September 11, nor on any of the 9/11 websites. But I now understand that I simply missed it. An excellent dialogue about the white plane appeared in July 2006 on the Loose Change Forum, an Internet discussion board sponsored by 9/11 film maker Dylan Avery.[10] Several months later Pilots for 9/11 Truth posted their own excellent forum discussion about this important evidence.[11] Although the cameraman has never been identified, there is every reason to believe the footage is bona fide.

As I have noted, the plane makes a banking turn in the video. The angle was lucky because it brought the plane's unique features and markings into plain view. Make no mistake, this was no ordinary aircraft. It belongs to the U.S. Air Force. The plane is an E-4B, the U.S. military's most advanced electronics platform. Even a casual comparison shows that the still-shot from the docudrama matches an official photo of the E-4B, from a USAF website.[12] See also the front cover (at bottom, and on page 39 in black-and-white). There is no mistake.

The plane is a modified Boeing 747-200. Notice the white color, the U.S. flag painted on the vertical stabilizer (i.e, the tail), and the blue stripe and insignia on the fuselage. The distinguishing feature, however, is the bump or pod directly behind the bulging 747 cockpit. The pod is clearly discernible in photos. No other plane has this piggy-backed appendage. It is unique to the E-4B and is integral to its military role as a state-of-the-art airborne command center. The pod contains a communication satellite-dish and perhaps other advanced electronic hardware. This is the same plane Linda Brookhart photographed near the White House.

How can we tell? Her vantage was not ideal — Ms. Brookhart was standing in the street looking up when she snapped the shot. Nonetheless, a careful inspection shows it to be the same plane. Notice, the aircraft in her picture has four engines and all of the characteristics of a Boeing 747. In addition to the white color, which is also a match, one other crucial detail establishes the identity. Notice the tiny blue spot near the rear of the plane. Several close-ups of an E-4B clearly show that this blue spot is simply the place where the blue stripes on the side of the fuselage come together at the rear of the aircraft. This spot can also be seen in the still-shot from the Spanish ABC network. No mistake. It is one and the same.

The spot is the only place on the 747 fuselage where the E-4B's otherwise conspicuous blue stripes are visible from below. This establishes a positive ID, because no other airplane has this combination of features.

Linda Brookhart explained to me that at the time of the evacuation she believed the White House was under attack. She was not the only one. Many others who were present, including government officials, felt the same way. On September 12, 2001, White House spokesperson Ari Fleischer told the press, "We have specific and credible information that the White House and Air Force One were intended targets of these attacks."[13] Attorney General John Ashcroft and Sean McCormack, representing the National Security Council (NSC), made similar statements.[14] So did Vice President Dick Cheney during his September 16, 2001 appearance on *Meet the Press*, cited in the previous chapter. During the interview, Cheney told Tim Russert that Secret Service agents evacuated him on 9/11 after "they received a report that an airplane was headed for the White House."[15] Whatever Cheney's role may have been, there is no reason to doubt this statement.

Barbara Riggs, who was the Deputy Director of the Secret Service on 9/11 (the first woman to hold that post), later offered another corroborating account. During a 2006 interview, Riggs stated that on September 11, 2001 she was in the Secret Service (SS) crisis center at agency headquarters, where she watched SS staff persons track two planes on radar, real-time. Both were approaching Washington. Riggs emphasized that everyone in the room at the time was operating under the assumption that the White House was a target.[16]

USAF photo of an E-4B.

Her statement is also important because it confirms the testimony of Secretary of Transportation Norman Mineta, discussed in the previous chapter. As noted, Mineta overheard a conversation in the White House bunker between VP Cheney and a young man, presumably a Secret Service staff person, who informed Cheney about an approaching plane. Later, Mineta identified it as AA Flight 77. The second plane mentioned by Riggs was probably United Flight 93, but we can't be certain. It might have been this mysterious white plane. If the E-4B's transponder had been set to a military code unreadable to the FAA (or Secret Service), the plane would have been indistinguishable on radar from a commercial plane with its transponder off.

In 2002, Presidential adviser Karl Rove indirectly corroborated this analysis. During an MSNBC interview Rove told NBC reporter Campbell Brown that when Bush left the classroom in Sarasota he immediately asked to be put in touch with the vice president.[17] However, as Rove tells it, they were unable to reach Cheney right away because "the Vice President was being moved literally, grabbed by his belt, lifted off the floor ... by a Secret Service agent and moved to the bunker *because the plane was approaching the White House"* [my emphasis]. To this day, we do not know which plane Rove was referring to. He probably did not know, himself. The exact time when Bush left the classroom is contested, but it could not have been later than 9:16 A.M. This would easily place Cheney in the bunker by 9:20 A.M., or earlier, which fits well with Mineta's timeline, and flatly contradicts the official story that Cheney arrived much later.

Pandemonium at the White House/Bush in Sarasota

Judging from news reports, the scene at the White House was pandemonium. According to the *Washington Post*, the Secret Service ordered staffers to file out in an orderly way, then screamed at them to run as fast as they could across Pennsylvania Avenue to Lafayette Park. Women were told to remove their high-heeled shoes so they could run faster. Some did not even bother to collect their shoes. They stepped out of them and kept right on going. The nearby sidewalks were littered with women's shoes. Other evacuees were advised "to remove the White House ID from around their necks so they couldn't be singled out by possible snipers outside the White House gates."[18]

This gives some idea of the tense atmosphere. It was no different on Capitol Hill, where House Speaker Dennis Hastert and other high officials were whisked to safety by security guards. Hastert later said two burly cops came up, grabbed him under each arm and carted him out of the building. Hastert, the third in line of succession, then flew by helicopter to Andrews AFB, where he and other cabinet officials boarded a plane to site "R," the secure facility near Camp David where the continuity of government (COG) backup team assembled to ride out the crisis. Deputy Secretary of Defense Paul Wolfowitz was also a part of this group.

Whereas VP Cheney and Speaker Hastert were hustled to safety by Secret Service agents, President Bush's experience in Sarasota, Florida was strangely different. When United Flight 175 hit the South Tower, Bush was sitting in a classroom with second graders. At 9:06 A.M. Andrew Card, Bush's chief of staff, came up and reportedly whispered in Bush's ear, "A second plane hit the other tower. America is under attack." By this point, the Secret Service should already have hustled Bush to safety. Given that the nation was under attack, an attempt on the president's life was a very real possibility.

After all, Bush's presence at Booker Elementary school was no secret. The press had widely reported his scheduled appearance. Standard procedure called for the Secret Service to remove the president to the nearest secure location, and this most definitely was not the school. In fact, Bush's continuing presence at Booker put the children in danger. According to Philip Melanson, an expert on the Secret Service, "You're safer in that presidential limo, which is bombproof and … bulletproof."[19] Yet, Bush's handlers allowed him to remain in the classroom for another ten minutes while the children and Bush took turns reading "My Pet Goat."

This incredible lapse of security has never been explained. Even when Bush got up and left the class, his casual demeanor is hard to fathom. Bush dallied at the school, delivered a short speech at 9:30 A.M., which was aired on national TV, then posed for a photo-op. His motorcade did not leave Booker Elementary until 9:34 A.M. Later, Andrew Card stated that the president first learned about the Pentagon strike and the threat to Air Force One during the short drive to the airport, which was 3-4 miles from the school.[20] It was only *then* that the Secret Service kicked into gear.[21] ABC News reporter Ann Compton, who was with Bush, called it "... a mad-dash motorcade out to the airport."[22] Kevin Down, a Sarasota police officer who was also present, described what he saw: "I thought they were actually anticipating a terrorist attack on the president while we were en route."[23] From these accounts, it would appear that Bush received the call about the Pentagon strike and Air Force One shortly after leaving Booker at 9:34 A.M.

Notice, this is *not* a close fit with the official story that the Pentagon crash occurred at 9:37-38 A.M., because one would expect a delay of at least a few minutes. For example, during ABC's live 9/11 coverage, which started at 8:51 A.M., Peter Jennings mentioned the plane circling the White House *before* he received word about the Pentagon strike. ABC's correspondent John McWethy was at the Pentagon, but he apparently was being evacuated and was out of action. The first indication of smoke came only at 9:42 A.M. Two minutes later Jennings mentioned a fire. Then came word of a plane crash. The full story emerged in bits and pieces.

By this time, there was genuine concern for Bush's safety. USAF Col. Mark Tillman, pilot of Air Force One, insisted on an armed guard at his cockpit door while the Secret Service ran an identity check on everyone aboard the presidential plane. At 9:57 A.M., when Tillman lifted off from Sarasota-Bradenton International Airport, he reportedly made a near vertical ascent. Dan Bartlett, the White House Communications Director, said, "It was like a rocket. For a good ten minutes the plane was going almost straight up."[24] Once aloft, Tillman chose to forego radio, so as not to reveal his location, and communicated with FAA air traffic controllers by telephone instead.

President Bush even refused his planned fighter escort. Four F-16s from the Minnesota Air National Guard were left sitting on the tarmac at Tyndall AFB in northern Florida. Instead, Bush scrambled fighters from his old Texas Air National Guard unit. They caught up with him en route to Barksdale AFB, in Louisiana.[25] The time of Bush's departure from Booker school (i.e., 9:34 A.M.), the short distance to the airport, and the fact that part of the drive was at high speed — all raise questions about the official story, including the actual time and circumstances of the Pentagon strike.

The White House Evacuation

The *Washington Post* reported that the White House evacuation com-
menced at 9:45 A.M. However, by some accounts it started much
earlier. Apparently, people left in stages.[26] Norman Mineta told the 9/11
Commission that the evacuation was already in progress when he arrived
in the PEOC (i.e., the presidential bunker) at 9:20 A.M.[27] Mineta said he
spoke briefly with Richard Clarke before descending into the bunker, and
Clarke confirms Mineta's account in his 9/11 memoir.[28] In a 9:52 A.M. live
broadcast, CNN's John King mentioned that the evacuation "had begun
about 30 minutes ago."[29] A story in *Newsweek* magazine reported that
staffers were leaving the West Wing at 9:30 A.M.

The time is important because the story also mentions the white plane,
possibly linking its appearance with the evacuation. The *Newsweek* story
mentions that security police urged staffers to "run, not walk, as fast as
possible," and shouted, "There's a plane overhead, don't look back!" Some
caught a glimpse of it, but apparently no one recognized it. The story
continues: "Several staffers saw a civilian airliner, reflecting white in the
bright sunlight, appearing to circle nearby."[30] From these accounts, it is
clear that the White House evacuation began in an orderly fashion, but
turned frantic.

Although none of the news reports cited above provide firm information about exactly when the E-4B was first spotted, other accounts
suggest the plane was already in the sky over Washington *before* the Pentagon strike. One of these reports aired in the U.K. two days after the attack. Mark Easton, anchor of Channel 4 News in England, reported that
"just before the crash a civilian plane was filmed over the city apparently
banking hard, and there were reports of a military plane circling the U.S.
Capitol. Moments later, the Department of Defense [i.e., the Pentagon]
was hit."[31]

In a separate story, CNN reported that U.S. Army Brig. General Clyde
Vaughn watched a commercial-size plane circle over Georgetown a few
minutes before the Pentagon crash. At the time Vaughn was eastbound on
Interstate 395, en route to the Pentagon.[32] In Gen. Vaughn's own words:
"There wasn't anything in the air, except for one airplane, and it looked
like it was loitering over Georgetown, in a high left-handed bank." The
CNN story correctly mentions that Georgetown is a part of the District
of Columbia and lies within the prohibited zone. As I have noted, commercial airliners arriving and departing from nearby Ronald Reagan avoid
this area, including Georgetown. Instead, they follow the nearby Poto-

mac River.[33] It is important to remember that people in different parts of Washington probably saw the white plane at different times.

Linda Brookhart says she snapped her photo *before* she saw the towering plume of smoke at the Pentagon. After returning home, she developed the film and notified the FBI. Days later, an agent came by and picked up a copy of the photo. But Brookhart did not hear back. She was never invited to testify. In fact, the 9/11 Commission never even contacted her.[34] With hindsight, this official lack of interest is not surprising, given that the 9/11 Commission's primary concern was to consolidate the official conspiracy story. Which, of course, meant ignoring everything else.

Although Brookhart's photo provides sufficient information to positively ID the mystery plane, the short segment from the Discovery Channel docudrama is important corroborating evidence. This footage of the E-4B appears in the Discovery Channel film in the context of the 9/11 evacuation of the White House, placing it in Washington on the day of the attack. However, we still do not know who filmed it. Nor does the footage include any visual evidence linking it to Washington. The segment is very brief and simply shows the E-4B banking against a backdrop of blue sky. For these reasons some have discounted it.

The Raw CNN Footage

Fortunately, it is not necessary to place undue weight on the Discovery Channel clip, because additional video evidence has since emerged that is even more compelling. In June 2007, "Pinnacle" was exploring CNN's video archive when he stumbled upon previously unknown raw video footage of the E-4B circling the White House on 9/11. The footage was filmed on the morning of the attack by another CNN cameraman at the White House, but never aired on television. Instead, it gathered dust in the CNN archive for nearly six years.[35] The 18-minute CNN video documents the White House evacuation and the fly-over in graphic fashion. When I learned about it, I contacted CNN and was able to acquire an unedited screener's copy. Ken Jenkins, a video expert, then vetted the footage. He believes it is bona fide.[36]

As it starts, the CNN cameraman and other members of the press are obviously on the White House grounds. A guard appears and instructs everyone to leave. As the camera rolls, the CNN reporter joins the exodus of journalists and staffers who are walking down the White House driveway. At this point, a voice is heard talking about "an explosion at the Pentagon." The CNN cameraman then exits through the White House gate.

CNN photo-grab of E-4B over Jackson Place, located across the street from the White House.

Source: CNN

In subsequent scenes, familiar Washington landmarks, including the old Executive Office Building, Lafayette Park and Jackson Place, are plainly in evidence. Suddenly, there is the shrill sound of sirens. Moments later, two red fire engines arrive in front of the White House, apparently in response to the fire alarm reported by the *Washington Post*.[37] About six minutes into the video, the camera suddenly pans up over Jackson Place and catches the white plane against a cloudless blue sky. As the camera zooms up, the four jet engines, white color, and even the blue spot on the fuselage, are all plainly visible. Later, I acquired the rights from CNN to publish three still-shots, which my webmaster pulled from the video.

From the video one can tell that the E-4B was flying at a slow speed, just as Bob Kur and General Vaughn claimed. The plane certainly appears to hang or "loiter" in the sky. Moving northeast, it banks and makes another much lower pass, filling about a fourth of the screen until it finally passes out of sight behind a large tree. In the bright sunlight, the blue stripe on the side of the plane and the communications pod behind the cockpit are plainly visible. Notice, this CNN close-up closely resembles the photo-grab from the Discovery Channel clip. The CNN video, however, is steadier and of better quality. The similarity is not surprising, because by this time security police had relocated the journalists from the White House to a press corral in Lafayette Park. Several of the existing segments of the E-4B were probably filmed from this same location. The total length of the E-4B segment in the CNN video is about twenty-nine seconds — much longer than any of the other known segments, which are only brief clips.

Later in the video, Secret Service agents are seen moving around on the White House roof. About 8-9 minutes into the film, smoke can be seen in the distance, behind the White House. At this point the camera shifts to several men standing on a sidewalk in Lafayette Park. They are using cell phones and apparently have just learned about the Pentagon strike. One says, "Did it actually hit the Pentagon?" Another voice says, "It's unclear. There's a fire over there." This dramatic CNN footage erases any shreds of doubt and proves that a U.S. Air Force plane, to be precise, an E-4B, circled over Washington at approximately the time of the Pentagon attack. (Required disclaimer: "Usage of this CNN material does not constitute an implied or express endorsement by CNN.")

More recently, additional evidence also came to light. We learned that the BBC captured yet another short video of the E-4B as it passed near the White House. This footage appeared in *Clear the Skies*, a 2002 BBC special report about the events of September 11. The special program aired on British television, but insofar as I know has never been shown in the U.S. Even so, the film is commercially available at amazon.com. This E-

CNN zoom shot of E-4B as it made a slow-banking-eastward turn over Jackson Place. Notice the white color, the four jet engines and the dot at the rear of the plane.

Source: CNN

45

CNN photo-grab of E-4B as it looped back, probably just east of the White House.

TCR 00:25:07·01
R PLAY LOCK

Source: CNN

4B segment is very similar to the clips already discussed and was probably filmed from Lafayette Park. However, it is distinguished by an audio component proving that at least one journalist on the scene did positively identify the white plane. As the film rolls, a voice can be heard saying, "It's the doomsday plane!"

The Doomsday Plane

Again, I must emphasize: this was no ordinary aircraft. The E-4B's official designation is the National Airborne Operations Center (NAOC), pronounced "Nay-ock." In former years, however, it was known as the National Emergency Airborne Command Post (NEACP), pronounced "Knee-cap." But the more common name is the one heard in the BBC film: the "doomsday plane," so called because its premier function is to serve as a flying command, control and communications post in the event of nuclear war or during a national emergency. For this reason, the U.S. Air Force keeps an E-4B on alert at all times.

A recent article in the *Air Force Civil Engineer* describes the plane as "a truly amazing" aircraft and provides more details about its impressive specs.[38] The $800 million plane has all of the advanced electronics needed for world-wide communication. This explains the "E" in its name, which stands for "electronic." The E-4B is not to be confused with the E-3 Sentry, which is the Pentagon's Airborne Warning and Control System (AWACS) radar reconnaissance plane. Fortunately, the two are easy to distinguish. The E-3 AWACS is a modified Boeing 707 — not a 747 — hence, is much smaller. The E-3 features a large radar dome (radome) attached above the fuselage, very different in appearance from the communications pod on the E-4B.

If the presidential plane, Air Force One, is a flying White House, then the E-4B is a substitute Pentagon. Its electronics cover the full radio spectrum, from extremely low frequency (ELF) to ultra high frequency (UHF). This enables the E-4B to communicate worldwide with all U.S. military commands, including tactical and strategic forces, naval ships, planes, nuclear-armed missiles, even submarines. The plane is outfitted with as many as 48 different antennae. One of these is wire-mounted on a spool at the rear of the aircraft. When in use, the wire is unreeled, dragging a small cone hundreds of feet behind the plane. In sum, the E-4B is a state-of-the-art communications platform and can serve as an airborne command center for all U.S. military forces in a national or world crisis.

The aircraft carries an electrical-generating plant to power all of its electronic hardware, which, incidentally, is also shielded against the electromagnetic pulse effects generated by nuclear explosions. The task of hardening the hundreds of miles of wiring in the plane was no small chore. According to a Boeing engineer who witnessed the work, braided shielding had to be installed around each and every wire bundle, which more than doubled the weight. The problem of shielding the pilots was solved in a novel way: The large windows in the forward cockpit were covered with the same screen mesh used in the windows of microwave ovens.[39] Even the plane's white color is a design feature, not simply cosmetic. Its intended purpose is to reflect heat away from the plane, hopefully enabling the E-4B to survive in a nuclear battlefield.

Like Air Force One, the E-4B can be refueled in flight, and therefore has essentially unlimited range. It can remain aloft for days at a time. When the president travels on Air Force One, an E-4B usually follows behind the presidential entourage, close at hand for reasons of national security. Strangely, however, it seems this protocol was not followed on September 11, 2001. In *Air War Over America*, the official U.S. Air Force account, author Leslie Filson writes that when Air Force One departed Sarasota-Bradenton airport, an AWACS plane was ordered to accompany the president.[40] If an E-4B had been with Bush in Florida, this would not have been necessary. At the time, the AWACS plane was participating in a military exercise off the Florida coast.[41] The U.S. government has never explained why a doomsday plane failed to accompany the president on September 11.

The E-4B also doubles as a mobile office for the Secretary of Defense. According to various reports, Donald Rumsfeld frequently used the plane. More recently, his successor, Robert Gates, traveled on an E-4B when he flew to London for talks with Prime Minister Tony Blair.[42]

"We See All"

The Air Force has a fleet of four E-4Bs, one of which, as noted, is always on alert. Collectively they are known as the "Nightwatch." The lead plane is designated as "Nightwatch-1," but each E-4B also has its own radio call sign.[43] Usually the fleet is assigned to Offutt Air Force Base, near Omaha, Nebraska. But individual E-4Bs are occasionally stationed at other bases. By the way, Offutt is also the home of USSTRATCOM, i.e., the U.S. Strategic Command (formerly SAC, the Strategic Air Command). The Nightwatch fleet is under the operational control of the Joint Chiefs of Staff,[44] in other words, the national command authority.

The E-4Bs are maintained by the First Airborne Command and Control Squadron, a part of the 55th Strategic Reconnaissance Wing. The wing's motto is *Videmus Omnia,* which is Latin for "We See All." Each E-4B has a crew of 64, and the plane can accommodate an additional 50 passengers, for a total of 114. The spacious 747 fuselage includes command and work areas, conference and briefing rooms, as well as an operations center or battle station. The plane also has a rest area, bunks for sleeping, even a galley stocked with a week's provisions. In 2005, the U.S. Air Force awarded Boeing Corporation a $2 billion contract to upgrade the Nightwatch fleet — an enormous sum considering there are only four of the planes. The stated goal of the five-year upgrade was "increased readiness."[45]

Practicing Armageddon

According to the *Omaha World-Herald,* on the morning of the September 11 attack, three of the E-4Bs were participating in a live command-level exercise known as Global Guardian.[46] The drill is an annual event, staged to test the readiness of the U.S. military's command and control procedures involved in waging thermonuclear war. The 2001 Global Guardian exercise started the week before September 11, under the directorship of Admiral Richard Mies, commander-in-chief of USSTRATCOM. It was reportedly in "full swing" when the attack began. NORAD was also a participant, along with numerous other commands. Previous Global Guardian exercises have involved the U.S. Space Command, the Air Combat Command, and the U.S. Atlantic and Pacific Fleets, among others.[47]

Since the 1990s Global Guardian has included mock terrorist attacks upon the military's computer and information systems. For example, during the 1998 exercise, a Red Team of mock terrorists attempted to disrupt USSTRATCOM's internal communications by hacking into its computers, and by tying up its phone/FAX lines with phony messages.[48] Although the details were not released, the staged "terrorist attacks" apparently were at least partly successful. Recent Global Guardian exercises have also included this sort of "attack" scenario. But it is not known if they were a part of the 2001 operation. The *9/11 Commission Report* says nothing about Global Guardian. As I have indicated, the only military excercise it mentions (in a footnote) is Vigilant Guardian, a NORAD exercise that involved simulated hijackings.[49]

Although the U.S. military has released few details about the 2001 Global Guardian exercise, we know that in previous years the drill included the loading of live nuclear weapons onto planes. This is troubling, especially in light of the August 2007 snafu at Minot AFB, which involved serious violations of longstanding Air Force protocols about the handling of nuclear weapons: A half-dozen nuclear-armed cruise missiles from Minot were "mistakenly" loaded under the wings of a B-52, then flown to Barksdale AFB, one of the embarkation points for U.S. troops and materiel en route to the Mideast.

It is likely that Global Guardian was the umbrella exercise for several other military drills also underway on 9/11, including Vigilant Guardian.[50] Even the names suggest a set of tiered exercises. A FEMA drill named Tripod was also in progress on 9/11 in New York City, and it too may have been tiered to Global Guardian. Tripod involved hundreds of government employees and its purpose, according to NYC mayor Rudy Giuliani, was to defend against a hypothetical biochemical attack.[51] Involvement of the E-4B in Tripod is quite likely, because one of the doomsday plane's secondary roles is to serve as a mobile command center for use by FEMA during national emergencies.[52] Although the flying command post apparently played no role in the Katrina disaster, FEMA is known to have used an E-4B during hurricane Opal in 1995.

Whereabouts on 9/11

Let us now review the whereabouts of the Nightwatch fleet on 9/11. According to the *Omaha World-Herald*, one of the E-4Bs was en route to Offutt AFB carrying a special high-level advisory panel chaired by Lt. General Brent Scowcroft. A source at the Pentagon confirmed to me that Secretary of Defense Donald Rumsfeld created this panel early in 2001 for the purpose of conducting an end-to-end review of the U.S. nuclear command-and-control system.[53]

This was unprecedented. Although the U.S. military once conducted a more limited fail-safe and risk reduction review (in 1991-93), never before had it undertaken anything so comprehensive as an end-to-end review. My source also identified the members of the panel. Without question, they were among the most senior national security experts in the land: including Maj. General Michael Carns, Dr. John Crawford, William Crowell, John Gordon, and Art Money, who by 9/11 had been replaced by Linton Wells. See my endnote for their impressive resumes.[54]

Obviously, the official 9/11 investigation should have interviewed all of these panelists about the Global Guardian exercise and the E-4B flight over Washington. At the very least, these most senior experts might have shed some light on the "security failures" of 9/11. Of course, this never happened.

Shortly after Flight 175 crashed into the South Tower, USSTRAT-COM reportedly terminated the 2001 Global Guardian exercise.[55] However, the E-4Bs remained aloft.[56] In his 2003 book about cyber-terrorism, *Black Ice*, Dan Verton, a former U.S. Marine Corps intelligence officer, writes that at about the time of the second strike on the WTC, an E-4B carrying civilian and military officials was preparing to lift off from an airport near the nation's capital.[57] Verton mentions that the E-4B was participating in a military exercise. No doubt this was Global Guardian. His book states that "they transitioned from exercise status to real-world status in the air."

Was this the plane that later circled over the White House? When I contacted Dan Verton about this, he informed me that he did not know. But I did learn a few additional details. Verton stated that his "longstand-ing source" is "a former senior military officer (with many stars)" who was aboard the E-4B on the morning of 9/11.[58] Verton does not know the exact departure time of the E-4B. In an email, however, he identified the airport as Andrews AFB. Later, this same E-4B flew to Offutt AFB, where Verton says he reached his informant by telephone, the day after the at-tack. The author of *Black Ice* currently writes for *Computerworld*.

In a 9/11 retrospective in the *Washington Post*, reporter Bob Woodward also mentioned the doomsday plane. Woodward wrote that on September

11, "Pentagon officials ordered up the airborne command post [i.e., the E-4B] used only in national emergencies."[59] The context of Woodward's story implies that the order to launch the E-4B was not given until *after* the Pentagon strike. This agrees with a September 12, 2001 story in the *Dayton Daily News,* which reported that shortly after 9:43 A.M., "An E-4B National Airborne Operations Center, a white 747 jumbo jet often confused with Air Force One, took off from Wright-Pat [Wright-Patterson AFB] for an undisclosed location. It returned later in the day. Wright-Pat is one of a few designated alternate bases for the flying command center."[60] From the story, it would appear that the E-4B departure from Wright-Pat was the designated alert plane and was sent up to assist NORAD in coordinating the military response to the "terrorist attack." The story makes no mention of Global Guardian. If these sources are correct, we have accounted for two of the four doomsday planes.

Schedule Change in 2001

Although the 2001 Global Guardian exercise was originally scheduled for October, the date was changed in March 2001 and moved up to September. The reasons for this change have never been disclosed. The timing of the schedule change is also curious, because, according to my Pentagon source, the first meetings of Rumsfeld's special advisory panel also occurred in March 2001. In previous years the military had always staged Global Guardian in October or November,[61] and, sure enough, the year after the 9/11 attack the date reverted back. The 2002 Global Guardian occurred in October, and this has continued to be the case.[62]

This raises disturbing questions. Why did the U.S. military change the date of Global Guardian in 2001? And why did the world's most sophisticated electronics warfare plane circle slowly over Washington during the September 11 attack? The cruising speed of the E-4B is 580 mph. Moreover, it normally fulfills its command and control mission at an altitude of 35-40,000 feet. Why was it seen "loitering" over Washington while the attack was in progress, essentially buzzing the roof tops?

During 2006, in a search for answers, my informant "Pinnacle" filed a formal Freedom of Information Act request with the Federal Aviation Administration, seeking two types of data: identification data, if any, from transponders, and the images of all radar tracks for Washington between 9:30-10:00 A.M. on the morning of September 11, 2001. The FAA completely ignored his request for radar images and simply responded that they had "no identification records." "Pinnacle" promptly filed an appeal, but as of this writing has received no decision. He also filed a FOIA request with the Secret Service for all relevant information, including radar data, and received a similar reply. "Pinnacle" was told that the Secret Service has "no records or documents of any kind relating to any aircraft whatsoever flying near or circling above the White House on 9/11 in the 9:30-10 A.M. time frame."[63]

"Pinnacle" also sent the basic facts covered in this chapter to his congressman, Rep. Adam Schiff (D-CA), along with a request that Schiff look into the matter. His congressman then made an official inquiry in Washington about "a four-engine white jet" observed and photographed near the White House on 9/11. Eventually, Rep. Schiff received a letter from the U.S. Air Force. It stated,

> This is in reply to you inquiry on behalf of [redacted] regarding his request for information relating to an unidentified aircraft that may have been in restricted airspace near the White House on September 11, 2001 between the hours of 9:30-10:30 A.M.
> *Air Force officials have no knowledge of the aircraft in question* [my emphasis].[64]

Curiously, Rep. Schiff received the above reply as a FAX at 8:12 A.M. on the morning of November 8, 2006, which was literally hours before Donald Rumsfeld resigned as Secretary of Defense. As I've noted, the command authority for the E-4B rests with the Joint Chiefs of Staff, so it's likely that Schiff's official inquiry was passed up the chain of command for a decision. The timing also suggests that Rumsfeld himself may have personally attended to the matter as one of his final actions as Secretary of Defense. Rumsfeld's last day on the job was no doubt a busy one as he cleared his desk of unfinished business. But why would Schiff's request for information require his personal attention?

In any event, it is obvious that the DoD lied to Congressman Schiff. No other conclusion is possible, because the evidence leaves no doubt about the presence and identity of the white plane. The questions I have raised bear repeating: Why did an E-4B circle the White House on September 11? And why did the U.S. military alter the schedule of Global Guardian in 2001, then revert back to the former schedule in 2002? Why the official denials? What are the U.S. Air Force, FAA, and Secret Service keeping from us?

In the next chapter I will suggest why the *9/11 Commission Report* is strangely silent on the matter of the white plane. As we will discover, the presence of this advanced Air Force plane over Washington calls into question the official story about what happened on September 11, 2001.

Endnotes

1. The ABC coverage from 9/11 has been archived at http://www.archive.org/details/abc200109110912-0954.

   The transcript of the same coverage was also archived: ABC News Special Report: "Planes crash into World Trade Center," ABC News, September 11, 2001, posted at http://www.fromthewilderness.com/timeline/2001/abcnews091101.html.

2. The transcript is posted at http://transcripts.cnn.com/TRANSCRIPTS/0109/11/bn.06.html.

3. The transcript is posted at http://transcripts.cnn.com/TRANSCRIPTS/0109/11/bn.05.html.

4. Richard A. Clarke, *Against All Enemies*, Free Press, New York, 2004, p. 7.

5. A video file of Bob Kur's NBC broadcast is archived at http://www.archive.org/details/nbc200109110954-1036. Also, an audio file is archived at http://alkali.colug.org/~kaha/whiteplane.mp3.

6. See at http://rawstory.com//news/2007/CNN_investigates_secret_911_doomsday_plane_0913.html.

7. The source here is John Judge. Go to http://www.ratical.org/ratville/JFK/JohnJudge/P56A.html Also see http://911exposed.org/P56.htm.

8. *The 9/11 Commission Report: Final Report of the National Commission on Terrorist Attacks Upon the United States*, W.W. Norton, New York, 2004, p. xvi.

9. Email from Linda Brookhart, March 25, 2007.

10. Credit for the ID goes to Matt H. (screen name: Bonez.) The discussion is posted at http://s15.invisionfree.com/Loose_Change_Forum/index.php?showtopic=9796&st=30.

11. This page has an excellent discussion of the mystery plane: http://z9.invisionfree.com/Pilots_For_Truth/index.php?act=ST&f=5&t=483.

12. At http://www.strategic-air-command.com/aircraft/command/e-4B_NOAC_Airplane.htm.

13. Press Briefings by Ari Fleischer, September 12, 2001, 4:05 PM EDT; also see CBS News, "Primary Target, The Pentagon," September 21, 2001.

14. Matthew Robinson, "President's flight dramatizes intelligence inadequacy," *Inside Washington*, Human Events Publishing, Inc., September 17, 2001.

15. "The VP appears on *Meet the Press* with Tim Russert," September 16, 2001. The interview is posted at http://www.whitehouse.gov/vicepresident/news-speeches/speeches/vp20010916.html.

16. "Spotlight on Barbara Riggs," President's Council of Cornell Women (PCCW) Newsletter, Spring 2006, posted at http://pccw.alumni.cornell.edu/news/newsletters/spring06/riggs.html.

17. Campbell Brown, "9/11 interview: Karl Rove," *NBC News*, September 11, 2002. Posted at http://www.msnbc.com/modules/91102/interviews/rove.asp?cpl=l&cp1=1.

18. Dan Balz and Bob Woodward, "America's Chaotic Road to War," first in a series, *Washington Post*, January 27, 2002.

19. This was reported by Susan Taylor Martin, "Of Fact, Fiction: Bush on 9/11," *St. Petersburg Times*, July 4, 2004. Melanson is the author of *The Secret Service: The Hidden History of an Enigmatic Agency*, Carrol & Graff, New York, 2003.

20. MSNBC, Transcript, "White House Chief of Staff Andy Card Discusses the Bush Administration's Actions on 9/11," *MSNBC News with Brain Williams*, September 9, 2002.

21. Insofar as I know, Barbara Honegger was the first to write about this. See her paper "The Pentagon Attack Papers,"which is attached as an appendix to Jim Marrs, *The Terror Conspiracy*, Disinformation Press, 2006. p.439.

22. BBC, September 1, 2002.

23. BBC, August 30, 2002.

24. Scott Pelley, "The President's Story," Part One, CBS News, September 10, 2003.

25. Leslie Filson, *Air War Over America*, Headquarters 1st Air Force, Tyndall AFB, 2003, p. 87; also see Scott Pelley, op.cit.

26. Thanks to David Ray Griffin for bringing this to my attention.

27. National Commission on Terrorist Attacks Upon the United States, Public Hearing, Friday, May 23, 2003. For the transcript go to http://www.9-11commission.gov/archive/hearing2/9-11Commission_Hearing_2003-05-23.htm.

28. Richard A. Clarke, *Against All Enemies*, Free Press, New York, 2004, p. 5.

29. "The White House Has Been Evacuated," CNN, September 11, 2001.

30. *Newsweek*, September 24, 2001.

31. Mark Easton, "Aboard the Hi-jacked Planes," *Channel 4 News* [U.K.], September 13, 2001.

32. In early April 2008, I spoke with General Vaughn on the telephone. He told me that on the morning of 9/11 he had just left a meeting at the Army-Navy Golf and Country Club, located in Arlington near Glebe Road, and was on his way to the Pentagon when he saw the strange plane banking over Georgetown. Vaughn says he watched it circle for about a half minute, but he refused to speculate about its identity. He arrived at the Pentagon in time to witness the impact. Vaughn told me that Flight 77 passed directly over the location of the new Air Force monument, just east of the Naval Annex.

33. Ian Christopher McCaleb, "Three-star general may be among Pentagon dead," September 13, 2001, posted at http://archives.cnn.com/2001/U.S./09/13/pentagon.terrorism/.

34. Emails from Linda Brookhart, March 25 and 27, 2007.

35. Title: White House Evacuation
Rec #: 18
Date: 09/11/2001
Slug: White House Evacuation
Dateline: U.S.; DC
Type: RAW
Reporter:
Length: 00:18:09:28
Source: R/CNN WX, R/CNN WX
Tape # : B24141#002
Record ID#: 2001011004966
Collection : Atlanta

CNN ID : 91040709
Video Config: Audio Config: Tape Format: BETA   Offsite Box#:
Description: 00:09:05:27 [B-roll employees evacuate White House &
the Old Executive Building after terrorist attacks in NY & DC and Sen Warner
comments on the attacks]---LS people running down steps away from Old Executive Bldg/ LS people walking out of Old Exec bldg/ MS security tells people
to get off Wht Hse grounds/ QS media set up as they announce "explosion at
the Pentagon"/ MS people file out of Wht Hse gate/ LS limos paused/ WS lrg
group walking away from the Wht Hse/ MS men waiting in st/ MS fire truck w
sirens GOOD AUDIO/ PB fire engine passes Old Exec bldg/ VS police cars
pass (tinted windows) as fire trucks etc arrive on scene/ LS *plane flying
above*/ MS people running across st/ VS people walking w bags etc/ WS
people running on sidewalk/ MS ambulance arriving GOOD AUDIO/ LS sharp
shooters walking on roof of Wht Hse/ PAN people looking as security blocks
off Lafayette Park in front of N faade of the Wht Hse/ VS people walking/
LS fighter plane flying above/ MS woman asking people to disperse/ Break/
RRAX/ SOT Sen John Warner (R-VA) "Capitol hill has responded w the right
precautions & closed our bldgs"/ RRAX/ SOT Warner "Another Pearl Harbor
for this country" (0:00) /
© 2006 CNN. All Rights Reserved.

A second CNN video, of shorter length (nine minutes), includes all of the key scenes, and may be viewed at the following link. First, you must register at CNN Image Source, then log in with your screen name and password. Each scene is represented by a key frame (or thumbnail). Explorer 6 or 7 is necessary to make the video play. (Good luck! It is not easy.) At http://imagesource.cnn.com:80/imagesource/search/Search.action?runSerializ-edSearch=&searchString=W3sicmVjbnVtIjoiOTEwNDA1MjAiLCJ0eXBlIjo3fSx7Im NvbGxlY3Rpb25zZIjpbIkFGUCIsIklNNQUdFU09VUkNFIl0sInR5cGUiOjF9XQ==.

36. The video was vetted by Ken Jenkins, a pioneer in the 9/11 truth movement. Jenkins holds a degree in electrical engineering from Carnegie-Mellon University, and has also done extensive postgraduate study in psychology. Ken has many years of experience in various technical aspects of the broadcast-video field. He has extensive personal experi-ence using video gear, cameras, and recorders. This includes working with high-end video crews both in the studio and in the field. Ken has also designed and built video cameras, including custom modifications and maintenance. He also had a side career in special effects design and implementation. In recent years Ken has worked as a producer. He presented his first PowerPoint and video productions about 9/11 truth in early 2002. More recently, he produced seven DVDs with leading 9/11 Truth author David Ray Griffin, including *9/11 – The Myth and the Reality*. Ken is a partner in 9/11TV.org, which has documented speakers at many 9/11 conferences and events. The resulting DVDs are distributed, in part, through local cable access channels nationwide.

37. Dan Balz and Bob Woodward, op. cit.

38. Lt. Col. James P. Zemotel, USSTRATCOM/J643, "CEs Still Have Aircrew Mis-sion," *Air Force Civil Engineer*, Vol. 14 #2, 2006.

39. Neil Chance, "Aviation History: Inside Boeing Flight Test and the Doomsday Air-plane," posted at http://www.wingsoverkansas.com/history/article.asp?id=804.

40. Leslie Filson, *Air War Over America*, Headquarters 1st Air Force, Public Affairs Of-fice, Tyndall AFB, 2003.

41. "Conversation with Major General Larry Arnold, Commander, 1st Air Force, Tyndall, AFB, Florida," *Code One*, Vol. 17, No. 1, 1st Quarter 2002, posted at http://www.codeonemagazine.com/archives/2002/articles/jan_02/defense/.

Another AWACS plane was in the vicinity of Pittsburgh, PA, and was also participating in a military exercise. Dave Forster, "UST grad guides bombers in war," *Aquin*, April 12, 2002, posted at http://www.stthomas.edu/aquin/archive/041202/anaconda.html.

42. Sally B. Donnelly, "Inside Bob Gates's Flying Fortress," *Time*, January 14, 2007.

43. Some of the better known names are: ADIOS, DEFY, GORDO and TANGY. Other possible E-4B call signs include ALVA, ANITA, BAMA, BLOKE, BONO, EL CID, FATLY, HEWIT, HORSE, LEICA, NAVEL, OLMIS, POLLY, SPICE, STOLE, UNTIL, UTTER, and VIGA. See http://www.henney.com/chm/callsign.htm.

44. "Up to $2B to Maintain and Upgrade USA's E=4B NAOC Fleet," *Defense Industry Daily*, Military Purchasing News for Defense Procurement Managers and Contractors, December 27, 2005, Posted at http://www.defenseindustrydaily.com/up-to-2b-to-maintain-upgrade-usas-e4b-naoc-fleet-01671/.

45. Ibid.

46. Joe Dejka, "Inside STRATCOM on September 11: Offutt exercise took real-life twist," *Omaha World-Herald*, February 27, 2002.

47. Col. Joe Wasiak, "Global Guardian '99," *The Collins Center Update*, Vol. 1, Issue 3, December 1999.

48. Ward Parker, "Incorporating IA into Global Guardian," *IA Newsletter*, IATAC, Vol 2, No 1, Summer 1998.

49. *The 9/11 Commission Report*, see Chapter One, Note 116, p. 458.

50. The number has continued to climb. At a 9/11 truth/peace conference held in Vancouver, Canada in June 2007 independent investigator Webster Tarpley argued that as many as twenty-five drills were either in progress on September 11, 2001 or had occurred in the previous months. To my knowledge, Tarpley's 2006 book is still the best synthesis of what is known about the various 9/11 drills: Webster Griffin Tarpley, *9/11 Synthetic Terror: Made in the USA*, Progressive Press, 2006.

51. "Long debunked rumor 'validated' by Giuliani," June 29, 2004, posted at http://prisonplanet.tv/articles/june2004/062904longdebunked.htm.

52. This is explicitly stated on the official USAF website: http://www.strategic-air-command.com/aircraft/command/e-4B_NOAC_Airplane.htm. See also "National Airborne Operations Center," Oct. 23, 2004, at http://www.fema.gov; Joint Chiefs of Staff, "J3 Operations: Functional Perspectives," at http://www.jcs.mil/j3.

53. Conversation with William L. Jones, support staff, U.S. Nuclear Command-and-Control System, October 22, 2007.

54. I will pass over Scowcroft, the chairman, because his background as a national security advisor is well known.

USAF Major General Michael Carns was a graduate of the first class of cadets at the U.S. Air Force Academy. He went on to become a pilot and logged 200 combat missions in an F-4E in Southeast Asia. During his long and distinguished career Carns commanded a fighter squadron and later a fighter wing, served as special assistant to the chief of staff of the Supreme Allied Commander Europe, was operational director of the Rapid Deployment Joint Task Force, commanded the 13th Air Force, and finished his career in Washington as Air Force Vice Chief of Staff. Carns is the recipient of the Silver

Star and the Distinguished Flying Cross. In 1995, soon after his retirement, Bill Clinton nominated him to become CIA Director.

Dr. John Crawford, a physicist, was a vice president and deputy director at the Sandia National Laboratories where he was responsible for all of Sandia's programs, operations, staff and facilities, and reported to the lab's director. Previously, Crawford was responsible for all nuclear weapons development programs in New Mexico, including the Trident II warhead program, cruise missile warheads, and the stockpile stewardship program. Crawford started at Sandia in 1962, and over the years managed or coordinated a wide range of research programs. He also served as a scientific advisor during the development of the National Ignition Facility (NIF).

William Crowell was president and CEO of the Cylink Corporation, one of the first security firms to develop and sell encryption-related software. Formerly, Crowell was a Vice President of the Atlantic Aerospace Electronics Corporation. After holding several senior positions at the National Security Agency (NSA), he was named Deputy Director of the NSA in 1994. He served on President Clinton's Expert Council (PEO), and has held various leadership roles on numerous defense-related panels involving national security issues and terrorism.

General John A. Gordon, a retired four-star general in the U.S. Air Force, was the Department of Energy's (DoE's) first Under Secretary for Nuclear Security and Administrator of the National Nuclear Security Administration (NNSA), an agency created by Congress in 1999 after allegations of Chinese espionage in the nuclear laboratories. Formerly, Gordon was an Associate Director and later a Deputy Director of the CIA. For several years he served as a special assistant to the president for defense policy and arms control. He has also served as director of operations for the U.S. Space Command.

Art L. Money, an engineer, was Assistant Secretary of Defense for Command, Control, Communications and Intelligence (C3I) until April 2001. Prior to his Senate confirmation Money held various high posts in the DoD, including Assistant Secretary of the Air Force. Formerly, he was Vice President and Deputy General Manager at TRW, an aerospace contractor. Money's background is in avionics and surveillance, including the design and development of airborne surveillance systems for intelligence gathering. Money was not on board the E-4B on 9/11, however. He retired in April 2001, after which, Linton Wells filled his position at DoD, and also inherited his seat on the advisory panel.

A graduate of the Naval Academy, Wells served on a variety of surface ships. Eventually he commanded a destroyer and subsequently a destroyer squadron. He retired as a Captain after a twenty-six year Navy career, only to return to work for the Secretary of Defense as a counter intelligence and networking specialist. A glance at Wells' resume confirms his extraordinary range of expertise. He holds BS degrees in physics and oceanography, a masters in math, and a doctorate in international relations from Johns Hopkins. Fluent in Japanese, he also studied at the Japanese National Institute for Defense Studies.

55. U.S. DoD, News Transcript, "Secretary Rumsfeld Interview with the Washington Post," January 9, 2002, posted at http://www.defenselink.mil/transcripts/transcript.aspx?TranscriptID=2602.

56. Joe Dejka, "Inside STRATCOM on September 11: Offutt exercise took real-life twist," *Omaha World-Herald*, February 27, 2002.

57. Dan Verton, *Black Ice: The Invisible Threat of Cyber-Terrorism*, McGraw Hill, Em-

eryville, CA., 2003, pp.143-144.

58. Emails from Dan Verton, August 16, 2007.

59. Dan Balz and Bob Woodward, op. cit.

60. Timothy R. Gaffney, "Wright-Pat Air Force Base Goes to Highest Alert: Base activates national command posts," *Dayton Daily News,* September 12, 2001.

61. *Space Observer,* March 23, 2001, p. 2; William Arkin, a military analyst, corroborated this in his 2005 book, *Code Names,* Steerforth Press, Hanover, NH, 2005, which mentions an October 22-31 date.

62. See the discussion about Global Guardian at http://www.globalsecurity.org/military/ops/global-guardian.htm.

63. Email from "Pinnacle," July 5, 2007.

64. Letter to Congressman Adam Schiff, November 8, 2006, signed by Lt. Col. Karen L. Cook, Deputy Chief Congressional Inquiry Division, Office of Legislative Liaison, Department of the Air Force, the Pentagon. See Appendix, pages 300 and 301.

3

Confirmation from CNN

The first article I posted on the Internet (in April 2007) about the E-4B fly-over was generally met with skepticism, if not stony silence. Although I did receive words of encouragement from some readers, many others were critical. Some of these critics complained about the grainy quality of the still shots. Others doubted their authenticity and insinuated that the photos had been retouched or faked. Still others were willing to concede that the video evidence might be genuine, and did show a U.S. Air Force E-4B. But even these individuals refused to believe that the footage had been filmed at the White House on the day of the attack. They argued that it was much more likely the E-4B video was from some other time or place.

They had a point, since, with the exception of Linda Brookhart's photo, there was no visual evidence linking the E-4B to Washington on 9/11. As the evidence accumulated, however, this argument became impossible to sustain. The breakthrough was "Pinnacle's" June 2007 discovery of the stunning footage in the CNN ImageSource archive. This video was the clincher because it obviously had been filmed at the White House on 9/11.

At this point there was a subtle shift. Many now agreed that the video footage and grainy photo-grabs might be genuine, and did show the world's most advanced military aircraft circling over the White House on 9/11. These same individuals, however, summarily dismissed the "conspiratorial" implications. They asked: *Why wouldn't an E-4B fly over Washington DC during a terrorist attack?* One view frequently expressed was that the doomsday plane was merely responding in a time of national crisis. These critics argued that the E-4B probably had been involved in a military exercise at the time of the attack, and was simply diverted — moved into position over the White House to help coordinate the defense of the nation's capital.

Yet, if this *were* the case, why the denials by the U.S. military? Surely, openly acknowledging whatever positive role the doomsday plane may have played would have demonstrated NORAD's resilience and its capacity to defend the nation. After the shocking "security failures," would not this have helped restore the public's confidence? Although it is possible that the E-4B's presence was innocent, given what we now know this seems unlikely, and it becomes more so with every passing day. As we will see, the debunkers of "conspiracy theories" invariably fall prey to their own assumptions.

By mid summer 2007, my E-4B research — compiled with "Pinnacle's" able assistance — was featured on several websites. Evidently, it had the effect of prodding (or shaming) CNN into action. On September 12, 2007, the day after the sixth anniversary of the September 11th attack, the Turner network aired a three-minute broadcast about the E-4B fly-over on *Anderson Cooper 360°*. The segment had been prepared by John King, and featured portions of CNN's raw footage, cited in the previous chapter, which had been gathering dust in the CNN archive for six years. This CNN video report is still posted on the Internet and is well recommended to readers.[1]

Not surprisingly, John King framed the story in the expected manner. It was, of course, taken for granted that the E-4B was on a legitimate mission when it buzzed the White House. All the same, the report was a breakthrough because it confirmed the basic facts. King based his report on consultations with two government sources who were knowledgeable about the incident. The sources refused to identify the plane, but they did confirm that it was a military aircraft. CNN was told that "the details are classified." However, the video evidence captured by CNN's own reporters was so compelling and so unambiguous that John King had little difficulty identifying the mysterious white plane as "among the military's most sensitive aircraft," namely, an E-4B, the so-called doomsday plane.

King also correctly noted that "six years later the Pentagon, the Secret Service and the FAA all say, at least for pubic consumption, they have no explanation of the giant plane that flew over the president's house as the smoke began to rise across the river at the Pentagon." King's report on CNN was important because millions of jaded Americans have become totally dependent on the national news media for their information about the world. For them nothing is real unless they see it on television. CNN's belated coverage finally made it possible for these Americans to accept the visual evidence as bona fide. This was not some bizarre hallucination from the conspiratorial fringe. The fly-over was very strange, yes, but it was no less real. It happened. The real question is why the U.S. Air Force still denies everything in the face of incontrovertible evidence.

I give CNN positive marks for airing this important evidence. Even so, John King's September 12 report on *Anderson Cooper 360°* still suffered from the familiar deficiencies that plague U.S. journalism. Today, television programming in our country has slumped to an all-time low. Most programs are little more than "filler." By this I mean, they fill the empty space between commercials, which are the true message and what the medium is really about. TV news, meanwhile, has largely become infotainment, geared not to educate and inform the citizenry but to manufacture consent for the official point of view while boosting a network's ratings.

Today's incarnation of Randolph Hearst's slanted yellow press of yesteryear specializes in drive-by reporting and the art of the killer sound byte, with a heavy emphasis on the whoopee factor. Spin is everything, content strictly secondary, and in-depth analysis almost nonexistent. Gone are the days when serious muckraking journalism did occasionally happen in our country. CNN's three-minute report was accurate insofar as it went. Unfortunately, due to its extreme brevity, CNN failed to do justice to one of the outstanding mysteries from September 11. John King neglected to mention a number of crucial facts, and spun the others.

In the CNN report John King implies a vague dismissal by the U.S. military when he states, "Ask the Pentagon, and it insists this is not a military plane." The particulars of the case, however, are a good deal more incriminating. By law, when the U.S. government receives a Freedom of Information Act request, it is not allowed to claim that it has no information simply because something is classified. The 2005 FOIA law explicitly states that in a case involving classified material the government must explain that the records exist, but are exempt. Assuming that CNN's government sources were correct, and the circumstances surrounding the E-4B fly over on 9/11 are indeed classified, the Air Force, FAA, and Secret Service were legally obligated to inform "Pinnacle" (who submitted these FOIA requests) of this fact. We are left to wonder why none of them did. See Appendix, page 302, for one official response.

Department of Defense regulations are also similar to the FOIA statute. Military regulations stipulate that in cases where information requested by a member of Congress on behalf of a constituent is classified and cannot be released, "the Member requesting the information shall be advised promptly of that fact and of the reasons for the determination."[2]

Clearly, the U.S. Air Force's letter of denial to Rep. Adam Schiff (D-CA) was in violation of military regulations.

The matter is more serious yet, because Rep. Schiff has a security clearance to view classified material. As the representative of California's 29th district, Schiff serves on two House sub-committees that deal with terrorism.[3] Indeed, Schiff himself has played a leading role on the issue by introducing legislation to strengthen security at U.S. facilities stocked with biological weapons. More recently, Schiff also authored a bill that would require air cargo to be screened for explosives. If the E-4B fly-over on 9/11 was indeed classified, the U.S. Air Force, at a minimum, was obligated to inform the congressman of this fact.

Why then, did they lie? Since when do U.S. national security interests require the Pentagon to deceive the nation's duly-elected representatives? Of course, President Bush bears the ultimate responsibility for such a policy, because the Nightwatch fleet falls directly under the national command authority, meaning the Secretary of Defense (at the time, Rumsfeld) who reports directly to the president. Furthermore, it is the White House that sets the tone for the government as a whole, including the military. More recently, we witnessed another ugly case when the Bush White House refused to allow Oregon Rep. Peter DeFazio to view the administration's contingency plans for Continuity of Government.

As a member of the Homeland Security Committee in the House, DeFazio has clearance to enter a secure "bubble room" in the Capitol and examine pertinent classified documents. DeFazio was understandably shocked at being denied access. He told Portland's *Oregonian:* "I just can't believe they're going to deny a member of Congress the right of reviewing how they plan to conduct the government of the United States after a significant terrorist attack." Then DeFazio added, "Maybe the people who think there's a conspiracy are right."[4] Both of these cases show the obsessive secrecy of the Bush administration, especially since 9/11. Given that transparency and openness are essential to representative democracy, what else can we conclude but that the U.S. has ceased to function as a republic?

Was there an After-Action Report?

If honest answers exist, they might be found in one or more "after action reports" describing the events of 9/11, at least one of which surely includes a discussion of the E-4B incident. Assuming that military personnel did their duty after 9/11 and filed such a report(s) through military channels, in all likelihood it (or they) came into the hands of Secretary of Defense Rumsfeld in the hours immediately following the 9/11 attack. There is reason to think that such reports once did exist, because so-called OPREP, or operational reports, are standard procedure in the U.S. military. In fact, they are required by military regulations. Of course, if these reports survived the shredder, today they are probably locked away in a desk or safe somewhere in the Pentagon, far from prying eyes.

A 1993 instruction document from the Joint Chiefs of Staff describes in detail the military's in-house reporting system in effect at the time of the 9/11 attack.[5] The reporting system is organized in a hierarchical manner, with lesser incidents requiring reports to lesser commanders. Only the most serious incidents require the highest level or so-called Pinnacle reports (OPREP-3 PINNACLE, abbreviated as OPREP-3P). My anonymous colleague adopted this as his personal screen name. This is not mere coincidence. It so happens that "Pinnacle" has devoted a considerable amount of time and energy investigating the U.S. military's internal reporting system.

The instruction document from the Joint Chiefs clearly states that in the case of a "significant event or incident" involving "national-level interest," a PINNACLE or highest level report must be filed with the national command authority, meaning the National Military Command Center, a secure office in the Pentagon which is the nerve center for U.S. nuclear war planning. Incidentally, this is the same office that proved dysfunctional on 9/11. A PINNACLE level report would also make the rounds of the Joint Chiefs of Staff and, as noted, would surely land on the desk of the Secretary of Defense. The instruction document defines a "reportable incident" as any event that "generates a high level of military action, causes a national reaction, affects international relationships, causes immediate widespread coverage in news media, is clearly against national interest, or affects current national policy." Obviously, the events of September 11, 2001 met every one of these criteria and without question would have been reportable. Did the appropriate officers file such internal reports in the hours after the attack? And, if so, do the reports still exist?

The instruction document goes on to describe the different types of operational reports (OPREPs), and the relevant procedures with each. The various sub-categories are identified by different code or flag names. For example, an OPREP-3 PINNACLE NUCFLASH (i.e., OPREP-3PNF) is the code name for any situation that creates a risk of nuclear war, such as an unauthorized nuclear detonation, the accidental or unauthorized launch of a nuclear capable missile or plane, or the detection of an unidentified object by a missile warning system. Another category, OPREP-3P EMPTY QUIVER (OPREP-3PEQ) is the code name for the seizure, theft, or loss of a nuclear weapon. OPREP-3P FRONT BURNER (OPREP-3PFB) is the code name for an attack on or harassment of U.S. military forces, a category under which a summary report about the events of 9/11 might well have fallen. At least one of the category names, OPREP-3P BROKEN ARROW (OPREP-3PBA), has become a part of popular American culture. Broken Arrow is the code name for an incident involving an accidental nuclear detonation, radioactive contamination, or the jettisoning of a nuclear weapon or component.

If it sounds familiar, this is because the code name Broken Arrow was leaked, and in 1996 became part of our lexicon when Hollywood produced a high-budget film by that name. The movie starred John Travolta, as a deranged Air Force officer who steals two nuclear weapons and proceeds to hold the nation hostage to nuclear blackmail. The screenplay suffers from more than a few corny lines, but the movie made up for it with lots of action, and the story was plausible enough to become a box office success. No one apparently noticed that Hollywood switched code names, preferring the sexier Broken Arrow to Empty Quiver, which, as noted above, is the actual OPREP-3 term for nuclear theft.

The Minot Incident

More recently, the U.S. news media reported a live case. As already mentioned, on August 30, 2007, U.S. Air Force personnel at Minot AFB in North Dakota "mistakenly" loaded six nuclear-armed cruise missiles under the wings of a B-52 bound for Barksdale AFB in Louisiana — the first reported unauthorized flight of nukes over U.S. airspace in nearly 40 years. The incident reached the news media only because USAF airmen leaked the story to the *Army Times* on September 5.[6] Retired AF General Eugene Habiger, who headed the Strategic Air Command (STRATCOM) from 1996-1998, told the *Washington Post*, "I have been in the nuclear business since 1966 and am not aware of any incident more disturbing."[7]

The security breach was not discovered until 36 hours later, when a ground crew at Barksdale AFB began removing the missiles. One can imagine the airmen's surprise on discovering that the missiles were nuclear-armed. At that point, the officer on duty alertly notified the National Military Command Center at the Pentagon. According to the *Post,* within hours an OPREP-3 BENT SPEAR report raced up the chain of command to Secretary of Defense Robert Gates, and reportedly even reached the desk of President Bush. The mishap was serious enough that it prompted the Air Force to order a one-day stand-down of the Air Combat Command so that officers could review safety procedures. *Yet, within the military's OPREP-3P reporting system a BENT SPEAR incident is regarded as less serious than a PINNACLE-level event, which surely characterizes the September 11 attack.*

Assuming that the U.S. military's internal reporting system functioned after 9/11, in accordance with regulations, this can only mean that at least one PINNACLE report reached Rumsfeld and the White House within hours of the attack. Indeed, given the complexity of events and the multiple "intelligence failures," in all likelihood there were several Pinnacle level reports, all bearing the same identification number. It also stands to reason that a copy of at least one of these would have been sent to the FAA, since the USAF E-4B violated the FAA prohibited zone, i.e., P-56, not to mention that agency's obvious role in cases of air emergencies and hijackings.

Did the Secret Service also receive a copy? This too seems plausible, because the White House also came under threat of attack on 9/11. It is the Secret Service, after all, not the U.S. military, which is the ultimate authority when it comes to the president's personal security. This includes the White House grounds and the airspace above the presidential mansion, which the E-4B clearly violated on 9/11. Therefore, it is reasonable to conclude that the Secret Service was also in the loop. But if the FAA and Secret Service received copies of said report, why then do both agencies now claim to have no information, as if the event never happened? Indeed, why is the whole matter surrounded by an aura of mystery and denial?

In fact, it is quite likely the USAF officer who was piloting the E-4B on 9/11 contacted the Secret Service directly by radio to notify the White House of his imminent approach, so as not to become an accidental victim of the Stinger missiles reportedly deployed on the roof of the president's house. According to one self-styled Internet expert, the E-4B has no missile defenses.[8] If this source is correct, the Secret Service surely learned — and still knows — the identity of the white plane and has no basis for pleading ignorance.

We can't be certain, but the facts suggest that the military's internal reporting system failed to function in the hours and days following the September 11 attack. Although author Dan Verton does not support "conspiracy theories" and attributes the so-called security failures of 9/11 to the fog of war, nonetheless, he evidently agrees with this conclusion. Verton informed me that on September 12, 2001, when he spoke (by telephone) with a high-ranking member of the Scowcroft advisory panel, his informant was then at Offutt AFB and "was still going through the events in question." Verton writes that his source was extremely displeased with the U.S. military's feeble response to the 9/11 attack and "mentioned that the after-action report would not reflect well on their performance" — an obvious allusion to the reporting system I have described. Did one or more OPREP-3P reports materialize after 9/11? Verton mentions such a report in his book,[9] but he later informed me that "[I] never saw it.... I have no idea if he [the informant] ever followed through, or if he did, if it was accepted/circulated ... the way things work with this administration, I'm sure it was circulated, only in a million thinly shredded strips."[10]

AC 360° Redux

CNN concedes that the video evidence it aired September 12, 2007 on *Anderson Cooper 360°* was never-before-shown raw footage from 9/11. However, the network has yet to explain why it "sat" on this important evidence for six years. We know that videos of the E-4B fly-over were shown in the U.K., in Spain, and probably in many other nations during the world coverage of 9/11. Yet here in America, the same evidence was kept out of the national news media for six years. The question is: Why? The circumstances suggest that this was an orchestrated effort — not accidental or coincidental.

During the days, weeks, and months following 9/11, there were many conflicting stories about the trajectory of Flight 77, including reports that the American Airlines flight made a pass over Washington and flew near the White House before striking the Pentagon. Bob Woodward was responsible for one such report, which appeared in the *Washington Post*.[11] In another report by NBC, Tom Brokaw cited government officials who claimed that Flight 77 had even circled the Capitol.[12] CBS followed suit with a similar story on September 21, 2001.[13] These and other such reports can still be found on the Internet, and some of them also include diagrams and maps describing the alleged flight path of AA Flight 77 over Washington.

Yet, even as these reports gained wide coverage and credence, CNN was in possession of video evidence that would have helped sort out and clarify what really did happen. Why then, did CNN withhold this important evidence from the nation? With hindsight, it would appear that within 24 hours of the attack someone in a high position at CNN made a decision to suppress this information. On September 12, 2001, the day after the attack, CNN posted a minute-by-minute timeline of 9/11. But strangely absent is any mention of the stories filed by Kate Snow and John King about the mysterious white plane.[14] Who made the decision to expunge the E-4B fly-over from the news? Here, I must emphasize: It is not my intention to single out CNN for special criticism. No doubt other networks were also in possession of similar evidence. Probably, they still are.

As this book went to press, we learned of two additional videos of the E-4B fly-over. Both actually aired on U.S. television, but with no contextual discussion, analysis, or follow-up. One short video was captured by an ABC cameraman as he was leaving the White House grounds. The footage is very similar to the CNN footage in that it shows the evacuation in progress. However, the overhead shot of the plane is very brief. Also, due to the sun's brightness, the film is overexposed, and the E-4B is only visible with contrast enhancement. ABC actually aired this evacuation segment at 10:42 A.M. on the day of the attack. The reporter mentions hearing a plane overhead, and in the segment White House police can be seen looking up at the sky. However, after 9/11, ABC dropped the issue and there were no follow-up reports.[15]

The other short video appeared on FOX in 2004. It even mentioned that a doomsday plane flew over the White House on 9/11.[16] However, there was no discussion by FOX of the above concerns, and nothing about the E-4B's possible role in the NORAD response. With these latest additions, there are eight known video segments of the E-4B fly-over.

The CNN report on *AC 360°* also suffered from another flaw. It neglected to discuss, or even mention, the E-4B's involvement in USSTRATCOM's 2001 Global Guardian exercise. One would think that the strange rescheduling of the 2001 drill from October to September, and the subsequent switch back in 2002, would have rated at least a sound byte, especially since the Pentagon gave no explanation about the schedule change. Why did John King not mention this in his report? The matter is important because it is well known that military exercises can provide cover for covert operations.

A serious in-depth television report would, at least, have mentioned these facts, thereby focusing a spotlight on the 911 Commission's failure to investigate them. Surely the function of the media is (or ought to be) to expose incompetence and malfeasance in high places. The Pentagon's rescheduling of Global Guardian was noteworthy in light of the 9/11 attack, and should have been thoroughly investigated by the 9/11 Commission. It wasn't. The commissioners failed to go there. Unfortunately, so did CNN, which thereby fumbled a chance to serve the national interest. CNN's absent-minded coverage served only to perpetuate the official omission.

CNN also missed another opportunity. John King failed to interview Brent Scowcroft or any of the members of Rumsfeld's special advisory panel. If Verton's account is correct, all of them were aboard the E-4B during its fly-over. Their identities were not classified information. I was able to learn their names simply by making a phone call to the Pentagon. (Imagine my surprise when a real person picked up and volunteered the details.) The CNN network has far more resources than I do, and certainly could have done this much, at the very least.

No doubt, the panelists have quite a story to tell about what they saw that day. The fact that their story has never been told has to be one of the more puzzling aspects of the U.S. media's collective amnesia about 9/11. No mistake, the flight of the white plane has all of the elements of a prime-time news story, one likely to send a network's ratings into the stratosphere.

"Pinnacle" captured the dark essence of it after discovering the raw CNN footage, when he likened the flight of the E-4B to an enormous predatory vulture circling ominously above the president's house, one of the symbols of our proud democracy. Given the cloak of secrecy surrounding the event, what else are we to think? The evidence suggests, and I believe we must conclude, that the decision to suppress the story came from above, and reflected the perceived narrow interests of the media's corporate ownership. Regrettably, those interests appear to be in sharp conflict with the best interests of our nation, and by this I mean the greater good.

One of the high points of the CNN report was a brief interview with Lee Hamilton, co-chair of the 911 Commission, who stated that he had "a vague recollection" of the 9/11 mystery plane. He claimed that his staffers had looked into the incident but never raised it as a relevant issue. Said Hamilton, "This never rose to the level of a discussion within the commission." His statement was important and called for further clarification. For example, who made the policy decision? One of the staffers? If so, which one? Surely the individual has a name. Another question: Was Hamilton in the loop?

Unfortunately, we have no answers because CNN failed to follow through. Whoever conducted the interview apparently forgot the essentials of journalism, i.e., the who, what, where and when. Nonetheless, the circumstantial evidence strongly points to Philip Zelikow, Executive Director of the commission.

Was Zelikow responsible for scrubbing the E-4B incident from the investigation? Why do I suggest this? Well, please consider the following remark by Lee Hamilton, made during an August 2006 interview on a Canadian TV program to CBC News host Evan Solomon:

> Yeah. A lot of things that came to the attention of staff did not come to the attention of the commission. Some of the things did come to the attention of the commission, and we didn't put 'em in, or at least we put 'em in at a lower level. *But many of the things did not come directly to my attention* [my emphasis].[17]

This is a remarkable admission, because, as co-chair of the commission, it was Hamilton's job to keep the investigation on track by providing sage leadership and guidance. Certainly this included the responsibility for supervising the staff and maintaining a firm grip on the agenda. Yet here Hamilton essentially admits that he either lost, or never had, control of the investigation. His statement is shocking and lends credence to the charges of a cover-up by numerous critics, including the families of the victims (especially the Jersey Girls), who were outraged that the day-to-day operational control of the commission was in the hands of a close associate of Condoleezza Rice, namely, Philip Zelikow.[18]

Were co-chairs Kean and Hamilton largely figureheads? Hamilton has called the "conspiracy theories" ludicrous, but what is truly ludicrous is the idea that the E-4B fly-over on 9/11 was not important enough to rise to the level of a discussion. Obviously, the E-4B crew, especially the pilot, not to mention the members of the advisory panel who may have been on board, were important ancillary witnesses to the events at the Pentagon. The E-4B pilot, for example, had he been interviewed, might have provided the commission with an eyewitness account at least as important as the testimony of Lt. Col. Steve O'Brien, the C-130H pilot who *was* interviewed and whose story, as we know, became a part of the official record.[19]

The E-4B's radar and other electronic data was also important evidence, and should have been subpoenaed and carefully studied by experts

The veritable workhouse of cargo transport, the Lockheed C-130H is about 100 feet long with a wingspan of 130 feet and propellers.

appointed by the commission. But, of course, none of this happened. In fact, Hamilton's remarks on CNN and his 2006 statement on CBC News demonstrated such blatant incompetence as to thoroughly discredit the official 911 investigation and its final report, which makes no mention of the E-4B, not even in a footnote. Indeed, I would argue that the raw footage aired by CNN on September 12, 2007 is sufficient grounds, in and of itself, for throwing out the *9/11 Commission Report* entirely and reopening the investigation.

By the way, Hamilton's grudging admission that commissioners were denied access to key information has been corroborated by at least one other member of the panel. Max Cleland, former U.S. Senator from Georgia, served on the 9/11 Commission for approximately one year, and during a November 2003 interview with Salon.com, shortly before resigning, he complained that as a panelist he did *not* have full access to all of the pertinent documents. Cleland compared the 9/11 investigation to the failed Warren Commission, and made it clear to Salon.com that he preferred to resign rather than participate in a cover-up.[20]

So, let us turn now to the important question: Why might Philip Zelikow seek to block an honest investigation of the E-4B incident? By now, the answer ought to be obvious. Some had already connected the dots within hours of CNN's September 2007 report on *Anderson Cooper 360°*.

One Internet blogger hit the nail squarely on the head when he posted the following headline: "If 9/11 was a surprise, why was the E-4B over DC?"[21] Exactly. No one has put it more succinctly. David Ray Griffin offers a more nuanced perspective in his latest book, which includes a chapter about the E-4B incident.[22] Griffin prefaces his remarks by stressing a point I have already made, but one that bears repeating. According to the official timeline, the U.S. military did not learn about the approach of Flight 77 until 9:36 A.M. (that time again!), barely two minutes before the Pentagon strike. Griffin writes,

> This short warning period ... gave the Pentagon time only to order an unarmed C-130H cargo plane, which was already in the air, to identify the approaching aircraft as a Boeing 757 before it crashed into the Pentagon.

As we know, the C-130H pilot, acting on orders, proceeded to shadow the alleged Flight 77 as it made its final approach. Yet, according to the official story, it was already too late. Given this short warning time, the U.S. military was unable to mount a defense. The E-4B's presence, however, constitutes a serious problem for this now-standard version of events. As I've already noted, Dan Verton's, and at least two other accounts, place the E-4B in the skies over Washington *before* the Pentagon strike, which, if true, punches a hole in the official story large enough to accommodate

The E-4B is 230 feet long with a wingspan of 195 feet and jet engines.

a Boeing 757 — or some other large aircraft. As we know, Flight 77(?) approached from the west and executed a 330-degree looping turn over Alexandria, Virginia, before making its final approach, a downward spiral that took just over 3 minutes. Griffin writes,

> ... a military plane over Washington [i.e., the E-4B] would have been in position to observe this maneuver after having seen Flight 77's approach to Washington. The 9/11 Commission's claim that the military had only 'one or two minutes' notice' of an approaching aircraft would become implausible.

Griffin is correct. As I have emphasized, this was no ordinary plane. The E-4B undoubtedly has advanced radar, in addition to state-of-the-art communications equipment, everything needed to electronically observe the approach of Flight 77(?) from many miles away. The cockpit of the E-4B was also an ideal perch from which to establish visual contact with Flight 77(?) long before its arrival. If the E-4B was in the Washington DC area, it was in excellent position and could have alerted the Pentagon and/or mustered whatever defenses were available, such as ground-to-air missiles. The airborne command and control plane was also well-placed to help direct the F-16 fighters from Langley when they arrived on the scene shortly before 10 A.M. Let us not forget, at this point the "terrorist" attack was still in progress. Hijacked Flight 93 was still over Pennsylvania and was believed to be heading toward Washington. As Secret Service Deputy Director Barbara Riggs has made perfectly clear, staffers at FAA headquarters still believed the White House was in grave danger.

Dan Verton writes in *Black Ice* that soon after the flying command post took off from Andrews AFB it "converted literally on the fly from exercise status to real world status."[23] This would indicate that the doomsday plane was available to assist in the NORAD response. Verton also mentions that the E-4B arrived at Offutt AFB later in the day. However, Verton offers no further details in his book about whatever role the E-4B may have played.

As noted, reporter Bob Woodward also mentioned the E-4B in his 2002 retrospective series in the *Washington Post*, writing, "Pentagon officials ordered up the airborne command post [i.e., the E-4B] used only in national emergencies."[24] Woodward likewise offered no further clues. It is not even clear from his article *which* E-4B he was referring to. Was it the

Wright-Pat departure? Woodward probably did not know himself, and simply repeated whatever his sources at the White House told him.

Nonetheless, his article does give the strong impression that the command post was sent up for the purpose of assisting the military's response to the 9/11 attack. While we have no information about the role played by the E-4B that departed Wright-Pat AFB after 9:43 A.M., one thing is certain: *The E-4B that buzzed the White House played no role whatsoever.* Far from helping to coordinate the defense of the nation's capital, it appears that the E-4B pilot did not even wait around for the Langley fighters to arrive, but simply left the scene.

In her book, *Touching History*, a 2008 account of the intense drama that unfolded in the skies over America on 9/11, Lynn Spencer mentions that the NEADS commander was unable to communicate with the Air National Guard and Langley pilots after they established a defensive combat air patrol over the nation's capital.[25] The reason? Radio works by line of sight, hence, requires an unobstructed path from transmitter to receiver. Due to the distance and the curvature of the earth, the radio signals from NEADS (located in Rome, NY) were not receivable in the DC area below 20,000 feet. The communication problems only added to the confusion. The matter was resolved, later that morning, when an E-3 AWACS arrived and began to serve as a high altitude communications hub. Gen. Larry Arnold stated that this particular AWACS plane just happened to be in the vicinity on "a training mission."[26] According to another source, it was in the skies over Pennsylvania.[27] But Arnold and the Air Force have yet to explain why the world's premier electronics platform, which was already on the scene, failed to assist in the defense of Washington.

Insofar as I am aware, there is no evidence that the E-4B was even in radio contact with any of the fighter pilots before, during, or after their delayed arrival, with the possible exception of one mysterious radio transmission that has never been explained. As reported by the BBC, Langley fighter pilot Major Dean Eckmann overheard a transmission at 9:33 A.M. while piloting his F-16 over the Atlantic. In Eckmann's own words: "They said, 'All aeroplanes, if you come within 30 miles of Washington DC, you will be shot down.'"[28] Who gave *this* order, and why? Did it come from the E-4B pilot? Was he warning off all planes, military as well as commercial, for the purpose of concealing his presence over the capital? In truth, we do not know. Yet, it is strange that the BBC story is nowhere mentioned in the *9/11 Commission Report*.

If the E-4B was on a legitimate mission, then how do we explain its odd behavior? There is also the matter of its low pass over the White House. As I have noted, the E-4B command-and-control plane is designed to fly at high altitude. Insofar as we know, the E-4B has no offensive weapons, and therefore had no reason to fly low over Washington. In fact, given that the "terrorist attack" was still in progress, the pilot's low flight path over the White House placed the E-4B in jeopardy. After all, there was no telling what might ensue. Anything was possible, including nuclear terrorism aimed at the Capitol or White House. For all of these reasons a bona fide command-and-control plane would have gone out of its way *to avoid* downtown Washington.

The E-4B's low pass over the White House also exposed the plane to accidental attack by the Secret Service, which is known to possess Stinger missiles. According to one source, already noted, the E-4B has no defense against ground-to-air missiles. But even if this report is incorrect, why take a chance? Either way, the E-4B's flight path is improbable, and hard to explain, unless, of course, the E-4B pilot had reason to be confident that his plane was not in danger. So, we see, the presence of the E-4B *before* the Pentagon strike and its strange behavior, taken together, deal a possibly fatal blow to debunkers of "conspiracy theories," who appear to have snared themselves in their own logic.

All of this establishes a clear motive and might explain why Executive Director Phil Zelikow could decide to suppress all information concerning the incident, just as he likely did in the case of Able Danger (as we will learn in a later discussion). From the standpoint of shoring up the official narrative, it was crucial that the potentially incriminating details about the E-4B never reach the eyes and ears of the commission members, at least not in any sensible form, lest the panelists decide on their own initiative to undertake a genuine investigation of the incident.

From the standpoint of the official story, this would have been a disaster — the equivalent of opening Pandora's box — for once begun, an honest inquiry might have led even the most purblind commissioners to stumble forward, in the direction of still more undesirable facts and ultimately to the troubling questions — and perhaps even some of the conclusions that I have already presented in this book. Did Zelikow take precautionary measures to insure this would not happen? Concealing the E-4B from the commissioners would have been easily done, since, as we know, Zelikow personally controlled the commission's agenda and the flow of information to the various panel members. As we are about to discover, however, the cover-up did not start with Zelikow.

Endnotes

1. A link to the CNN report is posted at http://rawstory.com//news/2007/CNN_investigates_secret_911_doomsday_plane_0913.html.

2. The DoD regulation in question is 5400.4. The verbatim wording is as follows: "4.3. Information Requested for Constituents. Information requested by Members of Congress for their constituents shall be tested for limitations on dissemination (see 3.1.2.) and handled in the same manner as if the constituent himself had written directly to the Department of Defense. If it develops that the information cannot be released, the Member requesting the information shall be advised promptly of that fact and of the reasons for the determination."

3. Rep. Adam Schiff is a member of the House Judiciary Committee and its Subcommittee on Crime, Terrorism and Homeland Security, as well as its other Subcommittee on the Constitution. He is also a member of the House International Relations Committee and its Subcommittee on International Terrorism.

4. Jeff Kosseff, "Congressman Denied Access to Federal Post-Terror Attack Plans," *Oregonian* (Portland), July 20, 2007.

5. Chairman of the Joint Chiefs of Staff Instruction, CJCSI 3150.03, December 1, 1993.

6. Michael Hoffman, "B-52 mistakenly flies with nukes aboard," *Army Times*, September 10, 2007.

7. Joby Warrick and Walter Pincus, "Missteps in the Bunker," *Washington Post*, September 23, 2007.

8. See the discussion at the following forum: http://www.abovetopsecret.com/forum/thread133996/pg1.

9. Dan Verton, *Black Ice: The Invisible Threat of Cyber-Terrorism*, McGraw-Hill, New York, 2003, p. 150.

10. Email from Dan Verton, September 24, 2007.

11. Dan Balz and Bob Woodward, "America's Chaotic Road to War," *Washington Post*, January 27, 2002.

12. NBC Network anchor Tom Brokaw stated that Flight 77 had circled both the Capitol and the White House before crashing into the Pentagon. This segment aired at 10:14 P.M. on September 12, 2001.

13. "Primary Target," CBS News, September 21, 2001, posted at http://www.cbsnews.com/stories/2001/09/11/national/printable310721.shtml.

14. CNN's original timeline may still be be viewed at http://archives.cnn.com/2001/U.S./09/11/chronology.attack/ Incidentally, five days after the 9/11 attack CNN posted a revised timeline that also failed to mention the incident. It may still be viewed at http://archives.cnn.com/2001/U.S./09/16/inv.hijack.warning/.

15. Credit for discovering this evidence goes to John Farmer, an independent 9/11 investigator. I will introduce him in the next chapter. See the ABC footage archive at http://www.televisionarchive.org/.

16. At press time, the Fox segment was posted at http://video.aol.com/video-detail/e-4b-on-fox-news/698085052.

17. *CBC News: Sunday*, "9/11: Truth, Lies and Conspiracy," Evan Solomon interviews Lee Hamilton, August 21, 2006: http://www.cbc.ca/sunday/911hamilton.html.

18. Philip Shenon, *The Commission*, Twelve, New York, 2008, pp. 166-174.

19. *The 9/11 Commission Report: Final Report of the National Commission on Terrorist Attacks Upon the United States*, W.W. Norton & Co., New York, 2004, pp. 25-26.

20. Max Cleland interview with *Salon*.com, November 21, 2003; also see Cleland's interview with Amy Goodman on *Democracy Now!* March 23, 2004.

21. Posted at http://correntewire.com/if_9_11_01_was_a_surprise_why_was_the_e4b_over_dc.

22. David Ray Griffin, *9/11 Contradictions*, Olive Branch Press, Massachusetts, 2008, see Chapter 21: Was a Military Plane Flying over Washington During the Pentagon Attack?

23. Dan Verton, op. cit., p. 150.

24. Dan Balz and Bob Woodward, "America's Chaotic Road to War," first in a series, *Washington Post*, January 27, 2002, posted at http://www.washingtonpost.com/wp-dyn/articles/A42754-2002Jan26_3.html.

25. Lynn Spencer, *Touching History: The Untold Story of the Drama that Unfolded in the Skies over America on 9/11*, Free Press, New York, 2008, p. 265.

26. "Conversation with Major General Larry Arnold, Commander, 1st Air Force, Tyndall AFB, Florida," *Code One*, Vol. 17, No. 1, 1st Quarter 2002. Posted at http://www.codeonemagazine.com/archives/2002/articles/jan_02/defense/.

27. The E-3 pilot was First Lieutenant Anthony Kuczynski, who was flying toward Pittsburgh, accompanied by two F-16s. Dave Forster, "UST grad guides bombers in war," *Aquin*, April 12, 2002. Posed at http://www.stthomas.edu/aquin/archive/041202/anaconda.html.

28. "Clear the Skies," BBC, September 1, 2002.

— 4 —

The E-4B Cover-Up

Our nation's capital is especially beautiful in the springtime when the cherry blossoms are at their peak. I say this from experience, having spent my youth in the DC area. Moreover, part of my family still lives in northern Virginia. So, it happened that I returned there in early April 2008 to complete the research for this book. My trip came about in the following way: In February 2008 I received an email from Rebecca McNerney, a well known analyst at the Department of Energy (DoE), who contacted me after reading my article on the Internet about "The 9/11 Mystery Plane." It seems that McNerney was an eyewitness on September 11, 2001. At the time, her office was located in the DoE building (sixth floor) at 950 L'Enfant Plaza, in SW Washington DC. In her email McNerney wrote: "Approximately 5-10 minutes after the Pentagon incident I saw a large white plane flying rather low from the White House over the National Mall toward the Capitol."[1] After some correspondence back and forth, McNerney agreed to meet with me in Washington for an interview, on site. Naturally, I was pleased for the opportunity to "see" what she saw on 9/11, through *her* eyes.

On September 11, 2001, McNerney, like millions of other Americans, was starting her work day when she learned about a tragedy unfolding in New York City. Someone two doors down had a TV on, and the people in her department gathered around watching in horror as the North Tower burned. Then came the second strike. When McNerney learned that the Pentagon was also under attack she hurried down the hall to her boss's office on the west end of the DoE, which has an unobstructed view across the Potomac. By this time a column of heavy smoke was billowing skyward. McNerney says she watched for a few minutes, in shock, then returned to her own office, located on the north side of the DoE. Moments later, she observed the large white plane cruising eastward toward the Capitol. McNerney is convinced it was the same plane described in my article.

She says she was terrified when she saw it. The strange white plane was low in the sky, obviously, where no commercial aircraft should *ever* be. She thought it was a suicide attack aimed at the Capitol. There was also the unsettling possibility that the DoE might be next. Seconds after it appeared, the white plane passed out of sight behind a nearby building. McNerney mentioned the strange aircraft to her colleagues but none of them had seen it. They thought she "was seeing things." Soon after, the order came to evacuate. The next hour was gridlock, as thousands of government employees simultaneously left Washington. McNerney says that during the long ride home she kept searching the skies, but she never again saw the white plane. In fact, over the next six years she never heard or read anything more about it, until she stumbled upon my article on the Internet.

We met at L'Enfant Plaza on April 4, 2008, and McNerney graciously walked me through her 9/11 experience. Although her department has since been relocated to a different building, she made prior arrangements for us to revisit her former office. I had assumed, wrongly, that the DoE was several miles from the Pentagon. Not so. The distance from L'Enfant Plaza is no more than about a mile. Her boss' former office on the sixth floor is spacious and commands a stunning vista across the river. The entire Pentagon looms large in the window.

McNerney's own former office has a more limited view-shed to the north, due to the proximity of other buildings in the sprawling government complex at L'Enfant Plaza. The E-4B was very low in the sky when she saw it, possibly as low as 500 feet. This is consistent with the videos of the E-4B captured from Lafayette Park. It would appear that the doomsday plane was losing altitude as it completed its loop over the White House. At that point, it probably swung east toward the Capitol. If this is correct, the time of day can have been no later than 9:41 A.M., when ABC's Peter Jennings reported the sighting at the White House.[2] But the fly-over must have happened before this, because one would expect a time lag of at least one or two minutes.

The 9:41 A.M. time is *not* guess work. Fortunately, as I have noted, someone at ABC had the presence of mind to embed a screen clock during the network's live coverage of September 11. This was not a video timer but a real-time digital clock set to Eastern Daylight Savings Time. From the standpoint of 9/11 truth, this clock was a lucky break because it provides us with an invaluable time-stamped record of that morning's horrific events from 8:51 A.M. (EDT), when ABC started its coverage, until about 9:54 A.M., when for some reason the clock was removed. Moreover, this entire record was later archived. So, it is easily accessible for study on the Internet. As I already noted, Jennings reported the plane circling the White House *before* he made his first comments about the Pentagon strike. For whatever reason, the time lag was longer with regard to the events across the river.

As the reader may by now have observed, Rebecca McNerney's testimony that she observed the white plane 5-10 minutes after the Pentagon strike is not a close fit with the official Pentagon crash time of 9:38 A.M. Therefore, her account must be added to the large body of other evidence which, taken together, calls into question the circumstances of the Pentagon strike.[3] I have come to view this as the most complex set of unresolved issues associated with 9/11. As such, it it is beyond the scope of this book and needs to be addressed and resolved by a new and fully empowered 9/11 investigation.

The Spot

Another goal of my trip was to identify the exact location where Linda Brookhart captured that stunning picture on the cover of this book. The search proved easier than expected, thanks to the building's distinctive architecture. I found the place after only a short stroll through the streets west of the White House. Brookhart was standing near the corner of 18th Street and Pennsylvania Avenue when she snapped the photo. She was facing east-south-east at the time, and was just outside the World Bank.

The spot is only one short block west-northwest of the White House. From where Brookhart stood you can actually see a part of the roof-line of the Old Executive Office Building. This fix on the location allows us to place the doomsday plane in the sky with considerable precision. No mistake, when Brookhart took the picture, the E-4B was almost exactly above the White House and was on a northeasterly heading. I documented the position with photos of the building and the street sign on the corner. As we proceed, this exact placement of the E-4B will turn out to be extremely important.

The RADES Radar Data

In October 2007, the cause of 9/11 truth received a major boost when the U.S. Air Force released its radar data from September 11, 2001. This was in response to a Freedom of Information Act (FOIA) request filed by an independent 9/11 investigator named John Farmer.[4] (He is *not* the same John Farmer who served on the 9/11 Commission.) This *other* Farmer is a semi-retired process-control engineer who also had a 12 year career in law enforcement. The radar data covers all four flights. The data stream starts at 5:30 A.M. EDT and extends to almost the entire day of September 11, 2001. The data files were packed onto four CDs and include Excel spreadsheets, powerpoint diagrams showing the various flight paths, and replay programs produced from the raw data.[5] (Special software is needed, however, to play them.) A cover letter explains that all of this material was compiled on September 13, 2001 by the U.S. Air Force's 84th Radar Evaluation Squadron (RADES), based at Hill Air Force Base in Utah, *at the request of the FBI.* John Farmer has since made this data freely available to other 9/11 investigators.[6]

The RADES radar data, as it has come to be known, is comprised of surveillance data from long-range radar facilities operated by NORAD and the FAA. However, it does *not* include returns from the FAA's more accurate short-range radars located at the major airports, including Andrews, Reagan and Dulles in the Washington DC area. Short-range radar is more accurate, because it scans every 4.5 seconds, as opposed to every 12 seconds in the case of long-range radar. Because I am primarily interested in the flight of the E-4B, I will limit this discussion to the radar coverage for Washington. Fortunately, a 9/11 researcher named Marco Bollettino created a helpful animation from the RADES radar data, which is readily accessible on the Internet.[7]

Bollettino used Camstasia software to record the screen while the RADES software video program was playing. He then added a NORAD (NEADS) audio-tape (channel 2) synchronized to run concurrently.[8] I am advised by Robin Hordon that we must be cautious of this NORAD tape, which has never been vetted for authenticity.[9] I respectfully mention this; however, I personally believe the addition of the audio was helpful because it allows us to follow the events of 9/11 real-time from the standpoint of the staffers at NEADS who were manning the radio transmitters. If we are careful we can authenticate it ourselves even as we study it.

The radar animation picks up the action at 9:29 A.M. as Flight 77(?) approaches from the west. It covers the Pentagon strike and the subsequent arrival of the Langley fighters. Readers are encouraged to watch the animation before reading the rest of this chapter (see endnote 7). Those who do will have no difficulty following my discussion. However, for convenience, I have also included diagrams that display the same information in a composite form. As we are about to learn, the RADES radar data is important not only for what it reveals, *but also because of what it fails to show.*

Before we begin, however, I need to inform the reader about a little-known 9/11 anomaly. For reasons that have never been disclosed, the RADES 9/11 radar data from NORAD's Northeast Air Defense Sector (i.e., NEADS) was time-lagged by 25.3 seconds. An official document indicates that the National Transportation Safety Board (NTSB) knew about the time lag by February 2002, if not sooner, and according to the same document, the lag was exclusive to the northeast sector.[10] The radar data from other NORAD sectors was unaffected and was in agreement, as usual, with Global Positioning Satellite (GPS) time. John Farmer was able to independently confirm this while studying the RADES radar data. In it he discovered a few data sets from NORAD's Southeast Air Defense Sector (SEADS), data that was *not* time-lagged.[11]

Official documents obtained by Farmer through a separate FOIA release indicate that the 9/11 Commission also knew about the unusual 25.3 second delay,[12] however, neither the commission nor the NTSB offered any explanation for it. In its study, the NTSB simply corrects the RADES data by adding 25.3 seconds, and insofar as I am aware, the 9/11 Commission fails even to mention the issue in its final report. As we know, the U.S. military was in the midst of numerous war games on September 11, and Farmer has suggested there may be a connection. "It seems reasonable," he speculates on his blog, "that as part of those exercises the radar data was being processed through some synthesizer which permitted the injection of 'false' exercise targets."[13] Although the time-lag issue has received scant attention, it could turn out to be one of the most important 9/11 anomalies. By the end of this discussion the reasons will be self-evident.

Let us start with the following graphic, which displays the composite radar track of the approaching AA Flight 77(?), including its descending 330-degree loop over Alexandria. Notice, the same composite image also shows the track of the C-130H transport, also a part of the official narrative, identified in the animation by its call sign as GOPHER06. The C-130H pilot, Lt. Col. Steve O'Brien, had just taken off from nearby Andrews AFB and was en route to his home base in Minnesota.[14]

By chance, his departure at 9:32 A.M. coincided with the high-speed approach of an unidentified aircraft from the west. O'Brien was in excellent position to observe the attack upon the Pentagon, and, no doubt, for this reason he was instructed by air traffic controllers at Reagan Airport to shadow the incoming aircraft. This he proceeded to do. O'Brien made an abrupt turn to the northeast and briefly tailed the plane — until the crash. Notice, the graphic shows his sudden course change. A number of eyewitnesses also reported seeing the C-130H flying behind and above the final approach of whatever hit the Pentagon.[15]

Lt. Col. O'Brien apparently flew over the Pentagon himself, observed the plume of smoke and flames, then swung around and was ordered to vacate the area. After which, he resumed his flight to Minnesota. His story includes one of the oddities of 9/11, because O'Brien also happened to be in the vicinity of Shanksville, Pennsylvania when Flight 93 went down shortly after 10 A.M.

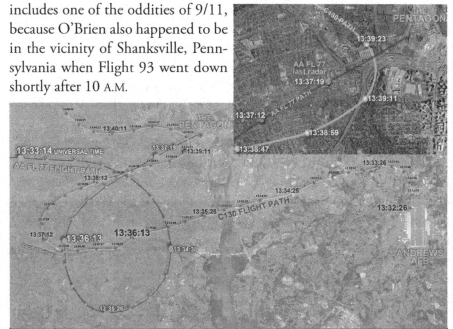

Flight paths of AA Flight 77 and the C-130H over Washington, based on the RADES radar data. Notice how the C-130H piot doubled back and trailed Flight 77 toward the Pentagon.

The Other Andrews Departures

According to the RADES radar data, there were only two other significant departures from Andrews AFB on 9/11 during the relevant time frame. The first plane, to be discussed later in this chapter, lifted off at 9:26 A.M., just as the national Ground Stop was going into effect. The other left Andrews at 9:43:57 A.M. (which I will round it off to 9:44 A.M.). The next diagram shows part of the composite flight path of this second plane, which has never been identified. Notice, its 9:44 A.M. departure time was nearly 18 minutes *after* the national Ground Stop at 9:26 A.M. We must ask, Why was this other plane allowed to leave Andrews in the first place? In fact, the same question can be raised about the C-130H, whose 9:32 A.M. departure was about six minutes after the Ground Stop.

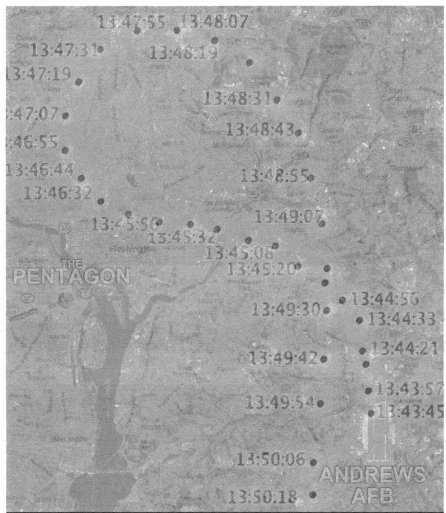

Initial flight path of Andrews 9:44 A.M. departure (VENUS77) showing loop over Washington, based on RADES radar data.

Readers who study the animation will notice that this plane is designated as M3_0310. Here, M3 is the standard Mode 3 transponder setting for both military and civilian aircraft. In fact, we know this was a military plane because it was also transmitting an M2 code (not mentioned in the animation), a military code not used by civilian aircraft. The diagram shows that after leaving Andrews at 9:44 A.M., the plane circled over Washington, then left the area on a southerly heading. At 9:50 A.M., as the plane continued south, three fighters from Langley AFB approached from the east (not shown in the first diagram). The F-16s were apparently tracking this plane, because they closed rapidly and overtook it about forty miles

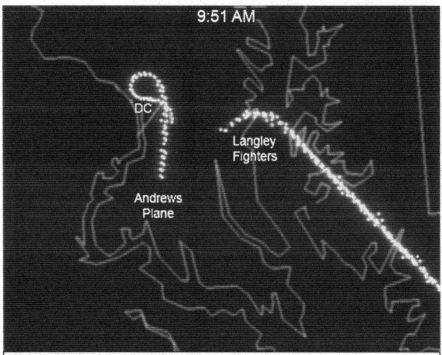

Detour of Langley fighters south of Washington and intercept of 9:44 A.M. Andrews departure, based on RADES radar data.

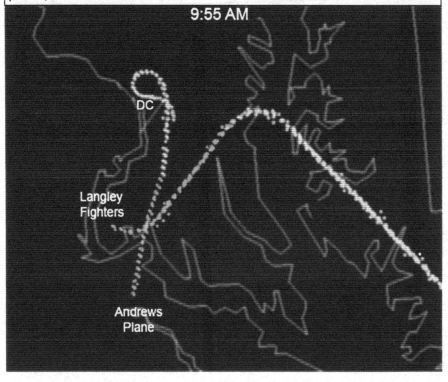

south of Washington. The preceding graphic images display the flight paths of the Langley fighters and this other plane. John Farmer generated both images from the RADES radar data.

The next diagram has been around for years, having been widely reported in the U.S. media coverage of 9/11. Notice, it shows the departure of the F-16s from Langley AFB, the initial wild-goose chase out over the Atlantic, the second wild-goose chase northwest toward Baltimore, and, finally, this loop south of Washington. But the media diagram gives no information about the 9:44 A.M. departure from Andrews, and there is nothing about the intercept. Although the diagram shows the roundabout detour south of the capital, this was *not* explained in the national news media at the time. The detour was never a part of the official story. Certainly the U.S. military never mentioned it. Nor does the 9/11 Commission in its 2004 final report. The question we should be asking is: *Why not?*

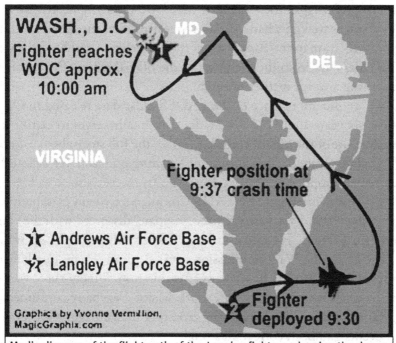

Media diagram of the flight path of the Langley fighters, showing the departure from Langley AFB and the three detours en route to Washington. They were first directed out to sea, then were sent to Baltimore, and were finally diverted south of Washington.

The commission surely knew about this intercept south of Washington. After all, the official investigation had the 84th RADES radar data in its possession.[16] While correlating the radar data with the 9/11 NORAD tapes, John Farmer discovered another part of the story. He found that

NEADS did not actually order the fighter pilots to intercept the plane, but simply instructed them to fly to a point on the map, a so-called "CAP point." As it happened, the fighters intercepted the plane from Andrews en route. (See endnote for the exact coordinates.)[17] If you listen closely to the audio you can actually hear this rendezvous information being transmitted by radio. The NEADS order, the CAP point, and the role of this other plane from Andrews have never been explained. *What are we to make of this?*

The detour is important because it delayed the arrival of the Langley fighters over Washington by 5-10 crucial minutes. Could this be why the Pentagon never informed us about this part of the story? No doubt this also explains why the 9/11 Commission perpetuated this cover-up in their final report, which makes no mention of the detour. However, we still do not know the details. Was the commission as a whole responsible for the cover-up? Perhaps. Then again, it may have been engineered by Phil Zelikow, who as we know had operational control over the agenda and the flow of information to the commissioners. Did Zelikow withhold the vital RADES radar data from the members of the official panel? This certainly is a promising area for further research.

So we see the importance of the RADES radar data released in October 2007, six years after 9/11. The radar data finally serves to clarify and correct this part of the official record. Even so, the full story about *why* the Langley fighters were deployed south of Washington has never been told. It is extremely important that we learn the truth, because, recall, when Michael Bronner interviewed NEADS Commander Kevin Nasypany for his September 2006 *Vanity Fair* article, Nasypany disagreed with the commission's final report. He told Bronner, "I knew where Flight 93 was. I don't care what [the 9/11 commission says]. I mean, I care but I made that assessment to put my fighters over Washington. Ninety-three was on its way in [to Washington] ..."[18] In short, Major Nazypany continued to insist that the commission was wrong, and that the Pentagon's earlier version of events had been correct all along!

Why does it matter? Because if Major Nasypany *did* know about Flight 93 and sent his fighters to Washington, how then do we explain this 40 mile detour south of the city which served only to cause further delay? It was another wild-goose chase, and — notice — that makes three in a row. Given that Flight 93 was over Pennsylvania at the time, i.e., in the north, why were the F-16s from Langley sent *in the opposite direction?* The failure of the 9/11 Commission to explain this key part of the story — allow me to repeat: it is nowhere mentioned in their final report — raises grave questions that can no longer be denied.

The flight of this second plane out of Andrews and the CAP point rendezvous certainly appear to have been scripted. Was all of this a part of some pre-planned war-game scenario? Was NEADS in the midst of an exercise even as the attack was in progress? Was the 9:44 A.M. Andrews departure a pre-arranged decoy sent to hold up the military response? The detour accomplished nothing except to delay the Langley fighters. *Was this the intent?* To summarize, was the detour south of DC a diversion, ordered for the purpose of allowing Flight 93 sufficient time to complete its suicide mission upon the nation's capital? I am well aware of the serious nature of these questions. I would argue, however, that they are now unavoidable, given that the *9/11 Commission Report* covered up this important evidence.

Of course, as we know, the likely final phase of the 9/11 "terrorist attack" never materialized, possibly because Flight 93's departure from Newark Airport was much delayed due to heavy runway traffic. Originally scheduled to depart at 8:01 A.M., Flight 93 did not finally get off until 8:42 A.M. — forty minutes late. Did this delay create insuperable problems for the conspirators? And were some of these conspirators also influenced by the fog of war? Did someone fail to receive word of a high-level clandestine decision to abort (in the case of Flight 93) until too late? Assuming treason, at some point a contingency plan would probably have kicked in. Was an order given at the last minute to shoot down Flight 93 to destroy evidence and silence potential witnesses? Unfortunately, these are the kinds of disturbing questions we must ask in light of the RADES radar data. They take on a special urgency as we hover on the brink of an expanded Mideast war — a war that followed 9/11 as surely as night follows day.

Touching History?

In June 2008, just before this book went to press, and *after* I had already written the above analysis, a new book about 9/11 appeared with the first published disclosure about the detour south of Washington. The book is Lynn Spencer's *Touching History* — already briefly mentioned in chapter one. Ms. Spencer is an excellent writer, and the fact that she also happens to be a commercial pilot was a huge asset in researching her account of the failed NORAD response on 9/11. Her gripping narrative captures the intensity of the moment, including the shock and full range of emotions experienced by the NEADS pilots, staffers, and FAA officials who were on duty that dreadful day. Spencer says she conducted hundreds of interviews.

I contacted the author because I was interested to know if she talked with Laura Brown, the FAA official who in 2003, as I noted in chapter one, informed the 9/11 Commission that the FAA set up phone bridges to the Department of Defense shortly after the first WTC impact. The Brown memo flatly contradicts the official story that the U.S. military was out of the loop. It was read into the record, but never appeared in the *9/11 Commission Report*. Fortunately, I did reach Spencer and exchanged several cordial emails, that is, until cognitive dissonance set in.

Ultimately, I learned more about her from this short dialogue than from her book. The author informed me that she did *not* interview Brown. In her email Spencer also volunteered the following editorial commentary: "It seems that two years after the fact, she [Brown] remembered the bits and pieces but not in a cohesive way. Sometimes in such circumstances, they blend (like Mineta's inadventant [*sic*] comments regarding AAL 77 - he was actually referring to UAL 93)."[19]

In short, Spencer discounted the testimony of Brown and also Mineta because, in her view, their memories from 9/11 were unreliable due to the passage of time. It is well known that memory gradually fades. Eyewitnesses also tend to to embellish or exaggerate their experience of a past event, and there is no reason to think this general phenomenon would not be true in the case of 9/11. I have a serious problem, however, with Spencer's peremptory dismissal of Laura Brown's testimony, because, in my opinion, that reflects a rather dogmatic point of view.

This is partly because Spencer admits that she never interviewed Brown, but also because (as the author informed me) she conducted her own interviews in 2006, in other words, *not two but five years* after the fact.[20] We are supposed to believe that Spencer's witnesses remembered correctly after five years, whereas Brown and Mineta became confused after only two. In fact, Spencer herself exaggerates the passage of time in the cases of Brown and Mineta, who actually gave their testimony in May 2003, i.e., *less than* two years after 9/11.

As I read *Touching History*, it became apparent that Spencer did not have access to the RADES radar data. This is unfortunate, because radar is a powerful tool — it could have been used as a "fact check" to confirm the testimony of her witnesses. Radar is, after all, an equal opportunity employer. It has no agenda and does not discriminate. It simply is what it is: an unbiased empirical record.

Well, what does the radar show? Assuming that the author reported accurately, the radar data shows that her own witnesses were not immune to the passage of time. The radar confirms that at least some of them embellished and/or confused the facts — the very thing for which Spencer

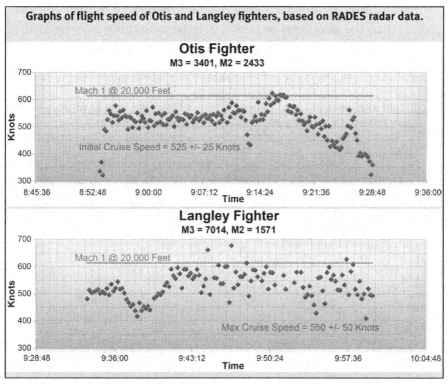

Graphs of flight speed of Otis and Langley fighters, based on RADES radar data.

cites Brown and Mineta. From the 9/11 radar data, it is possible to calculate the flight speed of the NORAD fighters, and when John Farmer did just that, he found that the Langley F-16s averaged about 630 mph (550 knots) en route to Washington — not 700 mph as Spencer states in her book (p. 182). While the difference is not huge, the data nonetheless shows the tendency to embellish. The speed crept higher with the passage of time.

In another case, Spencer writes (p. 43) that one of the Otis pilots broke the sound barrier as he passed 18,000 feet, shortly after leaving Otis AFB. But the radar data indicates this happened *later*, after the fighters left the holding pen south of Long Island. Another case of fuzzy memory. Incidentally, from the radar data, it is by no means certain the pilot *did* break the sound barrier. It was close. If he did it was only for a brief moment.[21]

Unfortunately, we cannot know how many other similar cases mar Spencer's narrative account. Radar will take us only so far, and due to the paucity of reference notes in *Touching History*, there is no way to independently check the author's sources. We are left to ponder how different Spencer's narrative might have been, had the author applied the same standard to all witnesses. If anything, the testimony of Laura Brown and Norman Mineta, recorded *less than two years* after 9/11, is arguably *more* credible than the interviews Spencer collected five years down the road.

As for the wild-goose chase south of Washington, Spencer was told by staffers that on the morning of 9/11, NEADS Weapons Director Steve

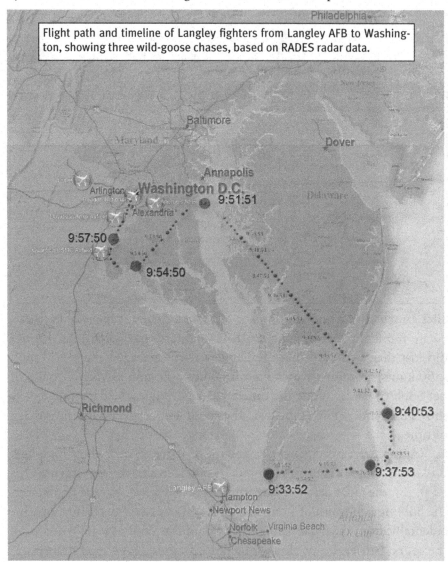

Flight path and timeline of Langley fighters from Langley AFB to Washington, showing three wild-goose chases, based on RADES radar data.

Citino made a mistake and gave the wrong coordinates to the Langley fighters. Supposedly, the miscue occurred at 9:40 A.M. According to Spencer, Citino later discovered his error, relayed the correct information, and at 9:51 A.M. "the three-ship [i.e., the formation of three Langley fighters] instantly turned toward the new coordinates [i.e., Washington]."[22] Spencer's timeline, however, is refuted by the RADES radar data (see the flight path diagram) which clearly shows that at 9:40 A.M. the Langley fighters were still in Whiskey 386, the holding pen off the Virginia coast.

At this point they had only just begun the *second* wild-goose chase, toward Baltimore. At 9:51 A.M. the fighters began to swerve, yes, but *not* in the direction of the capital. At 9:51 the F-16s were only starting, *not ending,* their third and final wild-goose chase, *away from* Washington. As indicated by the diagram, the Langley pilots did not finally get on the right track to the nation's capital until after 9:55 A.M. To be sure, the NEADS radar was time-lagged by 25.3 seconds, but even taking this into account, Spencer's timeline is still way off.

One of the weaknesses of *Touching History* is the absence of any critical analysis. Spencer never broaches the obvious question: Just how believable is it that NEADS could miss a city like Washington (on the third try) by at least forty miles? If there was a mistake, why was it not discovered and corrected much sooner? Surely NEADS was tracking the fighters on radar, and it must have been obvious that they were moving *away from* Washington. In the audio we can hear the NEADS radio crew speaking (channel 2), and at no point is there is any talk about a mix-up. Nor is anything said about a course correction.

After failing to ask the obvious, Spencer proceeds to confirm our worst fears with her blasé assertion that the detour of the Langley fighters south of Washington was of no great significance. She writes: "In retrospect, neither their airspeed nor their routing would have made a difference in their getting to Washington before American [Flight] 77."[23] Yes, true enough. But Spencer conspicuously fails to mention Flight 93, which, as noted, was still in the air. The last time I looked at a map, Pennsylvania was north of Washington— not *south.*

When I queried Spencer about the 9:44 A.M. Andrews departure, the author had no information. She mentioned that the flights out of Andrews AFB were beyond the scope of her research. Still, she offered an opinion: "I believe that the A/C [i.e., aircraft] that you are referring to were part of the COG [Continuity of Government] plan. This is a highly classified plan and not relevant to my book."[24]

I then showed Spencer the radar-generated diagram of the 9:44 A.M. departure circling over Washington, and posed this question: Is it reasonable that a COG plane, possibly loaded with high government officials, would have circled over the capital in the midst of a terrorist attack? The answer, of course, is an emphatic "No." The pilot would have peeled away from downtown Washington immediately after taking off from Andrews. Spencer apparently assumed that I was referring to the E-4B that flew over the White House. Perhaps she had seen one of my articles on the Internet about the white plane. Conceding my point about COG, she wrote back that she was not surprised

> ... that an airborne command and control plane was circling over the city. If I wanted to feed radar and radio data to the White House PEOC [i.e., the underground bunker below the west wing] - information that it did not otherwise have - that is exactly what I might do. But given that I am not privy to this classified information, I do not know what their mission was. I clearly do not have the curiosity or concern about it that you do.[25]

Although I restrained myself upon hearing this, I wanted to fire back: "Oh, really? Is that why they erased the E-4B from radar?" But, now, I am getting ahead of my story.

Once upon a time, in my younger days, I shared Lynn Spencer's implicit trust in the benevolence of the U.S. government. However, the mere act of living through the last half century cured me of that hang-up. After many painful disillusionments, today I know different. It does seem that blind faith and denial go together, and are but two sides of the same coin. Assuming a definitive account of 9/11 is one day written, it will not solely be based on some NORAD tapes and the fading memories of government eyewitnesses. It will be augmented with official FAA, Pentagon, and Secret Service documents, flight logs, air traffic control tapes, the RADES radar data, the short range radar, in short, with the whole panoply of physical and documentary evidence from which histories are normally constructed.[26] In fact, this is the very evidence that the 9/11 truth movement has been struggling for years to pry loose from a stonewalling government. If the U.S. military wanted the truth to be told, then, why did they not simply hand over all of this material in the first place? Was Spencer "blessed" like Michael Bronner and Bob Woodward with unique access to midwife a limited disclosure, not for truth-telling, but to shore up the official version of reality? From numerous passages in *Touching History* it is clear that Spencer is a firm believer in the "war on terror." No wonder Generals Eberhart, Myers and Arnold enthusiastically endorse her book.

So ended my short dialogue with Lynn Spencer.

However, we not quite finished with the 9:44 A.M. Andrews departure, which — I repeat — has never been identified. Consider the following image of this plane's extended flight path, also generated from the RADES radar data. Notice that after the intercept, the plane flew south and made a series of loops, which might signify a refueling rendezvous with a tanker. Then, the plane charted a bee-line across Virginia, West Virginia and Ohio. The radar track ends at 11:55 A.M. someplace over Indiana.

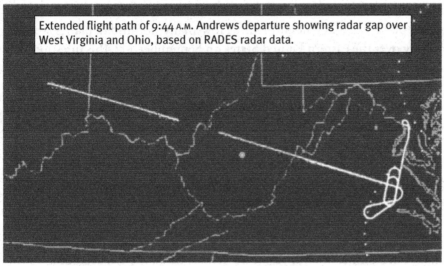

Extended flight path of 9:44 A.M. Andrews departure showing radar gap over West Virginia and Ohio, based on RADES radar data.

However, by extrapolating we can determine the plane's likely destination. The aircraft was, in fact, charting a direct route to Offutt AFB, near Omaha, Nebraska, home of USSTRATCOM and the E-4B Nightwatch fleet. Notice, also, the gap in the radar coverage over West Virginia and Ohio: curiously, the same region where Flight 77 disappeared on September 11. Was it by chance, or some accident, that neither the Pentagon nor the 9/11 Commission bothered to inform us about this gap in NORAD/FAA's long-range radar coverage? Insofar as I know, the gap has never been explained. I must emphasize, however, that I am a writer, not a radar expert.

In her email, Lynn Spencer guessed that this unknown departure from Andrews at 9:44 A.M. was the E-4B. She is not alone. Others have drawn the same conclusion.[27] This deserves careful consideration because the plane's probable destination is consistent with Dan Verton's account. In a

93

way, its time of departure also suggests that it might have been an E-4B. Notice, the plane lifted off from Andrews at almost the same time as the reported E-4B departure from Wright-Pat AFB, i.e., shortly after 9:43 A.M..[28] Did the national command authority order up not just one but *two* doomsday planes? This is possible. As I showed in chapter two, we have only accounted for two of the four E-4Bs in the Nightwatch fleet.

I should mention: There was yet another strange report on 9/11 about a large white plane over Martha's Vineyard. I learned about this from Colin Scoggins, who says the mysterious plane buzzed the local FAA tower soon after 10 A.M., and was sufficiently threatening that FAA officials ordered an emergency evacuation. Scoggins thinks it might have been a KC-10 from McGuire AFB in New Jersey. But no one knows for sure. The low-flying white plane was never identified.[29] How many doomsday planes were in the sky over the eastern United States on September 11? This question will redound through the remainder of this discussion.

If an E-4B left Andrews at 9:44 A.M., obviously, this cannot have been the same E-4B that buzzed the White House, because the time of departure is *three minutes after* the live report by Peter Jennings at 9:41 A.M. When Jennings was airing the live story about a mysterious plane over the White House, this *other* plane was still on the tarmac at Andrews. Moreover, the positional data is also wrong. A careful examination of its flight path over Washington confirms that although this other plane flew in the general vicinity, it never approached closer than about a mile of the presidential mansion, and this is a conservative estimate. Nor is there any chance of significant error regarding its position because, according to the U.S. Air Force, the RADES radar data should be accurate to within an eighth of a nautical mile.[30] Its departure time and flight path are simply incompatible with the confirmed sighting of an E-4B over the White House at, or before, 9:41 A.M.

The 9:26 A.M. Andrews Departure

It was only thanks to a lucky break that we learned about the earlier (i.e., 9:26 A.M.) departure from Andrews AFB. John Farmer had entirely overlooked this flight because for some reason the plane was not transmitting a military code, which is very unusual. (Its civilian code was M3_0512.) As Farmer put it: "Due to the clutter from Reagan, I filtered Andrews traffic by valid M2V bit (all military planes have this set to 1). M3_0512 has this set to 0, [which would indicate] a civilian plane. So it was lost in the Reagan NAP [i.e., National Air Port] clutter."[31] Fortunately, on June 11,

2008, "Pinnacle" received a batch of 9/11 documents from the FAA in response to a Freedom of Information Act (FOIA) request. The documents were from Reagan NAP and one of them indicated that a Boeing 747-200, code-named Sword31, was released to take off from Andrews AFB at 9:23 A.M. According to the documents, this other plane was *also* bound for Offutt AFB. (See Appendix, pages 303-306, for the FAA documents.)

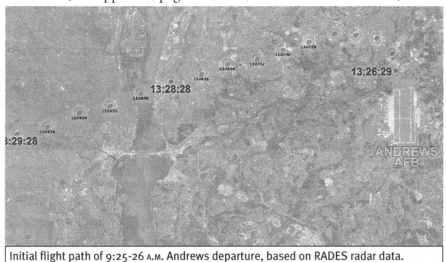

Initial flight path of 9:25-26 A.M. Andrews departure, based on RADES radar data.

When Farmer went back and rechecked the radar data, he found that the FOIA'd documents were correct. This departure from Andrews first appears on radar at 9:26 A.M. The first graphic shows the plane's flight path over Washington. The second shows the plane's extended radar track. Notice, it flew just north of the radar gap on the West Virginia-Ohio border. After making two course changes, it then also headed for Offutt AFB.

Notice that its flight path over Washington is the same as that of the C-130H, which left Andrews five minutes later. In fact, according to an

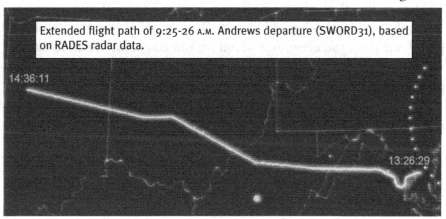

Extended flight path of 9:25-26 A.M. Andrews departure (SWORD31), based on RADES radar data.

95

official document this is a standard flight path for planes leaving Andrews and is known as the "Camp Springs One Departure" route.[32]

This 9:26 A.M. flight was probably the E-4B mentioned by Dan Verton in *Black Ice*. The time of departure is a reasonable fit with Verton's account. Recall, Verton claimed that a USAF doomsday plane left Andrews AFB at about the time the FAA was shutting down the airspace over New York City.[33] It would appear that the plane actually left Andrews just as the FAA shutdown was going national. One thing is certain: *This was not the E-4B that buzzed the White House.* As its radar track clearly shows, it never flew near the presidential mansion. *This can only mean that there were at least two E-4Bs in the skies over Washington on 9/11. There may have been three.*

The 9/11 Commission could have untangled this mystery, *if* the panel had been serious about providing "the fullest possible account of the events surrounding 9/11."[34] All of the information concerning the Andrews departures was pertinent to the official investigation, including the flight logs, the audio-tapes of radio communications with air traffic controllers, as well as the short-range radar data. The commission should have subpoenaed and reviewed all of this evidence. As we know, of course, nothing of the sort happened.

Consultation with 84th RADES

This completes our review of the significant departures from Andrews AFB during the relevant time frame. Notice, we have exhausted the possible candidates (two in number) by a process of elimination. Although one of these departures was probably a doomsday plane — and both may have been — neither was the E-4B that flew over the White House. We are left with an unsolved mystery.

Today, the physical presence of an E-4B over the White House on September 11, 2001 is beyond dispute. We have the videos, the Brookhart photo, the press and eyewitness accounts. On this basis, therefore, should we not expect that the plane was detected by radar? Yes, of course! This goes without saying.

Yet, incredibly, there is no hint in the RADES radar data that a plane flew anywhere near the White House. Where the radar track of the E-4B ought to be, there is nothing. So, how did a 230-foot Boeing 747 with a wingspan of 195 feet vanish into thin air? If we were talking about a stealth bomber, we might expect something like this. But a four-engined Boeing 747? Impossible!

In late April 2008, after puzzling over this vanishing act for many weeks, I contacted the 84th Radar Evaluation Squadron (RADES) at Hill AFB, Utah in search of answers. I spoke with a Mr. Jeff Richardson, who listened patiently to my story and, I felt, made an honest effort to be of assistance.[35] The conversation proved helpful. Richardson informed me that before 9/11, the FAA's short-range radar was used strictly for air traffic control at the various airports — it was *not* used for military surveillance, hence, was not plugged in to the NORAD system. This might explain why the FAA and Secret Service could track a plane locally without the U.S. military being in the loop. Of course, this does *not* explain why the 9/11 Commission failed to subpoena and study the FAA's short-range radar data.

I also learned more about the variables that affect radar coverage. These include the curvature of the earth, the proximity of the site, the height of the tower and also its elevation above sea level. Local topographic features, i.e., hills and ridges, or even tall buildings, are also a factor, because these can cause interference. Richardson suggested that any of the above might explain why the E-4B failed to show up on radar on 9/11 — assuming it was present. When I mentioned the eyewitness accounts and video evidence indicating that the plane flew as low as about 500 feet, this suggested to Richardson that the E-4B might well have dipped beneath radar.

I was not surprised to hear this. I already knew about one such case, and it bore out the principle. While investigating the Pentagon strike, John Farmer discovered that a security camera on the nearby Doubletree Hotel recorded the fly-by of a military helicopter at an estimated altitude of about 300 feet. Yet, this same fly-by escaped radar detection. The RADES radar data confirms that the helicopter left Andrews AFB at 9:13 A.M., flew west in the direction of the Pentagon, but disappeared over the tidal basin just west of the Potomac River.[36] Did something similar happen at the White House? *Did an E-4B fly under radar?*

I was open to this possibility. However, the more I studied it, the more the evidence failed to support it. Former air traffic controller Robin Hordon was already convinced from the RADES animation that NORAD/FAA radar was "seeing" the take-offs at Andrews AFB down to as low as 200 feet.[37] Surely the "low floor" at Andrews would also hold true at the White House, which shares similar topography. This part of Washington is about as topographically challenging as a pancake. Nor does the subdued DC skyline in the vicinity of the White House present any serious obstacles to radar. Downtown Washington's relatively low skyline is the result of building codes designed to enhance rather than compete with government monuments and buildings, including the president's house. The situation is different at the Pentagon, which lies at the base of a significant hill. This might explain why a helicopter was invisible to radar at 300 feet.

One of the variables affecting radar coverage is the curvature of the earth, which, fortunately, can be calculated with considerable precision. When John Farmer crunched the numbers, he found that Hordon was right. The nearest NORAD long-range radar facility to Washington is located at Plains, Virginia. The Plains tower is about 1,000 feet above sea level and is situated approximately 12 nautical miles west of Dulles International Airport and about 39 nautical miles from Andrews AFB. When Farmer did the calculation based on these numbers, he found that the curvature of the earth in no way impedes this tower's radar coverage of Washington. The relevant data are displayed in the following graph. Notice that the curvature of the earth only begins to effect radar coverage from the Plains tower (in a southeasterly direction) at a distance of about 50 nautical miles. Washington is well within this range. Farmer concluded, "I see nothing in the data that would limit acquiring a return for an aircraft above 200-250 feet in the Andrews or White House area."[38] (Needless to say, the graph would look very different if the calculation had been done in a westerly direction, due to the nearby Appalachian mountains.)

At this point, there was a new and surprising development. I received an email from Jeff Richardson at 84th RADES. Apparently my earlier call had piqued his curiosity. Richardson wrote to inform me that his point of view had changed as a result of studying the RADES radar data. He had gone back for another look and now agreed with Hordon and Farmer! Richardson wrote, "There are beacon mode C returns in the DC area, some below 500 feet, that would indicate the Plains radar had some low altitude coverage. If there was an E-4B in the area at 09:41 [A.M.], I can not explain why it was not in the recorded radar data."[39]

Evidently, after our phone conversation Richardson also explored some of the material on the Internet about the mystery plane, i.e., the E-4B fly-over. His email continued: "The few accounts I looked at seemed to show the aircraft in question much higher than 500 ft., and I would think more radars than just the Plains [tower] would have detected it." Readers who study the RADES animation will observe return clusters, i.e., multiple radar blips, for some of the aircraft, indicating returns from the three separate radar sites covering the area. The Plains radar facility is

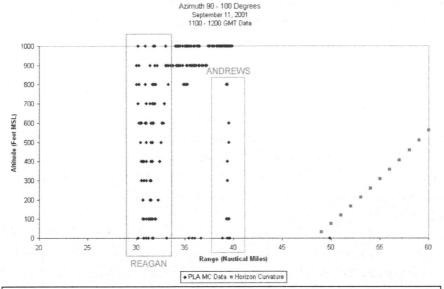

The Plains, VA Radar Site
Azimuth 90 - 100 Degrees
September 11, 2001
1100 - 1200 GMT Data

Graph showing long-range radar coverage of Washington DC area from Plains, Virginia radar tower. The returns from Reagan National Airport and Andrews AFB indicate that the tower was "seeing" down to ground level.

one of these. A second tower is located at Oceana, Virginia, not far from Langley AFB. A third is at Gibbsboro, New Jersey. The Plains facility, however, is by far the closest of the three to the Washington area, and for this reason it gives the most accurate returns.

A Covert Operation?

I was amazed and gratified by this development. It is extraordinary because it means we now have consensus on this issue — something I never dreamed would happen. The U.S. Air Force's 84th Radar Evaluation Squadron (RADES) now agrees with 9/11 investigators that the doomsday plane's loop over the White House should have been detected by NORAD/FAA long-range radar. Yet, it was not. So, how is this mystery to be explained?

This is the question, and in the face of continuing denials by Pentagon officials I believe we must consider all possibilities, including the "unthinkable." Was radar data intentionally withheld or scrubbed? This appears to be the case. But why would the U.S. Air Force go to the trouble of concealing a command-and-control plane? Surely this suggests that the E-4B was not on some innocent mission. Such a conclusion is further supported by the evidence presented in the previous chapters.

A covert operation would certainly explain the breakdown in the Pentagon's operational reporting (OPREP) system. In an email, Lynn Spencer complained to me that "the system did not work," but this truism fails to explain 9/11. The military's internal reporting system is not limited to "after action" reports, which I discussed in the previous chapter. A product of the Cold War, the OPREP system was intended to streamline the military response in the event of a nuclear attack, or threat of an attack, and surely the 9/11 "attack" would have been treated in a similar manner. The reporting system is capable of responding within minutes, not days or hours. Military regulations and the chain of command are clearly defined, and all roads lead to the office of the Secretary of Defense. This includes the National Military Command Center (NMCC), the nerve center of the Pentagon.

On 9/11 the NMCC should have functioned as the hub, receiving incident and situation reports from various sources and guiding the military response. But where was the leader, Secretary of Defense Rumsfeld? Incredibly, in the midst of the "attack" Rumsfeld abandoned his post.[40] Even as his command staff tried in vain to contact him, Rumsfeld walked out of the building to assist with the wounded on the lawn near the heliport. Here was a powerful clue. Although much has been made of the president's odd behavior on September 11, Rumsfeld's was no less strange. The only thing more bizarre is that the U.S. media did not even seem to notice.

Assuming a covert operation, only a few individuals in the U.S. military would have been privy to the true nature of the E-4B flight. Everyone else, both military and civilian alike, would have assumed without hesitation that the doomsday plane was simply responding to the "terrorist attack." True enough, its flight over the White House presented problems for the FAA and Secret Service, but neither of these agencies are subject to military regulations. Rumsfeld was the command authority, and in subsequent days he might easily have squelched any protests from this direction.

A covert mission might also explain the scheduled departure of a second E-4B from Andrews AFB just minutes before the "attack." This second E-4B was probably involved in Global Guardian, as reported. Yet, it might also unwittingly have provided cover for a clandestine operation. Witnesses on the ground would tend to confuse and merge the two flights. We are extremely fortunate to have the CNN footage and the amazing photo by Linda Brookhart, both of which make it possible to pinpoint the

E-4B's precise location. We are also extremely fortunate that someone at ABC posted a screen clock during the network's coverage.

The question "how did they do it?" is an intriguing one. Did the U.S. military exploit some new technological breakthrough on 9/11 that is being kept from us? I was reminded of the first use of stealth technology in combat during operation Desert Storm, when the Pentagon unveiled an entire fleet of fighter-bombers invisible to radar. The stealthy planes played a key role during the "shock and awe" phase of that war. Yet, prior to it, the government had successfully kept this radical new technology secret for years. I would agree that such a possibility seems far-fetched in the case of 9/11. However, we need to explore every avenue.

I am not the first to suggest that radar data was scrubbed by military hackers. If John Farmer is correct that the U.S. military may have utilized a 25.3 second break in the radar data stream to insert phony radar tracks during one of the exercises underway on 9/11, the delay might also just as easily have been used to erase other signals. According to former air traffic controller Robin Hordon, a 25.3 second time lag would allow more than enough time for a clandestine hacker to alter or erase a radar signal.[41] As noted, the time lag has never been explained.

If the E-4B's radar track was being scrubbed as the "attack" was in progress, this can only mean that the E-4B cover-up was not hastily improvised later for the purpose of "covering tail," i.e., hiding someone's incompetence. No, it was pre-planned, hence, by definition, was part of a conspiracy. We must be cautious, however. John Farmer informs me that the time lag could also be the result of computer processing, *done sometime later.* We simply do not know. But either way, the scrubbing of the E-4B's radar track, whether during the "attack" or after, amounts to the destruction of evidence, an extremely serious matter.

And let us not forget Flight 11. Recall, NEADS radar technicians had the precise coordinates, yet failed to locate the plane. So, here is another possible example of scrubbing. But what about the 25.3 second time lag itself? Might the time lag alone explain why NEADS technicians were unable to locate Flight 11? If the radar at Boston Center was on real time and the NEADS radar was lagged, even precise coordinates would have amounted to incorrect information. A Boeing 767 moving at 600 mph can cover a lot of distance — more than 4 miles — in 25.3 seconds. However, when I consulted former air traffic controller Robin Hordon about this, he discounted the possibility. Hordon says the NEADS radar techs are good, and would easily have overcome a 25.3 second difference. He thinks the radar signal from Flight 11 was erased.[42]

Let us also remember that the much-maligned 2002 National Transportation Safety Board (NTSB) flight path analysis of Flight 77 was built upon the RADES radar data.[43] This should make us wary of simplistic "fly-over" theories that could be distracting us from more important questions. But I will not speculate further about the E-4B's possible role. This is a question for a new 9/11 investigation. I believe that I have presented more than enough evidence to warrant such an inquiry.

John Farmer, who favors no particular theory about 9/11, has also found solid evidence that radar data may have been altered in the case of the Pentagon strike. Although most of his RADES radar research is quite technical and beyond the scope of this book, it is easily accessible on the Internet, and is well recommended to curious readers who are willing and able.[44] At my request, Farmer drafted a somewhat-less-technical paper summarizing his two-year investigation of the Pentagon event. (It is attached as an Afterword to this book.) He presents both physical evidence and eyewitness testimony that a second plane was in the vicinity at the time of the Pentagon strike. He thinks this other plane may have shadowed whatever struck the building. Farmer's paper is relevant to this discussion, because there is no hint in the RADES radar data that a second plane was in the area.

FAA's Short-Range Radar

As of July 2008, 9/11 truth activists were still awaiting the release of the FAA's 9/11 short-range radar, flight logs and various other official documents, under the Freedom of Information Act. All of this material, especially the short-range radar data, now looms large in light of the above discussion. "Pinnacle" filed one such request as early as 2006, and he thinks the release of additional records could be imminent. Recently, he learned from a source in the FAA that the agency has made a decision to release all of its 9/11-related data. "Now we will see," "Pinnacle" wrote in an email, "if the Freedom of Information Act is worth the paper it's written on." Other cases are also in the works. John Farmer has several pending FOIA appeals/requests.

When I spoke with Jeff Richardson at 84th RADES, he dashed cold water on such hopes. He mentioned that the FAA normally does not save short-range radar tapes. According to Richardson, the tapes are normally reused, which, of course, erases them in the process.[45] I was shocked to hear this, since there was nothing normal about 9/11. Surely we are on firm ground to expect that after the "worst terrorist attack" in U.S. history the FAA would have saved *all* of the evidence, including its short-range radar data.

Officials at Andrews AFB told John Farmer that the short-range radar from that base was indeed saved and that the FAA took possession of it shortly after 9/11.[46] However, according to Laura Brown, an FAA official, all of the FAA's radar data from 9/11 ended up in the hands of the FBI.[47] Unfortunately, at press time it was still unclear who has custody of the FAA's short-range radar data. If these records still exist, and if we ever get our hands on them, they are certain to give us a much clearer picture of what happened in the skies over Washington on September 11.

Note: On July 25, 2008, "Pinnacle" received a CD from the FAA loaded with yet another batch of FOIA'd 9/11 documents. The CD included flight progress strips (see Appendix, pages 307-310), which are used by air traffic controllers because they provide a handy summary of information about incoming flights and departures. FAA controllers typically update the strips in longhand. One strip indicates that on the morning of 9/11 a Boeing 747-200 arrived at Andrews at 7:28 A.M. (11:28 universal time). Its call sign was Word31. (Strangely, a different FAA document refers to this same aircraft as Sword31. Evidently the call sign was changed.) A later entry confirms what we already knew: This same aircraft departed Andrews at 9:25 A.M. (13:25 universal time) bound for Offutt AFB. The jackpot, however, was the presence of the telltale acronym, NAOC, *indicating that this aircraft was an E-4B.*

On August 20, "Pinnacle" received yet another CD from the FAA. This CD contained an audio from the Andrews AFB tower from 9/11 identifying the 9:44 AM Andrews departure (call sign: VENUS77) as "… a Boeing 747 NEACP" [Knee-cap] aircraft, confirming that this too was an E-4B. Recall, NEACP was the previous designation for the Nightwatch fleet. Curiously, the audio includes a 9:40 A.M. call from the Andrews flight manager informing air traffic controllers in the tower that the doomsday plane was headed for Offutt AFB and "is not going to wait," a possible reference to the national Ground Stop, which by then was in effect. Evidently, the E-4B pilot was under orders to get aloft, regardless.

In short, the newly released FAA records confirm that two doomsday planes took off from Andrews on 9/11. As we have already seen, both of these scheduled E-4B departures show up in the RADES long-range radar,

An E-4B on the ground and interior photos, showing Secretary of Defense Rumsfeld in his office, General Meyers in the briefing room and some of the work stations of the 48- to 112-man crew.

however, *neither* of them flew over the White House. The third E-4B, the one that did, remains a mystery.

Can it be mere coincidence that the Pentagon strike was book-ended by E-4B departures from Andrews — one shortly before and one just after — even as a third E-4B circled over Washington, a plane whose presence has never been explained? Let us remember: the US military denies it was there.

The first CD also contained another hugely important release: the short-range radar returns from Reagan NAP and Andrews AFB — exactly what 9/11 investigators had been hoping for! A preliminary analysis indicates that, as expected, the newly released short-range radar data was in real time, i.e. was not time-lagged. As this manuscript was headed out the door to the printer, John Farmer, Robin Hordon and Dennis Cimino, another 9/11 investigator, had begun a collaborative effort to analyze this new data, and were busily plotting it alongside, and comparing it with, the RADES radar data: searching in the vicinity of the White House for a radar track of the mystery plane ...

Stay tuned. This story is far from over.

Endnotes

1. Email from Rebecca McNerney, February 22, 2008.

2. The ABC coverage from 9/11 has been archived at http://www.archive.org/details/abc200109110912-0954.

The transcript of the same coverage was also archived: ABC News Special Report: "Planes crash into World Trade Center", ABC News, September 11, 2001, posted at http://www.fromthewilderness.com/timeline/2001/abcnews091101.html.

3. Insofar as I know, a senior military affairs journalist with the U.S. Navy by the name of Barbara Honegger was the first to compile this evidence. See Barbara Honegger, "The Pentagon Attack Papers," in Jim Marrs, *The Terror Conspiracy*, Disinformation Co., New York, 2006, p. 439; also posted online at www.patriotsquestion911.com, "Military, Intelligence and Government" category, scroll to Honegger.

The physical evidence includes at least two Pentagon clocks that apparently stopped working at the time of the attack, and, in addition, Army declassification specialist April Gallop's stopped wrist watch. The first wall clock stopped at 9:31:40 A.M., the other at 9:32:30 A.M. Gallop's wrist watch at shortly after 9:30 A.M. Notice, it is much easier to account for a clock that stopped *after* the official time of impact, than before it. One wall clock was in the heliport office just outside the Pentagon. The Smithsonian Institution preserved a photo of this frozen clock, which may be viewed at http://americanhistory.si.edu/september11/collection/record.asp?ID=19.

The other frozen wall clock was inside the west wing, and may be viewed at a U.S. Navy website: http://www.news.navy.mil/view_single.asp?id=2480.

Notice, this photographic evidence was preserved by two unimpeachable sources. From what I understand, the former was on display in the Smithsonian until recently. One website states, "The airplane actually struck the Pentagon at 9:38 A.M.; apparently the clock was six minutes slow." Yet, both clocks stopped within a minute of the same time. Were they *both* running 5-6 minutes slow? This is doubtful because, remember, these were military clocks. Anyone familiar with the U.S. military knows they do not run 5-6 minutes behind schedule. Being "on time" is an important part of military discipline. Indeed, it is one of the first lessons that grunts learn in boot camp. Judging from the photos, it appears that one of the clocks was battery-powered, a common type. The other may have been battery-powered, or was an electric wall clock. Both obviously stopped after a powerful shock wave knocked them off the wall. Shattered glass is even visible in one of the photos. In her paper Honegger mentions another famous historical event that was similarly frozen in time: the great San Francisco earthquake of 1906. In the aftermath of "the big one" the *San Francisco Chronicle* featured a front-page photo of a charred clock that stopped at precisely 5:12 A.M., marking the fateful moment when the massive quake rocked the city. She writes, "… a century after that devastating event the stopped clock serves as both the ultimate evidence and the symbol that captures it all." Honegger makes an astute point. Will the Pentagon clocks one day be viewed in a similar way?

There is other physical evidence, as well. The so-called "Naudet brothers video" includes a segment filmed inside a New York City fire station. In the moment when the first announcement about the Pentagon strike comes over the radio, a wall clock is plainly visible in the background. It reads 9:30 A.M., which, notice, closely matches April Gallop's frozen wrist watch. Another important piece of evidence is the original Federal Aviation Administration (FAA) "timeline document" from September 11, 2001. It was made public on September 17, 2001, one day before the Pentagon announced the official crash time of 9:38 A.M. The FAA document states that Flight 77 hit the Pentagon at 9:32 A.M., which is very close to the average of the two frozen clocks. The FAA's original timeline, however, soon disappeared down a collective memory hole and was forgotten. Fortunately, the document can still be viewed at the National Security Archive, a website maintained by George Washington University. Here is a link: http://www.gwu.edu/~nsarchiv/NSAEBB/NSAEBB165/index.htm.

Honegger also cites the testimony of a notable eyewitness: the soon-to-be Danish Foreign Minister, Per Stig Moller, who was in Washington on the day of the attack. When he heard a loud noise, Moller looked out the window, saw smoke rising from the Pentagon, and immediately checked his watch. The time was 9:32 A.M., a time that Moller subsequently reported in press interviews on his return to Denmark. Honegger also cites the case of Alberto Gonzales, who was President Bush's legal counsel on 9/11. On August 27, 2002 Gonzales gave an address at the Naval Postgraduate School in which he stated unequivocally that "the Pentagon was attacked at 9:32 A.M." Honegger, who works at the school, was present and cites the audio-tape recording of the address by the university. Gonzales' remark has long since been forgotten, but it shows that even within the Bush administration the official timeline did not take hold for many months. I should mention that Honegger thinks the initial blast wave was probably caused by planted bombs. In her paper she cites a videotaped testimonial of April Gallop taken under oath that the explosion happened literally the moment Gallop turned on her computer. Gallop worked in the most damaged part of the Pentagon. Honegger disputes the view that the frozen clocks recorded the moment of impact, although she doesn't rule out the possibility of a subsequent strike by a missile or a smaller plane, in the same part of the building. Although I disagree with Honegger about this, and suspect that the frozen clocks are the signature of an impact, I also feel that our best chance of resolving these issues and learning the truth is by means of a new investigation fully empowered with the authority to subpoena evidence.

According to John Farmer, the official Pentagon crash time is an average. In an email on May 11, 2008 he wrote, "There are two security video systems that recorded the event time at the Pentagon. The first is the Citgo station video and from it the best estimate for impact event is 09:40:37 – 09:40:38 (video time). The other would be the Doubletree north side camera, which records the fireball emerging at 09:34:11 (video time). The average of these two times gives 09:37:24. So as you can see, video recording systems time frames tend to vary a great deal.

"The official time of impact is given by the NTSB as 09:37:44. That time corresponds to the CSV file released by the NTSB which has had its time scale adjusted by the NTSB (refer to their release documents). However, the data stream stopped prematurely by all indications at around 6 seconds prior to impact, which means by their reckoning true impact time had to be 09:37:50. Using the NEADS time scale, impact time would have been at 09:37:27 and using SEADS time, 09:37:52.

"Another time source is the NORAD audio tapes, and the time (as can be seen in Marco's video) tends to agree with an impact time of between 09:37 – 09:38. I've measured the audio time variation in those tapes (using position markers) and during that time frame the time seems to be slow by around 16 seconds. So the empirical time sources discussed so far seem to indicate an impact time between 09:37-09:38, but closer to 09:38.

"Another less known empirical source is the Arlington County EMS tapes. Those are not available for distribution, but can be listened to by prior arrangement. Those I have spoken with who have listened to those tapes indicate agreement with the sources I've already discussed. Of course the FBI has custody of the 911 call center tapes and will not release those to the public, invoking law enforcement privilege."

All of which underscores my point that the final approach and the Pentagon strike are among the most complex of 9/11 issues and should be addressed, and hopefully resolved, in the course of a new investigation.

4. At http://911files.info/blog/?p=275.

5. In early 2008 I received a set of the discs from Farmer.

6. The RADES radar data can be downloaded from Farmer's website. See note four, above.

7. Email from Marco Bollettino, February 21, 2008. Please note: John Farmer has permanently posted the RADES radar animation at http://aal77.com/movies/pentagon.mixed.mpg.

As this book went to press, the animation was also posted at several other locations. Because videos have a way of disappearing from cyberspace, I am providing all of the known urls. Bollettino posted the animation at: http://www.viddler.com/explore/Ashoka/videos/1/.

Here are two others:
http://video.google.com/videoplay?docid=4392580422656090975.
http://video.google.com/videoplay?docid=4392580422656090975&q=rades+&ei=dVxuSK2aPIjkqgPA-7iYDw&hl=en.

8. From what I understand, the U.S. military has since released another batch of NORAD tapes. The new batch reportedly totals about 120 hours of material. However,

as of this writing I have not been able to locate and download this material for study. Presumably the channel 2 NEADS tape is a part of it.

Farmer explained how the audio was synchronized with the animation: "At the beginning of the audio tapes there is a tone at given time intervals. From those markers, it is only a matter of using the audio file position markers (in milliseconds) to determine the time of any point in the audio, which then can be matched to the RADES time. I wrote a program that reads those markers for each of the audios for my own use (on AAL77. COM for download). There is some variability in the timeline and at 2 hours the MCC audio loses around 16 seconds. So there is a potential 16 second time error in the audio, and a known 25.3 second error in the RADES time, but the synch should be good to +/- a minute at worst case (most likely less than that)." Email from John Farmer, July 15, 2008.

9. Email from Robin Hordon, May 19, 2008.

10. Daniel R. Bower, Recorded Radar Data Study, National Transportation Safety Board, Office of Research and Engineering, February 15, 2002. Posted at http://aal77.com/rades/anomaly/radardatastudy.pdf.

11. John Farmer, "NEADS Radar Time Anomaly," April 16, 2008, posted at http://911files.info/blog/?p=43.

12. The relevant documents are posted at http://911files.info/foia_documents/ntsb/ntsb_20070318_foia_documents.pdf.

13. Ibid.

14. Matthew L. Wald and Kevin Sack, "The Tapes: 'We have some planes,' Hijacker Told Controller," *New York Times*, October 16, 2001; also see *The 9/11 Commission Report*, p. 25-26.

15. http://911research.wtc7.net/pentagon/analysis/witnesses.html.

16. I learned this during my conversation with Jeff Richardson, at 84th RADES. See note 19 (below).

17. The cap point instruction is as follows: "QUIT 2-5 sent to CAP point, 38 25 N, 077 02 W." MCC OP. The reader can hear this information being transmitted by fast forwarding the animation to 09:45:33 EDT. Email from John Farmer, May 14, 2008.

18. Michael Bronner, "9/11 Live: The NORAD Tapes," *Vanity Fair*, September 2006, p. 285.

19. Email from Lynn Spencer, July 13, 2008.

20. Ibid.

21. Email from John Farmer, July 16, 2008.

22. Lynn Spencer, *Touching History: The Untold Story of the Drama That Unfolded in the Skies over America on 9/11*, Free Press, New York, 2008, pp.180-182.

23. Ibid.

24. Email from Lynn Spencer, July 13, 2008.

25. Ibid.

26. Apparently Lynn Spencer did try to FOIA FAA audio tapes, but was unsuccessful. Email from "Pinnacle," July 17, 2008.

27. Email from Marco Bolletino, February 21, 2008.

28. I should mention here that when John Farmer examined the radar data to fact-check

the Wright-Pat departure, he found that there were two departures from the base, one (M3_3462) at 9:30 A.M., the other (M3_6745; M2 = 4311) at 10 A.M. Notice, neither of these times is a close match with the departure time reported in the Dayton daily newspaper. The track of the first plane goes west. The track of the second goes southeast and shows that the plane flew in a holding pattern over the border between West Virginia and Virginia until mid-afternoon. The plane then returns to base after being replaced by another aircraft (M3_3162). Farmer speculates that this second departure was a tanker, as it flew in sync with another plane (from Langley AFB). Moreover, its holding pattern was in an area of frequent tanker activity. Farmer urges caution, however, in interpreting the radar data. He writes, "The radar coverage is limited ... and would catch it if it went north, east or west. Going directly south, depending on how fast it gained altitude, it could have been out of radar range by the time it reached operating altitude." Emails from John Farmer, May 17, 2008.

29. Email from Colin Scoggins, April 11, 2007.

30. Department of the Air Force, 84th Radar Evaluation Squadron (ACC), Hill Air Force Base, Utah, 13 September, 2001, Memorandum for Federal Bureau of Investigation (FBI).

31. Email from John Farmer, June 15, 2008.

32. Email from John Farmer, June 17, 2008.

33. Dan Verton, *Black Ice: The Invisible Threat of Cyber-Terrorism*, McGraw-Hill, New York, 2003, p. 144.

34. *The 9/11 Commission Report*, p.xvi.

35. Phone interview with Jeff Richardson, 84th RADES, Hill AFB, Utah, April 29, 2008.

36. Email from John Farmer, May 9, 2008.

37. Emails from Robin Hordon, March 2 and 3, 2008.

38. Email from John Farmer, May 2, 2008.

39. Email from Jeff Richardson, May 2, 2008.

40. Matthew Everett, "Donald Rumsfeld on 9/11: An enemy within," *Online Journal*, May 30, 2007. Posted at http://onlinejournal.com/artman/publish/article_2026.shtml.

41. Email from Robin Hordon, May 26, 2008.

42. Email from Robin Hordon,. July 23, 2008.

43. Email from John Farmer, April 13, 2008.

44. In addition to other research, Farmer has been correlating the RADES radar data with the NORAD tapes. Although the project is not done yet, it appears he has already made an important discovery. On one of the tapes Farmer found what may have been the call made by Colin Scoggins at 9:24 A.M. to NEADS that apparently gave rise to the phantom plane story. The transcript reads as follows: "13:24:02 Scoggins, Boston Military calls ID2. 'We did hear from Washington, there is an aircraft, they believe it is American 11 and he is southwest, only just don't have a point ...' ID2 OP."

Here 13:24:02 translates to 9:24 A.M. EDT. When Farmer checked the RADES radar data for this moment in time he discovered that incoming Flight 77(?) was exactly southwest of Washington. Obviously, the FAA had been tracking Flight 77(?), not some phantom plane southwest of New York. Since the 9/11 Commission had this same tape and surely reviewed it, the claim in their report (p. 26) that "We have been unable to identify the source of this mistaken FAA information" stretches the limits of credibility. So we see that Farmer's discovery provides additional strong support for Norman Mineta's version of events in the White House bunker on 9/11. Email from John Farmer, April 22, 2008. Check out Farmer's blog at http://911files.info/blog/. His RADES research is posted at http://911files.info/blog/?cat=4.

45. Phone interview with Jeff Richardson, 84th RADES, Hill AFB, Utah, April 29, 2008.

46. Emails from John Farmer, April 29, 2008 and May 9, 2008.

47. Email from David Ray Griffin, May 22, 2008.

5

Was 9/11 an Inside Job?

A s a result of the evidence presented in the previous chapters, I believe we must now broach the question more directly: Was 9/11 an inside job? Regrettably, there is considerable evidence that elements of the Bush administration were complicit in the 9/11 attack, and may even have helped stage it. Let us now examine some of what I regard as the most compelling evidence. However, the following discussion makes no claim to be comprehensive.

We know that within minutes of the "worst terrorist attack" in U.S. history, even before the collapse of WTC-2 at 9:59 A.M., U.S. officials knew the names of several of the alleged hijackers. CBS reported that a flight attendant on AA Flight 11, Amy Sweeney, had the presence of mind to call her office and reveal the seat numbers of the hijackers who had seized the plane.[1] FBI Director Robert Mueller later said, "This was the first piece of hard evidence."[2] In his memoirs CIA Director George Tenet emphasizes the importance of the passenger manifests, as does counterterrorism czar Richard A. Clarke.[3] All of which is very strange because the manifests later released by the airlines do *not* include the names of any of the alleged hijackers. Nor has this discrepancy ever been explained.

According to MSNBC, the plan to invade Afghanistan and "remove al Qaeda from the face of he earth" was already sitting on G.W. Bush's desk on the morning of 9/11 awaiting his signature.[4] The plan, in the form of a presidential directive, had been developed by the CIA and according to Richard Clarke called for "arming the Northern Alliance ... to go on the offensive against the Taliban [and] pressing the CIA to ... go after bin Laden and the al Qaeda leadership."[5]

A former Pakistani diplomat, Niaz Naik, tells virtually the same story. During a BBC interview, three days after 9/11, Niak claimed that senior American officials had informed him in mid-July 2001 that the U.S. would attack the Taliban "before the snows start falling in Afghanistan, by the middle of October at the latest."[6] Niak said he received this information in Berlin at a UN-sponsored international contact group on Afghanistan. He also predicted, correctly, that the U.S. attack would be launched from bases in Uzbekistan and Tajikistan. But how could U.S. officials know in mid-July that American forces would invade Afghanistan in October unless they had foreknowledge of the attack?

Foreknowledge probably also explains why General Richard Myers, the acting Chairman of the Joint Chiefs on 9/11, announced at the first post-9/11 meeting of Bush's National Security Council, held via video-conference the afternoon of the attack, that "there are forty-two major Taliban bombing targets."[7] But how did Myers come to have such detailed information about military targets in Afghanistan so soon after the 9/11 attack? This important detail belies oft-repeated claims that the U.S. military was not prepared to attack Afghanistan, and points to extensive war planning before 9/11. Journalist Steve Coll arrived at a similar conclusion while researching his 2004 book, *Ghost Wars*, an excellent history of the period leading up to the 9/11 attack. Coll interviewed two Clinton administration officials who informed him that "the Pentagon had been studying possible targets in the same spring [1998] that the CIA had been drawing up its secret plan to raid Tarnack Farm," located near Kandahar, Afghanistan, where bin Laden had taken up quarters at the invitation of Taliban leader Mullah Omar.[8]

According to Clarke, at the same meeting on the afternoon of 9/11, CIA Director George Tenet informed the president that "al Qaeda had committed these atrocities."[9] But, again, how did Tenet know this so soon after the attack, especially given that "security failures" had occurred, unless he had foreknowledge?

No Hard Evidence

On September 20, 2001, the Bush administration officially declared that Osama bin Laden was responsible for the 9/11 attack. Three days later, Secretary of State Colin Powell announced on *Meet the Press* that the government would soon release "a white paper" detailing the evidence against bin Laden. Later the same day, Bush faced questions from the press about Powell's remark and backed away from releasing any additional information.[10]

Bush explained that the government had a lot of evidence but that most of it was classified and could not be made public. Bush emphasized, however, that the evidence "leads to one person, as well as one global terrorist organization."[11] National Security Adviser Condoleezza Rice made a similar statement during an interview on FOX News. Said Rice, "We have very good evidence of links between Osama bin Laden, al Qaeda operatives, and what happened on September 11."[12] Rice refused to release any particulars, however, and, like Bush, claimed that the evidence was "classified."

As we know, the U.S. government never got around to releasing the promised white paper. Why not? Was it because the evidence was nonexistent? Or perhaps too weak to hold up in court? This was the view of journalist Seymour Hersh, who cited CIA and Justice Department sources to this effect in his regular column in the *New Yorker* magazine.[13]

Foreign intelligence agencies were also busily investigating the case, but fared no better. For instance, Germany's Chief Federal Prosecutor, Kay Nehm, admitted that there was no hard evidence linking bin Laden with the crime.[14] The lack of evidence prompted former German Chancellor Helmut Schmidt to speak out against President Bush's decision to invoke Article V of the NATO Treaty, mobilizing NATO's involvement in the war on terrorism. In Schmidt's own words: "Proof had to be delivered that the September 11 terror attack came from abroad. [Yet,] that proof still has not been provided."[15]

Osama did not cooperate by acknowledging his role in the attack — on the contrary. In a statement on September 16, 2001 carried by Arabic television service Al Jazeera, bin Laden categorically denied any involvement. Days later, he repeated this denial during an interview with the Pakistani newspaper *Ummaut*.[16] On November 3, 2001 *Al-Jazeera* released a third statement, in which bin Laden not only denied involvement but also accused the Bush administration of waging a "crusader war" against the Muslim world. To the best of my knowledge, none of these denials were reported in the U.S. media. Why not?

On October 1, 2001, British Prime Minister Tony Blair told the House of Commons that the case against bin Laden was proved beyond a shadow of doubt. Said Blair, "I have seen absolutely powerful and incontrovertible evidence of his [Osama Bin Laden's] link to the events of the 11th of September."[17] Several days later (on October 4), Blair's government went public with the evidence to which Blair had alluded — a "Bin Laden Dossier."[18] But the evidence turned out to be short of "incontrovertible," and in fact was shockingly thin. The *Independent* described it as "little more than conjecture,"[19] and an editorial in the *Guardian* (U.K.) concluded that the dossier was "almost worthless from a legal point of view."[20] The *Times* (London) agreed, observing, "There is no evidence presented [in the dossier] that directly links bin Laden to September 11."[21]

The Bin Laden Video and the Personification of Evil

Confronted with U.S. demands to hand over bin Laden unconditionally, the Taliban initially was defiant and refused. However, in early October 2001, two Pakistani Islamic parties persuaded the Taliban leadership to extradite bin Laden to Peshawar, Pakistan, where he would be held under house arrest and tried by an international tribunal.[22] The deal even included the extradition of bin Laden to the U.S. in the event of a conviction. However, Pakistani President Pervez Musharraf vetoed the arrangement, likely under pressure from the Bush administration. But why would the U.S. turn down an opportunity to bring the arch villain of 9/11 to justice for the crime of the century? Was it because, as already indicated, the U.S. had insufficient evidence to convict and faced the embarrassing likelihood of an acquittal?

In fact, the only evidence the U.S. government released linking bin Laden to 9/11 was a videotape which supposedly turned up by chance in Afghanistan. According to the State Department, U.S. military forces found the hour-long video in Jalalabad on December 9, 2001, shortly after the U.S. invasion.[23] It purportedly shows bin Laden and several of his al Qaeda comrades ghoulishly celebrating their successful attack upon America. The U.S. government released the tape on December 13, 2001 along with an English translation and a Department of Defense (DoD) press release. The latter included the following statement by Rumsfeld: "There was no doubt of bin Laden's responsibility for the September 11 attacks before the tape was discovered."[24]

The U.S. media made much of this confessional tape, as did political luminaries like New York City Mayor (and presidential hopeful) Rudy Giuliani, who told CNN that the tape confirmed that the U.S. military campaign against bin Laden was "more than justified." Giuliani added, "Obviously, this man is the personification of evil. He seems delighted at having killed more people than he anticipated, which leaves you wondering just how deep his evil heart and soul really is."[25]

In the video bin Laden brags about al Qaeda's role in staging the attack. But is the footage bona fide? Anyone who has seen the film knows that the main character bears only the most superficial resemblance to bin Laden, judging from well-known photos. In addition, there are major discrepancies. For example, the video shows bin Laden writing with his right hand, when according to the FBI he is a southpaw.[26]

Two independent translators and a third expert on oriental studies also took issue with the English translation of the Arabic released by the DoD. During the program *Monitor*, which aired on the German TV channel *Das Erste*, the three experts stated, "at the most important places where it [i.e, the video] is held to prove the guilt of bin Laden, it [i.e., the translation] is not identical with the Arabic."[27] The experts also disputed the U.S. claim that the tape proved foreknowledge. Gernot Rotter, professor of Islamic and Arabic Studies at the University of Hamburg, stated, "The American translators who listened to the tapes and transcribed them apparently wrote a lot of things in that they wanted to hear, but that cannot be heard on the tape no matter how many times you listen to it." While this does not necessarily exonerate bin Laden, it does raise questions. If, as Bush claimed, the U.S. had solid evidence of bin Laden's guilt, then why make false claims?

Evidently, the U.S. Federal Bureau of Investigation agrees with the skeptics. The FBI's online listing of "Most Wanted Terrorists" includes a webpage devoted to Osama bin Laden. According to this official post, which may be viewed by anyone with access to cyberspace, bin Laden is wanted by the FBI for the August 1998 attacks upon U.S. Embassies in Dar es Salaam, Tanzania, and Nairobi, Kenya, which killed over 200 people.[28] However, the page makes no reference to the events of September 11, 2001. Nor is there any mention of the video found in Afghanistan.

In June 2006, when blogger Ed Haas learned about this, he was understandably puzzled, and contacted FBI headquarters by phone seeking an explanation. Haas talked with Rex Tomb, the FBI's Chief of Investigative Publicity, who informed him: "The reason why 9/11 is not mentioned on Osama bin Laden's Most Wanted page is because the FBI has no hard evidence connecting bin Laden to 9/11."[29] Haas was dumbfounded, and said, "But how is this possible?" Tomb replied that "bin Laden has not been formally charged in connection with 9/11." He then explained why not:

> The FBI gathers evidence. Once evidence is gathered, it is turned over to the Department of Justice. The Department of Justice then decides whether it has enough evidence to present to a federal grand jury. In the case of the 1998 United States Embassies

being bombed, bin Laden has been formally indicted and charged by a grand jury. He has not been formally indicted and charged in connection with 9/11 *because the FBI has no hard evidence connecting bin Laden to 9/11* [my emphasis].[30]

This admission by the FBI is astonishing and raises fundamental questions about the war on terrorism, as well as the role of the U.S. media. Was Osama bin Laden convicted for the cold-blooded murder of nearly 3,000 innocent Americans in the U.S. court of public opinion by means of a media circus? Did the U.S. government and the corporate media collude to deceive the American people? If so, then a colossal miscarriage of justice has occurred.

Consider also the strange statement made by President Bush at a press conference on March 13, 2002. When asked about the progress being made to catch bin Laden, Bush replied, "We haven't heard much from him. And I wouldn't necessarily say he's at the center of any command structure. And, again, I don't know where he is. I, I'll repeat what I said. *I truly am not that concerned about him*" [my emphasis].[31] But why this almost lackadaisical attitude about the arch-villain whom Bush had promised to track down to the ends of the earth? What had become of the president's laser-like determination? Bush explained that bin Laden had ceased to be a terrorist threat due to the U.S. occupation of Afghanistan. Yet, by at least one account, the U.S. forces at Tora Bora displayed almost unbelievable incompetence during the pursuit of bin Laden, as a result of which the accused and most of his entourage escaped.[32] Was *this* the plan all along?

A no-less-strange remark made a few weeks later (April 6, 2002) by General Richard Myers, then Chairman of the Joint Chiefs, suggests that bin Laden's getaway had been approved at the highest level. Myers told CNN that "the goal has never been to get bin Laden."[33] I personally found his statement incomprehensible, since at the time Osama was public enemy number one. Did the U.S. allow bin Laden to escape because the Bush administration judged he was more valuable at large? We can't be certain, because by this time there were also numerous reports that bin Laden was dead.[34]

Did President Bush know when he made the statement noted above that bin Laden was already deceased? This would explain Bush's casual demeanor. Yet, either way, from the standpoint of propaganda it hardly mattered whether bin Laden was dead or alive. His larger-than-life reputation could be sustained simply by neglecting to confirm his death, and the legend is what counted. His persona could also be "spun" in various ways and made to serve political expedience. Indeed by this logic, bin Laden was even more valuable dead, because a living breathing bin Laden might at some point be apprehended, in which case the Bush administration faced the unwelcome prospect of a very public trial at which the terrorist would have an opportunity to tell *his side of the story* to a listening world. And this, of course, had to be avoided.

If we can believe the *9/11 Commission Report*, the case against bin Laden was greatly bolstered by the capture and subsequent confession in 2003 of the alleged 9/11 mastermind, Khalid Sheikh Mohammed (KSM). The problem, of course, as already noted in my introduction, is that the official story about the plot against America is wholly based on secret CIA interrogations that have never been independently confirmed, and must therefore be viewed as suspect. But even if we accept the testimony of KSM in 2003, this does not explain the rush to war in 2001. Nor does it explain President Bush's decision to go to war against Saddam Hussein — a decision reportedly made in July 2002.[35]

Previous cases of terrorism had already demonstrated the wisdom of proceeding with caution, since knee-jerk responses can (and do) misfire. For example, after the 1995 bombing of the Murrah Federal Building in Oklahoma City, U.S. investigators at first suspected a Mideast connection. But this was proved false, and similar errors were made after the 1988 downing of Pan American Flight 103 over Lockerbie, Scotland. Although initial evidence pointed to Syria or Iran, a thorough forensic investigation ruled them out and eventually implicated Libya.

The *9/11 Commission Report* itself describes the latter case as "a cautionary tale about rushing to judgment in attributing responsibility for a terrorist act."[36] So, why the rush to war after the September 11 attack? If the Bush administration had conclusive evidence that al Qaeda was responsible, why not release it? Was the Bush White House tight-lipped because the actual evidence would have exposed the complicity of the U.S. military and intelligence community? A stunning story that broke in the U.S. press in 2005 points to such a conclusion.

Able Danger

As it happened, a legitimate U.S. military counter-terrorist operation known as Able Danger was tracking Mohamed Atta and his cohorts as early as January-February 2000. The operation, based at Ft. Belvoir,

Virginia, was small but extremely high-tech, as it employed advanced computers to sweep the Internet, a methodology known as as data-mining. In May 2000, however, when Able Danger's success became known throughout the Defense Department, the officers who ran it were ordered to shut it down and destroy their data.[37] One officer reportedly was threatened with prison if he refused.

Later, the Pentagon attempted to block Senate Judiciary Committee hearings on Able Danger, and in 2005, when this failed, the Pentagon refused Able Danger staffers permission to testify before the committee.[38] One intelligence officer who later testified anyway, Lt. Col. Anthony Shaffer, was targeted for harassment. The question is why? Of course, the standard explanation is that the military bureaucracy made gross blunders and later sought to cover up their incompetence. But there is another possibility. Was Able Danger shut down because this honest operation "threatened" to unmask the covert planning for the September 11 "attack"?

What is clear is that the Pentagon's self-serving attempts to gag and discredit Lt. Col. Shaffer are not to be believed. In February 2006 Shaffer told the House Armed Services Committee that during the summer of 2000, he and other officers involved in Able Danger attempted on three separate occasions to warn the FBI about the terrorist threat posed by Mohamed Atta. But the meetings never happened. Each time they were canceled at the last minute by high-level Pentagon attorneys.[39] Nor has the Pentagon ever provided a satisfactory explanation as to why.[40]

Some time after the dissolution of Able Danger, Shaffer was reassigned to Bagram Air Base, Afghanistan, where in October 2003 he succeeded in bringing the existence of Able Danger to the attention of the 9/11 Commission. This apparently happened due to a chance encounter with Philip Zelikow, Executive Director of the commission, and several commission staffers who were then on tour — gathering firsthand information about the U.S. war on terrorism. Lt. Col. Shaffer told the House committee that after he briefed the commission staff about Able Danger's success in identifying Mohamed Atta and other alleged 9/11 hijackers, Zelikow came up, handed him his card, and asked him to "please contact me upon your return to the states so we can continue this dialogue."[41]

However, three months later when Shaffer did just that, he was surprised to discover that Zelikow was no longer interested in Able Danger. But why wouldn't he be? Then all hell broke loose, when Shaffer dutifully informed his commanding officer about the contact. From that point on, Lt. Col. Shaffer was subjected to the sort of military hazing that is usually reserved for green recruits. His security clearance was cancelled. He lost access to his office computer and all of his classified materials about Able Danger, which — he later learned — were destroyed. (Subsequently, the Pentagon dismissed his testimony, claiming it was unsupported by hard evidence, an obvious case of Catch-22.) Shaffer also learned that he was under investigation, although no formal charges were ever filed against him. He was told "off the record" that he had "pissed off" one or more high-ranking officers. Several of Shaffer's colleagues from Able Danger corroborated his story, but it didn't matter. His military career was over — destroyed.[42] Shaffer's testimony before Congress is riveting, and it is essential reading for anyone interested in 9/11 truth.

In their 2006 book *Without Precedent,* Thomas Kean and Lee Hamilton, co-chairs of the 9/11 Commission, deny that Able Danger had ever identified Mohamed Atta before 9/11.[43] But their assertion, much belated, is just not credible. Their own final report on 9/11 makes no mention of Able Danger. It is abundantly clear that even though Lt. Col. Shaffer notified the panel's staff about this important counter-terrorism operation, the commissioners made no attempt to investigate it, and since Kean and Hamilton failed to do so, how can they now credibly claim to know? Obviously, their denial is based on information they received, much later, from the Pentagon.

Kean and Hamilton write that their staff "received all of the Department of Defense documents on Able Danger and had found no mention of Atta."[44] But their claim is not persuasive, since we know that 2.5 terabytes of intelligence data about Able Danger had already been destroyed (in 2000), not to mention the information on Shaffer's hard drive (in 2004). The question for the co-chairs is simple: What assurance could they possibly have that the documents they received from the DoD about Able Danger tell the full story? Obviously, they do not. More to the point, why would Kean and Hamilton believe the Pentagon over the testimony of Lt. Col. Shaffer? As I have shown, the co-chairs already had good reason to believe that the Pentagon had deceived them in the hearings.[45]

Eavesdropping on bin Laden

The fact that Able Danger was shutdown in May 2000, long before Bush entered office, raises disturbing questions. Was covert planning for 9/11 already underway during the Clinton administration? It is curious that CIA Director George Tenet in 2002 told a closed session of a joint House-Senate panel investigating the 9/11 "security failure" that al

Qaeda's planning of the September 11, 2001 attack started as early as 1998.[46] But how could Tenet know this unless the CIA had been tracking bin Laden all along?

As a matter of fact, we know they were! According to several UPI reports, the National Security Agency (NSA) acknowledged in February 2001 that the use of advanced Echelon software enabled the U.S. intelligence community to eavesdrop on thousands of bin Laden's cell phone calls over a period of years. U.S. officials disclosed that even after bin Laden began to encrypt certain calls in 1995, his "codes were broken."[47] The date 1998 is doubly curious. That same year, Tenet informed the Senate Intelligence Committee that the CIA's strategy to defeat al Qaeda included the recruiting of al Qaeda operatives.[48] In his memoirs Tenet goes even further with an assertion that is remarkable for its candor. He writes, "... the [9/11] commission failed to recognize the sustained comprehensive efforts conducted by the intelligence community prior to 9/11 to penetrate the al Qaeda organization."[49] I had to re-read this passage several times just to believe my own eyes. Did the CIA recruit terrorists who were then used as patsies on 9/11?

Bush officials, of course, have steadfastly denied that the U.S. successfully penetrated al Qaeda before 9/11. But their denials are less than persuasive in light of Lt. Col. Shaffer's testimony about Able Danger, and also because we know that the monitoring of phone calls continued. After al Qaeda bombed two U.S. embassies in East Africa in August 1998, FBI investigators got lucky and stumbled upon an al Qaeda communications hub in Yemen. According to writer Lawrence Wright, this proved to be "one of the most important pieces of evidence the FBI would ever discover, allowing investigators to map the links of the al Qaeda network all across the globe."[50]

The hub was a private telephone — anything but high tech. The switchboard operator turned out to be the brother-in-law of Khalid al-Midhar, one of the nineteen alleged hijackers. His job in Yemen was simply to relay messages to and from various al Qaeda operatives, including bin Laden.[51] From phone records U.S. investigators confirmed a flurry of calls through the hub before the embassy bombings, and this pattern was repeated before the attack on the USS Cole in October 2000.[52] Indeed, it is unclear why U.S. intelligence agencies failed to prevent the attack on the Cole, because by this time they were surely listening. The al Qaeda hub was allowed to operate right up until September 11, 2001, and even after. Incredible as this sounds, U.S. and Yemeni authorities did not finally move in and close it down until 2002.[53]

Based on this evidence, gleaned from open sources in the U.S. media, we must conclude that the U.S. intelligence community was tracking al Qaeda's nearly every move before 9/11 — and had been for years — probably including the entry of the alleged hijackers into the U.S., their "flight training," and subsequent movements. The phone intercepts certainly continued. In June 2002 both the *Miami Herald* and the *Dallas Star-Telegram* reported that in the summer of 2001 the NSA even monitored phone conversations between alleged 9/11 lead hijacker Mohamed Atta and alleged 9/11 mastermind Khalid Sheikh Mohammed.[54] The papers reported that the NSA "did not recognize the significance of what they had."

Evidently, we are supposed to believe that the NSA did not pass along this important intelligence to the CIA. But this is absurd. After all, the NSA is a part of the U.S. Department of Defense and exists for the purpose of providing intelligence to the CIA and the U.S. military. The story in the *Miami Herald* even acknowledges this, citing an NSA official who stated under condition of anonymity that it was "simply not true" that the NSA failed to share the information with other intelligence agencies.[55] Of course they shared it. Incidentally, a Google search failed to locate the full text of either of these articles, which apparently have long since been scrubbed from the Internet. To the best of my knowledge they survive in cyberspace only as thumbnails.

What are we to make of all of this? Did elements of the U.S. intelligence community know about al Qaeda's multiple hijacking operation all along? Did they, then, covertly piggy-back their own planning on top of it, thereby insuring the attack's "success" while also manipulating it for their own ignoble ends? If true, this would easily explain why the Pentagon shut down Able Danger in May 2000. It would explain the Pentagon's gag order imposed upon the Able Danger staffers, which blunted a Congressional inquiry.

It would also explain the carefully orchestrated smear campaign aimed at Lt. Col. Shaffer, who did his patriotic duty and was made to pay a terrible price. It would explain why the DoD fed phony or incomplete information about Able Danger to co-chairs Kean and Hamilton, and other members of the commission, to persuade them that the data-mining effort was "insignificant." It would also explain why, time and again, during the period before 9/11, the CIA withheld critical information from the FBI, information which, had it become known, would have enabled the FBI to foil the 9/11 attack. The FBI was always just one or two critical pieces of information short of putting together the plot. Nor has the CIA disconnect ever been adequately explained.[56] The standard excuses, bureaucratic bungling and interagency rivalry, are simply not persuasive.

This interpretation would also explain why George Tenet lied during the 9/11 Commission hearings when he denied his meetings with President Bush in August 2001. Indeed, it might even explain why President-elect G.W. Bush retained Tenet, a Clinton appointee, as his CIA chief. The move was one of Bush's first decisions as president and was most unusual, especially given the neocons' scarcely concealed scorn for the Clinton administration.

However, it makes perfect sense, assuming that when Bush took office elements of the CIA and U.S. military were already deeply involved in the covert planning for the 9/11 attack. Continuity at the CIA would have been essential. As far as I know, author Ian Henshall was the first to make this connection.[57] And let us not forget: During the period before 9/11, the CIA Director visited the White House on a daily basis. Tenet personally briefed Bush on intelligence issues, an unusual chore for a CIA Director.[58] But, again, this becomes understandable, assuming that a major covert operation was in the works, one that entailed extreme compartmentalization. Only a very few individuals at the top would have been fully briefed.

Bin Laden in Dubai?

A no less shocking story, appearing in the prestigious French paper *Le Figaro* on October 11, 2001, points to the same conclusion. The story claimed that bin Laden was actually *under the protection* of U.S. security agencies prior to the 9/11 attack. According to *Le Figaro,* bin Laden checked in to the American Hospital in Dubai, one of the Arab Emirates located along the Persian Gulf, on July 4, 2001, just two months before 9/11, where he received medical treatment over a ten-day period for a serious kidney ailment.[59]

The story seems based in fact, because it includes many details: Bin Laden was reportedly accompanied by his personal physician, a nurse, four bodyguards, and at least one of his lieutenants. It also states that the local CIA station chief, evidently a well known figure in the tiny country, was seen entering bin Laden's hospital suite during his stay, and immediately after the meeting caught a flight back to the U.S. If the story is accurate, bin Laden held court from his hospital room, welcoming various members of his extended family, as well as prominent Saudis and Emiratis. It is no secret that bin Laden suffered from kidney disease. Pakistani

Prime Minister Nawaz Sharif had informed the Clinton administration about bin Laden's deteriorating health as early as 1998, during a state visit to Washington.[60]

A follow-up report in the *Guardian* (U.K.) on November 1, 2001 confirmed the above story and added further details, noting that bin Laden's Saudi guests included Prince Turki al Faisal, who was then head of Saudi intelligence. The article in the *Guardian* names French intelligence as the source of the story in *Le Figaro*. It also claims the information was leaked because the French were "keen to reveal the ambiguous role of the CIA and to restrain Washington from extending the war to Iraq and elsewhere."

Given that bin Laden was already wanted at the time for the U.S. embassy bombings in Nairobi and Dar es Salaam, why did the U.S. not arrange to have local authorities snatch the terrorist in Dubai, in order to bring him to justice? Of course, it goes without saying that bin Laden would never have visited the U.S. hospital in the first place had he not been confident of his protected status. Do we dare to connect these dots? Surely the story in *Le Figaro* suggests that elements of the U.S. intelligence establishment knew about the coming 9/11 attack and allowed bin Laden to remain free to play his assigned role as a patsy.

Such a conclusion is supported by powerful evidence that first came to light on November 6, 2001, when the BBC program *Newsnight* produced FBI documents showing that soon after G.W. Bush entered office, the White House ordered the FBI to "back off" from ongoing investigations of Osama bin Laden and other members of his family, some of whom were living in the U.S. at the time.[61] To the best of my knowledge, none of these stories from European and U.K. press were ever reported in the U.S. media. Again, why not?

Were elements of the U.S. government and intelligence community complicit in the events of September 11, 2001? Did they allow the attack to happen, or even help to stage it, in order to generate the pretext for a much more aggressive U.S. foreign policy which the American people would not otherwise support? Either way, the implications are shocking — so shocking that many of our fellow countrymen (and women) cannot bring themselves to even think such thoughts. Yet, it is a matter of record that the neoconservatives openly advocated an imperial shift in U.S. foreign policy before the November 2000 election.[62] Moreover, President Clinton was already moving in this direction, as I will show in a later chapter.

These are grave questions for our nation and we must not fail to address them. If there is any truth in them, we face a crisis unlike anything in our history. With this in mind, let us now return to the place where Bush's war on terrorism started, Ground Zero, in search of more answers.

Endnotes

1. According to another account the stewardess was Betty Ong. Lynn Spencer, *Touching History: The Untold Story of the Drama that Unfolded in the Skies over America on 9/11*, Free Press, New York, 2008, p.18.

2. "The President's Story," CBS News, September 10, 2003.

3. George Tenet, *At the Center of the Storm, My Years at the CIA*, HarperCollins, New York, 2007, pp.xix and 167; Richard A. Clarke, *Against All Enemies*, Free Press, New York, 2004. pp. 13-14.

4. Jim Miklaszewski and Alex Johnson, "U.S. planned for attack on al-Qaida," MSNBC and NBC, May 16, 2002.

5. Richard A. Clarke, op. cit., p. 26. Evidently the name of the plan was "Blue Sky." George Tenet, op. cit., pp. 130-131 and 171.

6. The three U.S. officials were Tom Simmons, a former U.S. Ambassador to Pakistan, Karl Inderfurth, former Assistant Secretary of State for Asian Affairs, and Lee Coldren, a former State Department expert on south Asia. George Arney, "U.S. 'planned attack on Taliban,'" *BBC News*, September 18, 2001.

7. George Tenet, op. cit., p. 23.

8. Steve Coll, *Ghost Wars: The Secret History of the CIA, Afghanistan, and bin Laden, from the Soviet Invasion to September 10, 2001*, Penguin Press, New York, 2004, p. 409, also see note 21, p. 628.

9. Richard A. Clarke, op. cit.

10. "White House Wavers on Publicizing bin Laden Case," UPI, September 24, 2001.

11. Transcript: President Freezes Terrorists' Assets: Remarks by the President, Secretary of the Treasury O'Neill and Secretary of State Powell on Executive Order, The Rose Garden, September 24, 2001, posted at http://www.whitehouse.gov/news/releases/2001/09/20010924-4.html.

12. *News Sunday*, FOX News, September 23, 2001.

13. Seymour Hersh, "What Went Wrong: The C.I.A. and the failure of American intelligence, *The New Yorker*, October 1, 2001.

14. *Guardian* (U.K.), September 17, 2001, p. 11; also see *Times* (London), September 28, 2001, p. 5.

15. Schmidt reportedly made the statement on German television on December 10, 2001. See the Webster Tarpley segment in the video by Barrie Zwicker, *The Great Conspiracy: The 9/11 News Special You Never Saw*, 2004.

16. *Ummaut*, September 22, 2001. The pertinent text reads as follows: "I was not involved in the September 11 attacks in the United States nor did I have knowledge of the attacks. There exists a government within a government within the United States. The United States should try to trace the perpetrators of these attacks within itself; to the people who want to make the present century a century of conflict between Islam and Christianity. That secret government must be asked as to who carried out the attacks.... The American system is totally in the control of the Jews, whose first priority is Israel, not

the United States ... I have already said that we are not hostile to the United States. We are against the system, which makes other nations slaves of the United States, or forces them to mortgage their political and economic freedom."

17. *Daily Telegraph* (London), October 1, 2001.

18. The full transcript may be viewed at http://paulboutin.weblogger.com/2001/10/05.

19. *Independent* (U.K.), October 7, 2001, p. 7.

20. *Guardian* (U.K.), October 5, 2001, p. 23.

21. *Times* (London), October 5, 2001, p. 8.

22. *Daily Telegraph* (London), October 4, 2001, p. 9; also see Milan Rai, "Afghanistan: The Unnecessary War," *Znet*, October 13, 2004.

23. The full video is posted at http://paulboutin.weblogger.com/2001/12/14.

24. As of this writing the press release is still posted and may be viewed at http://www.defenselink.mil/releases/release.aspx?releaseid=3184.

25. "Bin Laden on tape: Attacks 'benefited Islam greatly'," CNN, December 14, 2001, posted at http://archives.cnn.com/2001/U.S./12/13/ret.bin.laden.videotape/.

26. See http://www.fbi.gov/wanted/terrorists/terbinladen.htm.

27. Georg Restle, Ekkehard Sieker, "Bin-Laden-Video: Falschübersetzung als Beweismittel?", *MONITOR Nr. 485 am*, December 20, 2001. Posted at http://web.archive.org/web/20021218105636/www.wdr.de/tv/monitor/beitraege.phtml?id=379.

28. The page is posted at http://www.fbi.gov/wanted/terrorists/terbinladen.htm.

29. "FBI says, 'No hard evidence connecting Bin Laden to 9/11,'" *Muckraker Report*, June 6, 2006. Posted at http://www.teamliberty.net/id267.html.

30. Ibid.

31. President Bush Holds Press Conference, The James S. Brady Briefing Room, March 13, 2002. Posted at http://www.whitehouse.gov/news/releases/2002/03/20020313-8.html.

32. John F. Burns, "10-Month Afghan Mystery: Is bin Laden Dead or Alive?" *New York Times*, September 30, 2002.

33. *Evans, Novak, Hunt and Shields*, "Interview with General Richard Myers," CNN, April 6, 2002.

34. Giles Tremlett (in Madrid), "Al-Qaeda leaders say nuclear power stations were original targets," *Guardian* (U.K.), September 9, 2002; also see "Report: Bin Laden Already Dead," FOX News, December 26, 2001; "Israeli Intelligence: Bin Laden is dead, heir has been chosen," WorldTribune.com, October 16, 2002; "Musharraf: bin Laden likely dead," CNN, January 19, 2002.

35. George Tenet, op. cit., p. 309.

36. *The 9/11 Commission Report: Final Report of the National Commission on Terrorist Attacks Upon the United States*, Norton & Co., New York, 2004, pp. 75-76.

37. Army Major Eric Kleinsmith destroyed 2.5 terabytes of intelligence data about al Qaeda in May and June 2000, at the order of Tony Gentry, general counsel of the Army Intelligence and Security Command. This is an enormous amount of data. To get an idea just how large the number is, wrap your mind around this: It is the equivalent of 25% of the Library of Congress. Patience Wait, "Data-mining offensive in the works," *Government Computer News*, October 10, 2005, posted at http://www.gcn.com/

print/24_30/37242-1.html?topic=news.

38. Philip Shenon, "Pentagon Blocks Testimony at Senate Hearings n Terrorism," *New York Times*, September 20, 2005; also see Philip Shenon, "Second Officer Says 9/11 Leader was Named Before Attacks," *New York Times*, August 23, 2005.

39. Prepared statement of Anthony A. Shaffer, Lt. Col., U.S. Army Reserve, Senior Intelligence Officer, before the House Armed Services Committee, Wednesday February 15, 2006, full transcript posted at http://www.fas.org/irp/congress/2006_hr/021506shaffer.pdf.

40. The official explanations are so ridiculous they do not even deserve presentation.

41. Prepared statement of Anthony A. Shaffer, loc. cit.

42. Will Dunham, "Three more assert Pentagon knew of 9/11 ringleader," Reuters, September 1, 2005; "Navy Captain Backs Able Danger Claims," FOX News, August 23, 2005; also see Thom Shanker, "Terrorist Known Before 9/11, More Say." *New York Times*, September 2, 2005.

43. Thomas H. Kean and Lee H. Hamilton, *Without Precedent: The Inside Story of the 9/1 Commission*, Alfred A, Knopf, New York, 2006, pp. 294-295.

44. Ibid.

45. Dan Eggen, "9/11 Panel Suspected Deception by Pentagon," *Washington Post*, August 2, 2006.

46. John Diamond and Kathy Kiely, "Officials: Sept. 11 attacks were planned since 1998," *USA Today*, June 18, 2002.

47. Richard Sale, "NSA Listens to bin Laden," UPI, February 13, 2001; also see John C.K. Daly, "Analysis: U.S. Combs Airwaves for bin Laden," UPI, February 21, 2001; also see "U.S. Makes Cyberwar on bin Laden," UPI, February 9, 2001.

48. See the final report of the Joint Inquiry Committee, Appendix, p. 21; cited in Steve Coll, op. cit, p. 413.

49. George Tenet, op. cit., p.121.

50. Lawrence Wright, *The Looming Tower: Al Qaeda and the Road to 9/11*, Alfred A. Knopf, New York, 2006, pp. 277-278.

51. Lisa Myers, "Hindsight and the attacks on America," *NBC News*, July 21, 2004, posted at http://www.msnbc.msn.com/id/5479799/.

52. David Enser, Chris Plante and Peter Bergen, "USS Cole plot began after embassy attacks, investigator says," *CNN News*, December 20, 2002, posted at http://archives.cnn.com/2000/U.S./12/20/terrorism.threat.02/.

53. "U.S. links Yemen clan to Sept. 11 and East Africa attacks," MSNBC, February 14, 2002. archived at http://www.bouwman.com/911/Operation/Yemen/Feb-15.html.

54. *Dallas Star-Telegram*, June 7, 2002; also see *Miami Herald*, June 6, 2002.

55. *Miami Herald*, June 6, 2002.

56. For an excellent discussion of the many cases where the CIA withheld information, see Lawrence Wright, op. cit., chapters 16-20.

57. Ian Henshall, *9/11 Revealed: The New Evidence*, Carroll and Graf, New York, 2007, p. 64.

58. Tenet mentions this in his memoirs, op. cit., p. 137.

59. Alexandra Richard, "The CIA met bin Laden while undergoing treatment at an Amer-

ican Hospital last July in Dubai, *Le Figaro*, October 11, 2001 (translated by Tiphaine Dickson).

60. Steve Coll, op. cit., p. 442, also see note 14, p. 633.

61. Greg Palast and David Pallister, "FBI claims Bin Laden inquiry was frustrated: Officials told to 'back off' on Saudis before September 11," *Guardian* (U.K.), November 7, 2001.

62. The neocon strategy for global U.S. empire was outlined in a 2000 briefing paper, "Rebuilding America's Defenses: Strategy, Forces and Resources For a New Century." It may still be viewed at the Project for a New American Century (PNAC) website: http:// www.newamericancentury.org/publicationsreports.htm.

This enlargement from the above NOAA photograph details the immense devastation and the massive debris pile at Ground Zero.

6

Molten Steel
and Whispering Dust

You will whisper from the dust.
— Isaiah 29:4

Fires raged at Ground Zero for months following the worst "terrorist attack" in U.S. history. Indeed, the fires were not finally extinguished until six days before Christmas 2001, when the New York City fire marshal pronounced the blaze dead.

In the first hours after the attack, the fires hampered the search for survivors. Later, they hindered the cleanup. Joel Meyerowitz, a photographer from New York, documented all of this in his retrospective photo album, *Aftermath,* published in 2006. Armed with his trusty camera, Meyerowitz roamed the WTC ruin in the days and weeks after the attack. Although police ejected him from the site many times, he kept returning and eventually amassed an impressive photographic record of the crews working amidst twisted steel and smoking debris. Meyerowitz writes in his book that the ground was so hot that it melted the workmen's rubber boots.

But he was not the first to report the incredible heat. The earliest accounts of molten steel came from the first-responders. In 2002, Sarah Atlas, a member of New Jersey Task Force One Search and Rescue, was one of these. She told of seeing molten steel in the pile even as she searched in vain for survivors.[1] Another responder explained how he "crawled through an opening and down crumpled stairwells to the subway, five levels below ground," where in the darkness he saw "a distant, pinkish glow: molten metal dripping from a beam."[2] There were many such accounts, too many to dismiss.

Yet, this is exactly what proponents of the official 9/11 narrative have done. It is what they *must* do since the presence of melted steel or iron at Ground Zero cannot be reconciled with the official story, according to which nineteen Islamic extremists hijacked four commercial planes — in the process outsmarting the entire U.S. military establishment — and flew two of them into the World Trade Center and one into the Pentagon. The high-speed impacts and subsequent fires — we are told — fatally weakened the steel-frame twin towers, leading to a global structural failure in each case. The collapse of WTC-7 involved no plane crash and somehow was caused by fire alone, but exactly how has never been explained.

The accounts of molten steel are profoundly subversive to this official story, for reasons that will become clear as we proceed. And it is no wonder that for this reason supporters of the official narrative persistently ignore these eyewitnesses, when not actively trying to discredit them. *Never do they try to account for them.*

Debunkers of "conspiracy theories" frequently remind us that witnesses to a horrific event often give widely varying accounts, and on this basis we are supposed to conclude that the eyewitnesses at Ground Zero did not see what they say they saw. Either the witnesses were not competent to judge, or they were in a state of shock, or maybe they just got it wrong. Such blanket dismissals are often accompanied by a throw-away line, or a wave of the arm, some gesture that makes the testimonials go away as if by magic — along with the molten steel.

Occasionally, we get the *woo-woo* treatment. The critics roll their eyes, a none-too-subtle hint that the firemen or other trained professionals must have been drunk while on duty, or in an altered state, on drugs perhaps, or for whatever reason of unsound mind. Some even insinuate that the stories of molten iron are a colossal hoax, orchestrated perhaps by al Qaeda sympathizers to weaken our national will and divert us from our united purpose, i.e., the war on terror. According to this view, the eyewitnesses are not only wrong, they are traitors.

The problem with all of these arguments is the remarkable unanimity of the witnesses, nearly all of whom agree about what they saw — this and the physical evidence backing them up — which I will present shortly. Incidentally, we are extremely fortunate that physical evidence *did* survive, since the City of New York and the Federal Emergency Management Agency (FEMA) wasted no time removing the steel wreckage from the WTC site. According to a May 2002 Congressional report:

> In the month that lapsed between the terrorist attacks and the deployment of the BPAT team [FEMA's Building Performance

Assessment Team], a significant amount of steel debris — including most of the steel from the upper floors — was removed from the rubble pile, cut into smaller sections, and either melted at the recycling plant or shipped out of the U.S. Some of the critical pieces of steel — including the suspension trusses from the top of the towers and the internal support columns — were gone before the first BPAT team member ever reached the site.[3]

How do we explain this rapid removal of evidence? After a crime, it is standard procedure to cordon off the scene and sequester all evidence until it can be analyzed. Indeed, the removal or destruction of evidence is itself a serious crime. Local and federal authorities should have responded to the worst "terrorist attack" in U.S. history by immediately sealing off Ground Zero, until a team of forensic experts could examine the steel debris and determine the cause of the unprecedented structural failure. Never before, after all, had a steel-frame skyscraper collapsed due to fire, nor have any since. Yet on 9/11, three such "failures" occurred in a single day. From the standpoint of building design and public safety alone, the need for a thorough investigation was obvious.

Such investigations are, in fact, standard procedure after airline crashes and mid-air disasters. After the tragic 1996 crash of TWA Flight 800, which killed 230 passengers, federal agencies spent nearly $50 million raising the remains of the crashed Boeing 747 from the floor of the Atlantic Ocean, cross-examining eyewitnesses, and reconstructing the tragedy. After a massive salvage operation, investigators reportedly recovered 96% of the plane.[4] A similar effort after the Columbia space shuttle disaster spent nearly as much: about $40 million.[5]

Yet, after the worst "terrorist attack" in U.S. history, the preliminary FEMA investigation limped along on a budget of $1 million or less, which was plainly inadequate. FEMA was compelled to rely on volunteers. Three months later, Ron Hamburger, one of FEMA's lead engineers, complained that he still had not seen the blueprints of the collapsed buildings.[6] By then, of course, much of the steel had already been hauled away. Dr. Frederick W. Mowrer, a professor of fire protection engineering at the University of Maryland, told the *New York Times*, "I find the speed with which potentially important evidence has been removed and recycled to be appalling."[7]

In a January 2002 article, "Selling Out the Investigation," in *Fire Engineering Magazine,* editor Bill Manning complained about the destruction of evidence and called FEMA's investigation a "half-baked farce."[8] Manning was no "conspiracy theorist." But he was outraged by legitimate concerns about public safety. Did high-placed individuals order the rapid removal of steel to impede the investigation of the WTC collapse? But why would they do so if 9/11 was the work of foreign terrorists? We still do not know who gave this order. The Mayor's office refused to name the individual, despite written and oral requests from the *Times*.[9]

What is perfectly clear is that the eyewitnesses and the debunkers of "conspiracy theories" cannot both be correct. If the former are telling the truth, then the official story about what happened on 9/11 must be wrong — *very* wrong. The question about who is correct, therefore, is of paramount importance, and at the risk of seeming redundant I am going to present more testimonials, to establish the fact that we are not talking about a few eyewitnesses, but many. I will then review the physical evidence.

The witnesses who reported molten steel included firemen, city officials, contractors, workers, and trained professionals who toured the ruin. One of the latter, Dr. Keith Eaton, Chief Executive of the London-based Institution of Structural Engineers, later wrote in *The Structural Engineer* about what he saw, namely: "molten metal which was still red-hot weeks after the event," as well as "four-inch thick steel plates sheared and bent in the disaster."[10] A similar account came from Leslie E. Robertson, the engineer of record who helped to design the World Trade Center. Robertson's consulting firm Leslie E. Robertson Associates (LERA) worked in the WTC complex for 40 years, and at the time of the tragedy was still under contract to the Port Authority, which administered the WTC. In a keynote address before the Structural Engineers Association of Utah Robertson said, "... as of 21 days after the attack the fires were still burning and molten steel still running."[11]

In a subsequent interview, Robertson retreated from his statement.[12] But one of his own associates, Richard Garlock, was *also* a witness. Garlock, a structural engineer at LERA, was brought in after the WTC collapse to assess the danger to rescue teams who were then scouring the ruin for survivors. Garlock used the architectural plans of the WTC to help responders safely navigate the pile of wreckage. He also personally undertook a number of reconnaissance missions into the ruin. Later, during a PBS special, *America Rebuilds,* Garlock described his experience:

> Going below, it was smoky and really hot. We had rescue teams with meters for oxygen and carbon dioxide. They also had tem-

perature monitors. Here [explaining a photo] WTC 6 is over my head. The debris past the columns was red-hot, molten, running. I did some quick numbers with Gary Panariello, an engineer from Thornton-Tomasetti, to try and determine what the load on WTC-6 was, and how much of the lateral system of the building the contractor could take down. There were a lot of judgment calls ...[13]

Long after the search-and-rescue phase, the heat continued to hinder the cleanup. Another engineer described the conditions faced by work crews:

As rubble is removed from piles, random pockets of steel, glowing brilliant red, are uncovered. Sometimes new fires erupt. Sometimes the steel just glows because there is nothing left nearby to burn. A curious phenomenon, no fuel to burn, but something, heat migrating through the pile, continues to keep the steel at over 1,000° F. When that happens, work stops, equipment pulls back, and the firefighters put thousands of gallons of water on the piles to cool them down. Huge billowing clouds of steam are created, and we wait.[14]

The eyewitness raises an important point. Indeed, what burning fuel caused such intense heat in the wreckage? Although this engineer was unnamed, he was part of a team of health and safety engineers from Bechtel Group Inc. The team was led by Bechtel vice president, Stewart C. Burkhammer, P.E., CSP., who described the conditions at Ground Zero in an article published the following year in a professional journal:

The debris pile at Ground Zero was always tremendously hot. Thermal measurements taken by helicopter each day showed underground temperatures ranging from 400° F to more than 2,800° F. The surface was so hot that standing too long in one spot softened (and even melted) the soles of our safety shoes. Steel toes would often heat up and become intolerable. This heat was also a concern for the search-and-rescue dogs used at the site. Many were not outfitted with protective booties. More than one suffered serious injuries and at least three died while working at Ground Zero.[15]

Later, I will describe the thermal imaging. But, notice, the Bechtel engineer mentions 2,800°F, the melting point of steel. Ron Burger, a public health advisor at the National Center for Environmental Health, Centers for Disease Control and Prevention, also visited Ground Zero. Burger arrived the day after the attack and, after touring the site, compared the ruins to a volcano: "Feeling the heat, seeing the molten steel, the layers upon layers of ash, like lava, it reminded me of Mt. St. Helen's and the thousands who fled that disaster."[16]

Firemen used similar language, likening the site to "a foundry" or a "lava flow."[17] As the cleanup progressed, more evidence accumulated. Numerous witnesses reported seeing red-hot beams being pulled from the pile of wreckage. Sometimes the beams were dripping with molten steel.[18] 9/11 scholar David Ray Griffin compiled several of these eyewitness accounts in his 2007 book *Debunking 9/11 Debunking*, which I recommend to readers.[19]

Public health officials also toured the scene of destruction. One of them, Alison Geyh, Ph.D., an assistant professor of Environmental Health at Johns Hopkins, later wrote, "In some pockets now being uncovered they are finding molten steel."[20]

The witnesses included New York City sanitation workers, who helped with the cleanup by hauling scrap steel from Ground Zero to the Fresh Kills landfill. New York Department of Sanitation spokeswoman Kathy Dawkins explained that the waste "included everything from molten steel beams to human remains."[21]

The molten steel was even reported by Kenneth Holden, City Commissioner of New York, in his testimony before the 9/11 Commission. Holden described the atmosphere at Ground Zero as "surreal." He told the panel that the WTC site "was still so hot that molten metal dripped down the sides of the wall from Building 6."[22] Although Holden's statement is not mentioned in the commission's final report — a conspicuous omission, since he was a city official — it is supported by William Langewiesche, one of the few journalists who managed to gain access to the WTC foundation hole or "bathtub." In a 2003 book about the 9/11 disaster, *American Ground*, Langewiesche writes about "streams of molten metal that leaked from the hot cores and flowed down broken walls inside the foundation hole."[23]

The Molten Pools

As crews removed the mountain of wreckage, they discovered additional evidence: pools of molten metal where the towers had once stood, including at least one large pool at the bottom of the elevator shafts. Some of these pools were not found until three, four, even five weeks after 9/11. Contractors working on site confirmed these discoveries, including Peter Tully, president of Tully Construction of Flushing, New York, who was one of four contractors engaged by New York City to handle the cleanup. During an August 2002 interview Tully told the *American Free Press* that workmen had seen the molten pools.[24]

The same interview included a statement by another contractor, Mark Loizeaux, president of Controlled Demolition, Inc., who, six years before had ramrodded the cleanup of the bombed Murrah Federal Building in Oklahoma City. After September 11 Loizeaux was brought in for the same reason, i.e., to draft a clean-up plan for the WTC site. He told the *American Free Press*, "Yes, hot spots of molten steel were seen in the basements." Molten steel was also found under Building 7.

The reports were confirmed by Herb Trimpe, an Episcopalian minister who served as chaplain at Ground Zero for the American Red Cross. In a subsequent interview, Trimpe explained that he "talked to many contractors and they said they actually saw molten metal trapped, beams had just totally been melted because of the heat."[25] The eyewitnesses included volunteers, such as Guy Lounsbury, a member of the New York Air National Guard's 109th Air Wing, who volunteered at Ground Zero from September 22 to October 6, 2001. Lounsbury later wrote that a fireman told him "there was still molten steel at the heart of the towers."[26] A movie review of the documentary film *Collateral Damage* also cited testimonials by NYC firemen, who reportedly described heat so intense they saw "rivers of molten steel."[27]

Thermal Imagery

The fires were so intense that millions of gallons of water initially sprayed on the smoking ruins by NYC firemen had no effect. Nor did heavy rain on September 14. The pile continued to burn and produced heavy smoke emissions that interfered with the first attempts to study the site from the air. On September 15 mapping experts from Hunter College of NYC brought in a special laser camera (LIDAR) capable of penetrating the smoke, which they used in concert with global positioning to generate the first accurate maps and thermal images of Ground Zero. These maps became an important resource during the rescue and clean-up operations.[28] Thereafter, over-flights continued every two days.

On September 16, 2001 the National Aeronautics and Space Administration surveyed lower Manhattan from the air using an infrared spectrometer (AVIRIS), which confirmed dozens of "hot spots" in the wreckage. This work was done in collaboration with the U.S. Geologic Survey. The hottest spots were in the ruins of WTC 2 and WTC 7, where NASA recorded surface temperatures as high as 747°C (1,376°F).[29] The temperatures under the pile were no doubt *much* hotter — hot enough to evaporate rain and water long before it trickled to the bottom. Amazingly, molten steel was still being reported *two months after* the fires were officially declared out. As late as February 2002, NYC fireman Joe "Toolie" O'Toole reportedly observed a crane operator "lift a steel beam vertically from deep within the catacombs of Ground Zero. It was dripping from the molten steel."[30]

These reports have never been explained. Mark Loizeaux told the *American Free Press* that the continuing fires were fueled by "paper, carpet and other combustibles packed down the elevator shafts by the tower floors as they 'pancaked' into the basement." Manuel Garcia, a physicist, has suggested that cars left in parking garages under the WTC contained gasoline that may have fueled the fires.[31] Loizeaux and Garcia are probably both correct and, no doubt, there were other combustibles in the pile.

But the fact remains that none of these, nor any other fuels that are known to have been present in the World Trade Center, had sufficient potential energy to even approach the melting point of construction grade steel beams (2,800°F). For this reason the observed presence of molten steel or iron under the pile is extraordinary. Indeed, it is anomalous and cannot be reconciled with the official version of events. Surely this is why government officials have assiduously ignored these accounts, when not making vigorous efforts to discredit them.

Official Omissions and Denials

As noted, FEMA conducted the first official investigation of the WTC collapse.[32] In its report, released in May 2002, the agency theorized that the plane impacts and subsequent fires had weakened WTC-1 and 2, leading to their collapse. FEMA concedes, however, that "with the information and time available, the sequence of events leading up to the collapse of each tower could not be definitively determined."[33] The report also considers several possible fire scenarios for the puzzling collapse of WTC-7, a 47-story steel-frame building that was never hit by a plane, yet fell into its footprint at 5:20 P.M. on September 11. FEMA admits that with regard to Building Seven, even "the best hypothesis has a low probability of occurrence."[34] Although the FEMA report makes no mention of molten steel, a scientific paper attached to it as an appendix did mention some important evidence, which I will discuss shortly.

The second official investigation was the *9/11 Commission Report*, released in July 2004. Although the U.S. media often describes it as the definite record, in reality this highly selective report culled or excluded everything that did not agree with the official version of events, including, as noted, the testimony of NYC Commissioner Kenneth Holden, who told the panel he saw molten steel with his own eyes. The 567-page report never once mentions molten steel, nor does it discuss WTC-7. Evidently, the sudden collapse of a 47-story steel-frame skyscraper into its own footprint was not deemed important enough even to mention. These omissions are all the more glaring because the panel's mandate was "to provide the fullest possible account of the events surrounding 9/11."[35] It is also worth mentioning that the commission was made up almost entirely of lawyers and politicians, and as a group was sorely lacking in scientific credentials.

The third official investigation was prepared by the National Institute of Standards and Technology (NIST), an arm of the Bush administration's Department of Commerce.[36] NIST was tasked to pick up the investigation of the WTC collapse where FEMA left off. Three years later, in September 2005, NIST released a forty-three-volume 10,000-page report of its own that managed to avoid altogether the issue of the molten steel.[37] True, NIST did subsequently mention the issue — briefly — in a separate "Frequently Asked Questions" (FAQ) section that was added to the report a year later as a kind of afterthought, evidently for the purpose of making its findings both more accessible and acceptable to the public. This separate addendum dismisses the issue with the following bizarre statement:

> NIST investigators ... found no evidence that would support the melting of steel in a jet-fuel ignited fire in the towers prior to collapse. *The condition of the steel in the wreckage of the WTC towers (i.e., whether it was in a molten state or not) was irrelevant to the investigation of the collapse* since it does not provide any conclusive information on the condition of the steel when the WTC towers were standing [my emphasis].[38]

This statement by NIST dodges the key question. If the "jet-fuel ignited fires" did not melt the steel, *then what did?* Indeed, in that case, how do we explain the many eyewitnesses accounts? After disavowing the molten steel issue as "irrelevant," NIST then makes the following no less bizarre hedge:

> Under certain circumstances *it is conceivable for some of the steel in the wreckage to have melted after the buildings collapsed* [my emphasis]. Any molten steel in the wreckage was more likely due to the high temperature resulting from long exposure to combustion within the pile than to short exposure to fires or explosions while the buildings were standing.[39]

NIST never informs us what the "certain circumstances" that prevailed in the pile might have been. NIST also ignores the accounts of first responders who witnessed molten metal on their arrival at the scene within minutes or hours of the collapse. Obviously, the molten steel they encountered had been produced during or before the collapse — not after. In fact, NIST's above statement that "long exposure to combustion" may have produced pools of molten steel *after* the collapse is hogwash, since no one, including NIST, has identified an energy source in the rubble pile remotely capable of melting steel.

But I will go even further: NIST's statement is an affront to our intelligence, because the residual hot spots identified at the WTC site after 9/11 and the molten pools surely were related. There is no way to avoid the conclusion that both were the result of whatever caused the WTC collapse in the first place. Something on September 11, 2001 burned hot enough to melt steel in the twin towers. But such a deduction was evidently too obvious or too provocative for NIST scientists, who made a decision "not to go there," a decision — I should add — that appears to have been politically motivated. Certainly it had nothing to do with science.

When asked, "What caused the molten pools?" contractor Peter Tully suggested that perhaps jet fuel was responsible.[40] But on this point, at least, the NIST report is correct. It's easy to show that jet fuel was not the causative agent. Jet fuel simply does not burn with sufficient energy to melt steel — not even close. Many of the early reports by the U.S. and world press erred in this respect. In the emotional aftermath of 9/11, the press often mangled the science as badly as the twisted steel beams in the pile at Ground Zero. One report posted by the BBC on September 13, 2001 quoted experts who stated matter-of-factly that the burning jet fuel had melted the WTC's central columns, leading to the collapse.[41] The day after the attack, NewScientist.com asserted that "raging fires melted the supporting steel struts."[42]

That same day, the *Sunday Times* interviewed Hyman Brown, a civil engineering professor at the University of Colorado: "Steel melts," Brown told the *Times*. "90,850 liters of aviation fluid melted the steel. Nothing is designed ... to withstand that fire." Years before, Brown had worked as a project engineer in the construction of the WTC.[43] Incidentally, Brown was wrong about the amount of jet fuel. FEMA determined that the planes were not fully loaded and carried no more than 10,000 gallons, or about 40,000 liters, which was consumed within minutes.[44] Later, NIST agreed.[45]

On September 13, 2001 BBC radio interviewed Chris Wise, an engineer who gave this explanation:

It was the fire that killed the buildings. There's nothing on earth that could survive those temperatures with that amount of fuel burning. The columns would have melted, the floors would have melted, and eventually they would have collapsed one on top of the other.[46]

Elmer Obermeyer, the president of an Ohio engineering firm, also endorsed the meltdown theory in a story in the *Cincinnati Business Courier*. The paper noted that Obermeyer was a "guru in his field."[47] In October 2001 ScientificAmerican.com posted an article summarizing the results of a "9/11 panel" of MIT experts, one of whom, Eduardo Kausel, stated "that the intense heat softened or melted the structural elements — floor trusses and columns—so that they became like chewing gum, and that was enough to trigger the collapse.[48]

This is but a small sampling of the many erroneous reports in the media during those first emotional days. As Frank Gayle, one of the NIST's lead scientists, later pointed out: "Your gut reaction would be [that] the jet fuel is what made the [WTC] fire so very intense. A lot of people figured that's what melted the steel. Indeed, it did not, the steel did not melt."[49]

Gayle was seconded by Thomas Eagar, a professor of materials engineering at MIT:

The fire is the most misunderstood part of the WTC collapse. Even today the media report (and many scientists believe) that the steel melted. It is argued that the jet fuel burns very hot, especially with so much fuel present. This is not true.... The temperatures of the fire at the WTC were not unusual, and it was most definitely not capable of melting steel.[50]

When trained professionals get it wrong, we should not be surprised by the mistakes of journalists and politicians, few of whom are trained in physics. The fact is that jet fuel, which is essentially kerosene, will not burn in air in excess of about 1,832°F (1,000°C) — nowhere near the 2,800°F melting point of steel.[51] Even this 1,832°F upper limit is very difficult to achieve, since, as Thomas Eagar also pointed out, it requires the optimal mixing of fuel with oxygen during combustion, which can only be achieved in a laboratory, or on a stovetop. The clouds of black smoke that poured out of the twin towers on 9/11 were an obvious clue that the WTC fire burned at much lower temperatures, probably around 1,202°F (650°C) range, or even lower. This was due to the inefficient mixing of oxygen: why most building fires burn no hotter than around 932 -1,202°F (500-650°C).

But if the burning jet fuel did not melt the WTC steel beams, then how do we explain the eyewitness accounts? What were those fireman, engineers, workers, contractors and health professionals looking at? Were they all blind or incompetent? No, I think not, because compelling physical evidence supports their testimony — evidence that all three official investigations took pains to ignore. Much of this evidence was literally "in the air" over Manhattan in the days and weeks following September 11, 2001. As we will learn, it also posed serious health risks for local residents and workers involved in the cleanup.

"The Noise Kept Coming and Coming ... "

The plume of dust and smoke that poured out of the WTC on 9/11 was large enough to be visible from space. New Yorkers who were unlucky enough to be near the towers when they came down said it was like being in a tornado. Survivors told how, even as they fled for their lives, they could feel the intense heat behind them. One man who was 100 yards from the South Tower described the harrowing experience: "It was like being hit by hot gravel. The noise kept coming and coming. One second I was running and the next I was flying."[52] The man was lifted off his feet and propelled forward. Many others were thrown to the ground.

The dust consisted of hundreds of thousands of tons of pulverized asbestos, glass, gypsum, concrete and other construction materials, including paint, insulation, flooring, vermiculite, fiberglass, foam, plaster, computers, furniture, masonry, etc. Most of the cloud was comprised of coarser materials that soon deposited on the WTC site and in the surrounding neighborhood. Even so, the cloud was immense, and some of the dust continued to swirl over lower Manhattan until heavy rains cleared the air on September 14-15. Later, workmen stirred it up again when they brought in heavy equipment and started the cleanup. The ubiquitous dust was highly alkaline, with a PH as high as 12 due to the presence of so much cement, the main constituent of both gypsum and concrete. For this reason the dust was also extremely caustic. One expert described its impact on human tissue as "brutal." Others agreed. It was like breathing drano.[53] The coarser particles and asbestos contributed to the "World Trade Center cough" and other chronic ailments that have since afflicted nearly 70% of responders.[54] But the worst dangers were unseen.

The DELTA Group

The pile continued to emit an acrid plume for many weeks. In late September a team of atmospheric scientists from the University of California (Davis), known as the DELTA Group, arrived in New York with state-of-the-art equipment and set up a rooftop station about a mile NNE of Ground Zero. From there they proceeded to monitor the air from early October through late-December 2001.[55] Thomas Cahill, spokesman for the team, later told the press that the color of the plume is what initially drew his attention. Cahill is an emeritus professor of physics and atmospheric sciences at UC Davis. The color was "... all wrong. It was a light blue," he said. "My background is atmospheric physics, and the color of the plume tells me a lot. A light blue plume means very fine particles. Clearly, the pile was still hot and was giving off very fine particles."[56]

The data collected by the DELTA Group confirmed Cahill's early suspicions. The team measured extremely fine particulates down into the submicron (or nano) range that according to Cahill were "probably associated with high temperatures in the underground debris pile."[57] Toxic particles of this size are especially dangerous because they pass into the blood with ease via the lungs. The largest spike occurred in a sample taken in one 45-minute period on October 3rd: a whopping 58 µg (micrograms) of material per cubic meter, including transition metals, sulfuric acid, silica, i.e., glass, and many kinds of organic chemicals, some of which had never before been detected in the atmosphere. Many of the chemicals were known carcinogens. Although Cahill had spent the better part of a career testing air samples from pollution events around the world, he had never seen anything like this. "Even on the worst air days in Beijing," he said, "downwind from coal-fired power plants, or in the Kuwaiti oil fires, we did not see these levels of very fine particulates." Some of the metals in their fine-mode particle form, such as vanadium, turned up in the highest concentrations ever recorded in the United States.[58]

A Health Disaster in New York

Unfortunately, the impending health disaster in New York City immediately collided with politics. The Bush administration was determined to reopen Wall Street at the earliest possible date, and this, of course, meant that someone had to give the "all clear" in lower Manhattan.[59] As it happened, this unsavory political chore fell to Bush-appointee John L. Henshaw, Assistant Secretary of Labor for OSHA, who on September 16, 2001 dutifully stepped up to a microphone and announced that the air was safe to breathe. Said Henshaw, "Our tests show that it is safe for New Yorkers to go back to work in New York's financial district."[60] EPA Director Christie Todd Whitman made similar reassuring statements.

There was no reason for reassurance. In fact, the data gathered by Thomas Cahill's DELTA team showed that the air was most definitely *not* safe to breathe, especially in the vicinity of Ground Zero, and downwind. "By January," Cahill later told a reporter at UC Davis, "we had some numbers that were really scary."[61] He warned that the WTC cough and other acute respiratory problems then plaguing thousands of 9/11 responders was just the beginning. Cahill predicted many other health problems down the road, such as ischemic heart disease. According to Cahill, when very fine particulates of glass and metal enter the blood through the lungs, they can travel to the heart, where they build up and later cause swelling and weaken the heart muscle. Sufferers eventually die from cardiac arrest. "Almost surely," said Cahill, "in five to ten years we'll start to see heart attacks. People in their 40s."

As a result of the EPA's false assurances, precautionary measures at Ground Zero were lax: Less than a third of the clean-up workers bothered to wear face masks.[62] Yet, the DELTA Group's data indicated that "no one should have been allowed in without a double-canister respirator."[63] Cahill expressed outrage at the level of EPA incompetence, and charged that the Bush administration was responsible. When the EPA showed no interest in the DELTA Group's findings, the team released its data independently at a February 11, 2002 press conference. Two weeks later, Cahill was summoned to testify at a hearing in Washington, where he again contradicted the EPA.

His testimony on this occasion helped spark an internal EPA investigation, which culminated in an August 2003 report by EPA Inspector General Nikki Tinsley, the agency's in-house watchdog. Tinsley's report was stunning even by beltway standards. Tinsley conceded that the EPA had *no scientific basis* for issuing the "all clear" five days after the September 11 attack. The inspector also acknowledged that political interference had hobbled the EPA's response.[64] Tinsley revealed that the White House had instructed EPA Director Whitman to clear all EPA press releases with Bush's National Security Council, which then ordered the EPA to insert phony assurances and omit clearly-worded warnings.

The political fallout from this bombshell has yet to subside. In February 2006, U.S. district judge Deborah Batts allowed a class-action lawsuit against the EPA to proceed. The suit had been filed by attorneys for the victims.[65] The judge also blasted the Bush administration for negligence that could ultimately cost thousands of additional lives. Other suits against the city of New York on behalf of 8,000 recovery workers were also moving through the courts. By November 2006 at least 400 WTC responders had already been diagnosed with various cancers due to exposure to the deadly plume.[66]

In September 2003 Dr. Cahill presented a detailed paper of the DELTA Group's findings at a special symposium about 9/11 organized by the American Chemical Society.[67] Once again, Cahill contradicted the EPA's claims about air quality in a strongly-worded press statement that was widely reported in the U.S. media. "Two days later," Cahill said, "I heard from two independent sources that that press release ended up on George Bush's desk with a little yellow sticky note on it saying, 'Look what UC is doing to us.'"[68]

The Physical Evidence

When I reached Dr. Cahill by telephone early in 2007, he indicated that his team did not know about the molten steel at Ground Zero. Nonetheless, Cahill and the DELTA Group mention the high temperatures in a thorough summary of their research published in 2004. The article states that "infrared surveys showed surface temperatures in the collapse pile were as high as 30 K above ambient in October, and *much higher subsurface temperatures were inferred from the lower portions of removed steel beams glowing red*" [my emphasis].[69]

A crane lifts yellow-hot steel from the WTC ruin.

In fact, there is compelling evidence that some of the steel removed from the WTC ruin was much hotter than cherry-red. Color is an accurate gauge of temperature, and at least one photo taken during the WTC cleanup shows a forked claw-lift removing a piece of light-yellow steel, indicating a temperature of at least 1,900°F (1,038°C).[70] (Observe the bottom edge of the steel in the back cover photo.) From the color-temperature chart it is obvious that this steel is considerably hotter than cherry-red steel, which has a temperature of only about 1,450°F. Notice that the yellow-colored steel in the photo is also approximately 680°F hotter than molten aluminum.

The photo strongly supports the eyewitness accounts, because if molten steel were present, one would expect to find temperatures in the light-yellow heat range. Indeed, the confirmed temperature of 1,900°F is anomalous in and of itself, because this is well above the uppermost combustion temperature of jet fuel, or for that matter any other fuel known to have been present in the WTC. And, remember, this assumes the most favorable conditions for combustion, which certainly did not exist on September 11, 2001, nor afterward in the rubble pile. At very least, the photo is powerful evidence for an extreme energy source, as yet unidentified.

There is also compelling video evidence that steel did melt. Several remarkable videos of the South Tower, filmed just moments before it collapsed, show a large quantity of a bright white-yellow-orange liquid streaming out of the north side of the building on the 80th floor. The liquid is undoubtedly a molten metal of some kind.

Chart showing correlation of color and temperature.		
	F°	C°
Lead (Pb) Melts	621	327
Faint Red	930	500
Blood Red	1075	580
Aluminum (Al) Melts	1221	660
Medium Cherry	1275	690
Cherry	1375	745
Bright Cherry	1450	790
Salmon	1550	845
Dark Orange	1630	890
Orange	1725	940
Lemon	1830	1000
Light Yellow	1975	1080
White	2200	1205
Structural Steel Melts	≈2750	≈1510
Iron (Fe) Melts	2800	1538
Thermite (typical)	>4500	>2500

Source: Journalof911Studies.com

NIST downplayed this controversial event, concluding that the liquid was probably molten aluminum, possibly from United Flight 175, parts of which are believed to have come to rest in the northeast corner of the building, one or two floors above where the molten liquid was seen.[71] In fact, it is likely that some of the aluminum *did* melt, because the fires in the South Tower probably reached or exceeded the relatively low melting point of aluminum (1,220°F, or 660°C).

Nonetheless, in 2006 Dr. Steven E. Jones, then a professor of physics at Brigham Young University, challenged NIST's assertion that the liquid seen in the video was aluminum.[72] Jones pointed out that molten aluminum is characteristically silver in color, not yellow. While it is true that molten aluminum will begin to incandesce, i.e., to glow yellow, if additional heat is applied and its temperature is raised to 1,832°F (1,000°C), for all practical purposes this can only be achieved in a laboratory, because as soon as aluminum melts, it begins to flow. For this reason a container is required to raise the temperature of liquid aluminum beyond the melting point, and surely there was no such container on 9/11. On melting, the

145

aluminum would simply have flowed away from the heat source. Moreover, as Jones also pointed out, unlike iron, aluminum has low emissivity and high reflectivity, meaning that even when heated to an incandescent temperature (≈1,832°F) in a laboratory, it glows only faintly yellow — not brightly as in the photo.

NIST attempted to get around these problems by arguing that the molten aluminum was "very likely mixed with large amounts of hot, partially burned, solid organic materials (e.g., furniture, carpets, partitions and computers) which can display an orange glow, much like logs burning in a fireplace."[73] But NIST produced no empirical data to back up its claim. Evidently, NIST conducted no experiments on this, despite a $15 million research budget. The unsubstantiated claim aroused the curiosity of Dr. Jones, who together with several colleagues decided to test NIST's conclusion experimentally by adding these same organic materials to molten aluminum. When they did this in a labora-

Molten metal pours from the 80th floor of the South Tower minutes before it collapsed.

tory, however, they found no change in the silver color.[74] The organic materials did not readily mix with the aluminum, nor did the combination produce a bright orange or yellow color. Jones concluded that the metallic liquid seen flowing out of the South Tower on 9/11 was probably molten iron which had originated from the WTC steel. In his view, the evidence pointed to the use of a high temperature explosive such as thermite.

It is curious in this regard that when cleanup crews reached the bottom of the WTC pit, they made a surprising discovery, and one that supports Jones. The crews found large irregular masses of solidified slag. The lumps resembled meteorites and were in fact conglomerates of fused iron and other metals, with extruding pieces of pipe, steel and embedded chunks of concrete — further evidence that something had melted steel.

"The Deepest Mystery"

More evidence of an extreme energy source came to light during a preliminary metallurgical analysis of two steel samples recovered from the WTC ruin. One sample was from WTC 7, another from WTC 1. This work was performed by Jonathan Barnett and two other materials scientists from Worcester Polytechnic Institute. As noted earlier, this paper was included as an appendix to the FEMA report.[75] The scientists discovered that something had eroded one-inch thick flanges to half of their original thickness. Strangely, the edges of the steel were wafer-thin and curled up like a paper scroll. The samples showed "evidence of a severe high temperature corrosion attack upon the steel, including oxidation and sulfidation, with subsequent inter-granular melting."[76] The steel plate had been perforated and resembled Swiss cheese — the scientists actually used this metaphor. They concluded that at temperatures of about 1,800°F, "a liquid eutectic mixture containing iron, oxygen, and sulfur formed during this hot corrosion attack upon the steel." Notice, this temperature is far below the melting point of iron.

The scientists were in fact describing a well-known physical phenomenon: a eutectic mixture, in which the presence of one element (here, sulfur), has the effect of significantly lowering the melting point of another (in this case, iron). Barnett and his colleagues were shocked and baffled by the evidence, which they described as "very unusual." Notably, they could not explain how elemental sulfur and iron came to be mixed. This was a puzzler because structural steel has almost no sulfur content. The scientists acknowledged the possibility that "the phenomenon started prior to collapse and accelerated the weakening of the steel structure." Even as other FEMA experts explored a number of fire-induced collapse scenarios for WTC-7, Barnett told the *New York Times* that the explanations being considered "... would not explain steel members in the debris pile that appear to have been partly evaporated in extraordinarily high temperatures." The *Times* called the findings "perhaps the deepest mystery uncovered in the investigation."[77]

The Iron-Rich Spheres

In a stunning development, new evidence emerged in 2007 that may explain all of the above phenomena and could be the smoking gun from the collapsed World Trade Center. Dr. Steven Jones, whom I've already introduced, presented this new evidence in June during a riveting lecture and slide show at a 9/11 truth conference in Vancouver, Canada.[78] The evidence emerged in the course of studying the WTC dust, a sample of which Jones obtained from Janette MacKinlay, a New York City resident at the time of the 9/11 attack. MacKinlay's fourth floor apartment, located at 113 Cedar St. in Manhattan, was about 100 meters from the South Tower. She was away on September 11. However, when MacKinlay returned home a week later, she found her apartment filled with dust from the WTC. During the collapse it had flooded in through broken windows. MacKinlay preserved some of this dust in a plastic bag and, much later, sent the sample to Dr. Jones when she learned about his research. Jones also obtained a second dust sample from a Ph.D. scientist, who collected it from an interior window sill inside the Potter Building, located at 38 Park Row. This is about four blocks from Ground Zero. The sample was collected on September 14, 2001, just three days after the attack, as rescue operations were still underway, and before any major steel-cutting operations had begun.[79]

These samples were a lucky break, as they allowed Jones to study unaltered evidence from the WTC collapse. Jones soon discovered that the dust in both was rich in tiny metallic particles, which he extracted for laboratory analysis from the bulk sample using a simple magnet. When he studied the metallic particles, first under an optical microscope, then using an electron microscope, he found the same micro spheres previously reported in other studies of the WTC dust, including one by the U.S. Geological Survey (USGS).[80] The spheres ranged in size from 1 micron to 1.5 mm.

When Jones analyzed the metallic spheres using X-ray energy dispersive spectroscopy, he confirmed the USGS finding that the spheres were mostly iron, the primary constituent of steel. Some of the spheres were hollow, and their shape was clearly the result of surface tension, indicating that the iron had been in a molten state. But what energy source was responsible? As I have noted, the melting point of iron is 2,800°F, far above the highest combustion temperature of jet fuel or any other fuel present in the WTC.

Iron-rich sphere

Source: USGS Particle Atlas of WTC Dust

Further analysis revealed the likely answer. The same spectrograph also confirmed the presence of sulfur, aluminum, and copper, which Jones immediately recognized as significant, because this combination of elements happens to be the signature residue of thermate, a well-known high temperature explosive originally developed by the U.S. military. Thermate is an analogue of thermite, the use of which Jones had already suspected.

Here, finally, was hard evidence in the form of residues. Thermate differs from its cousin thermite in that it contains elemental sulfur, which has the effect of greatly lowering the melting point of iron to about 1,724°F (940°C). Thermite is occasionally used in demolition work to cut heavy steel beams, which it does very efficiently. Sulfur is sometimes added to speed up the reaction. The formula for thermate is relatively simple: fine aluminum powder is mixed with metal oxides (e.g., iron oxide and copper oxide) and elemental sulfur. Ignition triggers a violent reaction that reaches temperatures of 4,500°F, producing aluminum oxide (a white smoke) and large amounts of molten iron laced with sulfur.[81]

For a control, Jones staged a small-scale laboratory test, in which he used thermate to cut a steel bar neatly in two. The reaction produced a shower of sparks, another characteristic of this high-temperature explosive. The sparks were, in fact, tiny droplets of iron that condensed and hardened into tiny spherules, which Jones then gathered up for comparative analysis. When he studied them with an electron microscope, he found they were identical to those in the WTC dust. The resulting spectrograph was also a near-perfect match, showing the characteristic peaks in the same relative abundance. The chemical formula for thermate is somewhat variable, for which reason Jones had to estimate the relative proportions of the ingredients. Nonetheless, the match was very close.

In a separate study, Jones also analyzed a sample taken from the interior of a lump of slag pulled from the bottom of the WTC bathtub (the foundation hole). Here, again, he confirmed the presence of elemental sulfur. The use of thermate would explain the sulfur residues in the slag, and on the steel flange, cited earlier, as well as the erosion of the steel described by the scientists from Worcester Polytechnic. The use of thermate would also explain why various photos and videos of the WTC collapse show thick white smoke trailing from steel beams. The white smoke seen in the photos may well have been aluminum oxide. The use of thermate would also easily account for the yellow-orange molten metal seen pouring out of the South Tower moments before it collapsed.[82] As I've noted, a eutectic mix including sulfur could explain why the iron remained in a molten state, even though well below the melting point indicated by the color-temperature chart. Use of thermate could even account for another 9/11 mystery which has never been explained, namely, the extensive corrosive effects observed on many automobiles parked in the vicinity of the WTC. The corrosion was especially pronounced on the car roofs. In many cases the interiors were unaffected.[83] Obviously, whatever caused the corrosion showered down upon the cars from above.

For sake of comparison, Jones also analyzed a dust sample from the Stardust Hotel in Las Vegas, which was professionally demolished on March 13, 2007 using C-4, a different type of high-temperature explosive. The sample was gathered by 9/11 truth activists who were present to witness the destruction of the famous hotel. When analyzed, the Stardust sample was likewise found to contain iron-rich spheres. However, there were no residues of sulfur or aluminum, both of which are diagnostic for thermate. While the constituents of aluminothermic (i.e., thermite) explosives can vary — a number of different metal oxides can be used, including zinc oxide, zinc nitrate, potassium permanganate, and barium nitrate — nonetheless, according to Jones, the use of X-ray spectroscopy allows the metallic ingredients and elemental sulfur to be identified with considerable accuracy. Jones emphasizes that for this reason "the presence of the aluminothermic reaction signature is quite unambiguous."[84] As we are about to discover, his findings do not stand alone.

Corroborating Evidence

In April 2002, lawyers representing Deutsche Bank retained the R.J. Lee Group, a private consulting firm, to oversee several studies of the effects of 9/11 on the Bankers Trust Building in lower Manhattan. Located at 130 Liberty Street, across the street from WTC 2, the building suffered considerable damage on 9/11 as well as toxic contamination. After hiring an engineering firm to assess the structural damage, Deutsche Bank brought in the R.J. Lee Group to determine whether an environmental cleanup of the building was even feasible. The result was the most extensive microscopic investigation of WTC dust yet performed. All told, R.J. Lee scientists examined some 400,000 dust particles.[85]

In its December 2003 report, R.J. Lee noted that the WTC dust was very different from the background dust normally found in office buildings. The WTC dust possessed "a unique set of characteristics," which R.J. Lee thoroughly documented and catalogued. The particles of asbestos, plastic, gypsum, metal, and glass showed abundant evidence of having been formed in the presence of high temperatures. Some of the particles were vesicular in shape, with "a round open porous structure" and a "Swiss cheese appearance as a result of boiling and evaporation,"[86] language reminiscent of the Worcester Polytechnic paper. R.J. Lee also found that "various metals (most notably iron and lead) were melted during the WTC event, producing spherical metallic particles."[87] These included the same iron-rich spheres first identified by the USGS, and later by Jones. R.J. Lee's spectrographs of the hardened droplets (using the X-ray dispersive method) were also identical, and confirm the presence of the same elements found by Jones.[88] R.J. Lee attributed all of the heat-altered characteristics to the WTC conflagration.

R.J. Lee also found an abundance of mineral wool fibers in the dust, which is not surprising since mineral wool is a common insulation material and was used extensively in the WTC. The wool fibers had also been heat-altered, but one finding was of paramount interest. Amazingly, many of the fibers had a thin coating of lead-oxide, which indicated that the lead not only melted, but had been volatized. In short, the lead had reached the boiling point, i.e., 3,180°F (1,749°C) before vaporizing, after which it had condensed onto the surface of the wool fibers. Once again, R.J. Lee attributed these most unusual effects to the heat of the WTC conflagration.

Dr. Jones reviewed all of these findings in his June 2007 presentation, but took strong issue with R.J. Lee's conclusion that the WTC fire had produced the iron-rich spheres and the lead-coated fibers.[89] This was clearly impossible, because, as noted, office fires do not reach temperatures sufficient to melt iron, and come no where near the much higher boiling point of lead (3,180°F or 1,749°C). The NIST report admits that the WTC fires never exceeded 1,800°F (1,000°C),[90] which is far far below either of these temperatures. Here, then, was more compelling evidence for an extreme energy source on 9/11. As noted, thermate reaches temperatures of 4,500°F, easily hot enough to account for all of these effects.

In a separate line of research, Jones and his colleagues obtained unpublished spectrographic data from the USGS WTC dust study by means of a Freedom of Information Act request — and promptly made another important discovery. The unpublished data showed that the USGS had also found a tiny molybdenum-rich spherule, which had not previously been reported. This was extremely significant because molybdenum is a very hard metal, with an extremely high melting point: 4,753°F (2,623°C). The presence of this spherule indicates that something melted molybdenum on 9/11. Yet, how was this possible, since jet fuel and the other known combustibles in the WTC burn nowhere near this temperature? Here was yet more evidence for an extreme energy source.[91]

In his Vancouver lecture Dr. Jones made a final telling point: After crimes involving fires and explosions, it is standard forensic procedure to test for residues of high-temperature explosives.[92] Obviously, such tests should have been conducted after 9/11, which involved not only a major fire, but the most serious "terrorist attack" in U.S. history. Not only were there many eyewitness accounts of explosions (which I will discuss in the next chapter), in addition, as noted, one preliminary study by Jonathan Barnett and colleagues had *already* reported the erosion of steel and the presence of sulfur, both of which are most unusual and point to the likely use of explosives. Their findings were suspicious and, at very least, called for further research. Yet, by its own admission, NIST took a pass and failed to look for residues.[93] The agency attempted to justify its decision to skip this important follow-up work by claiming that the use of thermate to demolish the WTC was implausible, since many thousands of pounds of the high-temperature explosive would have been required — a claim sharply disputed by Dr. Jones, who estimates that around 1,000 pounds of thermate would have sufficed to demolish each tower.[94]

NIST's failure to test the WTC steel for residues of explosives was a grave omission, and one that undermines its conclusion that the WTC collapse was a global structural failure induced by the jet impacts and subsequent fires. The above evidence points to a very different conclusion, one with extremely serious implications for our nation. Perhaps this is why hundreds of professional architects and engineers have already signed a petition calling for a new and genuine investigation of the WTC collapse on 9/11.[95]

Endnotes

1. *Penn Arts and Sciences*, Summer 2002. Posted at www.sas.upenn.edu/sasalum/newsltr/summer2002/k911.html.

2. Marci McDonald, "Memories: They came to help at Ground Zero. What they experienced they can't forget," *U.S. News and World Report*, posted at http://www.usnews.com/usnews/9_11/articles/911memories.htm.

3. The Investigation of the World Trade Center Collapse: Findings, Recommendations, and Next Steps, Hearing Before the Committee on Science, House of Representatives, One Hundred Seventh Congress, Second Session, May 1, 2002, Serial No. 107–61, Hon. Sherwood L. Boehlert, New York, Chairman, posted at http://commdocs.house.gov/committees/science/≠hsy78961.000/hsy78961_0f.htm.

4. Max Ruston, correspondent report 2-222881, TWA investigation, New York, November 18, 1997.

5. Thomas H. Kean and Lee H. Hamilton, *Without Precedent: The Inside Story of the 9/11 Commission*, Alfred A. Knopf, New York, 2006, p. 45.

6. James Glanz and Eric Lipton, "A Nation Challenged: The Towers; Experts Urging Broader Inquiry in Towers' Fall," *New York Times*, December 25, 2001.

7. Ibid.

8. Bill Manning, "Selling Out the Investigation," *Fire Engineering*, January, 2002, posted at http://www.fireengineering.com/articles/article_display.html?id=131225.

9. James Glanz and Eric Lipton, "Experts Urging Broader Inquiry in Towers' Fall," *New York Times*, December 25, 2001.

10. Dr. Keith Eaton, *The Structural Engineer 3*, September 2002, #6.

11. James Williams, "WTC a Structural Success," *SEAU NEWS, The Newsletter of the Structural Engineers Association of Utah*, October 2001, #3.

12. The interview was part of a live debate with physicist Steven Jones, which aired on KGNU Radio, Denver, Colorado, on October 26, 2006. For the transcript visit "Jones v. Robertson," annotated by Gregg Roberts, posted at http://www.journalof911studies.

com/volume/200704/Roberts_AnnotatedJones-RobertsonTranscript.pdf.

13. Garlock's testimony from the PBS show is posted at http://www.pbs.org/americarebuilds/engineering/engineering_debris_06.html. For a profile about Garlock go to http://www.pbs.org/americarebuilds/profiles/profiles_garlock.html.

14. The account, dated October 21, 2001, is that of an unnamed Bechtel engineer. For links to the full article go to http://nielsenhayden.com/electrolite/archives/earchive_2001_10.html.

15. Jeffrey W. Vincoli, Norman H. Black, and Stewart C. Burkhammer, "Disaster Response: SH&E [Safety, Health and Environmental professionals] at Ground Zero. A firsthand account from the most dangerous workplace in the U.S.," *Professional Safety: Journal of the American Society of Safety Engineers*, May 2002, p. 21.

16. Francesco Lyman, "Messages in the Dust: What Are the Lessons of the Environmental Heath Response to the Terrorist Attacks of September 11?" The National Environmental Health Association, September 2003, posted at http://www.neha.org/9-11%20report/index-The.html.

17. At http://video.google.com/videoplay?docid=3060923273573302287&sourceid=docidfeed&hl=en.

18. Trudy Walsh, "Handheld Application Eased Recovery Tasks," Government Computer News, posted at http://www.gcn.com/print/21_27a/19930-1.html?topic=news.

19. David Ray Griffin, *Debunking 9/11 Debunking*, Olive Branch Press, Northampton, MA, 2007, p. 182.

20. *Magazine of Johns Hopkins Public Health*, Late Fall 2001. When I contacted Dr. Geyh, she confirmed the report. She stated that people involved in the clean-up effort told her they had seen molten steel in the debris.

21. Tom R. Arterburn, "D-Day: NY Sanitation workers' Challenge of a Lifetime." *Waste Age*, April 1, 2002, posted at http://wasteage.com/mag/waste_dday_ny_sanitation/.

22. Commissioner Holden's testimony before the 911 Commission is posted at http://www.globalsecurity.org/security/library/congress/9-11_commission/030401-holden.htm.

23. William Langewiesche, *American Ground: Unbuilding the World Trade Center*, North Point Press, 2003, p. 32.

24. Christopher Bollyn, "Seismic Evidence Points to Underground Explosions Causing WTC Collapse" *American Free Press*, August 28, 2002. http://www.serendipity.li/wot/bollyn2.htm.

25. Herb Trimpe, "A Day In September: The Chaplain's Tale," posted at http://archive.recordonline.com/adayinseptember/trimpe.htm ; also see Trimpe's book *The Power of Angels: Reflections from a Ground Zero Chaplain*, Big Apple Vision Publishing, 2006.

26. Guy Lounsbury, "Serving on Sacred Ground," *National Guard*, December 2001. Posted at http://findarticles.com/p/articles/mi_qa3731/is_200112/ai_n9015802.

27. "Unflinching Look Among the Ruins," *New York Post*, March 3, 2004.

28. LIDAR stands for Light Detection and Ranging. Maddalena Romano, "Mapping Ground Zero," *Geo News*, Hunter College, Department of Geography, City University of New York, Vol. 15, number 1, October 2001, pp. 1-5.

29. The results are posted at http://pubs.usgs.gov/of/2001/ofr-01-0429/thermal.r09.html.

30. Jennifer Lin, "Recovery Worker Reflects on Months Spent at Ground Zero," Knight-Ridder Newspapers, May 29, 2002.

31. Manuel Garcia, "The Thermodynamics of 9/11," *Counterpunch*, November 28, 2006. posted at http://www.counterpunch.org/thermo11282006.html.

32. FEMA's *World Trade Center Building Performance Study* is posted at http://www.fema. gov/rebuild/mat/wtcstudy.shtm.

33. Executive Summary, *World Trade Center Building Performance Study: Data Collection, Preliminary Observations, and Recommendations*, FEMA 403/May 2002, p. 2.

34. *World Trade Center Building Performance Study*, Chapter Five, WTC 7, p. 31.

35. *The 9/11 Commission Report, Final Report of the National Commission on Terrorist Attacks Upon the United States*, W.W.Norton & Co., New York, 2004, p. xvi.

36. At http://wtc.nist.gov/pubs/.

37. Ibid.

38. See question 13 at http://wtc.nist.gov/pubs/factsheets/faqs_8_2006.htm.

39. Ibid.

40. It is interesting that Lee Hamilton, co-chair of the 9/11 Commission, made a similar statement during a 2006 interview on Canadian television. When CBC host Evan Solomon asked Hamilton about Building 7, the co-chair prefaced his answer with a comment about the twin towers. According to Hamilton, the commission concluded that "the super-heated jet fuel melted the steel super-structure of these buildings and caused their collapse." Hamilton's statement revealed his ignorance not only of physics but also of the NIST report. 9/11: Truth, Lies and Conspiracy, Interview: Lee Hamilton, *CBC News Sunday*, August 21, 2006, posted at http://www.cbc.ca/sunday/911hamilton.html.

41. Sheila Barter, "How the World Trade Center Fell", BBC, September 13, 2001, http://news.bbc.co.uk/2/hi/americas/1540044.stm.

42. See http://www.newscientist.com/article.ns?id=dn1281.

43. "Kamikaze attackers may have known twin sisters' weak spot," Sundaytimes.com, posted at http://911research.wtc7.net/cache/disinfo/collapse/sundaytimes_kamikaze. html.

44. World Trade Center Building Performance Study: Data Collection, Preliminary Observations, ad Recommendations, FEMA 403/May 2002, Chapter Two: WTC 1 and WTC 2, p. 15.

45. NIST NCSTAR 1-5, Technology Administration, U.S. Department of Commerce p.180.

46. At http://news.bbc.co.uk/1/hi/england/1604348.stm.

47. "Carew Tower couldn't tolerate similar strike", *Business Courier*, September 14, 2001. http://www.bizjournals.com/cincinnati/stories/2001/09/17/story6.html.

48. Steven Ashley, "When the Twin Towers Fell", October 09, 2001, originally posted at www.ScientificAmerican.com. See the annotated version posted at http://911research. wtc7.net/disinfo/experts/articles/sciam01/sci_am1.html.

49. Andy Field, "A Look Inside a Radical New Theory of the WTC Collapse," *Fire/Rescue News*, February 7, 2004.

50. T.W. Eagar and C. Musso, "Why Did the WTC Collapse? Science, Engineering and Speculation," *Journal of the Minerals, Metals and Materials Society*, 53/12 (2001): 8-11. This paper is also posted at http://www.tms.org/pubs/journals/JOM/0112/Eagar/Eagar-0112.html.

51. Ibid.

52. See the film *911 Mysteries*, available at 911Mysteries.com.

53. Anthony DePalma, "Illness Persisting in 9/11 Workers, Big Study Finds," *New York Times*, September 6, 2006.

54. Robin Herbert, et al., "The World Trade Center Disaster and the Health of Workers: Five-Year Assessment of a Unique Medical Screening Program, *Environmental Health Perspectives*, Vol. 114, No. 12, December 2006.

55. DELTA stands for: Detection and Evaluation of the Long Range Transport of Aerosols.

56. Louisa Dalton, "Chemical Analysis of a Disaster: Scientists struggle to understand the complex mixture of aerosols released during and after the destruction of the World Trade Center," *Chemical and Engineering News*, October 20, 2003, posted at http://pubs.acs.org/cen/NCW/8142aerosols.html.

57. "Trade Center Debris Pile Was a Chemical Factory, Says New Study," September 10, 2003, posted at http://delta.ucdavis.edu/WTC.htm.

58. "Science briefs, Trade Center air laden with very fine particles, DELTA scientists find", *California Agriculture*, May-June 2002, posted at http://calag.ucop.edu/0203MJ/briefs.html.

59. Richard A. Clark, *Against All Enemies*, Free Press, New York, 2004, p.25.

60. EPA Response to 9/11, Press release: September 16, 2001, "EPA, OSHA Update Asbestos Data, Continue to Reassure Public about Contamination Fears," posted at http://www.epa.gov/wtc/stories/headline_091601.htm.

61. Mike Sintelos, "Air Crusader," *UC Davis Magazine On Line*, Vol. 24, Number 2, Winter 2007, posted at http://ucdavismagazine.ucdavis.edu/issues/win07/air_crusader.html.

62. Christopher Bollyn, "Depleted Uranium Released During Canadian Plane Crash: Little-Known Use of DU in Commercial Jets Exposed," *American Free Press*, October 22, 2004, posted at http://www.americanfreepress.net/html/depleted_uranium.html.

63. Ibid.

64. Inspector General Nikki Tinsley, the EPA's own watchdog, reported that the White House changed EPA press releases to "add reassuring statements and delete cautionary ones." "EPA-Gate: How BushMan LIED to New Yorkers," posted at http://archive.democrats.com/preview.cfm?term=September%2011%20Cleanup.

65. Jeff McKay, "Judge Says Government Misled Public on 9/11 Air Quality," CNSNews.com, February 6, 2006.

66. Kristen Lombardi, "Death by Dust: The frightening link between the 9/11 toxic cloud and cancer," *Village Voice*, November 28, 2006.

67. Thomas A. Cahill, et al., "Very Fine Aerosols from the World Trade Center Collapse Piles: Anaerobic Incineration?" American Chemical Society Meeting, New York, September 7-12, 2003.

68. Mike Sintelos, op. cit.

69. Thomas A. Cahill, et al., "Analysis of Aerosols from the World Trade Center Collapse Site, New York, October 2 to October 30, 2001," *Aerosol Science and Technology*, 38:2, pp. 165-183.

70. This photo was reportedly taken on September 27, 2001 by Frank Silecchia. Steven

Jones, "Why indeed did the WTC buildings completely collapse?" *Journal of 9/11 Studies*, September 2006, posted at http://www.journalof911studies.com.

71. National Institute of Standards and Technology (NIST) Federal Building and Fire Safety Investigation of the World Trade Center Disaster, Answers to Frequently Asked Questions. See question #11. Posted at http://wtc.nist.gov/pubs/factsheets/faqs_8_2006.htm.

72. Steven Jones, "Why indeed did the WTC buildings completely collapse?" *Journal of 9/11 Studies*, September 2006, posted at http://www.journalof911studies.com.

73. Ibid.

74. Ibid.

75. Jonathan Barnett, Ronald R. Biederman and R.D. Sisson, Jr., "Appendix C: Limited Metallurgical Examination," World Trade Center Building Performance Study, FEMA 403/May 2002.

76. Ibid.

77. James Glanz and Eric Lipton, "A Search for Clues in the Towers' Collapse," *New York Times*, September 2,2004.

78. Dr. Steven E. Jones, "Revisiting 9/11/2001: Applying the Scientific Method," *Journal of 9/11 Studies*, Vol. 11, May 2007, posted at http://www.journalof911studies.com/. To acquire a video of his June 2007 presentation in Vancouver, go to http://www.vancouver911truth.com/.

79. Dr. Steven E. Jones, et al., "Extremely high temperatures during the World Trade Center destruction," *Journal of 9/11 Studies*, January, 2008, posted at http://www.journalof911studies.com/articles/WTCHighTemp2.pdf.

80. Particle Atlas of World Trade Center Dust by Heather A. Lowers and Gregory P. Meeker, USDI, USGS, posted athttp://pubs.usgs.gov/of/2005/1165/508OF05-1165.html#heading08.

81. Dr. Steven E. Jones, "Revisiting 9/11/2001: Applying the Scientific Method," loc. cit.

82. Ibid.

83. Ibid.

84. Ibid.

85. Damage Assessment: 130 Liberty Street Property. WTC Dust Signature Report: Composition and Morphology, December 2003. Posted at http://www.nyenvirolaw.org/WTC/130%20Liberty%20Street/Mike%20Davis%20LMDC%20130%20Liberty%20Documents/Signature%20of%20WTC%20dust/WTC%20Dust%20Signature.Composition%20and%20Morphology.Final.pdf.

86. Ibid., p. 18.

87. Ibid., p. 17.

88. For a comparative look at the spectrographs from both studies see Dr. Steven E. Jones, et al., "Extremely high temperatures during the World Trade Center destruction," loc. cit.

89. Dr. Steven E. Jones, "Revisiting 9/11/2001: Applying the Scientific Method," loc. cit.

90. NIST NCSTAR 1 (Full Summary), Figure 6-36.

91. Dr. Steven E. Jones, et al., "Extremely high temperatures during the World Trade Center destruction," loc. cit.

92. Dr. Steven E. Jones, "Revisiting 9/11/2001: Applying the Scientific Method," loc. cit.

93. See question 12 at http://wtc.nist.gov/pubs/factsheets/faqs_8_2006.htm.

94. Dr. Steven E. Jones, "Revisiting 9/11/2001: Applying the Scientific Method," loc. cit.

95. To check how support for the petition has grown since this book went to press go to the following link: http://www.ae911truth.org/.

7

The NIST Report
and the
Question of Explosives

In August 2002 the U.S. Congress authorized the National Institute for Standards and Technology (NIST) to investigate the collapse of the World Trade Center on 9/11. The official mandate was not simply to conduct a building performance study, as some have claimed.[1] The primary stated objective of the investigation was to determine the cause of the collapse — no less.[2]

When NIST finally released its report in September 2005, numerous critics charged that the agency had ignored evidence of explosions in the World Trade Center, including the testimony of many eyewitnesses. NIST responded by asserting its scientific laurels. The agency insisted that its "200 technical experts" had conducted "an extremely thorough investigation." NIST boasted that its staff "reviewed tens of thousands of documents, interviewed more than 1,000 people, reviewed 7,000 segments of video footage and 7,000 photographs, analyzed 236 pieces of steel from the wreckage, performed laboratory tests and sophisticated computer simulations," yet found "no corroborating evidence for a controlled demolition." NIST also claimed that it had considered "a number of hypotheses for the collapse of the towers."[3]

Many Americans were persuaded by this snow job. Sad to say, few of our countrymen (or women) bother to read official reports, especially when they run to 10,000 pages. This has been a problem since at least the time of the Warren Commission report. The persistent individuals who *do* read reports, however, know that there are sound reasons to question all of the above, because a close reading of the NIST report shows that the agency *assumed from the beginning* that the Boeing 767 impacts and subsequent fires were responsible for the collapse of the twin towers. The report gives no consideration whatsoever to alternative hypotheses, including the leading candidate: explosives. Far from exploring other scenarios, NIST simply took it for granted that the impacts set in motion a chain of events leading to a catastrophic structural failure. Working backwards, NIST scientists searched for evidence that supported their predetermined conclusion. Everything else was ignored or excluded. If it is not already evident to the reader, this is no way to conduct a scientific investigation. NIST then had the audacity to imply that it arrived at its favored collapse model through an exhaustive process of elimination.

Most readers who browsed NIST's 2005 Executive Summary were probably not aware that NIST's stated conclusion was *really* an assumption. For example, consider this passage:

> The tragic consequences of the September 11, 2001 attacks were directly attributable to the fact that terrorists flew large jet-fuel laden commercial airliners into the WTC towers. Buildings for use by the general population are not designed to withstand attacks of such severity; building codes do not require building designs to consider aircraft impact.[4]

The comment about building codes is deceptive, because NIST readily concedes in its report that the towers survived the initial impacts. In fact, John Skilling, the structural engineer who designed the WTC, always claimed that they would. The towers survived, despite serious damage, because they were hugely overbuilt, redundant by design. Although the WTC's soaring lines gave the impression of a relatively light frame, in fact, the twin towers were extremely rugged buildings, engineered to withstand hurricane-force winds and even a direct hit by a Boeing 707, the largest commercial jetliner of the day. Some have argued that the newer Boeing 767s caused much more damage because of their larger size, but in fact, the two Boeings are comparable. Although slightly smaller, the 707 has a greater cruise speed of 600 mph (as compared with 530 mph for a Boeing 767). Assuming both were to crash at their cruising speed, the 707 would actually have greater kinetic energy.[5]

After the impacts on 9/11, the severed steel columns simply transferred the weight of the building to other undamaged columns. The NIST report even states that the towers would probably have stood indefinitely, if the impacts had not dislodged the fireproofing material that protected the steel from fire-generated heat.[6] Construction-grade steel begins to lose strength at 425°C (≈800°F) and is only about half as strong at 650°C (1,202°F). NIST argues in its report that the crashed jetliners damaged or dislodged 100% of the protective insulation within the impact zone, while also spilling many thousands of gallons of jet fuel over multiple floors. The resulting 800-1,000°C (1,440-1,800°F) blaze — the report claims — seriously weakened the now-exposed steel, leading to a global structural failure. In order to understand the official story, however, and to appreciate why it fails to explain the WTC collapse, it is necessary to know more about the World Trade Center and how it was built.

A State-of-the-Art Skyscraper

Upon its completion in 1970, the North Tower of the Trade Center soared 1,368 feet — 100 feet higher than the Empire State Building. In addition to being the world's tallest skyscraper, it was a state-of-the-art achievement of high-rise construction.[7] Designed by architect Minoru Yamasaki, the WTC was one of the first skyscrapers to feature large expanses of unobstructed floor space within a steel-frame building. Although commonplace today, this was a novel idea in the 1960s, as it required doing away with the forest of columns so typical of the skyscrapers of former years. Chief engineer John Skilling achieved the objective of open space with a double support system: the first tubular design, consisting of a dense array of 240 columns around the outer wall or perimeter, and a network of 47 huge columns at the core. The core columns supported about 53% of the weight of each building, and were massive, up to 52 inches wide.[8] The steel in these monster columns was seven inches thick at the base.[9]

The core columns were of two types: box columns at the foot of the buildings, gradually transitioning to rolled wide-flange beams ("I" beams) higher up. The core of each tower, including the elevators and stairwells, was surrounded by expansive office space. The perimeter wall supported 47% of the weight and also resisted the force of the wind. These exterior columns were reinforced with broad steel plates known as "spandrels," which girdled the building, like ribs, at every floor. Although the core columns gradually increased in size from top to bottom, for aesthetic reasons the external dimensions of the perimeter columns had to be the same all the way down, hence, required the use of heat-treated, i.e., high-strength, steel. This explains why Skilling's new tubular concept only became feasible in the 1960s, when high-strength steels first became available. Prefabrication and a modular design were other innovations that kept costs down and allowed for speedy construction.

Both inner and outer sets of columns were joined together by an innovative system of lightweight steel trusses. Each floor consisted of a truss assembly, over which was laid a corrugated steel deck — the bed for a poured four-inch slab of concrete. Although lightweight, the floor design was so sound that it easily supported the weight of libraries, file rooms, and heavy safes without the need for additional supports.[10] The lightweight truss assemblies were vulnerable to fire damage, however, because they consisted of rather thin steel members. For this reason, at the time of construction the trusses were spray-coated with protective insulation, 0.75 inch thick, and this was later upgraded to an average thickness of more than two inches.[11] (The technical term for the insulation is Spray-applied Fire Resistant Material: SFRM) The core columns had a fire-barrier of gypsum wallboard.

NIST argues in its report that the Boeing impacts jarred loose this protective insulation from the steel trusses and columns. The subsequent fires then weakened the exposed trusses, causing them to sag. This, in turn, pulled the perimeter columns inward. The fires also weakened both sets of columns, and at a critical point the perimeter wall buckled. NIST makes the claim that its investigation showed conclusively that the initiation occurred in the perimeter wall, triggering a global collapse.[12] Did the agency prove its case? Before I explore this question, however, it is important to understand what NIST did *not* investigate.

What NIST Failed to Investigate

Despite its broad charge to investigate the WTC collapse, NIST limited the scope of its investigation to the sequence of events from the first plane impacts to the onset of collapse. This means, of course, that NIST did not study the collapse itself. This narrow focus — some would call it sleight-of-hand — allowed NIST to sidestep a number of crucial issues. This was no doubt the intent, since investigating them would surely have led NIST scientists to some very different conclusions.

The first and foremost of these was the near-free-fall speed of the collapse. Videos filmed on 9/11 confirm that the towers plummeted as if there was almost no resistance whatsoever. But how can this be, given the enormous inertial mass of the building itself, which should have resisted and slowed the fall considerably? Even if we assume that the columns in the impact zone failed, the rest of the columns in the towers were untouched by the plane impacts and fires, suffering no loss of strength. These stone-cold columns should have resisted the fall.

Although the exact timing of the collapse of WTC 1 and 2 cannot be determined with precision because of the growing dust cloud, each collapse took approximately 10-12 seconds, only 1-2 seconds slower than the time for a billiard ball to free-fall from the WTC roof to the plaza below. But how can this be? By what special dispensation did the collapsing WTC violate the laws of physics? The reader will search the NIST report in vain for any discussion of this key anomaly. Why not? Obviously, because agency officials made a political decision not to go there.

No less puzzling was the fact that the collapses were total and nearly symmetrical. This means, of course, that when the collapses began all of the columns on that floor failed at precisely the same moment. But, again, how could this happen? Even if we assume that the plane impacts severed or damaged a number of columns in the impact zone, and even if we also assume that the fires weakened a number of other nearby columns, the majority of columns in the buildings and even on the affected floors were still at full strength at the moment of collapse. Yet, the collapses were total. The rubble from the buildings fell through the plaza level and piled up in the basements. Photos by Joel Meyerowitz and others show that the piles of wreckage were about six stories high, as evidenced by surviving portions of the perimeter wall. The wreckage reached the level of the column tree — a convenient reference point — where the larger exterior columns around the base divided into three smaller columns above.

The totality of the collapse is hard to explain because, as noted, the largest and strongest columns were in the lower part of the buildings. As they fell, the towers encountered increasing mass, i.e., resistance. For this reason, at least one engineer has argued that the WTC collapse should at some point have self-arrested.[13] This, however, has been disputed, and the matter remains controversial.[14]

Engineers obviously are fascinated by this question. Although a more detailed discussion is beyond the scope of this chapter, it is evident that media coverage has often served to confuse the issue rather than clarify. In a recent 9/11 documentary on the History Channel, for example, a debunker glibly described the events at Ground Zero as a "classic progressive collapse," as if this were a well-known or frequent phenomenon.[15] But this is plainly false, since — and I must emphasize it again — no steel-frame skyscraper had ever collapsed before 9/11, nor has any since.

There is an excellent reason why they do not fall down. Structural steel happens to be an extremely tough and forgiving substance — the reason it is the pre-eminent building material used in high-rise construction. As the *9/11 Commission Report* concedes, none of the New York fire chiefs anticipated a catastrophic structural failure on 9/11.[16] Had they believed a general collapse was possible, they would not have established their emergency command posts in the lobbies of both wounded towers. Nor would they have ordered hundreds of New York City firemen to begin the long climb up the stairwells to aid the victims and assist with the evacuation. As we know, 343 firemen perished. According to the official report, at least one fire chief did express concern about the danger of a *partial* collapse on the upper floors.[17]

No doubt, this individual was as shocked as everyone else by the totality and near-perfect symmetry of the ensuing collapses — both standard features of controlled demolitions and virtually unknown in random fire events. After I posted a critique of the NIST report in December 2006, I received a letter from a retired fireman who informed me that over the course of his twenty-odd years of service he had fought many types of fires, involving residential, commercial and industrial structures, including high-rise buildings. He explained that on a number of occasions, when his crew lost the battle to save a structure, "some of the times the building would collapse … in a random, haphazard, piecemeal fashion. Not once, did I personally witness one of those structures collapsing in the rather controlled … fashion as the WTC towers and Building 7."[18]

Another anomaly was the pulverization of material. Throughout history, concrete buildings have been known to collapse during powerful earthquakes, and when this occurs they typically fold up like an accordion, leaving a succession of concrete slabs, one piled on top of another, each plainly discernible in the rubble. But nothing like this occurred on 9/11. Photos of the mountain of wreckage at Ground Zero taken by Joel Meyerowitz and others show very few, if any, large chunks of concrete. The rubble pile consisted almost exclusively of twisted steel. The conspicuous absence of concrete is remarkable, since concrete was the main constituent of the 500,000-ton towers. As noted, each floor of the 110-story building, roughly an acre in size, consisted of a slab of poured concrete, most of which was pulverized during the collapse into small pieces and fine dust.

Some have attributed this to the force of gravity, but videos of the collapse clearly dispute this. The buildings were not pulverized as they hit the ground; they disintegrated in midair. As the South Tower started to collapse, for example, the entire upper section tipped as a unit, then inexplicably turned to dust before our eyes. As noted, much of the dust settled a foot deep on the sixteen-acre WTC site. The rest was deposited across lower Manhattan. Nor was the pulverization limited to concrete. Other construction materials also disappeared without a trace, including glass, office furniture, and tens of thousands of computers, not to mention the many victims. It's a fact that fewer than 300 corpses were recovered. Most of the victims were identified solely from body parts. Strangely, when workmen began to dismantle the badly damaged Deutsch Bank on December 8, 2006, they found more than 700 slivers of bone on the roof and within the structure.[19] This bizarre report has never been explained. (Incidentally, the E.J. Lee study determined that the building was beyond saving and recommended demolition.)

And there were other anomalies. The video record plainly shows that during the WTC collapse, perimeter columns weighing many tons were hurled as far as 500-600 feet from the towers. One remarkable photo of Ground Zero taken from above shows that entire sections of WTC-1's western perimeter wall were thrown over 500 feet toward the Winter Garden.[20] Could a gravitational collapse do this? Doubtful. The NIST report not only fails to adequately address any of these issues, *it doesn't even try.* The report makes reference to the "global collapse" of the towers, but we never learn precisely what this means because NIST never informs us. By sharply limiting the scope of its inquiry ahead of time, NIST rendered the truth unobtainable — an effective way to neuter an investigation.

With all of this in mind, let us now explore what NIST *did* investigate.

The Special Projects

The NIST investigation was comprised of eight separate projects, which together produced 43 volumes of supporting documentation. The projects included metallurgical studies, an impact analysis, an attempt to reconstruct the fires, and a computer model of the probable sequence of events leading to the collapse of each tower. Some of the agency's research was of excellent quality — some was not. But the main problem is that none of it lends credence to NIST's official conclusions.

Without question, the most serious obstacle NIST investigators faced was a lack of information about the dynamic conditions that existed in the core of the towers on 9/11.[21] To be sure, thousands of photographs and hundreds of hours of videotape made it possible to study in detail the damage to the WTC exterior, and to gain a reasonable understanding about conditions in the outer offices. Fires were often visible through the windows despite dense smoke, and structural damage in the impact zone, such as collapsed floors, was also discernible. However, as the NIST report states, "Fires deeper than a few meters inside the building could not be seen because of the smoke obscuration [*sic*] and the steep viewing angle of nearly all the photographs."[22] This is an important admission, and one that NIST repeats a number of times. For example, in one of the supplementary documents, NIST scientists qualify their analysis of the effects of the fire upon the steel with the following caveat:

> As conditions within the building core could not be determined from the photographic database, it was unknown what environment the recovered core columns may have experienced.[23]

As we will see, this candid statement haunts the entire report. In fact, the only physical evidence NIST had about the actual conditions at the core was the data it was able to glean from 236 steel columns, panels, trusses, and other smaller samples recovered from the WTC ruin.[24] Metallurgical testing of these steel samples was probably the most important work NIST carried out, because this was the foundation for the rest of the investigation.

The Metallurgical Studies

Thanks to the original labeling system used during the construction of the WTC, NIST was able to identify many of the samples it gathered, and to determine with precision their locations in the WTC. As it happened, a number of the columns were from the impact and fire zones.[25] Although the collection represented only 0.25 - 0.5 % of the 180,000 total tons of structural steel used in the two towers, NIST scientists believed their sampling was adequate to determine the quality of the steel and to evaluate its performance on 911.[26]

The metallurgical findings decisively refuted the pancake theory of collapse widely reported in the media after 9/11. The pancake enthusiasts, including MIT engineer Thomas Eagar, whom I have already cited, had argued that the weak link in the WTC was the point of attachment where the trusses connected with the inner and outer columns. These junctions, referred to as angle-clips, were made of relatively lightweight steel and were secured by steel bolts. During a 2002 *NOVA* television special, Eagar explained the pancake model and why in his opinion the trusses had failed:

> ... the steel had plenty of strength, until it reached temperatures of 1,100° to 1,300°F. In this range, the steel started losing a lot of strength, and the bending became greater. Eventually the steel lost 80 percent of its strength, because of this fire that consumed the whole floor ... then you got this domino effect. Once you started to get angle-clips to fail in one area, it put extra load on other angle-clips, and then it unzipped around the building on that floor in a matter of seconds. If you look at the whole structure, they are the smallest piece of steel. As everything begins to distort, the smallest piece is going to become the weak link in the chain. They were plenty strong for holding up one truss, but when you lost several trusses, the trusses adjacent to those had to hold two or three times what they were expected to hold.[27]

According to the pancake theory, when one floor collapsed it set in motion a chain reaction. Although initially this seemed plausible, it turned out that Eager seriously underestimated the robustness of the World Trade Center. The earlier 2002 FEMA study found no indication of substandard materials or construction. On the contrary, FEMA found that "many structural and fire protection features of the design and construction were ... superior to the minimum code requirements."[28] The NIST investigation bore this out. For example, NIST confirmed that the truss assemblies were not only bolted to the outer perimeter wall, *they were also welded,* hence were considerably stronger than expected — not prone to pancaking.[29] Nor could the pancake model explain the failure of the core columns.

The steel in the WTC also turned out to be significantly stronger than expected. Tests showed the yield-strengths of 87% of the steel samples exceeded the original specifications. For instance, the perimeter columns exceeded their specifications by more than 10%. The strength of the steel in the truss assemblies was also significantly higher than required. In many of the trusses, 50 ksi steel was used, even though the specifications called for only 36 ksi."[30] (1 ksi = 1,000 lb/per square inch.) NIST also tested a number of recovered bolts, and found that these too were stronger than expected, based on reports from the contemporaneous literature.[31] While all of these findings refuted the pancake theory, they also failed to support

NIST's own preferred collapse model. One need not be a rocket scientist to see that the stronger the steel, the less likely it was to fail on 9/11.

The Fire Tests: Core Weakening?

In a series of fire tests, NIST sought to address the alleged weakening of the WTC support columns. During a first-run, investigators placed an uninsulated steel column in a furnace where temperatures reached 1,100°C (2,012°F). During the test the surface temperature of the exposed column reached 600°C in just 13 minutes — the temperature range where significant loss of strength occurs. When the test was repeated with a column treated with SFRM insulation, the steel did not reach 600°C even after ten hours. NIST concluded that "the fires in WTC-1 and WTC-2 would not be able to significantly weaken … insulated … columns within the 102 minutes and 56 minutes, respectively, after impact and prior to collapse."[32] NIST interpreted these results as validating its theory that the critical factor on 9/11 leading to the global failure was the damage to and removal of the SFRM fireproofing insulation caused by the Boeing 767 impacts. But was this an unwarranted leap? Let us now explore this question.

NIST scientists developed a novel way to evaluate the impact of the fire on the WTC steel. According to the report, the approach was "easy to implement and robust enough to examine the entire component in the field."[33] They found that the original primer paint used on the steel beams and columns was altered by high heat. This made it possible to determine the level of exposure by analyzing the paint on the samples.[34] But the results were surprising. NIST found no evidence that any of the steel samples, including those from the impact areas and fire-damaged floors, had reached temperatures exceeding 1,110°F (600°C).[35] Sixteen recovered perimeter columns showed evidence of having been exposed to fire, but even so, out of 170 areas examined on these columns only three locations had reached temperatures in excess of 250°C (450°F).[36] Moreover, NIST found no evidence that any of the recovered core columns had reached even this minimal temperature.[37] The startling fact is that NIST's own data failed to support its conclusion that the fires of 9/11 heated the steel columns sufficiently to cause them to weaken and buckle.

How might we explain this absence of evidence? Shyam Sunder, NIST's lead scientist, probably offered a partial answer when he admitted that "the jet fuel … burned out in less than ten minutes."[38] Also, the actual amount of combustibles in the WTC turned out to be less than expected — considerably less. In its 2002 report, FEMA had noted,

... fuel loads in office-type occupancies typically range from about 4-12 psf [pounds per square foot], with the mean slightly less than 8 psf.... At the burning rate necessary to yield these fires, a fuel load of about 5 psf would be required to maintain the fire at full force for an hour ...[39]

Yet, when NIST scientists crunched the numbers, they found that a typical floor of the WTC did not even have this minimum level of combustibles. The average was only about 4 psf.[40] The shocking fact is that the twin towers were fuel-poor compared with other office buildings: a finding, notice, that does not support the frequent depictions in the media of a ferocious inferno raging beyond anything in human experience. More importantly, neither does it support NIST's favored collapse scenario.

Yes, the spillage of jet fuel ignited the combustibles, spreading the fires at a faster rate than would otherwise have occurred. Yet, for this same reason the fires also burned out sooner, because the fuel load was so low to begin with. Indeed, NIST scientists estimated that, on average, the WTC fires burned through the available combustibles at maximum temperatures (1,000°C) in only about 15-20 minutes,[41] after which, the fires began to subside. To make matters worse for the official collapse theory, NIST also found that "the fuel loading in the core areas ... was negligible."[42] It's easy to understand why all of these facts are downplayed in the NIST report. Taken together, they are fatal to NIST's collapse model, which requires that high temperatures be sustained. Fires that subside after only 15-20 minutes simply cannot weaken enormous steel columns and cause them to buckle.

I searched the NIST report in vain for any acknowledgment that the fire conditions in the laboratory test furnace were substantially different from the actual conditions on 9/11. Yet, this fact is undeniable, and calls into sharp question NIST's conclusion that damaged SFRM insulation was the critical factor. Although NIST took the position that "temperatures and stresses were high in the core area,"[43] on what basis did they reach this conclusion? As I've noted, NIST suffered from a persistent lack of information about the actual conditions in the core of the towers.

Surely, it is safe to conclude that the crashed Boeing 767s damaged and/or stripped away a substantial portion of the protective SFRM insulation from the steel beams and trusses in the impact zone. Exactly how much is not knowable. NIST acknowledges in its report that it had no hard evidence about the amount of protective insulation damaged or dislodged during the impacts.[44] Incredibly, however, the agency then asserts that all structural members in the debris path at the time of impact suffered 100% loss of insulation.[45]

The only physical evidence NIST presents in support of this dubious conclusion is a series of photos *of the exterior of the towers.* The photos do show that within the impact zone much of the SFRM foam insulation is indeed missing from the perimeter columns.[46] In places the original antirust paint is clearly visible on the exposed columns, indicating that the insulation is gone from these areas. NIST is also probably correct that the loss occurred during the impacts. But it does not follow on this basis that *all* of the insulation in the impact zone was similarly lost.

In fact, not only does the photographic evidence in the report *not* prove this, the photos show decisively that at least some of the insulation remained in place. *NIST even acknowledges this in its discussion of the photos.* For example, the report states that one photo "shows the absence of at least some, if not most SFRM from the center region of the outer web of the column." Here, "the absence of at least some" of the insulation can only mean that some of it also remained in place. The next passage goes on to describe one column in the same area on which the SFRM was "nearly intact."[47] In another section the report explicitly mentions that some of the insulation had apparently been treated with a special sealant, which "prevented the loss of SFRM in a great many locations where the SFRM was knocked off both above and below this location."[48] In short, NIST flatly contradicts itself regarding the disposition of the SFRM; and this is of crucial importance, because it means NIST's own data fail to support its conclusion.

For the sake of argument, however, let us for the moment ignore this glaring problem and assume that NIST's estimated total loss of SFRM is correct. As I will now show, even in this worst-case scenario there is virtually no chance that the fires on 9/11 weakened the WTC's core and perimeter columns within the allotted span of time.

A Vast Heat Sink

The reason is acknowledged nowhere in the NIST report, but ought to be self-evident. The WTC's support columns did not exist in isolation. The WTC was no laboratory furnace. The columns in each tower were part of an interconnected steel framework that weighed some 90,000 tons; and because steel is known to be at least a fair conductor of heat, on 9/11 this massive steel superstructure surely functioned as an enormous energy sink. The total volume of the steel framework was vast compared with the relatively small area of exposed steel, and would have wicked away much of the fire-generated heat.

Anyone who has repaired a copper water pipe with a propane torch is familiar with the principle. One must sit and wait patiently for the pipe temperature to rise to the point where the copper finally draws the solder into the fitting. While it is true that copper is several times more heat-conductive than steel, the fact that only three steel samples showed exposure to temperatures above 250°C indicates that the steel superstructure was indeed behaving as a heat sink. The fires on 9/11 would have required many hours, in any event much longer than the relatively brief allotted span of 56/102 minutes respectively, to slowly raise the temperature of each steel framework as a whole to the point of weakening even a few exposed members.

And there are other problems. Since in a global collapse all of the columns by definition must fail at once, this implies a more or less constant blaze across a wide area. But such was not the case on 9/11. As I've already noted, NIST found that the unexpectedly light fuel load in any given area of the WTC was mostly consumed in 15-20 minutes. At no time on 9/11 did the fires rage through an entire floor of the WTC — as Thomas Eagar implied in his interview.

The fires were not sustained, on the contrary they were transient.[49] This was especially true in WTC-1. The fires flared up in a given area, reached a maximum intensity within about 10 minutes, then gradually died down as the fire front moved on to consume combustibles in other areas. But notice what this also means: As the fires moved away from the impact zone into areas with little or no damage to the SFRM fireproofing, the heating of the steel columns and trusses in those areas would have been inconsequential. NIST's own data showed that, overall, the fires on floor 96 — where the collapse supposedly began — reached a peak 30-45 minutes after the impact and waned thereafter. *Temperatures were actually cooling across most of floor 96, including the core, at the moment of the collapse.*

But if this is correct, the central piers at that point were not losing strength, but regaining it.[50] How, then, did they collapse? Moreover, NIST's assertion that "temperatures and stresses were high in the core area" is not supported by its finding that the fuel load in the core was negligible.[51] On this point NIST again contradicts itself. For all of these reasons, NIST fails to explain in its report how transient fires weakened

WTC-1's enormous core columns and perimeter columns in the allotted span, triggering a global collapse.

The Fires in the South Tower

NIST determined that the fire behavior in the South Tower was substantially different: more continuous rather than transient, at least on the east side of the building where the remains of Flight 175 supposedly came to rest. This, in addition to more extensive impact damage, NIST informs us, explains why WTC-2 collapsed first, even though it was hit after WTC-1. It is now known, however, that NIST ignored important evidence that calls into question its assertion that fires were gravely weakening the core of WTC-2.

An audio-tape released in August 2002 by the Port Authority of New York, which apparently was lost or neglected for more than a year, is the only known recording of firefighters inside the towers. When city fire officials belatedly listened to it, they were surprised to discover that two NYC firemen actually reached the impact/fire zone of the South Tower about fourteen minutes before it collapsed. The long climb up the stairs was so arduous that most of the firemen, heavily burdened with equipment, were exhausted before they reached the 20th floor. However two, Battalion Chief Orlo J. Palmer and Fire Marshall Ronald P. Bucca, were in excellent physical condition. Palmer was apparently a marathon runner. On reaching the 78th floor sky lobby, they found many dead or seriously injured people; but they found no raging inferno. Palmer's radio exchange with other firemen shows no hint of panic or fear, as the following transcript shows:

> BATTALION SEVEN CHIEF (PALMER): Battalion Seven ... Ladder 15, we've got two isolated pockets of fire. We should be able to knock it down with two lines. Radio that, 78th floor numerous 10-45 Code Ones.
> LADDER 15: Chief, what stair you in?
> BATTALION SEVEN CHIEF: "South stairway Adam, South Tower."
> LADDER 15: Floor 78?
> BATTALION SEVEN CHIEF: Ten-four, numerous civilians, we gonna need two engines up here.
> BATTALION SEVEN CHIEF: Tower one. Battalion Seven to Ladder 15.
> BATTALION SEVEN CHIEF: I'm going to need two of your firefighters Adam stairway to knock down two fires. We have a house line stretched we could use some water on it, knock it down, okay.

LADDER 15: Alright ten-four, we're coming up the stairs. We're on 77 now in the B stair, I'll be right to you.

BATTALION SEVEN Operations Tower One: Battalion Seven Operations Tower One to Battalion Nine, need you on floor above 79. We have access stairs going up to 79, kay.

BATTALION NINE: Alright, I'm on my way up, Orlo.[52]

Here, Battalion Chief Palmer calls for more men and water to put out the isolated fires. His expression "10-45 Code Ones" refers to dead bodies, of which apparently there were many. The tape shows that the two firemen were not turned back by heat, smoke, or a wall of flames. They were able to function within the fire zone and were prepared to help the injured and combat the few isolated fires they found. Palmer even mentions that the stairway up to the next level, i.e., floor 79, was passable. Minutes later the building came down on their heads.

NIST knew about this evidence. The NIST report briefly mentions that firemen reached the 78th floor of WTC-2.[53] Inexplicably, however, the matter is simply dropped as if it had no bearing on the status of the fire in the core. The omission is conspicuous because, as I've stressed, NIST suffered from a persistent lack of information about the dynamic conditions in the interior of the buildings.[54] Here, then, was a real-time eyewitness account by trained professionals who were on the scene. Yet, NIST ignored it. Why? Well, obviously, because their words do not support the official story. Curiously, the *9/11 Commission Report* also briefly mentions this episode, but likewise fails to discuss its actual significance, no doubt for the same reason.[55]

According to NIST, the 78th floor of WTC-2 had fewer combustibles than other floors because it was a sky lobby, and on this basis the report leads us to believe that much more intense fires were raging several floors above the two brave firemen — fires that *did* cause fatal weakening of the columns. The problem for NIST, however, is that *survivors* from these higher floors tell a very different story. As we know, WTC-2 was unlike WTC-1 in that a number of individuals in the South Tower did manage to escape the impact zone via stairwell A, which luckily remained passable. (In his radio message Orlo Palmer refers to it as "south stairway Adam.")

One of these survivors was Stanley Praimnath, an employee of Fuji Bank who was on the 81st floor when Flight 175 crashed into the South Tower. In fact, the wing of the plane reportedly passed within twenty feet of him. Yet, Praimnath escaped without serious burns, and in his testimony mentions nothing about a raging inferno.[56] Brian Clark, another survivor, was an executive vice-president of Euro Brokers, based on the 84th floor. As Clark descended the stairs, he heard someone crying out for help. It was Praimnath, who at the time was still trapped on the 81st floor in the rubble. Clark found and freed the man, whereupon, the two escaped together down the stairs.

These two survivors are living proof that the official story cannot be right. Both were in the fire zone during and immediately after the impact, when the fires were most intense due to the spilled jet fuel. If the temperatures in the core were 1,000°C or higher, as NIST would have us believe, the two men would have died within minutes. Yet, both survived, and here is Clark's description of the fire: "You could see through the wall and the cracks and see flames just, just licking up, *not a roaring inferno,* just quiet flames licking up and smoke sort of eking through the wall" [my emphasis].[57] Quiet flames. No roaring inferno. It is not surprising that NIST chose to ignore the testimony of these survivors.

So, the known accounts of eyewitnesses do not support the official story regarding conditions at the core of WTC-2 — testimonials that NIST likely excluded from consideration for this very reason. But what about empirical evidence? Among the steel samples that NIST investigators recovered from WTC-2 were two core columns (C-88a and C-88b) from the impact zone. Actually, they were two different members from the same column (801). NIST pinpointed their location on floors 80 and 81, several floors above the firemen — very near the path of Flight 175. Both samples had been physically damaged, yet NIST found no evidence of the kinds of distortion, i.e., buckling, bowing, slumping, or sagging, that would be expected in cases of heat-weakened steel. Furthermore, although the samples came from within the fire zone, NIST was unable to show that the steel had been exposed to high temperatures.[58] This finding is so astonishing it bears repeating: The NIST report presents no physical evidence whatsoever that the fires in the core of WTC-2 were raging infernos.

On what, then, does the agency base its conclusion: "Dire structural changes were occurring in the building interior"?[59] The answer, apparently, is the following strange hedge:

> Note that these core columns represent less than 1 percent of the core columns on floors involved with fire and cannot be considered representative of any other core columns.[60]

In other words, we are supposed to accept NIST's theory about the fire solely on the basis of its opinion that a larger sampling of columns would have enabled NIST to prove its case. But this is hogwash! It simply is not the way science is done. Indeed, the paucity of evidence, if anything, calls into question NIST's earlier assertion that its sampling was adequate.

What is even more amazing is that NIST's own computer simulations of the WTC fires also tend to bear this out. Any curious reader who invests the time to review the relevant NIST document (i.e., CSTAR 1-5) will find page after page of color-coded graphic diagrams of these simulations, one set for each floor in the fire zone. Nearly all of them show that the core remained cool throughout the fires. The burden of proof was on NIST to demonstrate how the fires weakened the core columns in the allotted time, and the only reasonable conclusion one can draw is that the agency fails to present even a minimal case. But this also means, of course, that NIST likewise fails to explain the global collapse.

For the sake of argument, however, in order to show just how weak the official collapse model is, let us assume that the fires *did* burn hot enough and were sustained long enough, and caused numerous exposed columns in the impact zone to lose roughly half of their strength. As I will now show, even if this did occur, it still fails to account for the global collapse of either tower.

The Issue of Reserve Capacity

As the NIST report states,

> ... *both towers had considerable reserve capacity* [my emphasis]. This was confirmed by analysis of the post-impact vibration of WTC-2, the more severely damaged building, where the damaged tower oscillated at a period nearly equal to the first mode period calculated for the undamaged structure.[61]

The passage informs us that WTC-2 gave no sign of instability after the impact of Flight 175. Unfortunately, although NIST's summary report provides a wealth of information about how the World Trade Center was constructed, it fails to clarify the matter of the WTC's "considerable reserve capacity." At any rate, I scoured the report in vain for a clear discussion of this important issue. In frustration, I finally called NIST for assistance and was guided to several of the project reports and supplementary documents. I also consulted with Gary Nichols, an expert at the International Code Council, and with Ron Hamburger, a leading structural engineer. These conversations were an education. I learned that estimating the overall reserve capacity of a steel structure is by no means a simple matter. Numerous factors are involved. Moreover, there are different ways to approach the problem.

Perhaps the simplest measure of reserve capacity are the standards for the material components of a building. In the late 1960s when the WTC was constructed, the applicable standard was the New York City Building Code, which required a builder to execute computations for the various structural members to show they met the specified requirements. However, the code also allowed for actual testing of members in the event that computations were impractical. The testing standards applicable in 1968 give a reasonable idea of the required level of reserve strength in the steel columns and other materials used in the WTC. For example, in the most stringent test a steel member had to withstand 250% of the design load, plus half again its own weight, for a period of a week without collapse.[62]

Factor of Safety

Another widely used measure of reserve capacity is the so called "factor of safety." This varies for different structural elements, but for steel columns and beams typically ranges from 1.75 - 2.0.[63] The NIST report actually breaks down this more general figure into two separate and slightly different measurements for stress: yielding strength (1.67) and buckling (1.92).[64] For our purposes, however, the more general figure is adequate. So, for example, a steel column with a factor of safety of 1.75 must support 1.75 times the anticipated design load before it begins to incur damage.

While this value is typical of steel beams in general, the actual reserve strength of the steel columns in the WTC was higher. When NIST scientists crunched the numbers for the 47 core columns of WTC-1 (in the impact zone, between the 93rd and 98th floors) they calculated that the factor of safety ranged from 1.6 to 2.8, the mean value being 2.1.[65] This means that the average core column in the impact zone of WTC-1 could support more than twice its design load before reaching the yield strength, i.e., the point where damage may begin to occur. My grateful thanks to the NIST investigative team for helping me locate these numbers, which were buried in the report.

It is important to realize that the factor of safety is not a threshold for collapse, but a value beyond which permanent damage may *begin* to occur. As the NIST report admits, even "after reaching the yield strength, structural steel components continue to possess considerable reserve capacity."[66] This is why steel beams and columns typically do not fail in sudden fashion. The loss of strength is gradual. No doubt this helps to explain why, although fires have ravaged many steel frame buildings over history, none had ever collapsed — until 9/11 — nor has any since.

What all of this means, of course, is that even in the most improbable worst case, in which many or all WTC core columns lost half of their strength, there was still sufficient reserve capacity to support the building.

The Perimeter Wall

With regard to the WTC's perimeter columns, the factor of safety fluctuated from day to day and even from hour to hour, because, in addition to supporting 47% of the WTC's gravity load, the perimeter wall also had to withstand the lateral force of the wind, which is highly variable given the whims of Mother Nature. A single face of the WTC presented an enormous "sail" to the elements, for which reason John Skilling vastly overbuilt this part of the structure. According to the NIST report, the outer wall's factor of safety against wind shear on September 11, 2001 was extraordinary, i.e., in the 10-11 range.[67]

Why so high? The answer is simple: On the day of the attack there was essentially no wind, only a slight breeze.[68] For this reason nearly all of the perimeter wall's design capacity was available to help support the gravity load. As the NIST report states, "On September 11, 2001 the wind loads were minimal, thus providing significantly more reserve for the exterior walls."[69] When NIST crunched the numbers for a representative perimeter column in WTC-1 (column 151, between the 93rd and 98th floors), they arrived at a factor of safety of 5.7.[70]

Assuming this average figure is a typical value, we arrive at a reasonable estimate of the perimeter wall's amazing reserve capacity. Even if we subtract those columns severed or damaged by the impact of Flight 175, and the lost capacity due to the alleged (but unproven) buckling along the eastern perimeter wall, there was still a wide margin of safety, more than enough by several times over to support the outer wall's share of the gravity load, with plenty to spare.[71] I must emphasize: These are not *my* numbers. They are NIST's own figures.

The WTC's tremendous reserve capacity was no secret. In 1964, four years before the start of construction, an article about the planned WTC appeared in the *Engineering News-Record*. The article declared that "live loads on these [perimeter] columns can be increased more than 2,000 percent before failure occurs."[72] A careful reading of the piece also gives insight into why the plane impacts were not fatal to the integrity of the outer wall. The reason is simple: The perimeter columns were designed to function together as an enormous truss, specifically, a Vierendeel truss. The wall was inherently stable. After the plane impacts, it behaved like an arch, simply transferring the load to the surrounding columns. As the 1964 article states,

> ... the WTC towers will have an inherent capacity to resist unforeseen calamities. This capacity stems from its Vierendeel wall system and is enhanced through the use of high-strength steels.[73]

In short, NIST's own data fail to support its conclusions about the cause of the WTC collapse. The official theory requires the fatal weakening of both sets of columns, and NIST came up short on both counts due to insufficient evidence. Indeed, I would call it woefully insufficient.

Today, years after NIST released its report, it is increasingly obvious that NIST attempted to overcome the lack of physical evidence by resorting to computer simulations. This was problematic, of course, because computer models are no better than the quality of input and the accuracy of the programmer's assumptions. Architect Eric Douglas identified another issue in his 2006 analysis of the NIST report: "... a fundamental problem with ... computer simulation is the overwhelming temptation to manipulate the input data until one achieves the desired results."[74] Did NIST investigators fall prey to this tendency? Or were they somehow able to overcome the absence of physical evidence? I must ask the reader to bear with me a little longer while we explore these important questions.

NIST's Global Impact/Collapse Analyses

The purpose of NIST's global impact analysis (NCSTAR 1-2) was to estimate the structural damage to the WTC caused by the Boeing 767s. In this project NIST considered three different scenarios, ranging from less damage to extreme damage, with a moderate alternative (described as "the base") in the middle. As it happened, all three accurately predicted the impact damage to the WTC exterior at the point of entry, although with regard to WTC-1 the moderate case was slightly better match.[75] The three differed greatly, however, in predicting the number of severed columns at the WTC core, a datum that was obviously of great importance.

In the case of WTC-1 the lesser alternative predicted only one severed core column, the moderate alternative predicted three, while the extreme alternative predicted five to six. In the case of WTC-2 the disparity was even greater: The lesser alternative predicted three severed columns, the moderate five, and the extreme case no less than ten.[76] Although NIST never satisfactorily resolved these differences, it immediately threw out the less severe alternatives, citing two reasons in the summary report: first, because they failed to predict observable damage to the far exterior walls; and second, because they did not lead to a global collapse.[77]

On September 11, 2001, the North Tower sustained visible damage to the wall opposite the impact of Flight 11. This was caused by an errant landing gear and by a piece of the fuselage, which passed through the tower and came out the other side. Both parts were later recovered. During the second impact (of Flight 175), the same phenomenon was repeated: A jet engine was seen exiting WTC-2's opposite wall at high speed and was later found on Murray Street, several blocks northeast of the WTC. In its summary report, NIST leads us to believe that the observable damage to the far walls caused by these ejected Boeing 767 parts validated its simulations. Yet, in one of its supplementary documents NIST admits that "because of [computer] model size constraints, the panels on the south side of WTC-1 were modeled with a coarse resolution ... The model [thus] ... underestimates the damage to the tower on this face."[78] But, notice, this means that *none* of the three alternatives accurately predicted the exit damage.[79]

This admission, deeply buried in the 43-volume report, is fatal to NIST's first rationale for rejecting the lesser alternative, since it was no less accurate than the moderate and extreme cases. (Or, put differently: It was no more inaccurate.) Which, of course, means that NIST rejected the lesser alternative for one reason only: because it failed to predict a global collapse. The simulations for WTC-2 suffered from the same modeling defect. Once again, NIST rejected the lesser alternative, even though *"none of the three WTC-2 global impact simulations resulted in a large engine fragment exiting the tower"* [my emphasis].[80] Again, we can thank researcher Eric Douglas for digging deeper than the summary report. Otherwise, this flaw, tantamount to the devil lurking in the fine print, might never have come to light.

But NIST was undeterred by its own biased reasoning. Later, it also tossed out the moderate (base) alternative, and ultimately adopted the most extreme scenario in its subsequent global collapse analysis, even though, as noted, the lesser alternatives were just as accurate from a predictive standpoint as the extreme case. In fact, with regard to predicting the entry damage to WTC-1, as noted, the moderate alternative was actually a better match. The NIST report offers no scientific rationale for this decision, only the pithy comment that the moderate alternatives "were discarded after the structural response analysis of major subsystems were compared with observed events."[81] Here, of course, "observed events" refers to the ultimate collapse of the towers. Things get worse.

It would appear that NIST nearly failed to generate a collapse even with the extreme alternatives, which required further tinkering. As the report informs us: "Complete sets of simulations were then performed for cases B and D [the extreme alternatives for the two towers]. *To the extent that the simulations deviated from the photographic evidence or eyewitness reports, the investigators adjusted the input,* but only within the range of physical reality" [my emphasis]. [82] In other words, NIST scientists, working backwards from the collapse, tweaked the extreme alternatives until their computer model spat out the desired result, consistent with their original assumption that the 767 impacts and fires were responsible for the collapses on 9/11. Needless to say, the NIST report fails to give specifics about the "additional inputs." We are left to use our imagination.

The late Cornell astronomer Carl Sagan used to say that "extraordinary claims require extraordinary proof." By this tough but reasonable standard, the official explanation about the collapse of the WTC on September 11, 2001 was without question an extraordinary claim, because there were no historical precedents. I will say it again: No steel-frame skyscraper had ever collapsed due to fire-weakened columns. By this standard the official account required an extraordinary level of proof. Yet, as I have just shown, NIST failed to muster even a minimal evidentiary case. From the start, NIST's investigation was biased, hence unscientific. Indeed, its report is "a triumph" of circular reasoning.

The report actually left me slightly agog, in a state of mild shock at the disparity between NIST's research and its conclusions. NIST never overcame the lack of hard data about actual conditions at the WTC core — certainly not by resorting to computer models. Had its program been robust enough to properly characterize the far walls, investigators might have utilized the known exterior damage to those far walls to discriminate between the three alternatives and, thusly, to select the best choice, possibly validating the model. Failing this, NIST had no sound basis for rejecting the lesser and moderate alternatives. Both were at least as plausible as the extreme case. Why were they not given equal weight? The answer is obvious: that would have compelled NIST investigators to entertain the unthinkable, i.e., the possibility that some *other* causative agent was responsible for the WTC collapse. And what might that other agent be?

There is only one serious candidate: high-temperature explosives. Of course, NIST's failure to explain the World Trade Center collapse does not, in and of itself, prove that explosives were used. But it ought to inspire us to revisit this alternative with renewed interest, especially in light of the compelling evidence I have already presented. I was led to ask, *Is there other evidence for explosives, in addition to the tell-tale residues in the dust?* For example, were there eyewitnesses?

The Oral Histories

The answer is an emphatic *"Yes."* Many eyewitnesses reported hearing, feeling and seeing explosions at Ground Zero on 9/11; and their ranks swelled dramatically in 2005 when the city of New York released 503 oral histories of NYC firemen, paramedics and emergency medical technicians who were at the WTC on the day of the attack. The FDNY had gathered these interviews between October 2001 and January 2002 at the order of then-New York Fire Commissioner Thomas Van Essen, who later told the *New York Times* he wanted to preserve the accounts for historical reasons, "before they became reshaped by a collective memory." The department also made transcripts of the tapes: all told, some 12,000 pages of written testimony.

The city had withheld all of this material for several years because, as Nicholas Scoppetta, Van Essen's successor, told the *New York Times,* federal prosecutors advised him that its publication might impede the ongoing prosecution of alleged al Qaeda terrorist Zacarias Moussaoui.[83] The reason was flimflam. The histories obviously had no bearing on the Moussaoui trial. At any rate, this was the opinion of the NY state Court of Appeals, which ordered most of the material to be released, the result of a lawsuit filed by the *New York Times* and joined by the families of the victims. The oral histories were eventually made public in August 2005, and they are currently posted on the *New York Times* website.[84]

Notably, of the 503 testimonials, at least 118, i.e., 23% of the total, mention explosions in the WTC. This was the conclusion of Graeme MacQueen, former professor of religion at McMaster University, Hamilton, Ontario, who conducted a comprehensive review of the transcripts in 2006. MacQueen found no evidence that coercive measures had been used in gathering what he describes as "a remarkably rich body of narrative material."[85] In his opinion the responders gave their oral accounts freely and spontaneously, although some apparently read from written reports prepared ahead of time. In reviewing the material MacQueen found only a few cases where the questioner may have led the witness.

All told, MacQueen counted 177 unambiguous references to explosions in the accounts of 118 different witnesses. The number of references is higher than the number of witnesses because some responders were emphatic about explosions and mention them more than once. Although interpreting the histories was unavoidably subjective, MacQueen took pains to screen out cases that might be construed as ambiguous. For example, he excluded descriptive words like "roar," "rumble," "shake," and "earthquake" in the absence of more explicit language. Only the histories with unambiguous references to explosions were counted, i.e., those including words like "blast," "explosion," "secondary device," "bomb," "blow up," and "implosion."

MacQueen was impressed by the large number of eyewitnesses who reported explosions. He thinks the total would have been even higher but for the fact that many accounts show signs of revisionism. Notwithstanding Fire Commissioner Van Essen's laudable aim of collecting the histories while still fresh in memory, some responders evidently had already changed their minds by the time the interviews were conducted. MacQueen thinks these responders were probably influenced by the media's overwhelming tendency to describe the collapses as due to structural failure caused by the impacts and fires. As the transcripts show, some of the interviewees tiptoe around the issue of explosions, as if reluctant to use the word. These individuals probably had come to believe that their original impressions were mistaken. Even so, only two responders out of 503 explicitly denied that explosions had occurred. Seven others described the collapses solely in terms of a pancaking mechanism. MacQueen concludes that the oral histories lend strong support to the reality of explosions, while offering scant support for a non-explosive collapse scenario.[86]

I should mention that one self-professed debunker of "conspiracy theorists," Mark Roberts, has sharply criticized MacQueen's analysis of the oral histories.[87] On his website Roberts claims that MacQueen greatly exaggerated the number of references to explosions. Roberts did his own review and counted only thirty-one such cases, a number that is still significant, though much smaller. His criticism inspired me to conduct my own review.

I concluded that although a few of MacQueen's judgments (out of 118) may be questionable, this would be expected in any evaluation involving a subjective opinion. On the whole, I believe MacQueen conducted a competent survey, and I agree with his conclusions. I would add that while reading through the transcripts, I also noticed that several of the eyewitnesses went further and explicitly compared the collapses to controlled demolitions. For example, one New York City firefighter, Richard Banaciski, stated that "it seemed like on television [when] they blow up these buildings."[88] Thomas Fiztpatrick, an FDNY deputy commissioner, made a similar remark: "My initial reaction was that this was exactly the way it looks when they show you those implosions on TV."[89] A third firefighter, Kenneth Rogers, said that "it looked like a synchronized deliberate sort of thing."[90] Two other witnesses even wondered aloud if the United States was under a nuclear attack.[91]

Needless to say, Roberts, who himself agrees with the official narrative, fails to mention any of these cases, for reasons that should be obvious. This kind of omission no longer surprises me. It has been my experience that debunkers of "conspiracy theories" tend to be at least as selective in citing evidence as the official investigators.

Although the oral histories, were only made public in August 2005, according to the *New York Times,* the 9/11 Commission and NIST both gained access to the material long before this by bringing legal threats against the city of New York.[92] The 9/11 Commission actually drew upon the histories while drafting chapter nine of its final report, which covers the plane impacts and WTC collapse. Chapter nine makes reference to "our review of 500 internal FDNY interview transcripts."[93] A reader, however, will search the chapter in vain for any mention of the 118 responders who saw, felt and heard explosions.

In fact, in the entire 567-page *9/11 Commission Report* there is only one reference to explosions. The lone mention was drawn from interviews that the panel conducted in 2004, and is presented not as part of a discussion of an alternative collapse scenario (i.e., a demolition caused by explosions), but rather, for the purpose of discrediting the witness for even thinking such thoughts. Here is the text:

> When the South Tower collapsed, fire fighters on upper floors of the North Tower heard a violent roar, and many were knocked off their feet; they saw debris coming up the stairs and observed that the power was lost and emergency light activated. Neverthe-

less, those firefighters not standing near windows facing south had no way of knowing that the South Tower had collapsed; *many surmised that a bomb had exploded,* or that the North Tower had suffered a partial collapse on its upper floors [my emphasis].[94]

A reader who knows nothing about the oral histories will probably interpret this as an isolated case, and will judge that the firemen were simply mistaken. No doubt this was the drafters' intent.

NIST also acquired the oral histories, and likewise fails to discuss them in its final report. For this reason, NIST's categorical statement that it "found no corroborating evidence … that the WTC towers were brought down by controlled demolition using explosives"[95] is simply a lie. There is no other word for it, because NIST surely knew about the eyewitness accounts.

I should mention that a few debunkers of "conspiracy theories" have advanced more thoughtful arguments. In May 2007 Zdeněk P. Bažant *et al.* published a paper, "Collapse of WTC Towers: What Did and Did Not Cause It?" in which they attempt to show that "allegations of controlled demolition by planted explosives" have no scientific merit.[96] The authors argue that during the gravitational collapse, air was forcibly ejected from the buildings at high speed, causing loud sonic booms that some witnesses probably mistook for explosions. Their theory is plausible, but even if it is partly correct, it fails to account for all of the eyewitness accounts, since many witnesses reported hearing, seeing and feeling explosions well *before* the onset of the collapse. Graeme MacQueen has catalogued these accounts in his response.[97]

The sonic boom theory is also refuted by a separate group of at least fourteen eyewitnesses, who claim that an enormous explosion ripped through WTC-1 *even before Flight 11 struck the tower.* The spokesman for this group, William Rodriguez, had been a custodian at the WTC for twenty years. On the day of the attack he arrived for work at 8:30 A.M., and was in the B-1 basement of the North Tower talking with his supervisor when an enormous blast shook the room. Rodriquez is emphatic that the explosion came from below. He says the blast pushed him upwards, collapsed part of the ceiling, cracked the concrete walls, and even caused the sprinkler system to come on. Rodriguez thought a generator had exploded on a lower level. He goes on to say that, moments later, he felt the impact of Flight 11, high above.[98] A coworker agrees, and it is hard to dismiss their story because, as janitors, they were well acquainted with the building and surely would have known if a loud sound or explosion came from above or below.[99]

After the explosion, Rodriquez assisted a badly burned coworker, Felipe David, out of the building, then returned to help others. He freed several individuals trapped in an elevator, then used his master key to save a group of firemen stuck in a stairwell. Rodriguez climbed as high as the 39th floor, and he says that while assisting with the evacuation he heard and felt numerous other explosions. He was also one of the last people out of WTC-1 and survived only because he crawled under a fire engine, which shielded him during the collapse.

Rodriguez emerged as one of the genuine heroes of 9/11. He was feted at the White House and even testified before the 9/11 Commission — behind closed doors, at their insistence. But, of course, the final report makes no mention of his testimony about explosions. Rodriguez also contacted the FBI and made repeated attempts to reach NIST, without success.[100]

Rodriguez says he eventually did succeed in speaking with NIST officials at one of the agency's public hearings. Afterward, he described the experience: " ... I asked them before they came up with their conclusion ... if they ever considered my statements or the statements of any of the other survivors who heard the explosions. They just stared at me with blank faces."[101] Rodriguez says that at this point he realized the official investigation was a sham. Thereafter he began to speak out about his experience.

Audio-Visual Evidence

The many eyewitness accounts of explosions in the WTC are politically incorrect, but they are supported by physical evidence in addition to the residues found in the WTC dust. One example is Rick Siegel's dramatic videotape, which Siegel filmed from the New Jersey shore of the Hudson. But even to call it "dramatic" fails to do it justice. The footage is nothing short of astonishing. Siegel lived in Hoboken at the time, and on the morning of September 11, after hearing about the events at the WTC, he hurried down to the waterfront, set up his camera, and proceeded to capture most of the tragedy on film. The WTC was two miles away across the Hudson River. But Siegel overcame the distance thanks to his unimpeded vantage point, and because he used a tripod. However, the audio portion is what makes the footage so powerful. Siegel captured on a tape the enormous explosions that ripped through the South Tower moments before it fell. These were not tiny pops, but thunderous blasts that carried across the water. The explosions can be heard distinctly in the audio. Siegel's film, *911 Eyewitness,* is available for purchase on the Internet.[102]

My own reaction, the first time I watched it, was shock: To think that the networks never aired this important evidence! The video should have been on the six o'clock nightly news. After one large blast, a dust cloud is seen rising from the base of the WTC, at the level of the street, indicating that the explosion must have occurred on the lower levels, far from where Flights 11 and 175 impacted the buildings. Seconds later, the South Tower starts to collapse from the top down. Later in the tape a second series of explosions rocks the North Tower before it too falls. Siegel's video corroborates the many witnesses who heard, felt and saw explosions prior to the start of collapse.

Jim Hoffman, another 9/11 investigator, has criticized Siegel for the way he packaged his film, and Hoffman makes some good points.[103] *911 Eyewitness* was over-produced. Some of Siegel's supplementary analysis may also be questionable. Even so, his raw footage speaks for itself and is extremely important evidence. Nor did I see anything that made me doubt its authenticity. If the video is bona fide, and I strongly suspect this is the case, it proves that the many eyewitnesses who reported explosions in the WTC were telling the truth. Siegel should be encouraged to enlist experts to thoroughly vet his tape. Once this is done, some brave producer needs to air it on national television. *60 Minutes* would be an ideal venue.

Although it is common knowledge that the earth shook like an earthquake during the WTC collapse, it is less well-known that the shaking started well *before* the onset of the collapse — exactly what you would expect, assuming that large explosions ripped through each tower prior to collapse. This too was reported by numerous eyewitnesses. However, I will not review the accounts here, because others have already done so, and in my opinion quite adequately.[104] My point is that physical evidence also supports these accounts.

Luckily, an unknown cameraman captured a must-see short video of the onset of the collapse of WTC-1 from a nearby rooftop. Although his/her identity is unknown to this writer, the 2.6 MB video can still be downloaded from the Internet, where it has been posted for years.[105] The clip was featured in Dylan Avery's 911 documentary, *Loose Change (2nd Edition)*. Why is this footage important? Because the photographer, like Rick Siegel, had the presence of mind to plant the video-cam on a tripod.

As the film starts to roll, we are watching a close-up of the upper section of the North Tower. The building is ablaze, and smoke can be seen pouring from the upper floors. The video is of good quality, but even more importantly, it is steady thanks to the tripod. Suddenly, however, the frame noticeably vibrates for a *full second*, and then, about six seconds later the tower begins to crumble. This short clip provides compelling evidence that the witnesses who heard, saw, and felt tremors before the onset of collapse were telling the truth. Only an enormous explosion could shake the ground in this manner.

WTC-7 Report: Consigned to Limbo?*

Notice, I have not even discussed the case of WTC-7, which was not hit by a plane, hence had no spillage of jet fuel, and suffered only some exterior damage on its south side and relatively minor fires on several floors. Yet, at 5:20 P.M. on the afternoon of 9/11 this 47-story steel-frame WTC-7 dropped into its footprint like a stone. The *how* and the *why* evidently proved so troublesome to NIST's scientists that the agency chose to drop the issue from its September 2005 report. To this day, the collapse of WTC-7 has never been explained, certainly not by NIST, whose separate final report on the issue is long overdue. NIST's last press release on the matter, dated June 29, 2007, failed even to speculate about a release date. As of August 2008 a posting on the NIST website stated that the "final report for WTC-7 is not yet complete" and "will be released in draft form for public comment and posted on this website as soon as it is available."[106]

Right. Whenever *that* is ...

NIST may have consigned its WTC-7 report to bureaucratic limbo, but the absence of a report is no substitute for an explanation. In the meanwhile, time does not stand still. Even as NIST ducks the issue, the tide is turning against the official WTC collapse theory. Increasing numbers of experts are voicing doubts, and some have gone further. In 2007 two leading Swiss structural engineers stated in public that the collapse of WTC-7 was in their view a controlled demolition.[107]

Recently, a Dutch demolition expert named Danny Jowenko reached the same conclusion after a television crew showed him the video of the WTC-7 collapse.[108] At the time Jowenko had no knowledge about WTC-7, and did not even know that a third steel skyscraper had collapsed in New York on 9/11. Jowenko called it an obvious controlled demolition, and even though he was shocked when told the details, he did

* As this book was going to press, NIST finally released its long-awaited report. 187
Some preliminary comments are attached as an epilogue.

not back away from his opinion. The case epitomizes the seismic shift underway among professionals: a sure indication that a similar movement in public opinion cannot be far behind.

Endnotes

1. Ryan Mackey, "Examining Dr. David Ray Griffin's Latest Criticism of the NIST World Trade Center Investigation, *Journal of Debunking 9/11 Conspiracy Theories*, Volume 1, Issue 4, August 31, 2007.

2. NIST NCSTAR 1, Full Summary Report, WTC Investigation, Preface, xxxi.

3. Answers to Frequently Asked Questions, National Institute of Standards and Technology (NIST) Federal Building and Fire Safety Investigation of the World Trade Center Disaster, see question two, posted at http://wtc.nist.gov/pubs/factsheets/faqs_8_2006.htm.

4. NIST NCSTAR, Executive Summary, p. xlvii.

5. After the 1993 bombing of the World Trade Center, Skilling was asked if the towers were vulnerable to a terrorist attack. He replied that he designed them to withstand the impact of a Boeing 707, the largest commercial jetliner of the day. In 1993 Skilling evidently saw no reason to revise his original opinion in light of the more recent Boeing 767s, which are slightly larger: "Our analysis indicated the biggest problem would be the fact that all the fuel (from the airplane) would dump into the building. There would be a horrendous fire. A lot of people would be killed. The building structure would still be there." Eric Nalder, "Twin Towers Engineered To Withstand Jet Collision," *Seattle Times*, February 27, 1993.

Interestingly, one week before the September 11 attack, Skilling's partner, Leslie Robertson, spoke at a conference in Frankfurt, Germany. When asked what he had done to protect the towers from terrorism, Robertson confirmed Skilling: "I designed it for a 707 to smash into it." "Towers Build to Withstand Jet Impact." *Chicago Tribune*, September 12, 2001.

6. NIST NCSTAR 1-5, WTC Investigation, p. xlviii; also see NCSTAR 1-6, WTC Investigation, p. lxiv.

7. In July 1971 the WTC won a national award when the American Society of Civil Engineers (ASCE) named it "the engineering project that demonstrates the greatest engineering skills and represents the greatest contribution to engineering progress and mankind." Angus K. Gillespie, *Twin Towers: The Life of New York City's World Trade Center*, New Brunswick, Rutger's University Press, 1999, p. 117.

8. Curiously, the NIST report gives two different (and conflicting) figures regarding the load distribution. NIST NCSTAR 1-3C, WTC Investigation, p. 3, asserts that the WTC core columns supported 60% of the load, and the perimeter columns 40%, while NIST NCSTAR 1-2A, WTC Investigation, p. 87 gives the figures cited here.

9. NIST NCSTAR 1-3, p. 10.

10. "How Columns Will Be Designed for 110-Story Buildings," *Engineering News-Record*, April 2, 1964.

11. NIST NCSTAR 1-6 p. lxxi.

12. Answers to Frequently Asked Questions, National Institute of Standards and Technology (NIST) *Federal Building and Fire Safety Investigation of the World Trade Center Disaster*, see question two, posted at http://wtc.nist.gov/pubs/factsheets/faqs_8_2006.htm.

13. Gordon Ross, "Momentum Transfer Analysis of the Collapse of the Upper Storeys of WTC 1," *Journal of 9/11 Studies*, June 2006. Posed at http://www.journalof911studies.com/.

14. On the sixth anniversary of the September 11, 2001 attack, Cambridge University engineer Dr. Keith Steffen told the BBC that his calculations showed that the WTC's progressive collapse on 9/11 was a "very ordinary thing." "9/11 demolition theory challenged," *BBC News*, September 11, 2007.

15. *The 9/11 Conspiracies: Fact or Fiction*, A&E television networks, AAE 103790, 2007.

16. *The 9/11 Commission Report, Final Report of the National Commission on Terrorist Attacks upon the United States*, W.W. Norton & Co., New York, 2004, p. 302.

17. Ibid.

18. Email from Greg Bacon, February 25, 2007.

19. This strange development came to light in July 2006, long after the cleanup of the Deutsche Bank had supposedly been completed. The announcement prompted a sharp letter of protest from the attorney representing the families of the victims. For more details go to http://www.911citizenswatch.org/print.php?sid=906.

20. The photo is posted at http://www.geocities.com/debunking911/columnd.jpg.

21. NIST NCSTAR 1, Full Summary Report, WTC Investigation, p. 118; also see NIST NCSTAR 1-2, WTC Investigation, Executive Summary, p. xli.

22. NIST NCSTAR 1, Full Summary Report, WTC Investigation, p. 124.

23. NIST NCSTAR 1-3C, WTC Investigation, p. 217.

24. NIST recovered 12 core columns from the WTC, but only one (in two separate pieces) from WTC 2 turned out to be from the area affected by the impacts/fires. A number of flanges from the core were also recovered. See Table 5-2 in NIST NCSTAR 1-3, WTC Investigation, p. 35.

25. NIST NCSTAR 1-3, WTC Investigation, p. 39.

26. Ibid.

27. The *NOVA* special "Why the Towers Fell" aired in 2002. The text of the *NOVA* interview with Thomas Eagar is posted at http://911research.wtc7.net/disinfo/experts/articles/eagar_nova/nova_eagar2.html.

28. FEMA: Executive Summary: WTC Building Performance Study, p. 2.

29. NIST NCSTAR 1-3, WTC Investigation, p. 10; also see p. 23.

30. NIST NCSTAR 1, NCSTAR 1-3, WTC Investigation, p. 115.

31. NIST NCSTAR 1, NCSTAR 1-3, WTC Investigation, p. 116.

32. NIST NCSTAR 1, Full Summary Report, WTC Investigation p. 130.

33. NIST NCSTAR 1-3C , WTC Investigation, p. 218.

34. Ibid.

35. NIST NCSTAR 1, Full Summary Report, WTC Investigation p. 88.

36. NIST NCSTAR 1-3, WTC Investigation, p. 101.

37. Ibid.

38. Andy Field, "A Look Inside a Radical new Theory of the WTC Collapse," *Fire/Rescue News*, February 7, 2004. Sunder made a similar statement during an October 19, 2004 presentation. See "World Trade Center Investigation Status," S. Shyam Sunder, lead investigator, Building and Fire Research Laboratory, NIST. This paper can be downloaded as a pdf file at http://www.nist.gov/public_affairs/agenda_oct192004.htm.

39. FEMA, *World Trade Center Building Performance Study*, Chapter Two: WTC 1 & 2, 2002, p. 22.

40. NIST NCSTAR 1, Full Summary Report, WTC Investigation, p. 76.

41. NIST NCSTAR 1, Full Summary Report, WTC Investigation p. 127.

42. NIST makes this important point in two separate places in the text. NIST NCSTAR 1-5, WTC Investigation, pp. 49 and 51.

43. NIST NCSTAR 1-6, WTC Investigation, p. lxvix.

44. NIST NCSTAR 1-2, Executive Summary, p. xli.

45. NIST NCSTAR 1-5, Executive Summary, p. xliv.

46. NIST NCSTAR 1-3, WTC Investigation, see photos and discussion pp. 49-55.

47. Ibid.

48. NIST NCSTAR 1-3C, WTC Investigation, p. 24.

49. NIST NCSTAR 1, Full Summary Report, WTC Investigation, p. 126-127.

50. NIST NCSTAR 1-5, WTC Investigation, p. 121.

51. NIST NCSTAR 1-6, WTC Investigation, p. lxvix; also see NIST NCSTAR 1-5, WTC Investigation, p. 51.

52. Jim Dwyer and Kevin Flynn, *102 Minutes: The Untold Story of the Fight to Survive Inside the Twin Towers*, Times Books, 2005, p. 206; also see Jim Dwyer and Ford Fessenden, "Lost Voices of Firefighters, Some on 78th Floor," *New York Times*, August 4, 2002; also see Christopher Bollyn, "Feds Withhold Crucial WTC Evidence," *American Free Press*, August 8, 2002.

53. NIST NCSTAR 1, Full Summary Report, WTC Investigation, p. 44.

54. NIST NCSTAR 1-2, WTC Investigation, p. 5.

55. *The 9/11 Commission Report*, p. 301.

56. Praimnath's testimony is posted at http://www.ambassadorspeakers.com/ACP/speakers.aspx?name=STANLEY%20PRAIMNATH&speaker=375.

57. "The Fall of the World Trade Center," BBC Two, Thursday, March 7, 2002, posted at http://www.bbc.co.uk/science/horizon/2001/worldtradecentertrans.shtml.

58. NIST NCSTAR 1-3, WTC Investigation, p. 95.

59. NIST NCSTAR 1, Full Summary Report, WTC Investigation, p. 43.

60. NIST NCSTAR 1-3 WTC Investigation p. 95.

61. NIST NCSTAR 1, Full Summary Report, WTC Investigation p. 144.

62. In the code, this was sub-article 1002.0, Adequacy Of The Structural Design. See NIST NCSTAR 1-1A, WTC Investigation, p. 32.

63. Conversation with Ron Hamburger, structural engineer, Dec 7, 2006.

64. NIST NCSTAR 1-2, WTC Investigation, p. 66.

65. In the NIST report, the reserve capacity data is expressed in the form of demand/capacity ratios, which is simply another way of expressing the factor of safety. I use the latter because I feel it's more comprehensible to the average layperson. Personal communication, December 14, 2006. See NIST NCSTAR WTC Investigation 1-6, Figure 8-9, p. 233.

66. NIST NCSTAR 1-2, WTC Investigation, p. 66.

67. NIST NCSTAR 1-2, WTC Investigation, p. cxii; also see NIST NCSTAR 1-2, WTC Investigation, p. 84.

68. The NIST report states: "... on the day of the attack the towers were subjected to in-service live loads (a fraction of the design live loads) and minimal wind loads." NIST NCSTAR 1-2 WTC Investigation, p. liv.

69. NIST NCSTAR 1-2, WTC Investigation, p. 66.

70. I received clarification about this from the NIST WTC Investigation Team, personal communication, December 14, 2006. The number 5.7 is derived from values presented in Figure 4-35, NIST NCSTAR 1-6, WTC Investigation, p. 101.

71. NIST NCSTAR 1-2, WTC Investigation, p. 66.

72. "How Columns Will Be Designed for 110-Story Buildings," *Engineering News-Record*, April 2, 1964.

73. Ibid.

74. Eric Douglas, R.A., "The NIST WTC Investigation — How Real Was The Simulation?" A review of NIST NCSTAR 1, *Journal of 9/11 Studies*, December 2006, p. 8. Posted at http://www.journalof911studies.com/.

75. NIST NCSTAR 1-2, WTC Investigation, Executive Summary, p. lxxxvii. NIST also admitted this in its global impact study., which states "... in terms of structural damage condition in exterior columns, Case Ai and Case Bi and similarly Case Ci and Case Di damage sets were identical." NIST NCSTAR 1-6D, WTC Investigation, p. 10.

76. NIST NCSTAR 1-2, WTC Investigation, Executive Summary, p. lxxv.

77. NIST NCSTAR 1-2, WTC Investigation, p. lxxv.

78. NIST NCSTAR 1-2B, WTC Investigation, p. 344.

79. NIST NCSTAR 1-2B , WTC Investigation, p. 345.

80. NIST NCSTAR 1-2B, WTC Investigation, p. 353.

81. NIST NCSTAR 1, WTC Investigation, p. 142; also see NIST NCSTAR 1-6D, WTC Investigation, pp. 131, 174, 150 and 239.

82. NIST NCSTAR 1, Full Summary Report, WTC Investigation, p. 142.

83. Jim Dwyer, "City to Release Thousands of Oral Histories of 9/11 Today," *New York Times*, August 12, 2005.

84. The FDNY testimonials are posted as pdf files at http://graphics8.nytimes.com/packages/html/nyregion/20050812_WTC_GRAPHIC/met_WTC_histories_full_01.html.

For a convenient look at some of them go to http://www.911review.com/coverup/oral-histories.html.

85. Graeme MacQueen, "118 Witnesses: The Firefighters' Testimony to Explosions in the Twin Towers," *Journal of 9/11 Studies*, August 21, 2006. Posted at http://www.journalof911studies.com.

86. Ibid.

87. Roberts' article is posted at http://forums.randi.org/showpostphp?p=1997183&postcount=1.

88. Oral history of Richard Banaciski, # 9110253, posted at http://graphics8.nytimes.com/packages/html/nyregion/20050812_WTC_GRAPHIC/met_WTC_histories_full_01.html.

89. Oral history of Thomas Fiztpatrick, # 9110001, posted at http://graphics8.nytimes.com/packages/html/nyregion/20050812_WTC_GRAPHIC/met_WTC_histories_full_01.html.

90. Oral history of Kenneth Rogers, # 9110290; posted at http://graphics8.nytimes.com/packages/html/nyregion/20050812_WTC_GRAPHIC/met_WTC_histories_full_01.html.

91. Oral histories of Richard Smiouskas, # 9110210 and Paul Mallery, # 9110312, posted at http://graphics8.nytimes.com/packages/html/nyregion/20050812_WTC_GRAPHIC/met_WTC_histories_full_01.html.

92. Jim Dwyer, op. cit.

93. *The 9/11 Commission Report*, p. 554.

94. Ibid., p. 306.

95. Answers to Frequently Asked Questions, National Institute of Standards and Technology (NIST) Federal Building and Fire Safety Investigation of the World Trade Center Disaster; see question two, posted at http://wtc.nist.gov/pubs/factsheets/faqs_8_2006.htm.

96. Zdeněk P. Bažant, Jia-Liang Le, Frank R. Greening and David B. Benson, "Collapse of World Trade Center Towers: What Did and Did Not Cause It?" Structural Engineering Report No. 07-05/C605c, Department of Civil and Environmental Engineering, Northwestern University, May 27, 2007 (Revised June 22 and December 15, 2007).

97. Graeme MacQueen, "Sonic Booms in the Collapse of the Twin Towers?" *Journal of 9/11 Studies*, letters, June 11, 2007, posted at http://www.journalof911studies.com/letters/SonicBoomExplanation3.pdf.

98. "The Heroism of William Rodriguez: Amazing Testimony from Inside the World Trade Center Towers on 9/11," transcript of Rodriguez's presentation at the American Scholars Symposium, June 25, 2006; posted at http://arabesque911.blogspot.com/2007/05/heroism-of-william-rodriguez-amazing.html.

99. Greg Szymanski, "Second WTC Janitor Comes Forward With Eye-Witness Testimony Of 'Bomb-Like' Explosion in North Tower Basement," arcticbeacon.com, July 12, 2005.

100. Deanna Spingola, "William Rodriguez, a 9-11 Survivor," *The Conservative Voice*, August 25, 2005, posted at http://www.theconservativevoice.com/articles/article.html?id=7762.

101. Greg Szymanski, "WTC Basement Blast and Injured Burn Victim Blows 'Official 911 Story' Sky High," arcticbeacon, June 24, 2005.

102. At www.911eyewitness.com.

103. Jim Hoffman, "Rick Siegel's 9/11 Eyewitness: Sensationalism and Pseudo-Science," posted at http://911review.com/reviews/911eyewitness/index.html.

104. David Ray Griffin, "Explosive Testimony: Revelations about the Twin Towers in the 9/11 Oral Histories," January 26, 2006; posted at http://www.mindfully.org/Reform/2006/911-WTC-Twin-Towers26jan06.htm.

105. At http://www.whatreallyhappened.com/shake.html.

106. NIST Status Update on WTC-7 Investigation, June 29, 2007, http://wtc.nist.gov/pubs/.

107. The first was Dr. Hugo Bachmann, a professor of structural engineering, who stated, "In my opinion WTC-7 was with the highest probability brought down by controlled demolition, done by experts. *Tages-Anzeiger,* September 9, 2006 posted at http://tagesanzeiger.ch/dyn/news/ausland/663864.html.

The other engineer was Professor Jörg Schneider, who stated, "WTC-7 was with great probability brought down by explosives." Posted at http://tagesanzeiger.ch/dyn/news/ausland/663864.html [See also http://www.danieleganser.ch/e/zeitungsartikel/index.htm and http://journalof911studies.com/articles/Intersecting_Facts_and_Theories_on_911.pdf.

108. The video of the interview is posted at http://www.911blogger.com/node/3231.

FBI TEN MOST WANTED FUGITIVE

**MURDER OF U.S. NATIONALS OUTSIDE THE UNITED STATES;
CONSPIRACY TO MURDER U.S. NATIONALS OUTSIDE THE UNITED STATES;
ATTACK ON A FEDERAL FACILITY RESULTING IN DEATH**

USAMA BIN LADEN

Date of Photograph Unknown

Aliases: Usama Bin Muhammad Bin Ladin, Shaykh Usama Bin Ladin, the Prince, the Emir, Abu Abdallah, Mujahid Shaykh, Hajj, the Director

DESCRIPTION

Date of Birth:	1957	**Hair:**	Brown
Place of Birth:	Saudi Arabia	**Eyes:**	Brown
Height:	6' 4" to 6' 6"	**Complexion:**	Olive
Weight:	Approximately 160 pounds	**Sex:**	Male
Build:	Thin	**Nationality:**	Saudi Arabian
Occupation:	Unknown		

Remarks: Bin Laden is the leader of a terrorist organization known as Al-Qaeda, "The Base." He is left-handed and walks with a cane.

CAUTION

USAMA BIN LADEN IS WANTED IN CONNECTION WITH THE AUGUST 7, 1998, BOMBINGS OF THE UNITED STATES EMBASSIES IN DAR ES SALAAM, TANZANIA, AND NAIROBI, KENYA. THESE ATTACKS KILLED OVER 200 PEOPLE. IN ADDITION, BIN LADEN IS A SUSPECT IN OTHER TERRORIST ATTACKS THROUGHOUT THE WORLD.

CONSIDERED ARMED AND EXTREMELY DANGEROUS

IF YOU HAVE ANY INFORMATION CONCERNING THIS PERSON, PLEASE CONTACT YOUR
LOCAL FBI OFFICE OR THE NEAREST U.S. EMBASSY OR CONSULATE.

REWARD

The Rewards For Justice Program, United States Department of State, is offering a reward of up to $25 million for information leading directly to the apprehension or conviction of Usama Bin Laden. An additional $2 million is being offered through a program developed and funded by the Airline Pilots Association and the Air Transport Association

www.fbi.gov

The 9/11/01 "terrorist" attack is is not mentioned on Osama bin Laden's Most Wanted poster/webpage because the FBI has no hard evidence connecting bin Laden to 9/11.

8

9/11 Conundrums

According to the official story, the plan to attack America on 9/11 was carried out by a core group of four Islamic extremists based in Hamburg, Germany: Mohamed Atta, Ramzi Binalshibh, Marwan al-Shehhi, and Ziad Jarrah. Determined to strike a blow against imperialism — we are told — the group initially sought to join the Islamic resistance movement in Chechnya, which at the time was battling the Russians. Their plan became untenable, however, when it was learned that the Chechnyan border had been closed. The aspiring jihadists made their way to Afghanistan instead, where they supposedly arrived in late November 1999.

Almost immediately they were granted an audience with the legendary figure of Osama bin Laden. According to the story, bin Laden had been planning an attack on America since March-April of 1999, when he supposedly approved a hijack plan conceived by one of his top lieutenants, Khalid Sheikh Mohammed. (Here, I must remind the reader that it is still impossible to separate fact from myth — I am merely recounting the official history.) Bin Laden was reportedly overjoyed by the arrival of these fresh recruits, all of whom were well educated, had lived in the West, and spoke several languages, including English. From what is known of Atta, he was apparently fluent in German, French, and English, in addition to his native Arabic. For these reasons the aspiring terrorists had extremely high value from the standpoint of jihad.[1]

The four supposedly swore allegiance to bin Laden, who selected Mohamed Atta to be their leader. After some basic training at bin Laden's camp they returned to Germany in January 2000 and began the methodical planning which led to the September 11 attack. One of the first steps, of course, was to emigrate to the United States. To conceal their visit to Afghanistan, the group reported their passports lost or stolen and were duly issued new and unblemished travel documents. At this point they applied for visas.

By March 2000 the group was searching the Internet for information about American flight schools. Two members of the group, Mohamed Atta and Marwan al-Shehhi eventually enrolled at Huffman Aviation, located in Venice, Florida. Another, Ziad Jarrah, was accepted for training at the Florida Flight Training Center (FFTC), also in Venice. The fourth member, Ramzi Binalshibh, failed to obtain an entry visa to the U.S., probably because of his Yemeni background, and had to forego flight instruction. Binalshibh remained in Germany, where he helped in a support capacity. His eventual replacement was Hani Hanjour, who allegedly piloted Flight 77 into the Pentagon.

The *9/11 Commission Report* states that in the fall of 2000 Atta, al-Shehhi and Jarrah successfully completed their courses at the Venice flight schools. Atta and al-Shehhi received their pilot's licenses in December 2000.[2] Here, however, the official narrative breaks down, because in no way did the flight training at Huffman and FFTC prepare the three jihadists to pilot Boeing 767s and 757s — just one of many sizable holes in the official conspiracy theory.[3] As we know, in the days after the 9/11 attack the world press swarmed into Venice, Florida, looking for a sensational story about Mohamed Atta and the other pilots. One of the feature attractions was Rudi Dekkers, owner of Huffman Aviation. Dekkers became an instant celebrity, made the rounds of the national media, and even testified before Congress. He told reporters that his school offered flight instruction in light aircraft only, not commercial jetliners.[4]

His statement should have raised eyebrows, because there is a galaxy of difference between a small Cessna and a commercial Boeing jetliner. The *9/11 Commission Report* offers very little in in the way of clarification on this vital point. It merely states that the terrorists subsequently prepared for the 9/11 attack by training on flight simulators.[5] End of story. We are supposed to fill in the blanks and leap to the conclusion that during the remaining nine months of their lives, the al Qaeda pilots somehow and somewhere picked up the necessary skills to fly large airliners into tall buildings — a considerable leap, as we are about to learn.

In June 2002, FBI Director Robert S. Mueller told the Joint Intelligence Committee that in late December 2000 Mohamed Atta and Marwan al-Shehhi showed up at the SimCenter flight school at Opa-locka Airport, near Miami, for a single session in a Boeing 767 flight simulator. Another statement by the FBI to this effect can be found in the transcript of the trial of Zacarias Moussaoui.[6] At the trial, the FBI produced a financial document indicating that Atta and al-Shehhi paid $2500 for the session.[7] However, the FBI released no further details. In the course of researching this book, I made strenuous efforts to learn more about the 767 training session, and I did manage to reach the office of an executive of Pan Am International (which owns Opa-locka). However, he refused to speak with me on the telephone. Later, I contacted Judy Glass, the PR person for Pan Am, who promised that she would look into the matter and get back to me with the details. But she never did. Months later, when I again attempted to reach Ms. Glass, she would not even return my calls. Obviously, for whatever reason, Pan Am International is refusing to release any information about the reported 767 simulator session. The question is *why?*

Evidently, Atta and al-Shehhi also purchased time at Opa-locka in a Boeing 727 simulator. In this case, fortunately, the *New York Times* was able to dig up some details.[8] Henry George, an instructor at the school, later told the *Times* that each of the hijackers spent a grand total of three hours in the simulator. Atta paid George the handsome fee of $1500 for the privilege. The ringleader Atta is known to have worn a money belt, and on occasion flashed large amounts of cash. There are even stories of Atta tossing hundred-dollar bills at people.[9] Evidently, something similar occurred on this occasion. George explained that it was not a formal training program in jet flight, but "a mini mini introduction." He said the two spent most of their time in the simulator practicing maneuvers and turns, although they also did take-offs and landings. Said George, "They did not seem to have the skill to pilot real jetliners, although they could turn the planes."

A Boeing 727 has three engines, rather than two, and features an old-fashioned cockpit with analog gauges and dials — very different from the digital instrumentation of a Boeing 767, which requires special training. A 727 is also much smaller and more maneuverable than a 767. Nonetheless, a few hours in the 727 simulator would have given Atta and al-Shehhi at least the feel of a large jetliner. Crucially, the story mentions nothing about whether the two practiced suicide runs at buildings, and we must conclude on this basis they did not. If they had, it is certain that George, who supervised their sessions, would have noticed. The only other possibility is that he failed to mention the fact to the *Times*, which is just not credible, given what happened on 9/11. Nor would the *Times* have failed to recognize a blockbuster story. Imagine the sensational headline: *TERRORISTS PRACTICED CRASHING JETLINER!* The header alone would have sold out the entire edition.

I am not trying to be flip or cute. The point is deadly serious. As we are about to learn, crashing large commercial airplanes into tall buildings is neither simple nor easy. It requires the practiced skills of a professional, hence would entail considerable training ahead of time. This is why U.S. Air Force pilots spend hundreds of hours in the air practicing approaches and bombing runs. They do this in peacetime to hone flight skills which must be second nature in wartime. As with anything else, practice makes perfect. One of the biggest problems with the official 9/11 narrative is that there is absolutely no evidence that the alleged hijackers had the requisite level of skill needed to fly Boeing 767s or 757s, let alone make suicide runs. Indeed, the available evidence indicates that they were barely able to fly *small* planes.

We know, for example, that in September 2000. Atta and al-Shehhi flunked a "stage I rating test" at Jones Aviation, another Florida flight school, located in Sarasota. After flunking the test, the two quit the school in frustration. It was not an advanced program either, but a basic course. Later, the instructor told the *Washington Post*, "They chose to go back to Huffman, We didn't kick them out, but they didn't live up to our standards."[10]

That the two continued to struggle with basic skills is shown by the following incident. Just days after receiving their pilot's licenses (in December 2000), Atta and al-Shehhi reportedly rented a small plane (a Piper Warrior) from Huffman Aviation and flew to Miami International Airport.[11] After they touched down, the plane's engine stalled and died while they were taxiing on the runway. At that point the two men turned off the controls, climbed out of the cockpit, and simply abandoned the plane on the tarmac — a definite "no-no" in the aviation business. After walking away, Atta and al-Shehhi rented a car and returned to Venice.

Later, the abandoned Piper was towed to a nearby hanger and checked out by a qualified plane mechanic. But he found no mechanical problems. The engine had apparently flooded, nothing more. Atta and Shihhi lacked even the basic know-how to restart the motor of a small plane. Incidentally, their rookie mistake was also a violation of FAA regulations. If you or I had done what they did, we would have faced consequences, at the very least a stiff fine, possibly worse. But Atta and al-Shehhi did not even receive a reprimand. Why not? Were they protected? An honest investigation would have pursued these questions. But there is not a peep about any of this in the *9/11 Commission Report*.

"Sim" Trials in Phoenix Raise Questions

The following remarkable story by a flight instructor named Dan Govatos speaks directly to these issues, and casts further doubt on the official narrative. The story aired on May 15th, 2007, during a radio interview hosted by Mike Swenson.[12] Govatos is a professional pilot with twenty-years experience, and flew for two major airlines. At the time of the 9/11 attack, he was employed as an FAA-authorized flight examiner at a training facility in Phoenix, Arizona. On the morning of 9/11 he was in a Boeing 737 flight simulator working with a class of pilots who had nearly completed their 737 training. Govatos was giving the trainees their "check ride," that is, their final test in the simulator, when they emerged on a break and learned about what was happening in New York. By now, the story is familiar. Someone had a television on in the break room, and like everyone else in America that day Gavatos and his pilots found themselves staring in awe and disbelief at the TV screen.

Needless to say, they were horrified by what they were seeing. The WTC had been hit, and columns of smoke were pouring out of the towers.

The training facility was located at a Phoenix airport, which was soon shut down due to the national Ground Stop. Govatos and his pilots were unable to go home that day. They spent the night at the airport, and the next morning Govatos said, "Hey guys, let's try something. Let's see if we can hit those buildings. Like we saw happen." Govatos led his class back into the simulator and set the "sim" program for New York. After which, they all took turns trying to crash the Boeing 737 into the World Trade Center. These were not novices, by the way.

Although the pilots had not flown 737s professionally, each of them had many years flight experience. But none of them could do it, not even after ten high-speed runs at the building, and — remember — this was a Boeing 737, which is smaller and more maneuverable than a Boeing 767. The pilots only succeeded in hitting the towers when they slowed down to near-landing speeds. This is important because, according to the official story, the impacts on 9/11 occurred at high speed: Flight 11 hit the North Tower at approximately 440 mph, and Flight 175 was ripping along at 540 mph when it plowed into the South Tower.

During the radio interview Govatos discussed the experience in the simulator that day, and why his pilots had failed to replicate the impacts at the World Trade Center.

People do not realize how difficult it is to hand-fly a jetliner at those high speeds. Particularly with a novice, whose experience is limited to small planes, there is a tendency to over-control everything.

You've got to understand, when you're going 300 knots in a Boeing airliner and you move the controls like you would expect to do in a little airplane, you couldn't stand the "G' forces. Everything has to be fingertip control. Even pilots who have logged thousands of hours of flight time have an extremely difficult time controlling a large airplane at those speeds.

This is one reason why commercial pilots usually rely on the autopilot, which has been standard equipment on the large jetliners for many years.

Govatos also mentioned that due to the high level of difficulty, his pilots repeatedly tripped the crash-logic built into the Boeing flight program, which froze the simulator. Each time this happened, they had to stop and reset the machine. After numerous failed runs, Govatos himself finally succeeded in hitting the tower. But he says he knew, even before the sim trials, "Something is not right." Meaning: with the official story.

During the same show, Swenson also interviewed another experienced pilot, Rob Balsamo, one of the founders of Pilots for 9/11 Truth. Balsamo explained that while he was producing the documentary film *Pandora's Black Box*, which analyzes the National Transportation Safety Board's report on Flight 77, he likewise practiced crashing a Boeing 757 into the Pentagon, in this case using a Microsoft flight program. Balsamo, an seasoned pilot, said it took him at least five to six attempts to approximate the final approach of Flight 77. Yet, as we know, whoever was at the helm of Flight 77 (assuming it *was* Flight 77) managed it on the first try.

When asked by Swenson to comment on the descending Top Gun loop maneuver that Hani Hanjour supposedly made in his final approach, Balsamo replied, "A lot of people say it was an impossible turning maneuver. But that is not the case. It is actually the opposite. It was a very graceful, in fact, a professional maneuver, well within the envelop of the aircraft. However, when the aircraft descended and rolled out of its turn on the last straight leg to the Pentagon, *that* maneuver itself … When you look at the yoke movement, you can tell that somebody, whoever was at those controls, was a professional and knew how to fly the aircraft."[13]

A Closer Look at Hani Hanjour

Many pilots agree with this assessment. According to the *Washington Post*, "… aviation sources said the plane [Flight 77] was flown with extraordinary skill, making it highly likely that a trained pilot was at the helm."[14] However, if this is true it poses major problems for the official 9/11 narrative, because there is overwhelming evidence that Hani Hanjour, the terrorist who supposedly flew Flight 77 into the side of the Pentagon, was even less qualified than Atta and al-Shehhi. Let us review this evidence.

Barely five feet tall and slight of build, Hani Hanjour was a native of Taif, a popular resort city in Saudi Arabia. By all accounts, he was shy and mild-mannered, even to the point of being timid. Hanjour was religious, but apparently not very ambitious. As a young man he cultivated no dreams of flying airplanes, but aspired only to become a flight attendant. Later, his older brother Abulrahman encouraged him to aim higher. Even so, as we are about to discover, Hani's aptitude for learning was rather limited.

His older brother Abulrahman was also responsible for Hani's first and second trips to the U.S. His brother was in the business of exporting used American cars to Saudi Arabia, which involved frequent travel back and forth. Abulrahman had connections in the States, and in the spring of 1996 he arranged for Hani to stay in Miramar, Florida with a couple he had known: Susan and Adnan Khalil. After his arrival in America, Hanjour roomed with the family for at least a month. Later, Susan Khalil described him as socially inept, with poor English, and "really bad hygiene."[15] Susan said her husband had to remind Hani to bathe and change his clothes.

In April 1996 Hani moved to Oakland, California, where he studied English for several months at Holy Names College. During this period he lived with a family who described him as a "quiet, introverted individual."[16] While in Oakland, Hanjour enrolled at the Sierra Academy of Aeronautics, but attended only one half-hour class and never returned. In the fall Hanjour moved to Scottsdale, Arizona and enrolled at Cockpit Resource Management (CRM), a flight school where he trained for three months. But the results were less than satisfactory. According to Duncan K.M. Hastie, owner of the school, Hani was "a weak student" who was "wasting our resources."[17] Hani withdrew from the program, then later returned in 1997 for several more weeks of instruction.

This "on and off" pattern of behavior was typical of the man. Hastie says that over the next three years Hanjour called him at least twice a year, and each time wanted to return for more training. By this point, however, it was obvious to Hastie that Hani had no business in a cockpit. Hastie refused to let him come back. "I would recognize his voice," Hastie said. "He was always talking about wanting more training. Yes, he wanted to be an airline pilot. That was his stated goal. That's why I didn't allow him to come back. I thought 'You're never going to make it.'"[18]

Rejected by CRM, Hanjour enrolled at nearby Sawyer Aviation, also located in the Phoenix area. Wes Fults, a former instructor at Sawyer, later described it as the school of last resort. Said Fults, "It was a commonly held truth that, if you failed anywhere else, go to Sawyer." Fults remembers training Hanjour, whom he described as "a neophyte." He says Hani "got overwhelmed with the instruments" in the school's flight simulator. "He had only the barest understanding of what the instruments were there to do," said Fults. "He [Hanjour] used the simulator three or four times, then disappeared like a fog."[19] I must emphasize to the reader that I'm not making this up. Other accounts in *Newsday,* the *New York Times,* as well as stories by the major networks, all corroborate the portrait of general ineptitude. Even the FBI confirms the basic story.[20]

Yet, somewhere along the way Hani qualified for a pilot's license. According to the FBI, this occurred in April 1999 while Hani was enrolled at Arizona Aviation, another of the numerous flight schools he attended.[21] The FBI document offers no further details. Nor does the *9/11 Commission Report,* which only briefly mentions the school. The pertinent line reads, "[In 2000] Hani began refresher training at his old school, Arizona Aviation."[22] Notice, again, the implied pattern of "on-again, off-again" behavior.

Although Hani Hanjour arrived sooner and spent more time in the U.S. than the other alleged hijackers, he never mastered the English language. Hani never learned to write English, and by all accounts his spoken English was atrocious. Incidentally, this sets Hani apart from Mohamed Atta and the other better-educated members of the Hamburg cell. It also raises a red flag, because in the U.S., fluency in English is required to obtain a pilot's license.

Hani's poor English and his sub-standard piloting skills actually prompted one flight school, Jet Tech, to question the authenticity of Hani's FAA-approved pilot's license. Jet Tech was another of the schools in the Phoenix area where Hani sought continuing instruction. Peggy Chevrette, Jet Tech's operation manager, later told FOX News, "I couldn't believe that he had a license of any kind with the skills that he had."[23] She explained that Hani's English was so bad it took him five hours to complete an oral exam that should normally have taken about two hours. Nor did Hani's answers impress the Jet Tech flight instructor: on the contrary. The instructor's evaluation notes,

> ... student [Hani] made numerous errors during [his] performance ... [and displayed] a lack of understanding of some basic concepts. The same was true during review of systems knowledge. The root cause is most likely due to the student's lack of experience.[24]

Early in 2001, Chevrette contacted the FAA to convey her concerns about Hani. In fact, she called a number of times. Eventually a federal inspector, John Anthony, showed up at the school and examined Hani's credentials. But Hani's papers were in order, and Anthony took no further action. The inspector even suggested that the school provide Hani with an interpreter. This surprised Chevrette, because it was a violation of FAA rules. "The thing that really concerned me," she later told FOX News, "Was that John had a conversation in the hallway with Hani and realized what his skills were at that point and his ability to speak English."[25] Evidently, Anthony also sat in on a class with Hani.

Although FOX News was unable to reach Anthony for comment, FAA spokesperson Laura Brown defended the FAA employee. "There was nothing about the pilot's actions" she said, "to signal criminal intent or that would have caused us to alert law enforcement."[26] This is true enough. The Jet Tech staff never suspected that Hani was a terrorist. According to Marilyn Ladner, vice-president Pan Am International, the company that owned Jet Tech, "It was more of a very typical instructional concern that 'you really shouldn't be in the air.'"[27]

At least one FAA inspector, Michael Gonzales, disagrees. Gonzales, who is also the president of a professional organization that represents FAA inspectors, told the Associated Press, "There should have been a stop right then and there." Gonzales thinks Hani should have been re-examined, as required by law.[28] Although Pan Am dissolved its Jet Tech operation shortly after 9/11, a former employee who knew Hani expressed amazement "that he [Hani] could have flown into the Pentagon. He could not fly at all."[29]

According to the official narrative, in the weeks before the September 11 attack at least two of the alleged hijackers, i.e., Hani Hanjour and Ziad

Jarrah, rented small planes at local airports on the outskirts of New York and Washington DC for the purpose of familiarizing themselves with the intended targets. But at least one of these ventures did not go according to plan. During the second week of August 2001, Hanjour attempted to rent a plane at Freeway Airport in Bowie, Maryland, about twenty miles from Washington. Although Hani presented his FAA license, the airport manager insisted for safety reasons that an instructor first accompany him on a test flight to confirm his piloting skills. During three such flights in a single-engine Cessna 172, instructors Sheri Baxter and Ben Conner observed what others had before them: Hanjour had trouble controlling and landing the aircraft. Even though Hami had a license and a log book showing 600 hours of flight time, Freeway's chief instructor Marcel Bernard refused to rent him a plane without additional lessons.[30] Let us remember, this was just weeks before the 9/11 attack.

The *9/11 Commission Report* acknowledges Hani's poor English and his sub-standard piloting skills.[31] It also mentions that flight instructors had urged him to give up trying to become a pilot. But the report then dodges crucial questions: First, why did the FAA grant Hani Hanjour a pilot's license in the first place? Second, who was responsible? And third, how did Hani come to have 600 hours of flight time in his log book? The high number suggests that the log book may have been falsified. But one will search the official report in vain for any discussion of these important questions.

Instead of providing answers, the report cavalierly states that Hani qualified for a license because he "persevered." But this is absurd. In fact, it is an obvious case of deception, because clearly Hanjour's English and piloting skills never improved. What is more, the 9/11 Commission surely knew this. The basic facts were readily available, having been established by the press in open-source accounts in the days and weeks following 9/11, long before the start of the official investigation.

The Other Four

It now appears that Hanjour may have exploited a loophole in the FAA system to obtain his pilot's license. For many years the FAA has allowed private contractors to certify pilots, and agency records show that Hani Hanjour did indeed obtain certification in this manner, that is, by hiring a private examiner. This was first reported by the *Dallas Morning News* in June 2002. According to the story, Hanjour was certified in April 1999 as an "Airplane Multi-Engine Land/Commercial Pilot" by Daryl Strong, one of the FAA's 20,000 designated pilot examiners. Les Dorr, an FAA official, defended the agency's longtime policy of outsourcing the certification process.

But a critic, Heather Awsumb, took issue with it. Awsumb is a spokesperson for the Professional Airways Systems Specialists Union, which represents more than 11,000 FAA and Defense Department employees. She pointed out that the FAA does not have anywhere near enough staff to oversee the 20,000 designated inspectors, who have a financial interest in certifying as many pilots as possible. This might also explain how Hani evaded the language requirement. Said Awsumb, "They receive between $200 and $300 for each flight check. If they get a reputation for being too tough, they won't get any business." She added that the present system allows "safety to be sold to the lowest bidder."[32]

While this might explain how Hani Hanjour obtained his pilot's license, it does not begin to account for the final approach of Flight 77 (or whatever hit the Pentagon). Given the facts, the official narrative cannot possibly be correct, because it is obvious that Hani Hanjour was completely incapable of flying a Boeing 757 airliner, and therefore could not have crashed Flight 77 into the Pentagon at 530 mph on the morning of September 11. This brings us to the vital question: If not Hani Hanjour, who or what was at the helm?

The facts impel us to examine all of the possibilities, which thankfully are few in number. According to the official narrative, on the day of the attack Hanjour was accompanied by four other al Qaeda terrorists, the so called "muscle hijackers." Their job was to seize the cockpit, subdue the crew, and control the passengers. Did the FBI simply err when it identified Hani Hanjour as the pilot? Perhaps one of these *other* jihadists was flying the plane: Nawaf al Hazmi, Khalid al Mihdhar, Majed Moqed, or Salem al-Hazmi.

Two of the men, Nawaf al Hazmi and Khalid al Mihdhar, *did* study at a U.S. flight school. According to the *Washington Post*, the two began flight lessons in May 2000, several months after their arrival in the U.S., at which time they enrolled at Sorbi's Flying Club near San Diego.[33] As in Hani's case, the project did not go well. Rick Garza, who was the flight instructor at Sorbi's at the time, says the two men spoke little English, yet were impatient and wanted to learn to fly large Boeing jets. "They had zero training before they got here," he said, "so I told them, they had to learn a lot of other things first. It was like dumb and dumber, I mean, they were clueless. It was clear to me they were not going to make it as pilots."[34]

After a half dozen ground lessons and two flights, Garza sat the two men down and told them: "This is not going to work out." Garza says they offered him extra money if he would continue the training, but to his credit, Garza refused. So ended their plans to become suicide pilots. This rules out both al Hazmi and al Mihdhar.

Another alleged hijacker, Majed Moqed, also a Saudi, reportedly studied law at King Fahd University before dropping out, after which he was recruited by al Qaeda.[35] A law student certainly did not fly a Boeing jetliner into the Pentagon. Scratch Moqed.

We will probably never know the true identity of the last member of the alleged hijacker crew. Although the name released by the FBI was "Salem al-Hazmi" — supposedly the younger brother of Nawaf al Hazmi — we now know this name was merely an assumed identity. Within weeks of 9/11, it was revealed that several of the alleged hijackers in fact were not dead, but were alive and well. This includes the real Salem al-Hamzi, who at the time apparently was working at a government-owned petrochemical complex in the city of Yanbu, Saudi Arabia.[36]

After the attack Salem saw his photo in the newspaper and was shocked to learn that the U.S. government had accused him of hijacking Flight 77. During an interview, Salem told reporters he had never been to the United States. He also explained that someone had stolen his passport during a trip to Cairo three years before 9/11. Evidently the impostor reversed the "z" and "m" in his surname, i.e., from "Hamzi" to "Hazmi," the spelling that appears on a New Jersey driver's license, which — we are told — was recovered at the Pentagon crash scene.[37] Everything else was a match, including the photo, as noted, the birth date, and other personal information. The facts clearly point to a case of identity theft. However, the story also has a curious twist that could be trivia, but then again, just might turn out to be extremely important.

Recall the bin Laden video released by the U.S. government in December 2001, which purportedly features Osama bin Laden sitting around with comrades boasting about al Qaeda's involvement in the 9/11 attack. According to the Bush administration, the one-hour-long video is proof of bin Laden's involvement. Yet, as I have noted, experts dispute the DoD's translation from the Arabic, and many doubt that the character in the video is actually bin Laden. No one has explained why bin Laden, a known southpaw, is seen in the film writing with his right hand. But here is the twist: shortly after the footage was released, CBS reported that the names of several of the nineteen alleged hijackers are mentioned in the video by bin Laden himself, apparently in the context of praising them as martyrs.[38]

The names include one Salem Alhamzi, who, I think, we may fairly judge to be the same individual we have been discussing. Curiously, the spelling reported by CBS was "Hamzi," [39] rather than "Hazmi," the significance of which is unclear. Without more information we cannot be certain why the "z" and "m" were switched. *What is certain is that the real bin Laden (assuming his guilt) would have known the hijacker's actual name.*

So why, after just taking credit for the crime of the century, would bin Laden heap praise upon an assumed identity? This makes no sense. Surely bin Laden would have praised the jihadist by his actual name, rather than praising an alias. If this somewhat speculative analysis is on target, then it is more evidence of fakery. Did the perpetrators slip up when preparing the script for the video, by mentioning the assumed name? If so, covert operators are human like the rest of us and do sometimes make mistakes. On a scale of one to ten, this was a whopper.

Some, no doubt, will argue that the unidentified man who posed as Salem al-Hazmi, whoever he was, was the actual pilot of Flight 77. But this is a slim reed on which to defend the official narrative, and in the view of this writer is no more than grasping at straws.

The 9/11 Conundrums

We have followed the tracks into a forest of detail. Let us now step back and revisit the big picture. From the moment we acknowledge the high likelihood that explosives were used on 9/11 to demolish the World Trade Center, we are compelled to entertain a new point of view, and by this I mean through the eyes of the perpetrators. Surely the planting of charges in the towers was a major undertaking, and took weeks or months to complete. Yet, once the decision was made, the evildoers were fully committed.

The "planes operation" had to move forward, and the margin for error was small. The operation was complex. There were many things that could go wrong, any one of which threatened to expose the plan. There was a significant danger, for instance, that the explosives would be discovered prematurely. Moreover the planes had to hit the specified buildings on target, point blank, and no mistake about it. A botched crash might also expose the operation.

Given all of this, is it reasonable to suppose that the perpetrators would place their trust in four rank amateur pilots who between them had zero experience flying large Boeing airliners? I think not. In fact, the very notion is absurd. There was no certainty that Hani Hanjour and the others would even be able to locate the buildings, let alone hit them on the first attempt. In fact, the plan was so complex that the chances for success were rather low, that is, without expert assistance. Obviously, the terrorists needed help to complete their suicide mission — a great deal of it. We are compelled to ask: What kinds of assistance were the insiders prepared to deliver? How did they insure the success of the operations? Above all: *How was it all done?*

These conundrums have led 9/11 investigators down a multitude of pathways in the search for answers, including — it must be admitted — a number of blind alleys. In the following pages I will present my own research into one of the conundrums of that day.

Endnotes

1. I need to mention that this usage of the term jihad is outside the mainstream within Islam. Although my knowledge of the Muslim religion is only rudimentary, as I understand it, the term usually refers not to terrorism nor even war but to the struggle within the individual for truth and spiritual liberation. In a wider sense, it is the struggle for peace and social justice.

2. *The 9/11 Commission Report, Final Report of the National Commission on Terrorist Attacks Upon the United States*, W.W. Norton & Co., New York, 2004, pp. 226-227.

3. Investigative writer Daniel Hopsicker spent many months in Venice tracking down various parts of the story that never made it into the official account. According to Hopsicker, Atta and al-Shehhi were also enrolled at Professional Aviation, a flight school at Charlotte County Airport, located near Punta Gorda, which is just down the road from Venice. Hopsicker also found evidence of a long history of CIA activity in Punta Gorda and thinks Atta's sojourn in Charlotte County was dropped from the official narrative for this reason. We also know that Atta and al-Shehhi checked out the Airman Flight School in Norman, Oklahoma, but chose not to enroll. Daniel Hopsicker, *Welcome to Terrorland: Mohamed Atta and the 9/11 Cover-Up in Florida*, Madcow Press, Venice, FL, 2004, pp. 86, 90-100.

4. Ibid., p.131.

5. *The 9/11 Commission Report*, p. 227.

6. Statement for the Record, FBI Director Robert S. Mueller III, Joint Intelligence Committee, Joint Investigation into September 11th, Closed Hearing, June 18, 2002; U.S. District Court for the Eastern District of Virginia, Alexandria Division, Criminal No. 1:01cr455, United States of America vs. Zacarias Moussaoui; also see David Firestone and Dana Canedy, "FBI Documents Detail the Movement of Hijackers," *New York Times*, September 15, 2001.

7. John Farmer found this information in the FBI Chronology. According to the document, the session happened on December 31, 2000. The document is numbered 0573000259772 and mentions Sun Trust Bank. Email from John Farmer, July 16, 2008.

8. Statement for the Record, FBI Director Robert S. Mueller III, Joint Intelligence Committee, Joint Investigation into September 11th, Closed Hearing, June 18, 2002; US District Court for the Eastern District of Virginia, Alexandria Division, Criminal No. 1:01cr455, United States of America vs. Zacarias Moussaoui; also see David Firestone and Dana Canedy, "FBI Documents Detail the Movement of Hijackers," *New York Times*, September 15, 2001.

9. Daniel Hopsicker, op. cit., p. 40.

10. Steve Fainaru and Peter Whoriskey, "Hijack Suspects Tried Many Flight Schools," *Washington Post*, September 19, 2001. Also see Statement for the record: FBI Director Robert S. Mueller III, loc. cit.

11. "Suspected WTC hijackers abandoned plane on a Miami taxi way," CNN.com, October 17, 2001.

12. Interview with Dan Govatos and Rob Balsamo by Mike Swenson on Revolution Radio, May 15, 2007. The best part of the interview is included in the following terrific video. "Could the Hijackers have hit the buildings?" posted at http://www.911blogger.com/blog/1015.

13. Ibid.

14. Marc Fisher and Don Phillips, "On Flight 77: 'Our Plane is Being Hijacked,'" *Washington Post*, September 12, 2001.

15. Amy Goldstein, Lena H. Sun and George Lardner Jr. "Hanjour an Unlikely Terrorist," *Cape Cod Times*, October 21, 2001.

16. Ibid.

17. Ibid.

18. Ibid.

19. Ibid.

20. Statement for the record: FBI Director Robert S. Mueller III, Joint Intelligence Committee Inquiry, Joint investigation into September 11, closed hearing, Joint House/Senate Intelligence Committee Hearing, June 18, 2002.

21. Ibid.

22. *The 9/11 Commission Report*, pp. 226-227. One of the staff reports, not included in the final report, confirms the FBI document, and states that Hani Hanjour "completed flight training and received FAA pilot certification. Hanjour received his commercial multi-engine pilot certificate from the FAA in March 1999." Steven Strasser, *The 9/11 Investigations: Staff Reports of the 9/11 Commission*, 2004, The Four Flights, Staff Statement No. 4, pp. 4-5.

23. "FAA Probed, Cleared Sept. 11 Hijacker in Early 2001," FOX News, May 10, 2002.

24. Hani's evaluation and other documentation of his time at Jet Tech were entered as evidence during the trial of Zacharias Moussaoui. Training Records, Hani Hanjour, B-737 Initial Ground Training, Class 01-3-021, Date: 2/8/01, Jet Tech International, posted at http://www.vaed.uscourts.gov/notablecases/moussaoui/exhibits/prosecution/PX00021.pdf.

25. "FAA Probed, Cleared Sept. 11 Hijacker in Early 2001," FOX News, May 10, 2002.

26. Ibid.

27. Jim Yardley, "A Trainee Noted for Incompetence," *New York Times*, May 4, 2002.

28. "Report: 9/11 Hijacker Bypassed FAA," AP, June 13, 2002.

29. Ibid.

30. Thomas Frank, "Tracing Trail of Hijackers," *Newsday*, September 23, 2001.

31. *The 9/11 Commission Report*, pp. 226-227.

32. Kellie Lunney, "FAA contractors approved flight licenses for Sept. 11 suspect," GovernmentExecutive.com, June 13, 2002.

33. Amy Goldstein, "Hijackers Led Core Group," *Washington Post*, September 30, 2001.

34. Edward Helmore and Ed Vulliamy, "Saudi Hijacker 'was key to bin Laden'," *Observer* (U.K.), October 7, 2001.

35. At http://en.wikipedia.org/wiki/Majed_Moqed.

36. David Harrison, "Revealed: the men with stolen identities," *Telegraph* (U.K.), September 23, 2001; also see Dan Eggen, George Lardner Jr. and Susan Schmidt, "Some Hijackers' Identities Uncertain," *Washington Post*, September 20, 2001.

37. The alleged hijacker's New Jersey driver's license reads "Salem al-Hazmi," the same spelling that also appears in the *9/11 Commission Report*. However, the surname can also be spelled "al-Hamzi." The same is true of the other alleged hijacker, Nawaf al Hazmi, whose last name may also be spelled al Hamzi. Such variants are a curious oddity when translating Arabic into English.

38. "Bin Laden Names Hijackers on Tape," CBS News, December 20, 2001.

39. Ibid.

The Flying Patsies?

When you have eliminated the impossible, whatever remains, however improbable, must be the truth.
— Sir Arthur Conan Doyle, "The Sign of Four," 1890

On June 1, 2001 the U.S. Joint Chiefs of Staff issued a new order that changed official policy in cases of aircraft piracy, i.e., hijackings. The new order (CJCSI 3610.01A), signed by Vice Admiral S.A. Fry, Director of the Joint Chiefs of Staff, replaced the existing order (CJCSI 3610.01), which had been in effect since July 1997. When I learned about this, I was immediately intrigued. The date, just three months prior to 9/11, suggested more than mere coincidence. The June 2001 order was like a red flag shouting an insistent question: Why did the U.S. military alter its hijack policy just a few months before 9/11? It is a fair question. Why, indeed?

When I first examined the document, which, by the way, is still posted on the Internet, my excitement increased.[1] The June 2001 order states that when hijackings occur, the military's operational commanders at the Pentagon and at the North American Aerospace Command (NORAD) must contact the office of the Secretary of Defense for approval and further instruction. At the time, of course, this meant Donald Rumsfeld. Was this new order evidence of a policy change made for the purpose of engineering a stand-down on 9/11? This seemed plausible, assuming that a group of evildoers within the Bush administration wanted a terrorist plot to succeed for their own twisted reasons. And what might those reasons be? Well, just possibly, to create the pretext for a much more aggressive U.S. foreign policy, one that the American people would not otherwise support.

On the other hand, would the Joint Chiefs be so naive as to effect a stand-down on 9/11 by means of an ordinary administrative memo, thus leaving a paper trail to the crime of the century? Several prominent 9/11 investigators evidently thought so. One of them was Jim Marrs, an accomplished journalist, who discusses the June 1, 2001 Pentagon order in his excellent book, *The Terror Conspiracy.*[2] Filmmaker Dylan Avery was another. Avery mentions the order in a similar context in his popular video, *Loose Change 2nd Edition.*[3] So does Webster Griffin Tarpley in his engaging book, *9/11 Synthetic Terror,* one of the deepest examinations of 9/11 in print.[4] Initially, I was sympathetic to their conclusions, however, after studying the document more closely I began to have second thoughts. Fortunately, the previous July 1997 order is also available for download via the Internet.[5]

Close inspection of the two documents, side by side, shows that the previous order *also* required notification of the office of the Secretary of Defense in cases of hijackings. In fact, there was almost no change in the language on this point. It would appear that the basic policy remained in effect, and can be summarized as follows: *Although operational commanders have the authority to make decisions of the moment in cases of hijackings, they are also required to notify the office of the Secretary of Defense, who must be kept in the loop and who may chose to intervene at any time.*

Side by side, the two documents are almost identical. But there is one difference. The new order includes an extra passage in the policy section that mentions two new kinds of airborne vehicles, "unmanned aerial vehicles (UAVs)" and "remotely operated vehicles (ROVs)." The order states that, henceforth, these are to be regarded as "a potential threat to public safety." But why would two new categories of aerial vehicles require the drafting of a new order, especially since the basic policy did not change? I puzzled over this for some time, until I stumbled upon a news story about the Global Hawk, which prompted further investigations and ultimately convinced me that the June 1, 2001 Pentagon order may indeed offer a clue about what happened on September 11, 2001.

The answer is not obvious. The technology I will now describe certainly was not on my radar screen. Like most Americans, I went about my affairs over the course of years blithely unaware that technological advances were altering our world beyond recognition. While it is certainly true that new technologies hold amazing potentials to improve our lives and free us from drudgery, make no mistake, they can just as easily enslave us. Nor is it likely that technology's most hopeful possibilities will be realized so long as its cutting edge remains shrouded in secrecy for "reasons of national security," a phrase that in my view is one of the most abused expressions in our language.

But I will go even further: If ordinary citizens do not soon awaken to the insidious dangers that new technologies pose to our freedoms, the faceless individuals and nameless puppeteers who command these technologies will succeed in imposing their hidden agendas upon us. In that case, the experiment in self-government that began with the drafting of the U.S. Constitution more than 200 years ago will have reached a dark end. History will come to view us in the same way that we currently look upon the democracies of ancient Greece, i.e., as just another of humanity's great-but-failed experiments.

Here, I would add a further point: In his important book *Nemesis, The Last Days of the American Republic*, Chalmers Johnson, an expert on Japan and U.S. foreign policy, claims that as much as 40% of the Pentagon budget is "black," meaning: hidden from public scrutiny.[6] If the figure is accurate, it makes my point.

A Cautionary Tale: The Flight of the Global Hawk

On April 23, 2001, just weeks before the Pentagon issued the new hijack order, an unmanned aircraft, the RQ-4A U.S. Global Hawk, completed its maiden 7,500 mile flight from Edwards AFB in southern California to Edinburgh AFB in South Australia.[7] The nonstop 8,600 mile passage across the Pacific took just 22 hours and set an endurance record for an unmanned vehicle. The drone returned to California in early June, after a dozen joint exercises with the Australian military. The previous year, the Global Hawk had made a similar transatlantic run to Europe, where it participated in NATO exercises.

You might be thinking: OK, but so what — what is the big deal with the Global Hawk? How does it relate to 9/11? I will answer the second question in a moment. Rod Smith, the Australian Global Hawk manager, answered the first when he said, "The aircraft essentially flies itself … from takeoff, right through to landing, and even taxiing off the runway."[8] The drone follows a preprogrammed flight plan, although ground controllers constantly monitor it and ultimately remain in control. The jet-powered craft is 44 feet long, has the wingspan of a Boeing 737, and can remain aloft for 42 hours. It flies at extremely high altitudes, up to 65,000 feet, and has a range of 14,000 nautical miles. The Global Hawk is aptly named — the bird truly has a global reach. Its cruising speed is nothing special, about 400 mph, but its ability to reconnoiter vast areas of geography is remarkable. In a single flight, the drone can surveil an area the size of Illinois: more than 50,000 square miles. It comes equipped with advanced

213

radar, infrared and electro-optical sensors, which combined can return up to 1,900 high-resolution images during a single flight. These are impressive specs by any standard.

The U.S. military wasted no time putting the Global Hawk to work gathering intelligence. The bird flew during Operation Enduring Freedom, Bush's October 2001 invasion of Afghanistan, and subsequently saw wide use in Iraq. During one year alone, Global Hawk drones flew at least 50 combat missions over Iraq and Afghanistan and logged 1,000 hours of flight time. By the way, during the summer of 2006, the Israelis used similar technology during their aerial campaign against Lebanon. In fact, it was they who pioneered the use of surveillance drones during a previous (1982) invasion of their northern neighbor. The U.S. first used drones the following year, when Ronald Reagan ordered the invasion of Grenada, a small island nation in the Caribbean. According to various reports, Global Hawk surveillance of Iran is ongoing.

Development of the Global Hawk began in 1995, with the first air trials in 1998 at Edwards AFB. However, the technology is much older. In his film *Loose Change 2nd Edition* Dylan Avery included a video segment from a NASA test flight carried out in 1984, also at Edwards AFB. During the 16-hour exercise, ground pilots remotely controlled a Boeing 720, guiding it through 10 successful takeoffs, numerous approaches, and 13 landings. The test ended with a pre-planned crash.

The Pentagon's use of drones for target practice during war games has been routine for many years. In fact, there is ample evidence that the U.S. military first experimented with remote-controlled aircraft as early as World War II. At the time, the U.S. air command was suffering heavy losses over German-occupied Europe as a result of intense flak barrages. It was hoped that the introduction of remote-controlled bombers would stem the losses by reducing the exposure of air crews to withering German anti-aircraft fire. The experiments involved B-17s and B-24s packed with explosives — known as "Weary Willies." The air crew would take off, then bail out after a chase plane took over control. The crew in the chase plane would then guide the unmanned bomber, essentially a flying bomb, into its target.

The experimental program failed however. Weary Willies were ineffective weapons because they flew very slowly, and thus were easy targets. The missions were also extremely hazardous. One of them cost the life of the elder brother of President John F. Kennedy. Lt. Joseph P. Kennedy Jr. was piloting one of the converted bombers when the aircraft, loaded with ordnance, exploded prematurely.[9] The program was scrapped in 1944. However, after the war the U.S. resumed ROV research, and in the 1950s made rapid progress with radio-controlled planes. As we are about to learn, even greater strides apparently were made during in the 1970s.

The True Beginning?

In late September 2001, a few weeks after the World Trade Center attack, George W. Bush mentioned ROV technology during some comments to the press. The president was passing through Chicago's O'Hare International Airport and paused to discuss airline safety. According to the *New York Times*, Bush mentioned that his administration was considering several measures, including federal grants for stronger cockpit doors and new transponders that cannot be turned off. Bush also talked about installing video cameras so that pilots could monitor the passenger section of commercial jetliners.[10] Then, Bush said,

> We will look at all kinds of technologies to make sure that our airlines are safe, including technology to enable controllers to take over a distressed aircraft and land it by remote control.[11]

Bush implied that this helpful technology belonged to the future. However, there is strong evidence it already existed at the time he spoke — and even before 9/11. A few days after his press briefing, the Raytheon Corporation announced that on August 25, 2001, "a government-industry team had accomplished the first precision approach by a civil aircraft using a military Global Positioning System (GPS) landing system." During three months of trials, Raytheon and the U.S. Air Force had conducted a series of experiments at Holloman AFB, New Mexico. The test flights involved a Fed-Ex Express Boeing 727-200 equipped with a Rockwell-Collins GNLU-930 Multi-Mode Receiver.

Raytheon's contribution was a military GPS ground station developed under a U.S. Air Force contract, involving a Joint Precision Approach and Landings System (JPALS) program.[12] The auto-landing followed a series of sixteen successful approaches, during which the aircraft was guided by the JPALS ground station. According to Fed-Ex spokesperson Steve Kuhar, a senior technical advisor: "... the consistency of the approaches allowed us to proceed to actual auto-landings with very little delay." The press release boasted that "Raytheon is the world leader in designing and building satellite-based navigation and landing solutions for civil and military applications." The date of the successful auto-landing was two weeks before the September 11 attack.

Nor is this the only case. Other high-tech firms also do similar research. In fact, after the 9/11 attack there was a considerable amount of discussion within the industry about new civilian ROV applications. For example, soon after September 11, Tom Cassidy, president and CEO of General Atomics Aeronautical Systems, sent Transportation Secretary Norman Mineta a letter in which he discussed the feasibility of using remote control technology to prevent future acts of terrorism.[13] Cassidy's firm developed the Predator, a remote-controlled reconnaissance and attack plane which has been in use by the U.S. Air Force since 1994. The Predator is a distant cousin of the Global Hawk. Cassidy informed Mineta that it would not be difficult to adapt the same technology for commercial aircraft:

> Such a system would not prevent a hijacker from causing mayhem on the aircraft or exploding a device and destroying the aircraft in flight, but it would prevent him from flying the aircraft into a building or populated areas.

One small high-tech Arizona company named KinetX went so far as to submit a serious proposal to the Federal Aviation Administration for just such a system. The Tempe-based KinetX developed its proposal in concert with another Arizona firm named Cogitek. In a white paper the two companies claimed that their National Flight Emergency Response System (NFERS), as they called it, would prevent future 9/11-style hijackings. They insisted that a prototype could be up and running within a year. The white paper described NFERS as "the integration of existing technology for the purpose of transferring cockpit operations to a secure ground station in case of an emergency." The paper stated, "It is important to note that *the essential technology exists now*" [my emphasis].[14]

In 2006, Dr. Lyman Hazelton, chief scientist at KinetX, posted additional details about the NFERS system on a web blog dedicated to security issues. Hazelton explained that NFERS "uses strong crypto, a command-able autopilot in a physically secured section of the aircraft, and the IRIDIUM satellite phone system (which we helped to design and are still working on now)."[15] He then added, "We tried hard to think through the security process for the system, and I think we did a good first cut. We certainly have all the technology to make it happen ... "

The FAA never responded to their proposal, however, according to the KinetX website.

In January 2006 the Boeing company announced a patent for similar technology.[16] Boeing's "auto-land system" reportedly involves an onboard processor. Once activated, it overrides the cockpit controls and guides a hijacked plane to an emergency landing. The system can be preprogramed into the plane's autopilot, or operated remotely by ground controllers. It can be activated in several different ways: either directly by the pilot during a hijacking-in-progress; or indirectly by sensors installed in the cockpit door, which would be tripped by forcible entry; or, lastly, by ground controllers via a remote link.

At issue, is whether Boeing's auto-land system was truly a new development in 2006. Or did the aircraft giant merely pull preexisting hardware off the shelf, as KinetX had proposed in 2001 with its NFERS system? The Pentagon's June 1, 2001 order strongly suggests that, from the standpoint of the U.S. military, ROV technology had come of age by the spring of 2001, several months *before* 9/11. Curiously, in 2008 Secretary of Defense Robert Gates confirmed as much during an address to the Air University, in which he mentioned that "we now have more than 5,000 UAVs [Unmanned Aerial vehicles], a 25-fold increase since 2001."[17]

We need to ask: When was the last time that the U.S. military developed a new technology *after* private industry, or even simultaneously? It is well known that military research & development programs always receive the best available resources, funding, and expertise. For this reason the military almost always leads the way in technology, usually by at least ten years, sometimes by much more. The emergence of the Internet is an obvious example. As we know, the U.S. military developed cyberspace many years before the Internet exploded into the civilian sector. Does it not stand to reason that ROV technology also followed a similar development path?

All of which raises disturbing questions. Did George W. Bush wander off his crib sheet in late September 2001 in his remarks to the press about aircraft safety? Did the president blunder when he mentioned ROV technology in the same breath with 9/11? One does not need a Ph.D. in rocket science to know that what holds for the goose is also true for the gander. Obviously, the same ROV technology designed to foil hijackers might also be used to commit acts of terrorism, i.e., to fly planes into tall buildings. It just depends on who is at the controls. It's tempting to wonder how much (or how little) George W. Bush knew (and presently knows) about September 11. It's a fair question, and here is another: Did Bush unwittingly come within a whisker of giving the game away?

Joe Vialls' "Back Door" Theory

According to the late aeronautical engineer, Joe Vialls, the technology to capture planes via remote control has been around a very long time. If Vialls is correct, the U.S. military developed ROV technology as far back as the mid-1970s, in response to a sharp upsurge in terrorist hijackings during this period. The goal of the project, which, according to Vialls, involved two American multinationals in collaboration with the Defense Advanced Research Projects Agency (DARPA), was to facilitate the remote recovery of hijacked American aircraft. Vialls claimed that the effort succeeded brilliantly in developing the means: first, to listen in on cockpit conversations in a target aircraft; and, second, to take absolute control of the plane's computerized flight control system through a remote channel. The aim was to cut the hijackers out of the control loop while empowering ground controllers to return a hijacked plane to a chosen airport, where police would deal with the terrorists.

To be truly effective, however, the new technology "had to be completely integrated with all onboard systems," which could only be achieved by incorporating the system into a new aircraft design. According to Vialls, this is exactly what happened. A high-level decision was made, and Boeing quietly included a "back door" into the computer designs for its 767 and 757 commercial jetliners, which at the time were still on the drawing boards. Both planes went into production in the early 1980s.

Vialls shocked even Internet users when he posted all of this on his website in October 2001.[18] He contended that the system, although designed for the best of intentions, fell prey to a security leak. Somehow the secret computer code fell into the hands of evildoers within the Bush administration, who surreptitiously used the remote channel on 9/11. Thus armed with the secret codes, the perpetrators easily activated the hidden channel built into the transponders and simply took over the flight controls. Whether or not the alleged nineteen hijackers were actually on board remained uncertain. But the issue clearly was of secondary importance, since the jihadists were not flying the planes.

Vialls cited evidence in support of his thesis. Crucially, not one of the eight commercial pilots and copilots aboard the four allegedly hijacked planes on 9/11 sent the standard signal alerting FAA authorities that a hijacking was in progress.[19] Sending this signal, or "squawking," as it is called, takes only a few seconds and is done by activating a cockpit device known as an ELT (emergency locator transmitter). A pilot simply keys-in a four-digit code — 7500 — and the letters "HIJK" flash on a screen at ground control. The fact that not even one of the pilots or copilots managed to transmit this standard SOS on 9/11 was suspicious: the first indication to Vialls that the planes were being flown by some remote means.

Another clue was the near total loss of radio contact. Although an electronic failure can disrupt the radio link between a pilot and ground control, this would not explain the loss of radio contact in three out of four planes. Vialls concluded that the pilots lost the ability to transmit after the evildoers commandeered the transponders.

Additional evidence turned up in a video of the last seconds of Flight 175, which had been briefly posted on the Internet. According to Vialls, the footage was anomalous because it showed the plane executing a steep diving maneuver during its final approach that exceeded the normal software limitations of a 767. Boeing jets are designed with liability concerns in mind, as well as passenger safety. Flight control software prevents a pilot from making steep turns that pull substantial "G" forces. Such turns run the risk of injuring passengers, especially the aged and infirm, which can result in costly lawsuits. This was strong evidence — Vialls argued — that the plane was under remote control.

The Critics Respond

Debunkers had a field day trying to discredit Vialls and his remote control scenario. What is truly surprising is that, many years later, his ideas continue to have traction despite the debunkers, whose more thoughtful criticisms I will now discuss. Some of them pointed out that the flight controls on Boeing 767s and 757s, while fully computerized, are not fly-by-wire designs like some newer planes, including the Global Hawk. On the contrary, they are mechanical beasts with hydraulically assisted cable and pulley controls. For this reason, these critics assert, a Boeing pilot always has the option of "turning off" the autopilot and flying manually.[20] One anonymous critic who claimed to be a Boeing maintenance technician argued that even in the worst case, a 757 or 767 pilot could simply pull the electrical breakers, shutting down the power supply to the onboard computers. This would allow him to regain control and fly the old fashioned way, that is, by the seat of his pants, though, no doubt, with considerably more difficulty. Such criticisms, I fully acknowledge, are plausible and may even be correct. The problem is that under the circumstances it is impossible to evaluate them without additional information. Unfortunately, short of hacking into Boeing's corporate files there is no way to determine whether the company engineered a hidden override system into its 767s and 757s. Nor can Vialls help us, because, unfortunately, he died in 2005.

The story has a no less intriguing sequel. Vialls also contended that in the 1990s, officials at Lufthansa airlines made a shocking discovery. By chance, after taking delivery of a fleet of Boeing jetliners, they stumbled upon the hidden ROV system, at which point, because of the obvious security concerns, Lufthansa went to considerable trouble and expense to remove the original flight control system and replace it with one of German design. As far as I know, this story remains unconfirmed. But neither has it been discredited, and there is yet another twist. In 2003 Andreas von Buelow, a former minister of research and technology in the German government, authored a book, *Die CIA und der 11. September. Internationaler Terror und die Rolle der Geheimdienste* (The CIA and September 11: International terrorism and the role of secret services [PIPER VERLAG, MUNICH]), in which he discussed Joe Vialls' remote control theory while calling for a new 9/11 investigation.

In his book, von Buelow made a stunning charge of his own. Von Buelow claimed that the 9/11 attack was not the work of Islamic extremists, but was an inside job orchestrated by the CIA. As a former high official in the German defense ministry, was Von Buelow privy to the details about Lufthansa's experience with Boeing? At the present, unfortunately, there are many more questions than answers. For this reason, I call on Lufthansa and Boeing to come to our assistance by disclosing their corporate records to an independent team of inspectors. I would add that von Buelow has not backed away from the controversial opinions expressed in his book. In radio interviews he has argued that the "hijacked" planes on 9/11 were most likely guided by some form of remote control. He thinks 9/11 was a covert operation carried out by a small group within the U.S. intelligence community, numbering fewer than 50 people.[21]

The Latency Period Issue

Other critics came at Vialls from a different direction. They claimed that potential 9/11 conspirators would never use ROV technology because of the so called latency period issue. They pointed out that flying planes by remote control involves a troublesome time delay, which makes precision flying difficult if not impossible.[22] These critics typically cite the astronomical accident rate for drone aircraft, which is 100 times higher than for manned planes. Take, for instance, the Predator, as noted, a cousin of the Global Hawk. Out of 135 of these unmanned surveillance-and-attack planes delivered and used in military operations, at least 50 have crashed, and 34 others have suffered serious accidents.[23] Such numbers do not inspire confidence, and on this basis critics argued that any 9/11 perpetrators within the U.S. government would have instantly rejected ROV technology out of hand as far too unreliable.

The above argument sounds plausible, but is easily refuted. A look at the specifications for the Global Hawk shows that there are two very different ways to remotely control an aircraft, only one of which involves a time delay. The first is by means of a remote link, e.g., a communications satellite, which does indeed involve a latency period. The second method, however, is direct line-of-sight, which involves no such delay. Evildoers determined to fly planes into the World Trade Center might, therefore, have overcome the latency period issue by setting up a local command center, for example in WTC-7. Rooftop cameras or other equipment might also have been employed to provide a real-time video feed. Once the local controllers established visual contact, they might have switched from the remote link to line-of-sight. After which, guiding the planes into the towers would have been a simple matter. The final approach was the only portion of the flight where "slop" in the controls would have mattered.

In March 2007, after I posted the above analysis on the Internet, I heard from a pilot with more than 45 years flying experience. He wrote, "If there truly is a back door and a remote control operation is possible, then it would be a simple matter to have remotely done 9/11." According to this pilot, a simple transmitter in a window of each tower, or on the roof, would have provided all of the necessary guidance for a "routine autopilot coupled approach."[24]

In fact, the autopilots on today's airliners are so advanced that pilots seldom touch the controls. A Boeing autopilot, officially termed the "flight director," is perfectly capable of flying a commercial airliner from take-off to landing. According to pilot and former air traffic controller Robin Hordon:

> ... when a commercial jet approaches its destination, the flight director interfaces with transmitters located at the end of a runway and makes the adjustments. All the pilots have to do is sit back, monitor the controls, and watch the airplane land it-

self, even in zero-zero conditions [i.e., zero visibility due to fog or stormy weather].[25]

In June 2007, Hordon delivered an address to a Vancouver, BC 9/11 truth conference about a range of issues, including remote control technology. Although Hordon does not necessarily agree that it was used on 9/11, he admits it is a possibility. Said Hordon, "Could an aircraft be remotely controlled in flight right now? Absolutely. In a heartbeat. Because the technology is there."[26]

Locked Doors

Curiously, at the time of the 1993 World Trade Center bombing, dozens of workers fled heavy smoke by climbing to the roof, where they were rescued by police helicopters. But no such exodus to safety occurred on 9/11. Many people trapped on the upper floors *did try* to reach the roof, however they could not because they found the doors locked. We know this from cell phone calls made by frantic victims. One can imagine their horror, after fleeing toxic smoke, heat and flames, only to discover that there would be no escape. Surely at that point, hundreds of trapped souls must have known they were doomed. In their 2003 book *City in the Sky*, authors James Glanz and Eric Lipton state that the locked-door policy went into effect shortly after the 1993 bombing.

> For a variety of reasons, the Port Authority had decided, with the agreement of the Fire Department, to discourage the use of helicopters in emergencies at the building. Ordinary building occupants were never briefed on the policy change after 1993, and there were no signs explaining that the doors were locked, although the Port Authority's emergency drills directed people down the stairs, not up ... "[27]

The *9/11 Commission Report,* released in July 2004, affirms all of this, and also mentions that the doors were locked "for security reasons." But it offers no further details.[28] Questions remain, because there is reason to think the people trapped in the South Tower should have been able to reach the roof despite the policy. While the North Tower was famous for its 107th floor restaurant, Windows on the World, the South Tower had its own popular tourist attraction. Known as "Top of the World," it featured the highest observation deck in America, allowing a unique

360-degree panoramic vista of New York City and environs.[29] Weather permitting, tourists could also ride an escalator from the enclosed 107th floor deck to an outdoor viewing platform mounted on the roof. Photos confirm that a flood of tourists indeed visited the WTC roof nearly every day. There were also shops on the 107th floor that catered to tourists. The official investigation never explained why WTC security personnel, who surely had keys to the open air platform, failed to use them on 9/11. The official report makes no mention of any of this.

Assuming that 9/11 was an inside job, the locked-door policy obviously was convenient for the perpetrators. The abandoned helicopter rescue system also eliminated any chance that survivors would live to tell stories about bombs exploding in the core of the buildings. Due to the smoke and heat, helicopter rescue would have been difficult, but not impossible.

This might even explain the demolition of WTC-7, assuming the building housed the local command center. Such an operation would have involved a substantial amount of incriminating hardware which could not be removed after the fact without running grave risks. It would have been much safer, from the standpoint of the perpetrators, to destroy the evidence by "pulling " Building 7.

The Lone Gunman

On March 4, 2001, six short months before 9/11, the Fox network aired a pilot television program called *The Lone Gunman*. The title of the premiere was "Scenario 12-D." The show was fictitious: about a strange military exercise gone awry, but it was no less prophetic. In the story a faction within the U.S. government stages a phony terrorist attack for the purpose of provoking a U.S. military response abroad. The deeper reason, as the riveting dialogue makes clear, is because "the arms market is flat." Evidently, a powerful sub-group of industrialists and their co-conspirators within government view false-flag terrorist operations as a perfectly acceptable means for priming the economic pump, thus driving up arms production and sales. Need I mention that, in the real world, the profits generated by this particular industry are exceeded only by the illegal drug trade?

And what is the act of "terrorism?" Why, the very thing we have been discussing! Using remote access, the evildoers commandeer a Boeing 727 during a commercial flight over the northeastern United States. (Notice, this was the same model used by Raytheon in the remote tests later that year.) Of course, the controllers are safely on the ground. In one scene we see them huddled around a lap-top computer in a dimly-lit room, in the process of busily steering the plane toward — you guessed it — the World Trade Center!

For maximum effect, we are informed that the airliner is fully loaded with 110 passengers and is carrying 16,000 gallons of jet fuel. The tension mounts as the derelict plane moves closer to its doom. The pilot orders the electrical power cut, then calmly warns the unsuspecting passengers to return to their seats and fasten their seat belts. (As if this would make any difference.) Meanwhile, his crew struggles to regain control of the ship. At the last instant the pilot achieves a manual override and pulls up the nose — just in time to miss the South Tower by inches. In one scene we are even shown a graphic of the flight path, which, believe it or not, is almost identical to the final approach of Flight 175.

At this point, you will probably not be surprised to learn that nothing came of FOX's hijack pilot program. The network dropped the series after a few months, and to my knowledge nothing has been heard of it since.[30] Was the program just a bizarre coincidence? We are left to wonder. Debunkers of "conspiracy theories" always take delight in pointing out that such scenarios are ridiculous in real life "because the government cannot keep secrets." Maybe they are right. Did someone "on the inside" leak the planned attack to a confidante in Hollywood? How else would the producer know the shape of things to come?

To this writer, the maturation of ROV technology in the period immediately prior to 9/11 feels rather too close for comfort.

Endnotes

1. The June 1, 2001 order can be downloaded at www.dtic.mil/doctrine/jel/cjcsd/cjcsi/3610_01a.pdf.

2. Jim Marrs, *The Terror Conspiracy*, Disinformation Company Ltd., 2006, p. 38.

3. To his credit, Avery does not mention this issue in his sequel, *Loose Change: Final Cut.* I am informed by David Ray Griffin, who served as a consultant on the final edition, that Avery & company changed their minds.

4. Webster Griffin Tarpley, *9/11 Synthetic Terror: Made in USA*, Progressive Press, 2006, p. 200.

5. The July 1997 order can be downloaded at www.dtic.mil/doctrine/jel/cjcsd/cjcsi/3610_01.pdf.

6. Chalmers Johnson, *Nemesis: The Final Days of the American Republic*, Henry Holt & Co., New York, 2006, pp. 9 and 115.

7. Documented at http://www.fas.org/irp/program/collect/global_hawk.htm. See also

http://www.airforce-technology.com/project_printable.asp?PROJECTID=1280.

8. "Robot plane flies Pacific unmanned," ITN News, posted at http://web.archive.org/web/20010707000937/http://itn.co.uk/news/20010424/world/05robotplane.shtm.

9. My thanks to Rowland Morgan for first bringing this to my attentionin an email, August 26, 2007.

10. *New York Times*, September 28, 2001.

11. Jeff Long, "Landing by remote control doesn't quite fly with pilots," *Chicago Tribune*, September 28, 2001.

12. Raytheon News Release. "Raytheon and Air Force Demonstrate Civil-Military Interoperability for GPS-Based Precision Landing System," Marlborough, MA., October 1, 2001.

13. Jeff Long, op. cit.

14. Cited in Jim Marrs, *The Terror Conspiracy*, Disinformation Company Ltd., 2006, p. 137.

15. See Dr. Hazelton's post at http://www.schneier.com/blog/archives/2006/07/remote-control_a.html#c107421.

16. John Croft, "Diagrams: Boeing patents anti-terrorism auto-land system for hijacked planes," posted at http://www.flightglobal.com/articles/2006/12/01/210869/diagrams-boeing-patents-anti-terrorism-auto-land-system-for-hijacked.html.

17. Text of Gates' Air Force Comments: Defense Secretary spoke about challenges at Air University, MSNBC, April 21, 2008, posted at http://www.msnbc.msn.com/id/24240541/.

18. The page has been archived at http://geocities.com/mknemesis/homerun.html.

19. This was reported by CNN's Wolf Blitzer on 9/11. "Government Official Has New Evidence Regarding Hijacked Airlines," CNN Live Event/Special, September 11, 2001, 23:52 ET. Posted at http://transcripts.cnn.com/TRANSCRIPTS/0109/11/se.07.html.

20. The following site is home to a group of the most indefatigable debunkers on the Internet: http://911myths.com/html/remote_control.html.

21. An audio file of one of these interviews is available at http://www.prisonplanet.tv/audio/200406vonbuelow.htm.

22. For an interesting discussion and additional sources go to: http://911myths.com/html/remote_control.html.

23. This was reported by the *Wall Street Journal*, online edition. Go to: http://online.wsj.com/article/SB115491642950528436.html?mod=todays_us_marketplace.

24. Email from "old geezer pilot," February 25, 2007.

25. Jeremy Baker, "The First Fifteen Minutes of September 11: Former Air Traffic Controller Robin Hordon speaks out on 9/11, NORAD, and what should have happened," PrisonPlanet.com, March 12, 2007.

26. Ibid.

27. See the account in James Glanz and Eric Lipton, *City in the Sky: The Rise and Fall of the World Trade Center*, Times Books, New York, 2003, p. 252.

28. *The 9/11 Commission Report: Final Report of the National Commission on Terrorist Attacks Upon the United States*, W.W. Norton & Co., New York, 2004, pp. 279-281, 294, 317. The report states that a "lock release order" was issued at 9:30 A.M., which would have unlocked all areas in the complex controlled by the WTC's computerized security

system, including the doors to the roof. The order was never executed however. Why not? According to the report, because of "damage to the software controlling the system, resulting from the impact of the plane." Of course, assuming perpetrators had planted explosives, they must have had access to the WTC security system, including the computers, which they surely would have disabled as a part of their plan.

29. At http://en.wikipedia.org/wiki/World_Trade_Center.

30. My thanks to "Pinnacle" who provided information about the WTC observation deck and *The Lone Gunman.*

10

Clinton Set the Stage for Bush

A t the end of the Cold War, the peoples of the earth shared a rare moment of history. The United Sates stood alone as the sole planetary superpower. The American star which had been rising since the Second World War reached its apogee. For whatever reason, it seemed that destiny had selected the United States for a special role: to guide the community of nations into a period of unparalleled peace and prosperity. With the fading of East-West tensions this and much more seemed within reach. For a brief time, it did appear that almost anything was possible. And why not? After all, the United States faced no serious military rivals. The U.S. dollar was the favored currency in international exchange, and had been for decades. English was the *lingua franca* of science, diplomacy and commerce. Most of the world acknowledged U.S. leadership. American culture was widely imitated. All of this, taken together, was unprecedented. Never in history had one nation achieved this much global influence. America had both the prestige and the power to shape the future of humanity, for better or ill.

Legacy of the Cold War

T he world was desperate for a new vision. This was true for many reasons, but primarily because the titanic struggle between capitalism and Communism had been so destructive. The forty-five-year Cold War had been waged on many fronts and in the most improbable places. It was an ideological war, not a clash of civilizations. As the vying spheres of influence ebbed and flowed across the continents, numerous nations were drawn in. Proxy wars raged along the tectonic margins and at the friction points where

East and West collided. Neither side could defeat the other militarily without destroying itself, because the epic struggle was governed by a mad doctrine: Mutually Assured Destruction (MAD). It was a fitting acronym for an insane time. It was also a cruel paradox. For decades, the world, rigged to a trip wire, could neither stand still nor move forward. The added rub, which I believe most people sensed intuitively, was that the precarious balancing act could not be sustained indefinitely. Of course, looking back, it is clear that the Cold War itself, I mean the idea of the Cold War, was a carefully cultivated illusion: a false reality. But that is another story.[1]

Certainly the consequences were real enough. Citizens of the planet who lived through the period know what it means to live wedged between impossible alternatives — the unthinkable on one hand and the unendurable on the other. Millions were crushed beneath these wheels. Indeed, some nations were utterly destroyed beyond hope of recovery. The list of victims is long, and includes Afghanistan, Angola, Cambodia, Chile, the Dominican Republic, Haiti, East Timor, Ethiopia, Granada, Guatemala, Honduras, Indonesia, Laos, Mozambique, Nicaragua, Panama, Somalia, Sudan, and Viet Nam. No doubt there are others ...

Even as the Cold War trampled on the rights of indigenous people everywhere, it despoiled the global environment. Toxic mayhem on a vast scale accompanied the nuclear arms race. Entire regions were affected, and many were ruined or left permanently scarred. The open wounds from the heyday of uranium mining still deface the landscapes of the American southwest. Navaho children still play on the tailing piles, amidst the radioactive dust left behind by soulless corporations that appeared on the scene, eager to make a fast buck, boomed briefly, then disappeared or were swallowed, in turn, by still larger corporations with even less of a conscience. Even worse scars can be found in the former Soviet republics, where whole provinces were poisoned by catastrophic accidents at Sverdlovsk and Chernobyl, and entire ecosystems, such as the Aral Sea region, were despoiled by central planning gone amok.

Dashed Hopes

By any measure, the toll of the Cold War was incalculable, and it is no wonder that when the corrupt old Soviet state finally collapsed, the world's response was "good riddance!" The dismantling of the Iron Curtain was attended by joyous celebration in Europe. For a brief time, hope soared. Here in the U.S., there was even talk of a peace dividend. *Have we forgotten?* Everywhere people dared to believe that the victory of the West presaged a new era of international cooperation, now desperately needed to address a long list of pressing global problems, among them Third World poverty, overpopulation, the challenge of sustainable development, the energy crisis, AIDs, and the environment.

Most importantly, at long last *real* progress toward nuclear disarmament was finally within reach. All eyes at this moment turned to the West and especially to Washington for leadership. Yet it is now painfully obvious, and has been for most of George W. Bush's presidency, that humanity's once high hopes have been dashed. All that remains is the question: *How did this happen?* It is a difficult question, admittedly, but if we are ever to find our way back and regain a measure of hope, I believe we must face it honestly.

Today, many Americans hold G.W. Bush personally responsible for the wars in Iraq, Afghanistan and elsewhere that have caused America's increasing isolation in the world. Many also blame Bush for the sinking dollar, the deepening economic crisis and the general decline in our fortunes. While I am no friend of the Bush administration, I do not entirely agree with this view, because I take issue with those who still naively believe in a partisan solution. The truth is more complex.

In fact, the previous Democratic administration of William Jefferson Clinton bears a large measure of responsibility for the disasters that have befallen us. In many ways the Clinton White House set the stage for George W. Bush. Dr. Helen Caldicott, the tireless campaigner against nuclear oblivion, writes that she got the wake-up call about Clinton in 1999, when she was invited to attend a meeting in Florida about the weaponization of space. Caldicott was aghast as she listened to knowledgeable individuals describe current U.S. military planning for space. Like many of us, she had trusted Bill Clinton, and naively believed he was taking care of the nation's business. Suddenly, Caldicott realized she had been living in a fool's paradise:

> To my horror I found that seventy-five military industrial corporations such as Lockheed Martin, Boeing, Raytheon, TRW Aerojet, Hughes Space, Sparta Corp, and Vista Technologies had produced a Long Range Plan, written with the cooperation of the U.S. Space Command, announcing a declaration of U.S. space leadership and calling for the funding of defensive system and "a seamlessly integrated force of theatre land, sea, air and space capabilities through a world-wide global defense information network." The U.S. Space Command would also "hold at risk" a finite number of "high-value" earth targets with near instantaneous force applica-

tion — the ability to kill from space.... I also discovered that the much-vaunted missile defense system was to be closely integrated with the weaponization of space, and that all of the hardware and software would be made by the same firms, at the combined cost of hundreds of billions of dollars to the U.S. taxpayers.[2]

The plan envisaged "full spectrum dominance," that is, U.S. military domination of land, sea, air and space. Although U.S. planners sought to portray this next generation of technological wizardry as defensive, in actuality, the planned systems, if implemented, amounted to a major break with the 1972 ABM Treaty and with longstanding U.S. commitments to maintain the peaceful status of outer space. The cold hard logic of dominance meant that the project was offensive in nature. But why? Exactly who was to be targeted? Which enemies? Remember, this was 1999. The Cold War was over and had been for years.

It was obvious to Caldicott that a precious opportunity was being squandered, perhaps forever. The new space weapons threatened to trigger a new global arms race and, very likely, another cycle of world conflict. Caldicott writes that she staggered home from the meeting determined "to become re-involved in educating the public about the impending catastrophe associated with the mad plans of the U.S. Space Command and its associated corporations ... "

The Critical Path: Swords into Plowshares

The point is that not even one of the new weapons systems being planned was needed. In fact, the grand plan for space, if implemented, would have benefited no one but a few arms manufacturers and, of course, the bankers who finance such deranged schemes — all at immense cost to the U.S. taxpayer. As noted, the plan to weaponize space was in direct conflict with then-current U.S. foreign policies, and was diametrically opposed to the limited nuclear arms reductions then in progress; yet, it was being presented as in the best interests of America: a case of mendacity so brazen one wonders how the selfish individuals who dreamed it up could sleep at night.

As I've noted, the end of the Cold War presented America and the world with a golden opportunity to move in a new direction, one that, in fact, was essential for the survival of our planetary civilization. As a younger man, I was a great admirer of the late inventor R. Buckminster Fuller. He is probably best known for the geodesic dome, but Fuller also popularized the notion of the "critical path," an expression used by engineers, and one that means exactly what it suggests.[3] The idea is that if we are to become sustainable on "spaceship earth" and avoid destroying our planetary home, we must learn to live within the physical limitations or budget imposed by Nature. This requires that we drastically reduce our human "footprint" by becoming much more efficient in the way we use energy and natural resources.

Fuller was a firm believer in human ingenuity, and he often argued that our predicament called for a designer revolution on various levels, both economic and social. None of the steps in the critical path are optional, from the standpoint of survival. Taken together, they should be understood as the minimum requirements necessary for the long-term success of the human enterprise. While experts often disagree, at the end of the Cold War the single most urgent step in the critical path should have been obvious to every thinking person, including the newly elected President Bill Clinton, who entered the White House in 1992 on a wave of high hopes.

As the first Democratic U.S. president to be inaugurated in the post-Cold War era, Bill Clinton's number one priority should have been to meet with our Russian neighbors at an early date, and to negotiate with them a mutual halt in nuclear weapons production and research, as well as a rapid build-down of existing nuclear stockpiles and delivery systems. It was also imperative that Clinton give firm direction to the U.S. military. The Pentagon had to be made to understand that because the Cold War was now thankfully over, the nation must chart a new path, one requiring the urgent redeployment of resources away from the nuclear weapons industry. A key part of this redirection would be the announcement of a vital new mission for the national weapons labs (Lawrence, Los Alamos, and Sandia). Henceforth, the labs would cease most weapons-related research/development and would redirect their considerable talents in a positive direction, the new mission being a Manhattan-scale project to solve the nation's long-term energy problem.

The goal would be to wean America away from its unhealthy dependence on coal and foreign oil. Clinton would instruct the labs to engineer a phased transition toward abundant and clean energy alternatives at the earliest possible date; to make this happen he would press Congress to appropriate the needed funding. Efforts would focus on a range of promising technologies, but especially wind, solar, tidal, and hydrogen.

Meanwhile, the nuclear establishment would be stripped of its vast subsidies. Although in a bygone era these may have been justified, the nuclear establishment had failed to produce a long-term energy solution. Indeed, the enormous monies lavished upon it over decades of preferential treatment had succeeded only in creating a bureaucratic dinosaur. The nuclear industry had become a part of the problem itself and was now an impediment to change. Why? Because its enormous subsidies undermined healthy market forces, and were frustrating the development of more promising energy alternatives. Henceforth, nuclear power would have to compete on an equal playing field with solar, hydrogen, wind energy, etc.

Another key objective would be to achieve the economies of scale necessary to bring down the costs of clean and renewable alternatives. The project would envision whole new sectors of the economy, greatly enhanced national productivity, boosted foreign earnings, not to mention millions of high-paying new jobs — not offshore *but right here in the U.S.* Meanwhile, resources would also be redirected to a long list of outstanding social and environmental problems. At the top of the list: the urgent cleanup of the toxic mess created by the nuclear establishment during a profligate half-century of out-of-control weapons development. This alone would cost an estimated $350 billion (in 1995 dollars, according to the Department of Energy), a whopping figure that does not even include the costs associated with cleaning up the mess at the Hanford reservation, the Nevada Test Site, and the Savannah and Clinch nuclear facilities, all so contaminated that a solution may not even be feasible.

Some will argue that the above visionary plan was (and is) unrealistically utopian — too much to expect of any U.S. president, let alone the Clinton White House. But I take strong exception with this viewpoint, because in the 1990s the transition I have described was already within reach. Few major technological breakthroughs were needed. Many of the important alternatives were already "on the shelf" and could have been brought to maturity without undue economic strain. Some, no doubt, would have been mainstream long since but for bureaucratic inertia and because powerful vested interests have actively suppressed them — the same interests, I would add, that have sought to keep America addicted to oil. No, what was needed more than anything was strong leadership in the White House — to beak through the inertial barriers and confront the vested interests. What is the role of a U.S. president, after all, if not to use the power of the office (the "bully pulpit") to catalyze changes that are needed for the good of the nation as a whole. Indeed, this is precisely why a president must stand above special interests.

In the early years of his presidency, Clinton did not lack for popular support. A solid majority of the American people elected him because they wanted change, and they looked to Clinton to make the tough decisions. This is not just my opinion. Numerous commentators have pointed this out. No question, Bill Clinton entered office with tremendous political capital. Yet, incredibly, he never used it. The crucial factor was leadership and he simply failed to deliver. There are various theories as to why. Dr. Caldicott's frank assessment will make Democrats squirm, but in my opinion it carries the ring of truth. Caldicott thinks Clinton lacks the necessary strength of character, and she has it about right. I would go further, but, again, that is another story.[4]

Clinton's Nuclear Policy Review: A Diminished Presidency?

Like other newly elected presidents, Bill Clinton soon ordered a policy review of U.S. nuclear weapons doctrine. The review was of vital importance, and its successful completion required Clinton to become personally involved. This also meant taking charge at the Pentagon as the commander-in-chief. Unfortunately, instead of asserting his authority, Clinton vacillated, as if he were unclear himself about priorities and objectives. Eventually he delegated the nuclear policy review to mid-level officials who were easily outmaneuvered by hard-liners in the military. The Pentagon generals opposed any changes in U.S. nuclear policy, and they won a decisive victory. It was a major defeat for Clinton and one from which he never recovered. Caldicott speculates that Clinton thereafter sought to compensate for his loss of standing by using military force abroad on more occasions than any president in two decades. She may be right. Clinton's subsequent attempts to placate the Pentagon certainly were no substitute for strong leadership, and this probably explains why, even today, Clinton is generally viewed with contempt within the U.S. armed services. Soldiers naturally respect strength and revile weakness.

However, Clinton's diminished presidency did not become evident for some years. Certainly none of this was immediately obvious. At the 1995 Nonproliferation Review Conference, the Clinton administration, to all appearances, achieved a major success by persuading a majority of nations to agree to an indefinite extension of the Nonproliferation Treaty (NPT). This success was probably due to Clinton's vocal support for the Comprehensive Test Ban Treaty (CTBT), and because the U.S. delegation agreed to a list of noble principles reaffirming the U.S. obligation under Article VI of the NPT to take steps in the near future toward complete nuclear disarmament. The world did not then know that Clinton was about to trample on those same principles, by succumbing to a deal with hard-line elements within his own administration. Surely this in itself is an indication of Clinton's failed leadership, for only a weak president would ever agree to such a back-room deal.

What was the deal? The U.S. Department of Energy, representing the national weapons labs, agreed to back Clinton's support of the Comprehensive Test Ban, but *only* if Clinton agreed to preserve the labs' traditional role as nuclear overseers; and this, of course, meant preserving the nuclear arsenal itself. In this way was born the Stockpile Stewardship and Management Program, otherwise known as Manhattan II. Although its stated purpose seemed innocuous enough: to insure the safety and reliability of the U.S. nuclear stockpile, in reality the program was geared to maintain various nuclear research and development programs at roughly Cold War levels for many years into the future. Additionally, the package created new computational and simulation programs to compensate for the anticipated ratification of the Comprehensive Test Ban Treaty.

We also know that nuclear research was also allowed to continue at Los Alamos — in secret — a clear violation of the NPT. This came to light in 1995, when Dr. Don Wolkerstorfer, a Los Alamos manager, mentioned a new bunker buster, the B-61-11, during a radio debate.[5] (The B-61-11 is a variable-yield nuclear penetrator, maximum yield: 340 kilotons.) The following year, Department of Defense spokesperson Kenneth Bacon revealed that other new earth penetrators were *also* in the works. Bacon told reporters, "We are now working on a series of weapons, both nuclear and conventional, to deal with deeply buried targets."[6]

There are indications the labs were also moving ahead with an even more ambitious program to develop the next generation of nuclear weapons. On April 25, 1997, the physicist Hans Bethe, the most senior surviving scientist from the original Manhattan Project, sent a letter to President Clinton. One day, it may have historic significance. In the letter Bethe urged the president to halt research on new weapons designs, including a pure fusion bomb, long viewed as the Holy Grail of nuclear weapons designers.

The great physicist, who headed up the theoretical division at Los Alamos during the development of the atomic bomb, had been retired for years. Yet, Bethe maintained contacts in the labs and so was well informed about the types of research programs that were underway. He informed Clinton that the U.S. already possessed more than sufficient weaponry for its security, and he urged,

... the time has come for our Nation to declare that it is not working, in any way, to develop further weapons of mass destruction of any kind. In particular, this means not financing work looking toward the possibility of new designs for nuclear weapons. And it certainly means not working on new types of nuclear weapons, *such as pure-fusion weapons* [my emphasis].[7]

Bethe deserved to be taken seriously. After all, he earned the 1967 Nobel Prize in physics for describing the fusion process that drives the stars. In his letter, Bethe further wrote that because "new types of weapons would, in time, spread to others and present a threat to us, it is logical for us not to pioneer further in this field."

Although the famous physicist affirmed his support for the stewardship program, Bethe also cautioned that computational experiments could be used to design new categories of weapons, even in the absence of underground testing. He urged Clinton not to fund such programs. This was sage counsel, because it is believed that Israel managed to evade international detection while clandestinely developing nuclear weapons by this very means, i.e., through the use of computational models and computer simulations. Israel has never signed the NPT and is believed to have staged only a very few small nuclear tests — possibly as few as one.[8] Yet, the dearth of live testing did not prevent Israel from developing a large and advanced nuclear arsenal. Six weeks later, Clinton sent Bethe a polite reply that deftly side-stepped all of the points the scientist had raised (see endnote 7).

Just five months later, in November 1997, Clinton issued a presidential directive, PDD-60, formalizing the outcome of his nuclear policy review. Most of the document remained classified, but more than enough was released to serve notice to the world that the United States was now a far more serious threat to the Nonproliferation Treaty than any terrorist or rogue state. Clinton's directive flew squarely in the face of the noble principles he had agreed to at the 1995 NPT conference. It reaffirmed the logic of the Cold War and announced a cornucopia of new spending to be showered upon the nuclear establishment over the next two decades. The directive announced that the U.S. would maintain the status quo, namely, the Cold War triad of nuclear forces (i.e., bombers, ICBMs and submarines) as well as the hair-trigger launch-on-warning posture. The U.S. insisted upon the right to nuclear first-use and even the right to use nukes against non-nuclear states that might somehow threaten U.S. "interests."[9]

These shocking revelations were unprecedented. The U.S. also rejected a Russian proposal for deeper cuts in the number of strategic warheads. Instead, the U.S. would move ahead with plans to upgrade the U.S. Trident missile force and the B-2 bomber. The U.S. would also resume production of plutonium pits, which are the fissile cores used in nuclear weapons. The directive reaffirmed the new emphasis on sub-critical nuclear testing and advanced computer modeling procedures: *the very thing Hans Bethe had cautioned against.* Additionally, the U.S. announced that it would resume production of tritium, an isotope of hydrogen used in thermonuclear weapons. The stated purpose was to provide additional supplies for the stewardship program.

Because tritium has a half-life of just twelve years, the tritium gas used in nuclear weapons decays and periodically must be replenished. Even so, the explanation was dubious, since tritium can be scavenged from deactivated weapons and recycled. Given even modest reductions in the size of the U.S. nuclear force, in 1997 there was at least a thirty-year supply of tritium for the stewardship program.[10] This hinted that Hans Bethe was correct, and the U.S. was already secretly developing the next generation of nukes. As if all of this were not enough, the directive also announced that the U.S. would complete construction of a brand-new National Ignition Facility (NIF) at the Lawrence Livermore laboratory, where the world's most powerful lasers would be used to study nuclear fusion — another clue.

These policies had been decided with no public debate or consultations with Congress. It certainly now appears that Clinton made a bargain with the devil. Perhaps he acted in the mistaken belief that the much-anticipated ratification of the Comprehensive Test Ban by the U.S. Senate would allow him some flexibility — a chance to later rescind at least some of his newly announced policies. As we know, of course, things took a rather different turn. In 1998 the Republican-controlled Senate rejected the Test Ban, dealing Clinton another stinging defeat. In any event, it is obvious today that Clinton's attempts to placate the militarists in his administration backfired, with the unfortunate result of locking the U.S. into a Cold War posture for many years to come, even though the Cold War was long over. All of which raises serious questions about Bill Clinton's style of leadership, or lack thereof.

The Repeal of Glass-Steagall

Now, with the benefit of hindsight, it is also evident that Clinton's character issues were not limited to placating generals. The more fundamental problem was that instead of serving the people who had elected him, Clinton chose to serve a tiny group of very rich and powerful men. Most assuredly, Clinton was looking after their interests in 1999 when he signed a bill repealing the 1933 Glass-Steagall Act.[11] The average American knows nothing about this, and probably has never even heard of it, so I will be brief.

It is enough to know that Glass-Steagall was enacted during the Great Depression for a sound reason: because in the roaring '20s Wall Street bankers had shown they were incapable of regulating themselves. Glass-Steagall created a regulatory firewall that separated commercial banking from Wall Street investment banking and insurance. This eliminated conflicts of interest and other abuses within the banking community. By the 1990s, however, the important firewall was under attack from bankers who viewed the New Deal as an aberration. Federal Reserve Chairman Alan Greenspan crusaded for deregulation, and during Clinton's second term he finally succeeded.[12]

Clinton's signature on the bill repealing Glass-Steagall opened the floodgates to the so called securitization revolution, and the result has been a disaster for our nation: derivative schemes as far as the eye can see, wild speculation, a vast real estate bubble, the sub-prime crisis, and pyramids of debt that now saddle the U.S. economy with tens of trillions in liabilities, not to mention the ongoing meltdown of the U.S. dollar. Wall Street banking became a legalized skimming racket, set up to fleece naive investors who dare to play the game at their own risk. Would a president committed to the best interests of our nation as a whole have signed such a bill? Of course not!

Clinton's Expansion of NATO

For many years during the Cold War, the North Atlantic Treaty Organization had been the first line of defense against a possible Soviet attack on Western Europe. But when the old Soviet state collapsed in the early 1990s during the presidency of Mikhail Gorbachev, NATO's original purpose also ceased to exist. Later, when the Berlin Wall came down, President George H.W. Bush assured Gorbachev that the U.S. would not expand NATO into eastern Europe, *if* Russia did not oppose the reunification of Germany. The agreement was mutually beneficial, and the Russians were true to their word. However, during his second term Clinton reneged on Bush's promise, by proposing to admit eastern European nations to the

NATO alliance, starting with Poland, the Czech Republic, and Hungary. Clinton's Secretary of State, Madeleine Albright, went on tour promoting the new plan. She argued that NATO expansion was a good idea because it would stabilize central Europe politically and economically.

Thoughtful critics, however, such as former Senator Sam Nunn (D-GA), a longtime expert on U.S. nuclear policy, begged to differ. Nunn pointed out that because Moscow would naturally view the eastward expansion of NATO as a grave threat to its national security, the probable consequence would be exactly the opposite. Clinton's plan for NATO would stall progress toward arms reductions, destabilize Europe, and might even lead to a new Cold War. Critics also warned that the U.S. taxpayer would likely pick up much of the tab for NATO expansion to the tune of many billions of dollars, most of which would end up in the bank accounts of various arms merchants. Yet, in 1998, with almost no debate, the U.S. Congress closed ranks behind Clinton and voted to support NATO expansion.

With hindsight, the critics were correct. Despite facile claims by the Clinton administration to the contrary, the expansion of NATO into eastern Europe was not in the best interests of the United States, nor in the best interests of Europe. At the time, the relatively poor nations of eastern Europe did not have money to waste on U.S. armaments. Their top priority was (or should have been) to improve the quality of life of their people, which meant rebuilding their infrastructure after the disaster of Communism. Of course, Washington promised that in return for purchasing our weapons, the U.S. would support their entry in the European Union (EU), which most of western Europe opposed at the time.

Yet, this enticement was an illusion, because their purchase of large quantities of U.S. weapons actually slowed their economic recovery, and this more than anything delayed their entry into the EU. No, the sole beneficiaries of NATO expansion were the U.S. arms makers and their financial backers on Wall Street, who saw in the breakup of the former Soviet bloc an opportunity to enrich themselves. They can only be compared with the carpetbaggers who infested the southern states after the American Civil War for the purpose of exploiting the defeated Confederacy.

The U.S. arms industry, the world's largest, spent millions successfully lobbying the U.S. Congress and the Clinton administration to expand NATO, and their lobbying paid off handsomely (for them). Subsequently, they cashed in on a vast new arms bazaar. Clinton had already signaled his obeisance to these powerful interests as early as 1995, when he issued

Presidential Directive 41, which announced that arms sales were essential for preserving U.S. jobs.

The 1995 directive instructed U.S. diplomats to get busy and boost foreign sales of U.S.-made weapons for the good of the U.S. economy. Obviously, Clinton found it easier to maintain the status quo, however perilous for the nation, than use the considerable power of his office to change that reality and move America away from the weapons economy built up during the Cold War. When Moscow protested the expansion of NATO, Clinton brushed aside Russia's concerns with characteristic aplomb. The president defended NATO expansion as a force for good. Indeed, his casual demeanor seemed to make light of this quaint Russian idea that NATO might somehow threaten Moscow. How absurd.

As the Bush Administration continues preparation to install an anti-ballistic missile (ABM) system in Poland and a new ABM radar site in the Czech Republic, virtually on Russia's doorstep, and as we hover on the brink of a wider Gulf war that could easily "go nuclear," it is crystal clear that Moscow's concerns about its security were well-founded. The real issue is why Bill Clinton, a Rhodes scholar, was purblind at the time. The fact is that the expansion of NATO was never about the stability of Europe. It was never about U.S. or global security. It was always about one thing: the sale of weapons for profit.

Now, as the world situation deteriorates each day, all of this has become more obvious. But where is the outrage? Why is this key issue not being raised in the political discourse? Have we lost the capacity to distill even the simplest and most obvious lessons from recent history? Are we now witnessing for this reason the terminal phase of America's "race to the bottom"? Has our political culture been so dumbed down that our nation is beyond redemption? If so, our terminal condition is largely the result of media consolidation, which Bill Clinton also surely hastened by signing the 1996 Telecommunications Act (and, as I recall, amidst much pomp and circumstance).

Republican presidential candidate John McCain has declared that the U.S. occupation of Iraq and the "war on terror" will continue for 100 years. Such statements are insane, and obviously so, yet McCain's prompted no strong rebuke from Democratic leaders Barack Obama and Hillary Clinton. Why not? Is militarism so fashionable that the Democrats are afraid to challenge McCain's rabid warmongering for fear of being labeled as "weak" or "unpatriotic"?

Someone (anyone) with a mind to care should corner Hillary Clinton and ask her this pointed question, on camera: *Why did your husband put* the interests of the weapons manufacturers and bankers above the interests of our nation and our planet? Why, Hillary?

Why, indeed? Because the plain truth is that Bill set the stage for the disasters that have overtaken us. Perhaps the real issue, today, is whether any politician in America has the integrity to answer a simple question.

Endnotes

1. For a deep analysis of this question, see Fletcher Prouty, *JFK, The CIA, Viet Nam, and the Plot to Assassinate John F. Kennedy*, Birch Lane Press, New York, 1992.

2. Helen Caldicott and Craig Eisendrath, *War in Heaven: The Arms Race and Outer Space*, The New Press, New York, 2007, p. ix; also see Helen Caldicott, *The New Nuclear Danger*, The New Press, New York, 2004.

3. Buckminster Fuller, *Critical Path*, St. Martin's Griffin, New York, 1982.

4. I for one would like to hear from Bill's own mouth why, while serving as governor of Arkansas, he did not shut down one of the largest cocaine smuggling operations in U.S. history. It passed through Mena, Arkansas, a small town in Bill's own backyard. For the full story see Daniel Hopsicker, *Barry and the Boys: The CIA, the Mob, and America's Secret History*, Madcow Press, Venice, FL, 2001.

5. Broadcast by radio station KSFR in Santa Fe, New Mexico, on July 18, 1995. For more details about the B-61-11 go to http://en.wikipedia.org/wiki/B61_nuclear_bomb.

6. Office of the Assistant Secretary of Defense (Public Affairs), DoD News Briefing, Tuesday April 23, 1996. The Clinton administration also sponsored the creation of a closely related military program, the Underground Facility Analysis Center (UFAC), a multi-service "consortium dedicated to detecting, identifying, characterizing and assessing for defeat adversarial underground facilities or hardened and deeply buried targets." For more details see Maj. Mark Easterbrook, "Underground Facility Analysis Center," Military-geospatial-technology.com, October 18, 2007.

7. The text of Bethe's letter, and Clinton's reply, have been posted by the Federation of American Scientists. http://www.fas.org/bethecr#letter.

8. Mark Gaffney, *Dimona: The Third Temple?* Amana Books, Brattleboro, 1989, chapters 4 and 5.

9. For an excellent discussion of PDD-60, see Rear Admiral Eugene Carroll, USN (ret), "The NPT Review — Last Chance?" *The Defense Monitor*, Vol. XXIX, No. 3, 2000. Posted at http://www.cdi.org/dm/2000/issue3/NPT.html.

10. Kenneth D. Bergeron, *Tritium On Ice*, MIT Press, 2002. Also see Charles D. Ferguson's review in the March/April 2003 issue of *The Bulletin of the Atomic Scientists*, (vol. 59, no. 02) pp. 70-72.

11. The 1999 bill was the Gramm-Leach-Bliley Act, aka the Financial Modernization Act.

12. For an excellent discussion, see F. William Engdahl, "The Financial Tsunami, Part III: Greenspan's Grand Design," January 24, 2008, posted at http://www.321gold.com/editorials/engdahl/engdahl012408.html.

Why the War on Terror Is a Fraud

B ill Clinton helped prepare the way for the neocon invasion of America. Yet, as we know, a "catalyzing event" separates Clinton from Bush: the earthquake of September 11, 2001, a day so pivotal that we now categorize world history as either pre- or post-9/11. The collapse of the World Trade Center was arguably the most dramatic human-caused catastrophe ever captured on film, and so painful to watch that many of us would rather forget. Many Americans have no doubt tried.

But 9/11 was not only a tragedy for America. It was tragic for the planet. The political shift to the right that followed in its wake here in the U.S. also set in motion a polarizing sea-change in world affairs. Other governments copied the U.S. response, citing the "threat of terrorism" as a convenient excuse to curtail civil liberties and crack down on political dissidents. The pattern was global. Additionally, the events themselves were a shared experience, a fact that, in my opinion, many Americans still do not fully appreciate. The same horrifying images circled the earth at the speed of light and ultimately reached an audience of at least several billion people: everyone with access to a television screen.

Surely this helps to explain the vast outpouring of sympathy for America following the attack. Condolences came from every direction. In many foreign cities there were spontaneous demonstrations in honor of the victims. In Tehran, for example, thousands of people gathered in the streets for candlelight vigils. An entire stadium of Iranian soccer fans reportedly paused for a moment of respectful silence. These impromptu Iranian acts of commiseration with America are ironic, in retrospect, since Iran is in the cross-hairs — under increasing attack by the Bush administration.

Most Americans are probably unaware that in the period immediately following 9/11, the governments of Iran and Syria supplied the Bush administration with intelligence information about terrorism, and in other ways supported the U.S. response to 9/11. Iran and Syria not only offered to help track down the alleged perpetrators, i.e. Osama bin Laden and the members of al Qaeda, they also made it clear they were prepared to go much further. Both offered major concessions that held the potential to transform the political landscape of the Mideast for the better.

Nothing less than a comprehensive regional peace settlement was within reach. Yet I would bet that very few Americans know that these initiatives ever happened, let alone why they failed. But, of course, this is not surprising, since many of the events I will discuss in this chapter went unreported in the U.S. media. Shocking, but true.

In fact, the long-troubled U.S.-Iran relationship showed signs of new life *before* the 9/11 attack. Early in 2001, during the first days of the Bush administration, positive statements by Secretary of State Colin Powell were reciprocated by Iran's Foreign Minister Kamal Kharrazi. As the diplomats tested the waters, U.S. oil companies waited in the wings, hoping for a breakthrough. Both nations had much to gain from improved relations. But to understand why this is so, we need to review some history.

Strategic Importance of Iran

During the 1990s, Iran was still struggling to recover from its bloody war with Saddam Hussein (1980-1988), which ravaged the region and caused great damage to the oil infrastructure in the Gulf. In the aftermath, Iran's oil exports lagged far behind the years of peak production in the 1970s under the Shah. The resulting economic consequences for the country were severe, because Iran is heavily dependent on foreign earnings from oil. Nor did the U.S. play a helpful role — on the contrary. During the Iran-Iraq war the U.S. had provided arms to both sides — a morally bankrupt policy — and after the war ended, Washington used its considerable influence to hinder Iran's recovery.

It did this by discouraging international investment, which Iran desperately needed to return its oil production to pre-war levels. In 1995 President Bill Clinton also punished Iran by imposing formal economic sanctions, a negative policy that largely backfired, as European and Russian investors moved in to exploit the "vacuum" left by the U.S.[1] No wonder U.S. oil companies chaffed under Clinton's punitive policy, which put them at a disadvantage.[2]

The stakes were immense. At issue were some of the last great oil and gas fields on earth awaiting development, located not only within Iran but across a wide swath of Central Asia. Known as the Caspian Sea basin, the region stretches from Azerbaijan in the west to Kazakhstan and Turkmenistan in the east. All of this was up for grabs, and U.S. oil companies wanted their share of the action, which, of course, meant gaining access.

A mere glance at a map shows that the most direct and efficient route for getting oil/gas out of this land-locked region lies through Iran, which at the time already possessed a functioning north-south network of pipelines. The few additional needed spur lines could have been constructed for a small fraction of the cost of the alternative routes through Turkey and Afghanistan, routes favored by the Clinton administration for reasons having to do with domestic politics.

U.S. oil companies openly questioned the wisdom of these alternative routes. The line through Turkey, for example, had to pass through the politically unstable Caucasus and also through a portion of the Kurdish homeland. Although it was completed in 2005-2006, the pipeline through Turkey continues to entail serious risks of disruption. Leery investors eventually abandoned the other project through Afghanistan for the same reason. They deemed it much too risky.

The facts of geography also explain why Conoco and Mobil lobbied Clinton to waive sanctions — as it happened, unsuccessfully — so that they might reap immense profits from lucrative energy swaps. A swap of crude oil or gas might work as follows: Iran would supply oil for export directly from its fields in the Persian Gulf while receiving an equivalent amount for its own energy needs from newly developed fields in neighboring Turkmenistan or Kazakhstan.[3] Swaps promised enormous profits to investors by eliminating the need to transport oil/gas over great distances. Clinton rejected these proposals.

But in 2001 there was every reason to suppose that the newly elected President Bush would cater to them. After all, Bush was an oil man himself, and many officials in his administration, such as Condoleezza Rice, came directly from the oil industry. Even Vice President Richard Cheney was on record opposing sanctions, despite his hawkish views. In 1996, while CEO of Halliburton, Cheney called sanctions against Iran "self-defeating."[4] His company was well-positioned to profit from energy swaps.

In fact, at the time Halliburton was *already* doing business with Iran — violating Clinton's sanctions in the process. This was probably illegal and later prompted a criminal investigation of the corporate giant by the U.S. Justice Department.[5] Cheney's remark reflected the cynical view: Policy be damned. Business is business. Let us enrich ourselves.

As we know, after the 2000 election Cheney flip-flopped, suddenly morphing into the most outspoken critic of Iran in the Bush administration. How strange that the U.S. media never held Cheney accountable, either for his sanctions busting or for his unexplained about-face. Strange indeed.

In the real world, the strategic importance of Iran had been obvious since at least World War II, when Franklin Delano Roosevelt kept Stalin in the war against Hitler with a Lend-Lease line of supply through Iran, whose government was then friendly to the West. As fighting raged on the eastern front, some $18 billion in U.S. arms and materiel was off-loaded from ships in the Gulf and transported north by rail to the U.S.S.R..[6] Entire factories were disassembled and sent to the Soviet Union in this way. Without Iran's vital assistance it is doubtful the Soviets could have resisted the Nazi onslaught.

Later, Iran was repaid for its loyalty to the West with treachery: In 1953 the CIA overthrew the popular Iranian Prime Minister Mohammad Mossadegh, who had committed the unpardonable crime of insisting on a fair price for Iran's oil in the global marketplace. In his place, the CIA installed a tyrant, the Shah, who, though despised and feared at home, remained a compliant U.S. puppet for many years. Those who wonder, "Why do they hate us?" would do well to study this dark episode in U.S. history, which lies at the root of the present crisis.[7]

Common Ground

After 9/11, the government of Iran issued a strong condemnation of the World Trade Center attack. Soon, the U.S. and Iran discovered mutual interests in Afghanistan. Both nations were staunchly opposed to al Qaeda and the Taliban, whose retrograde form of Sunni Islam was much too extreme even for Iran's fundamentalist mullahs. In fact, Iran was already supporting two Afghan factions opposed to the Taliban, one led by Rashid Dostum, an Uzbek warlord based in the north. The other was a Shi'ite community of three to four million Hazaras in central Afghanistan.[8] Let us now briefly review Iran's strong opposition to the Taliban.

After 1995, as the Taliban military forces spread out from their southern Pashtun stronghold in Kandahar and extended their grip over non-Pashtun areas of Afghanistan, the movement's inflexible leaders showed no interest in broadening their base to reflect the country's great diversity of ethnic and religious groups. Wherever the Taliban went, they imposed draconian rule, based on a reactionary interpretation of Sunni Islam known as Wahabbism, an import from Saudi Arabia.

In this respect, the Taliban was a drastic departure from the more tolerant Islamic traditions, such as mystical Sufism, which had flourished in Central Asia for centuries, but which, unfortunately, had been destroyed by the Soviet occupation and by years of civil war. The Taliban's persecution of Shi'ites became intense. Afghani Shi'ites were given three choices: convert, leave the country, or die. A number of massacres followed, carried out by both sides, and the result was an even worse polarization of a country already in an advanced stage of disintegration. The Taliban drew most of its military, financial, and political backing from just two sources, Saudi Arabia and Pakistan. The U.S. also provided aid until 2001. The opposition, later known as the Northern Alliance, received support from a long list of neighbors, including India, Iran, Russia, Tajikistan, Turkmenistan, Uzbekistan and even far-off Turkey.

The Taliban also defied its critics by openly harboring the renegade scion of a wealthy Saudi family, one Osama bin Laden, who during the 1980s had endeared himself to the Afghan resistance because of his connections and vast fortune, which he used to spread Wahabbism.[9] Even as the Taliban expanded its sphere of influence, Iran managed to keep opposition forces alive — just — through an intensive airlift of military and logistical support.

Tehran was nearly drawn into the conflict itself in 1998, when Taliban fighters entered the Iranian Consulate in Mazar-el-Sharif, in northern Afghanistan, and murdered eleven Iranian officials. The bloody incident sharply escalated tensions in the region after it was revealed that several Pakistani intelligence officers (from ISI, the Pakistani equivalent of the CIA) were involved in the atrocity. Both Iran and Pakistan had opposed the Soviet presence in Afghanistan, but each backed different factions of the Afghan resistance. Iran's response was to mobilize its regular army and to conduct military exercises along the border with Afghanistan. As many as 200,000 Iranian soldiers participated in these exercises. The Taliban massed a smaller force to repel a possible Iranian invasion. The tense standoff was only defused when UN-mediators persuaded Mullah Omar, the Taliban leader, to release a number of Iranian prisoners. It was the first time the reclusive and enigmatic Omar had ever met with an international official.[10]

This was the context for improved U.S.-Iran relations after 9/11. As U.S. forces prepared to invade Afghanistan, Iran supplied the U.S. with intelligence about the Taliban's military assets, including targeting information, all of which proved invaluable.[11] The Iranians also allowed America to use airfields in eastern Iran, helped with search and rescue, and even advised the U.S. on how to navigate the complex ethnic rivalries and political fault lines during the delicate negotiations with the Northern Alliance.

After weeks of cooperation, the U.S.-Iran talks picked up momentum. At a December 2001 conference in Bonn, Germany, convened to set up a post-Taliban government, Iran played a helpful role by persuading the various opposition groups to moderate their demands.[12] Whatever their distrust of the U.S., the mullahs of Iran had decided it was in their interest to help the Americans oust the Taliban. For a brief time it even appeared that the backdoor channel might develop into a true rapprochement. Let us now examine why this did not happen.

Bush's "Axis of Evil"

On January 3, 2002, as U.S. occupation forces were consolidating their hold on Afghanistan, the Israelis intercepted a ship in the Red Sea, the *Karine A*, loaded with military arms. The ship had left port in Iran and was apparently bound for the Palestinians in Gaza.[13] Israel's neocon allies in the Bush White House had opposed the dialogue with Iran from the start, and now they seized upon the incident. After a brief struggle over policy, the hard-liners prevailed — with Bush's backing. Three weeks after the seizure of the *Karine A,* George W. Bush delivered his famous "axis of evil" speech, in which he lumped Iran with Iraq and North Korea as the world's worst purveyors of state terrorism. Iran was also condemned for undermining the Mideast peace process.

The reality, of course, was quite different, since in 2002 there *was no existing* U.S.-brokered Mideast peace process. Clinton's Camp David initiative was long dead, and at the start of his presidency G.W. Bush had adopted a "hands off" policy regarding the Israeli-Palestinian conflict. In fact, this was a major departure from longstanding U.S. policy in the region. Although past U.S. Presidents Reagan, G.H.W. Bush, and Clinton were heavily biased toward Israel, they still maintained official U.S. support for UN Security Council resolutions calling upon Israel to withdraw from territories seized during the 1967 Six-Day War. Past presidents had also maintained at least the pretense of serving as a regional peace broker. Bush's abandonment of this legacy was tantamount to open support of Israel's continuing land seizures, expanding settlements, and its harsh treatment of the Palestinians, which former President Jimmy Carter, aptly compared to Apartheid.[14] For this reason G.W. Bush's "hands off" policy was an embarrassment to every American concerned about a just resolution of the Palestinian issue. By this time, the second *Intifada* was underway, violence in Palestine was increasing, and, as usual, Yassir Arafat's Palestine Liberation Organization was being blamed.[15]

Viewed in retrospect, it is likely that G.W. Bush's uncritical support for Israel originated in the personage of Israeli Prime Minister Ariel Sharon, who entered office shortly after Bush (in February 2001) on a hard-line platform of "no land for peace" and no negotiations with the Palestinians. The newly elected Prime Minister Sharon had a long history of violently opposing peace talks. As a young Israel Defense Forces officer, Sharon had personally led unprovoked border raids against Palestinian villages in the 1950s, attacks that murdered hundreds of Palestinians and ultimately destroyed then-Israeli PM Moshe Sharett's historic 1954 peace initiative with Egyptian President Abdul Nasser.[16]

This was no doubt the intended purpose of the clandestine raids, which Sharon, true to form, staged without PM Sharett's knowledge or consent. The peace talks with Nasser had shown signs of progress, which Sharon and other Israeli hawks viewed as anathema. Although Sharon's unsavory involvement in what can only be called terrorism has been known to scholars for many years, the full story has never been honestly reported by the U.S. media. Had it been, Bush would likely have faced bipartisan pressure in 2001 to distance himself from Sharon, just as he did in the case of Arafat.

Many years later, while serving as Housing Minister, Sharon played a major role in the rapid expansion of illegal Israeli settlements in the occupied territories. Sharon even bragged that the settlements were "the deciding factor" that prevented then-PM Yitzhak Rabin from agreeing to a complete withdrawal from the territories in exchange for peace.[17] As we know, of course, Rabin was nonetheless assassinated anyway for pursuing a political compromise.

Sharon was also the architect of Israel's fateful 1982 invasion of Lebanon, the aim of which was to annihilate the PLO. At the time, Sharon served as Defense Minister in the government of PM Menachem Begin. After the war it was revealed that Sharon had deceived Begin, the entire Israeli cabinet, and even his own staff about the full extent of his invasion plans.[18] In addition to using banned cluster bombs supplied by the U.S., Sharon also attacked Syrian positions, threatening a wider war. Later, he was found personally responsible by Israel's Kahan Commission for the massacre of as many as 2,000 Palestinians at the Sabra and Shatila refugee camps, located in West Beirut.[19]

Although the actual killing was the bloody work of the Lebanese Phalange, a Maronite Christian faction, the militia only gained access to the camps because the Israeli army violated the U.S.-brokered cease-fire, reoccupied Beirut, and allowed them in. Indeed, there were witnesses, including a Jewish nurse, even an American Congressman, who saw the ring of Israeli soldiers around the camps.[20] The massacre brought international dishonor upon America, because the Reagan administration had guaranteed the safety of those same refugees during the negotiations which brought about the PLO's departure from Lebanon.[21]

Reagan later "punished" Israel for its aggression and for putting America in the position of betraying its word by opening the spigot of U.S. aid to Israel wider than ever. In subsequent years the level of aid continued to grow, and currently stands at roughly $3 billion/year: a flood of cash and credit that Jewish Voice for Peace describes as "the greatest transfer of wealth from one nation to another in history."[22] Much of this aid, I should mention, has been used to construct even more settlements, meaning that U.S. taxpayer dollars, far from making things better, have only added fuel to the fire.

At the time of the *Karine A* incident in January 2002, PM Sharon was even then preparing another military offensive against the Palestinians, which he unleashed in late March 2002. It turned out to be the largest such operation since the 1967 Six-Day War. In fact, this probably explains the controversial arms shipment. The Palestinians were surely well informed that a large Israeli military offensive was in the works, and were likely attempting to acquire arms for their own defense. Of course, the U.S. government often regards even self-defense as "terrorism."[23]

Sharon's military offensive continued through the spring of 2002. During this period, the Palestinians in the West Bank endured a nightmare of incursions by the Israeli army into their towns and communities. This included the wholesale leveling of urban areas with American-supplied Caterpillar bulldozers, in addition to the usual helicopter rocket attacks, targeted assassinations, checkpoints, curfews, torture, and many other forms of harassment. Sharon had declared open season on the Palestinians, hundreds, perhaps thousands of whom were killed and many more wounded, imprisoned, or made homeless.

What remained of the West Bank economy collapsed at this time. Most of the population was reduced to bare subsistence and became dependent on international food aid. For the first time malnutrition became a serious problem. Many Palestinian families lived on the edge, a meal or two away from starvation. During this period, Israel also reduced to rubble most of the infrastructure (valued at hundreds of millions of dollars) built-up during the Oslo peace process. This included administrative and police buildings, radio stations, helicopter and port facilities, water utilities, electric generating plants, even schools — everything needed by a society.

But this was precisely the point: to erase the efforts of the Palestinians to create their own nation. The Israelis also stole or destroyed the Palestinian Authority's computers and everything else they could carry off: administrative documents, legal and medical records, cultural materials, census information, and the like. As the nightmare deepened, Amnesty International and other human rights organizations cited Israel for most of the violence.[24] Yet, true to form, U.S. government officials, members of Congress, and the U.S. media continued to portray the crackdown in the familiar way: Israel was merely "defending itself." The Palestinians had brought this holocaust upon themselves because of their suicide bomber attacks and because Arafat had rejected former Israeli PM Ehud Barak's "generous peace offer."

Yet, an honest assessment would have correctly placed at least an equal measure of blame at the doorstep of Israel and the White House,[25] while also recognizing the right of the Palestinians to defend themselves against Israel's military attacks, some of which involved advanced weapons supplied by the U.S. The heavy bias in the U.S. toward Israel was nothing new. Blaming the victims has long been a staple of U.S. politics and press coverage of the Mideast conflict. For this reason, i.e., because of the lack of honest reporting, most Americans probably failed to detect the dark irony in Bush's "Axis of Evil" speech, which stigmatized Iran for state terrorism: exactly what Israel was doing to the Palestinians. The speech set the tone for the policy of vilification that has continued.

Abdullah's 2002 Peace Proposal

On the eve of Sharon's attack upon the West Bank, crown prince Abdullah, heir to the throne of Saudi Arabia, offered to negotiate a sweeping peace treaty with Israel. The new peace offer, unveiled at a March 2002 meeting of the Arab League held in Beirut, was ratified by every Arab leader in attendance.[26] It proposed to end the Arabs' longstanding conflict with Israel. But it also went much further, offering Israel normalized relations, in other words, full trade and cultural ties — in short, an end to the bitter conflict. The sole condition was that Israel abide by UN Security Council resolutions, which call on it to withdraw from the occupied territories, i.e., the West Bank and Gaza, and allow the Palestinians to develop their national homeland.

The new Arab peace offer elicited no comment from PM Sharon. It was briefly mentioned by the U.S. media, but then simply dropped out of the news, probably because the White House, taking its cue from Sharon, chose to ignore it. In fact, Bush's silence should have prompted headlines in all of the major U.S. papers. Due to the U.S. media's failure to cover this important story, I would bet that few Americans are aware the Arab peace offer even happened. Nonetheless, it was important, possibly even historic, because it had the backing of every Arab leader and, therefore, might have led to a comprehensive settlement of the world's most serious longstanding conflict. That is, *if* the U.S. and Israel had responded favorably.

The shocking picture I have just described will dumbfound many Americans, so far removed is it from the familiar version of Mideast history presented in the U.S. media. Many will find it incomprehensible, like a fable from another planet. Yet, most of the facts I have cited were recently confirmed by two former members of G.W. Bush's own National Security Council, Flynt Leverett and Hillary Mann, currently husband and wife, both of whom served as senior Mideast policy experts during Bush's first term. Leverett worked at the CIA for a number of years before becoming an advisor to then-Secretary of State Colin Powell. Mann served as Condoleezza Rice's Iran expert and on the National Security Council. Both were directly involved in the secret negotiations with Iran in the aftermath of 9/11. Leverett also worked on the Palestinian issue. For this reason both have firsthand knowledge of what went down and why these initiatives failed.

Although Leverett and Mann are politically conservative, they are pragmatists, not ideologues. They did not agree with Bush's "hands off" policy, particularly his blind support for Ariel Sharon. Both understood the importance of making diplomatic progress on the Palestinian issue and the no less urgent need for pro-active diplomacy with Iran to stabilize the Gulf region and avoid a wider Mideast war. As time passed, both became increasingly alarmed by the colossal arrogance and stupidity they witnessed in Bush's White House, and by the drift of events toward a wider Mideast conflagration, so much so that after leaving the Bush administration, the two began to speak out, even in the face of threats and attempts by the White House to muzzle them. Leverett and Mann's story was even featured in *Esquire* magazine.[27] The story they tell, although profoundly disturbing, is pertinent in this context because it both confirms and fleshes out the picture I have already sketched.

Leverett tells how, in December 2001, after Syria and Iran had been cooperating with the U.S. for some weeks after 9/11, Secretary of State Colin Powell floated a proposal at the White House. Henceforth, the U.S. would adopt a *quid pro quo* approach with both nations, essentially rewarding them for their helpful intelligence, either by removing them from the official terrorist list or by creating a special status for them, the point being to start an open-ended dialogue that could move forward, step-by-step, fostering cooperation on a broader range of issues. Powell's proposal was astute, but went nowhere.

Cheney and Donald Rumsfeld hated the idea, as did Stephen Hadley, a deputy national security advisor, who then drew up a policy memo, which became known as Hadley's Rules:

> If a state like Syria or Iran offers specific assistance, we will take it without offering anything in return. We will accept it without strings or promises. We won't try to build on it.[28]

Obviously, since diplomacy is a two-way street, Hadley's new policy seemed perversely designed to prevent any further improvement in relations. Yet, for weeks Iranian officials had been telling Mann they wanted an expanded dialogue with the U.S., without preconditions. According to Mann, the Iranians made it clear that "they were doing this because they understood the impact of this attack [i.e., 9/11] on the U.S., and they thought that if they helped us unconditionally, that would be the way to change the dynamic [between the two countries] for the first time in twenty-five years."[29] Here, then, was a historic opportunity to reshape the troubled U.S.-Iran relationship. Yet, the Bush White House would have none of it.

In the subsequent period, Leverett worked directly with crown prince Abdullah's foreign-policy advisor, Adel Al-Jubeir, who was then in the process of drafting the 2002 Saudi peace proposal discussed above. By this time Sharon's military offensive against the Palestinians was in full swing. In April 2002, Secretary of State Powell traveled to Israel and twice crossed the Israeli lines, walking through "no man's land" to visit Arafat, whose compound (what remained of it) was under siege. The purpose of his visit was to explore "political horizons." However, a few days later, while Leverett was meeting with senior U.S. officials at the David Citadel Hotel in Jerusalem, he received a call from Washington. It was Stephen Hadley, who instructed him to "tell Powell he is not authorized to to talk about a political horizon."[30]

The reason? Rumsfeld and Cheney were opposed to peace talks — end of story. Leverett had to give the bad news to Powell, who was understandably furious. For the previous ten days the Secretary of State had been conferring with various world leaders about the Palestinian issue, and now the White House had pulled the rug out from under him. Leverett does not explain why Powell did not immediately resign to protest this treatment, and the insane policy. Resigning would have shown moral strength, but evidently Powell's loyalty to Bush or perhaps his own ambition (or both) got the better of him.

Weeks later, as Sharon's military offensive continued, crown prince Abdullah flew to Texas to visit Bush at his ranch. The octogenarian sheikh was anything but the stereotypic playboy prince. In fact, Abdullah was one of the few in the royal family who, despite great wealth, still embodied the traditional values and simplicity of the old desert lifestyle. On his arrival in Crawford, Abdullah immediately confronted Bush with a blunt question and said he wanted an equally direct answer. "Are you going to do anything about the Palestinian issue?" the prince asked.

When Bush became evasive, Abdullah stood up and said, "That's it. The meeting is over." Abdullah's direct language caused a panic among Bush's aides. As *Esquire* reports, "No Arab leader had ever spoken to the president like that."[31] Yet, the crown prince could not be dismissed, either. Saudi Arabia was a key U.S. ally and absolutely vital to the world's oil supply. Bush, Rice and Powell beat a hasty retreat into an adjoining room for a quick consultation. Minutes later, Bush returned and promised Abdullah that he would give the Palestinian issue his utmost consideration. This apparently satisfied the crown prince. The upbeat U.S. press coverage of the meeting between the two leaders in Texas belied the near-rupture in U.S.-Saudi relations. Powell later referred to it as "the near-death experience."

Soon after, the King of Jordan *also* pressed Bush to resolve the Palestinian issue, during a state visit to Washington. In fact, during this period, i.e., the run-up to the 2003 invasion of Iraq, U.S. officials heard this same urgent refrain many times from various world leaders. No state in the Mideast, with the exception of Israel, wanted another war against Saddam Hussein. Instead, they wanted the U.S. to focus on the Palestinian issue. In response, over the next few months Leverett and others in the administration dutifully worked on a road map for peace. Leverett even promised the King of Jordan that a U.S. peace plan would be announced by year's end. However, it never happened.

Why not? For the reasons I have already indicated. Around Thanksgiving, Leverett received a call from the Jordanian foreign minister who informed him that he had just learned from Rice that the road map was off the table. The Jordanian diplomat felt betrayed and, according to *Esquire,* told Leverett, "Do you have any idea how this has pulled the rug out from under us, from under me? I'm the one who has to go into Arab League meetings and get beat up.... How can we ever trust you again?"[32]

Later, Leverett learned from Rice that PM Sharon had personally called Bush with a request to cancel the road map for peace. From the details presented in the *Esquire* article, it is apparent that Rice, like Powell, was simply incapable of providing the president with a policy assessment that deviated from what he wanted to hear. Once again, Sharon had scuttled a peace initiative, this time before it had even begun, and by means of a simple telephone call. This was the creature Bush described as "a man of peace."[33]

The bigger question, of course, is why the President of the United States would be so easily swayed — diverted from longstanding U.S. commitments to UN Security Council resolutions on Palestine, not to mention Bush's personal promise to crown prince Abdullah. Brent Scowcroft, a retired four-star general and former national security advisor to Presidents Ford and G.H.W. Bush, may have provided the answer when he later told the *Financial Times* of London that "Sharon just has Bush wrapped around his little finger. I think the president is mesmerized."[34] After the remark Scowcroft was immediately sacked from his position as chairman of Bush's Foreign Intelligence Advisory Board, a position he had held since

2001.[35] You may recall that Scowcroft also chaired a special advisory panel which conducted an end-to-end review of US nuclear forces.

I would add that two prominent American scholars, John J. Mearsheimer and Stephen M. Walt, present a more nuanced view of these events in their important book, *The Israel Lobby,* in which they argue that President Bush's halting attempts to pursue a road map were effectively countered at every step by the influential Israel lobby. Yet, the two scholars arrive at essentially the same conclusion: In the end Bush supported policies advocated by Sharon, even though this was not in the best interests of the U.S.[36]

G.W. Bush's unconditional support for Israel apparently dates back to 1998, when Bush, then governor of Texas, went on a tour of Israel organized by Matthew Brooks, head of the Republican Jewish Coalition. Later, Brooks discussed the high point of the trip, as reported by Ron Hutcheson in an August 3, 2006 McClatchy wire story:

> If there's a starting point for George W. Bush's attachment to Israel, it's the day in late 1998 when he stood on a hilltop where Jesus delivered the Sermon on the Mount, and with eyes brimming with tears read aloud from his favorite hymn, 'Amazing Grace.' He [Bush] was very emotional. It was a tear-filled experience. He brought Israel back home with him in his heart. I think he came away profoundly moved.[37]

Assuming the story is accurate, and not just myth-making, it reveals G.W. Bush's vacuous grasp of Scripture. Brooks never explained how the Sermon's spiritual passages, such as "The meek shall inherit the earth," "Blessed are the peacemakers," and "Blessed are they who hunger and thirst for justice ... " were somehow transmogrified into support for an Israeli system of Apartheid more virulent than anything that existed in South Africa. During the same tour, Bush reportedly accompanied Ariel Sharon, then Foreign Minister, on a helicopter ride over the occupied territories, and this too made a lasting impression.

Bush referred to it during the first meeting of his National Security Council, held on January 30, 2001. According to then-Treasury-Secretary Paul O'Neill, who was present, Bush mentioned the ride with Sharon before declaring that it was time to end U.S. efforts to achieve peace with the Palestinians. "I just don't see much we can do over there, at this point," Bush said.[38] Secretary of State Colin Powell objected, however, and pointed out the obvious: that the consequences of unleashing Sharon would be dire, especially for the Palestinians. Bush simply shrugged. "Maybe that's the best way to get things back in balance," he said. "Sometimes a show of strength by one side can really clarify things."

The Opening with Syria

After 9/11, the Syrian government also shared intelligence information with the U.S., as reported by Seymour Hersh in *The New Yorker*.[39] Syrian President Bashar Assad ordered the intelligence sharing with the CIA for the purpose of improved relations. Assad wanted off the U.S. State Department list of states that sponsor terrorism. The Syrian government had extensive files on Islamic extremism because of its own long-running struggle with the Muslim Brotherhood. In the course of tracking the Brotherhood, the Syrians had penetrated many other extremist cells in the Middle East and Europe, and thus were even able to provide the CIA with dossiers on a number of the alleged 9/11 hijackers. The intelligence was current and of excellent quality.[40]

In another case, the Syrians supplied information about a terrorist plot to attack the U.S. Navy's 5th Fleet headquarters in Bahrain, located in the Persian Gulf. Thanks to this information, the U.S. was able to thwart the attack and save American lives. Remarkably, the Syrians even allowed the CIA to undertake a sensitive intelligence-gathering mission inside their country — in Aleppo, near the Turkish border. The Syrians made it clear they were prepared to go even further and to provide the U.S. with detailed information about controversial Saudi links to Islamic terrorism. As Robert Baer, a former CIA field officer, put it: "The Syrians know that the Saudis were involved in the financing of the Muslim Brotherhood, and they for sure know the names."[41]

When Hersh interviewed Syrian President Assad in Damascus, the Syrian leader drew a distinction between international terrorists like al Qaeda and those Assad described as the "resistance," that is, groups such as Hezbollah, Hamas, and Islamic Jihad who are fighting for their land and their freedom. Even so, Assad told Hersh he was prepared to curtail the activities of such groups in Syria in return for improved relations with Washington. In the end, however, Syria received nothing for its intelligence assistance. The promising backdoor link with Damascus drew sharp fire from Donald Rumsfeld, who accused Syria of supplying arms to the Iraqi insurgents.

Rumsfeld also claimed that Saddam had smuggled his weapons of mass destruction into Syria for safe-keeping. The charges were never substantiated and, in fact, were absurd, but Rumsfeld prevailed. Early in 2003 he demanded Syrian participation in the operational planning for the invasion of Iraq, then imminent. Although Bashar's father, Hafez Assad, had joined the U.S.-led coalition against Saddam during the first Gulf war, the son wisely declined. With the start of "Shock and Awe" in March 2003, the diplomatic opening with Syria passed into oblivion without much notice.[42]

Iran's Peace Offer

According to Mann and Leverett, even after Bush's deeply insulting "Axis of Evil" speech in 2002, the Iranians continued to show up in Geneva for backdoor talks with the U.S. The secret negotiations went on for another year, and culminated in April 2003 with a detailed Iranian proposal for a comprehensive Mideast peace.

At this time Bush and the neocons were flying high. The U.S. military was then in the victorious mopping-up phase of the Iraq invasion. Mann was back at the State Department, and told *Esquire* she learned about the peace offer from the Swiss ambassador, who FAXed her a two-page summary. Switzerland was then serving as the intermediary and had conveyed the offer to the U.S. on Iran's behalf. This was not unusual, since despite the secret channel, the U.S. and Iran still had no formal relations.

The Iranian offer encompassed the full range of issues, and from the two-page summary it was clear to Mann it had come from the highest level, that is, from Iran's Supreme Leader, Ayatollah Ali Khamenei. Mann was startled as she read one concession after another. There were offers to provide more help on the terrorism issue by ending support for Hamas and Islamic Jihad. Iran also offered to disarm Hezbollah in Lebanon and to accept much tighter oversight by the International Atomic Energy Agency (IAEA) over its nuclear program. Iran even offered to recognize Israel. The Iranians had signed-on to Abdullah's 2002 peace offer.[43]

With hindsight, Tehran's motivation is apparent. Iran's leaders were convinced that the U.S. planned to attack *them* after finishing with Iraq, hence their initiative to accommodate Washington and hopefully stave off a confrontation. Here, then, was a golden opportunity for the Bush administration — now at the height of its influence — to achieve nearly all of its objectives in the Gulf vis-à-vis Iran. Yet, incredibly, the White House not only ignored the peace offer but even lodged a formal complaint with the Swiss government about their ambassador's "meddling." In short, it was another display of American hubris. Incidentally, in March-April 2006, Iran's leaders repeated their call for negotiations with the U.S. and, once again, were rebuffed.[44]

Israel's Role

But why reject a peace offer that would have accommodated the most important U.S. interests in the region, while moderating Iran's behavior in the bargain? The answer is so straightforward, it eluded me for the longest time, just as, I suspect, it has also eluded many Americans. Negotiating with Iran's leaders was out of the question because *that* would confer legitimacy upon the government of Iran — something the Bush White House has been loath to do. Why? Because since at least 2002, the Bush policy on Iran has been regime change, not peaceful coexistence. You do not negotiate with a government you are seeking to overthrow. The goal of the neocons is to install some new puppet in Tehran who will take orders from Washington. Who knows? Perhaps Reza Pahlavi, the son of the late Shah.[45]

But how did the policy of regime change arise? *Indeed, where did it come from?* It is a question that the U.S. media has never honestly explored. The fact is that the policy arose in Israel after the conclusion of the 1991 Gulf War and, some years later, was adopted by the neocons. In 1991 Operation Desert Storm greatly weakened Saddam Hussein's military power, and for this reason the Israeli government shifted and began to view Iran as its main adversary in the region. Indeed, the dust had scarcely settled after the First Gulf War when Israel launched a campaign to prepare its own people for a future conflict with the new nemesis. According to the late dissident scholar Israel Shahak, all of the Hebrew newspapers in Israel "… shared in the advocacy of this madness, with the exception of *Ha'aretz*, which has not dared to challenge it, either."[46] To my knowledge the war of words chronicled by Shahak in his important 1997 book *Open Secrets* has never been mentioned in the U.S. media.

Israeli Prime Minister PM Yitzhak Rabin's government then launched a parallel effort to persuade its American ally of the growing nuclear threat from Iran. As I have noted, in the 1990s U.S.-Iran relations were at low ebb. President Bill Clinton was outraged by Iran's opposition to his Oslo Peace Process. (Given the benefit of hindsight, however, Tehran's reasons at the time now appear astute and almost prophetic.) As mentioned, in 1995 Clinton hardened his policy of containing Iran with an executive order imposing a package of sweeping economic sanctions. Clinton even punished a dozen Russian companies for their nuclear and military trade with Iran, especially transfers of missile technology.

The concern was not only with Iran's resurgent nuclear program, but also with its continuing development of a delivery vehicle, namely, the Shahab-3 missile. Experts worried that the missile would eventually be capable of targeting U.S. bases in the Gulf, as well as Israel.[47] As I have noted, Clinton had little success persuading the European allies to support his sanctions policy. Clinton's reluctance to confront Israel over its expanding settlement policies in the West Bank surely had much to do with this, not to mention the U.S. double standard about Israel's nuclear weapons program. The world looked to Washington for leadership, but instead saw hypocrisy. Throughout the 1990s the policy of the European Union toward Iran was one of "critical engagement."[48]

In November 2002, shortly after G.W. Bush announced his new policy of "preventive war," Israeli PM Sharon openly called on the U.S. to bring about regime change in Tehran after first dealing with Saddam Hussein.[49] The call was repeated in April 2003, just weeks after the U.S. invasion of Iraq, this time by Daniel Ayalon, the Israeli ambassador to Washington. In a press statement, Ayalon called for regime change in Syria and Iran, to be achieved by "diplomatic isolation, economic sanctions, and psychological pressure."[50] The ambassador stopped just short of advocating a U.S.-led war against the two countries.

Ayalon noted that while the overthrow of Saddam Hussein had created new opportunities for Israel, it was "not enough." "We have to follow through," Ayalon told a sympathetic conference of the Anti-Defamation League. "We still have great threats of that magnitude coming from Syria, coming from Iran." Ayalon also criticized the European Union for its commerce with Iran and even advocated a suspension of diplomatic ties. "Governments should not allow visits by Iranian leaders such as President Sayed Mohammed Khatami and Foreign Minister Kamal Kharrazi," said the ambassador. "And foreign leaders should not visit Iran. I don't think this is the way to deal with them, because the more the regime is isolated, the shorter its days ..."

Yet, the Iranian leaders named by Ayalon were anything but radicals. In fact, Khatami and Kharrazi were both moderates who favored improved ties with the West, especially the U.S. Ayalon went on to express a delusional hubris rivaling that of Cheney and Rumsfeld in the case of Iraq: "... and, as I mentioned, there is fertile ground in Iran to have a regime change there. Seventy percent of the population [of Iran] are really ready for regime change. They have tasted, they have been experiencing, before, democracy and Western cultures and they are yearning for it."

Israel's Nuclear Agenda

In recent years, the neocons have echoed the increasingly strident statements of Israeli officials about Iran. In 2005 Vice President Cheney hinted that "the Israelis might well decide to act first, and let the rest of the world worry about cleaning up the diplomatic mess afterwards."[51] In October of 2007, Bush himself warned that Iran's nuclear program could trigger World War III.[52] Hard-liners like Joe Lieberman openly support a "preventive" attack on Iran's nuclear sites and even liberals, like Hillary Clinton have adopted a hard line. Of late, the news has been filled with scary reports that Israel, or the U.S., or both jointly, intend to stage an attack in the near future. One report even claimed that the Israeli Air Force was rehearsing the use of nuclear bunker busters.[53] Unfortunately, the reports can not be dismissed, because of Israel and America's past history of attacking other nations. Yet, IAEA Inspector-general Mohamed El Baradei, recipient of the 2005 Nobel Peace Prize, has insisted on many occasions that there is no hard evidence for an Iranian nuclear weapons program.[54]

The charges against Iran are especially dubious in light of Washington's own hypocrisy on the nuclear issue. There is no question that Iran, which is a signatory to the Nonproliferation Treaty, has the right to develop nuclear power for peaceful use. One may disagree with Tehran's decision to do so — I do, because I oppose the nuclear path in general — but clearly Iran is within its rights under Article IV of the treaty. The U.S. had no problem supplying nuclear technology to the dictatorial Shah of Iran in the 1970s. In fact, several of the neocons, including Donald Rumsfeld, were personally involved in arranging transfers of U.S. technology at that time. Bush's ongoing nuclear trade with India and his massive support for nuclear-armed Pakistan, both of which developed the Bomb while refusing to sign the NPT, point to the real problem: Washington's selective and even arbitrary interpretation of its own treaty.

And then, of course, there is the 800-pound gorilla, namely, Israel, whose undeclared nuclear arsenal makes a mockery of U.S. attempts to portray Iran as a rogue state. It could even be argued that Washington's refusal to openly acknowledge Israel's nuclear status is a strong indicator that the nuclear nonproliferation regime is kaput — has already disintegrated.

Stupid and inflammatory statements by Iranian President Ahmedinejad have been seized upon and portrayed as a *casus belli,* and while I agree that his remarks have been unhelpful, it appears they were intentionally mistranslated. Nor, in any event, does Ahmadinejad control Iran's nuclear program. That power rests in the cautious hands of the Supreme Mullah. The whole issue is a red herring: an attempt to cast the policy of regime change in defensive terms and make it more palatable. The bottom line is simply that Israel, with U.S. backing, seeks to maintain its nuclear hegemony in the region.

For many years the shared wisdom was that nuclear weapons might be justified in Israel's case, due to the country's unique security problems, having to do with Israel's small size. Nukes might be acceptable, so the thinking went, because Israel would then feel secure enough to negotiate a lasting peace settlement with its neighbors. But it hasn't worked out that way. As it happened, a strong Israel simply had no incentive to negotiate. Period.

In a thoughtful article that appeared in *Ha'aretz* in September 2005, Baruch Kimmerling, a professor at Hebrew University, conceded what scholars have long known: that the country's nuclear weapons are linked to Israel's illegal military occupation of the Arab West Bank. As Kimmerling phrased it, Israel's nukes "in the basement are a guarantee that no pressure, foreign or domestic ... can force Israel into genuine territorial concessions."[55] Clearly, Kimmerling's assessment is correct: For many years the country's nuclear monopoly has tempted Israel's nation's leaders to forego negotiations and simply to impose their will upon the neighborhood. This explains the expanding settlements, the invasion of Lebanon in 1982, the security wall, the cantonization of the West Bank, and the recent unilateral withdrawal from Gaza. And why else would Israel dismiss a 2002 Saudi peace initiative that offered not just recognition but full normalized relations, including full trade, economic ties, cultural exchanges, in short, an end to the conflict, if Israel would abide by UN Security Council resolutions on Palestine?

There will likely be no diplomatic solution on Iran nor on the Mideast peace front so long as our own leaders view Israel's nukes as a non-issue, their underlying assumption being, of course, that Israel needs them to survive. Others pooh-pooh the matter, but in my opinion this is the crux of it. We need a rude awakening, and let us pray it does not come in the form of a mushroom cloud. The truth is that Israel's nukes are weapons of mass destruction, pure and simple, whose very existence is a moral obscenity, just like all such weapons: an affront to God and every living thing on this planet. We need to start thinking about them in these terms.

Of course, Israel's supporters invariably downplay the dangers. They rationalize the shocking fact that Israel has targeted a large swath of humanity with annihilation by arguing that Israel's WMDs are not a concern, since Israel has neither used its nukes nor threatened to use them; anyway the arsenal is necessary for Israel's survival in a tough neighborhood. But no matter how often these phony arguments are repeated, the facts cannot be made to support them. If Israel possessed only a few atomic weapons of last resort, the Samson option (as Seymour Hersh refers to it) might be reasonable.

However, the vast size of Israel's weapons arsenal, the strong likelihood it includes hydrogen bombs, tactical nukes including neutron weapons, and a multiple array of advanced delivery vehicles, including nuclear-armed cruise missiles, not to mention chemical and biological weapons, indicates that Israel's policy is not primarily defensive in nature. The large size of Israel's arsenal is probably due, in part, to the technological imperative. Israel's war economy developed a momentum of its own.

But this is a flimsy excuse and no justification. Israel's WMDs are clearly meant to project power and to this extent they have already been used. One need not pull the trigger of a revolver to use it, and the same is true of the bomb. The people of the Mideast understand this very well. After all, they have lived in the long shadow of Israel's arsenal of 200-400 nukes for many years.[56]

Déjà Vu?

As the Mideast crisis deepens, it is hard to escape the feeling we have been through all of this before, as indeed we have: during the run-up to the 2003 attack on Saddam Hussein, who, like Ahmadinejad, was compared with Hitler and also falsely accused of developing weapons of mass destruction.

In his 2007 memoir, former Federal Reserve Chairman Alan Greenspan acknowledges that despite all the talk about WMD, oil was the primary reason for the 2003 U.S. invasion of Iraq. "I am saddened," Greenspan writes in his book, "that it is politically inconvenient to acknowledge what everyone knows: the Iraq war is largely about oil."[57] Certainly the Iraqi people did not need to be reminded by Greenspan. They knew the truth from the first days of the U.S. occupation of Baghdad, when the U.S. military broadcast America's real intentions by assigning troops to protect the oil ministry, while allowing Iraq's thirteen national museums — the nation's crown jewels — to be ransacked. Later, the U.S. military claimed it did not have sufficient resources to protect the museums, but this is nonsense. A few tanks would have sufficed. The full extent of the losses may never be known, since in many cases the inventories of the holdings are also missing. But it is safe to say that the destruction to Iraq's 6,000-year historical legacy was incalculable.

This, of course, in addition to the tens of thousands of dead and wounded Iraqis and the vast damage to the nation's infrastructure wreaked by "Shock and Awe." Several days after the museums were looted, Iraq's National Library & Archives was also burned, along with the Library of Korans at the Ministry of Religious Affairs. An Iraqi citizen would have had to be brain dead — on life-support — to miss the symbolism. Imagine our reaction if foreigners invaded the U.S. for the purpose of liberating America, then presided over the looting of the Smithsonian and the destruction of the U.S. Archives and Library of Congress. Paul Zimansky, an archaeologist at Boston University, called it "the greatest cultural disaster of the last 500 years." Eleanor Robson, a fellow of All Souls College, Oxford, agreed. Said Robson, "You'd have to go back centuries to the Mongol invasion of Baghdad in 1258 to find looting on this scale."[58]

Let us remember, we are not just talking about Iraq's cultural heritage. Mesopotamia, the land between the rivers, as the ancient Greeks referred to it, was the cradle of western civilization, and this includes the U.S. Yet, Secretary of Defense Rumsfeld brushed off the looting as a non-event, comparing it to the "untidy" aftermath of a soccer match.[59] One is left speechless by this kind of mentality, which Iraqis and others are correct to label as "American-style barbarism." If the archaeologists are right, U.S. crimes in Iraq have exceeded even the worst plundering of artistic treasures by the Nazis during World War II.

In May 2003, the Bush White House underscored the criminal nature of the U.S. invasion by decreeing that, henceforth, U.S. oil companies would be immune from any legal challenges under Iraqi law. In other words, they were free to despoil the environment and swindle the Iraqi people of their liquid gold without fear of ever being held accountable.[60] In 2007, the Iraqi government announced, probably at the instigation of Washington, that it would refuse to honor a pre-existing drilling contract with Lukoil, a Russian oil company.[61] Cancelation of the contract, which pre-dated the U.S. invasion and had been negotiated by Saddam himself, cleared the way for the oil ministry to open up the rich West Qurna oil field to new bids by U.S. and other "approved" oil companies.

All of this surely confirmed, to anyone paying attention, that the neocon plan from the beginning was to divvy up the spoils of war among the "coalition of the willing." I should mention, however, that there is no evidence the U.S. oil industry helped formulate the new policy. In fact, it appears that the oil companies were wary of Bush's war plan, despite the enticements.[62] Oil companies are motivated by profit, but they are not stupid. To prosper they need political stability, which probably explains why the major U.S. oil companies have long supported a Mideast peace settlement.

Their support dates from the presidency of Richard Nixon, when Secretary of State William Rogers first advocated such a plan.[63] Unfortunately, Rogers was outmaneuvered by Henry Kissinger, Nixon's top adviser, whose primary goal was shielding Israel. This became the U.S. policy, and it has not changed over the years except to become ever more entrenched. Without question, the increasing hostility toward America that has resulted from U.S. support for Israeli Apartheid and for dictatorial Arab governments has made life much more difficult for U.S. oil companies trying to do business in the region.

Redrawing the Map

The Iraqi people had good reason to doubt the sincerity of U.S. rhetoric about planting the seeds of western democracy — propaganda that in any event was aimed more at Americans than Iraqis. Many in the U.S. who initially supported the U.S. invasion have criticized Bush and Cheney for their "mishandling" of the war and for failing to provide for Iraq's post-war recovery. Leading Democrats like Hillary Clinton, for example, have harped on this issue. What Clinton and the rest fail to understand is that the necons never planned for Iraq's recovery, because their plan from the outset was to dismember the country. The war was "largely about oil," yes, but this was by no means the full story.

The neocons' grand design, ambitious in scope, called for redrawing the regional map to benefit Israel and the U.S. The plan was to partition Iraq into pieces, and one of the keys to its success was persuading Jordan's Hashemite rulers to go along. Surely this is why Vice President Cheney pitched the U.S. war plan to Jordanian crown prince Hassan at a London meeting in July 2002.[64] Pro-U.S. dissident Iraqis were also present. The grand design was no secret and was even discussed in the Israeli press.[65] Of course, it was never mentioned in the U.S. media. Here the plan to redraw the map was considered a hard-sell. This is why Americans were kept in the dark — fed lies about weapons of mass destruction and "spreading democracy."

The Hashemite family had once ruled Iraq as well as Jordan. Indeed, Jordan's present King Abdullah is the second cousin of the last Iraqi monarch, Feisel II, who as a young prince fought alongside (and was greatly esteemed by) T.E. Lawrence during the fierce desert campaign that defeated the Ottoman Turks in World War I. The campaign is recounted in Lawrence's war memoir, *Seven Pillars of Wisdom*, and was made famous in the Hollywood film *Lawrence of Arabia*. Feisal ruled the kingdom of Iraq until the 1958 revolution, which eventually brought Saddam Hussein to power.

The point is that the Hashemites had never relinquished their claim to the throne, and it seems this became the neocon hook. In return for Jordan's support, the neocons offered to restore Hashemite rule. Hassan would be installed as the new king of Iraq, or Jordan would simply be allowed to annex most of the country, including Baghdad, which would cease to be a capital city. The Kurdish region in the north would remain autonomous, but would nominally also be a part of the new Hashemite realm. The U.S. would insist upon a permanent military presence there to allay Turkish concerns about Kurdish nationalism. The southern Shi'ite portion of Iraq was to be split off and remain a rump state. Or: more likely, it would be folded into Kuwait.

Jordan was the key to making all of this happen. But, of course, there was a price. In return for much expanded Hashemite influence in the region, Jordan, at some point, would be required to accept a new influx of Palestinian refugees who would be "encouraged" to emigrate from the West Bank by the Israeli army. (This in addition to the large Palestinian refugee population *already* living in Jordan.) The forced transfer would allow Ariel Sharon to complete the Jewish settlement of territories seized in the 1967 war — unopposed. In essence, Jordan would become the Palestinian homeland. Hashemite concerns about political instability caused by so many refugees would be mitigated by Jordan's expansion to include millions of additional Iraqis. The Palestinians would remain a minority population.

Jordan would also agree to allow the construction of a new pipeline across its expanded territory, from Kirkuk to Haifa, Israel. This would allow oil from Kurdistan to reach the world market, and would also permanently solve Israel's energy problems.[66] Haifa would become, in the words of Israeli Infrastructure Minister Yusef Paritzky, "the Rotterdam of the Middle East."[67] The Kurds would be encouraged to flood the world market with oil, driving down the price to $15/barrel or under. This would undermine OPEC (the Organization of Oil Exporting Countries) and perhaps even destroy the cartel once and for all, while stimulating economic growth in the U.S. and the West. The multinational oil corporations would survive the price collapse because of their diversification.[68]

In his memoirs, former CIA Director George Tenet admits that "the decisions we made tended to fracture Iraq, not to bring it together."[69] The key decisions he refers to include the May 2003 disbanding of the Iraqi army and the purging of the Baath party, both of which had many untoward effects. 40,000 Iraqi school teachers, for example, were thrown out of work simply because of their Baath party membership. Viewed in retrospect, these decisions appear to have been perversely designed to render the country prostrate. Was this the goal, all along: to insure that Iraq would never again challenge Israel?

We know the names of the policy-makers. When Tenet says, "we," he means Donald Rumsfeld, Paul Wolfowitz, Douglas Feith and, no doubt, Dick Cheney. Although these men destroyed Iraq, they did not succeed in redrawing the regional map because they failed to anticipate the depth of Sunni (and Shi'ite) resistance.[70] They also vastly underestimated the vulnerability of Iraq's oil infrastructure to sabotage.

Nor have I seen any evidence that the Jordanians signed on to the U.S. war plan. In short, it was another case of American hubris — but on a colossal scale. In March 2007, while delivering a speech on on the fourth anniversary of the U.S. invasion, the late Lt. General William Odom, former director of the National Security Agency called the neocons' blunder "the greatest strategic disaster in U.S. history." Odom then added, "And the longer America stays [in Iraq] the worse it will be. It's time to 'cut and run.'"[71]

The Crisis with Iran

Unfortunately, we now face an even worse disaster. What happened in Iraq may be repeated in the case of Iran, only magnified several times over. The sovereign nation of Iran, the world's fourth largest oil producer, has three times the population of Iraq and five times the size. Clearly, an attack on the country would be madness. This is true for many reasons, not the least of which is the vulnerability of our naval forces to cruise missile attack. In March 2007, after years of evading the issue, the U.S. Navy finally confirmed research that I had posted about this issue on the Internet as early as 2004.[72]

Pentagon officials acknowledged that despite six years of warnings from weapons testers, the U.S. Navy still had no effective defense against the latest Russian anti-ship missile, known in the West as the Sizzler.[73]Moscow manufactures advanced cruise missiles largely for export and aggressively markets them on the world market. The weapons are a cash-cow for Russia, and though the details are not known, Iran may well have acquired them in significant numbers. If so, this means that a U.S. attack on Iran would almost certainly provoke a counter-attack upon the U.S. Fifth Fleet on patrol in the Persian Gulf.

In a story carried by Bloomberg.com, Orville Hanson, who has evaluated weapons for the U.S. Navy for 38 years, described the Sizzler as a "carrier destroying" weapon. The missile is a sea skimmer. It flies about thirty feet above the ocean, initially at subsonic speeds. However, about ten nautical miles from its target, a rocket-propelled warhead separates and accelerates to three times the speed of sound. As the missile makes its final approach, it performs very high-speed defensive maneuvers, including sharp-angled dodges, which make it extremely difficult to track and intercept. Thomas Christie, the Navy's top weapons testing official, acknowledged to Bloomberg that, since 2001, he had received assurances that the Navy planned "to fully fund the development and production" of missiles that could replicate the Sizzler in order to learn how to defend against it. But, said Christie, "They haven't."

By March 2007, the Pentagon considered the threat so serious, according to an official budget document, that Deputy Secretary of Defense Gordon England gave the Navy just weeks to explain how it planned to counter the Russian-made missile. Charles McQueary, director of the Pentagon's weapons-testing office, warned that if no answer was forthcoming, he would block ship and weapons productions programs until the matter was addressed.[74] McQueary threatened to halt nearly $80 billion in new contracts, including Northrop-Grumman's planned start-up of a new $35.8 billion CVN-21 aircraft-carrier. Other defense contractors that would be affected included General Dynamics and Raytheon. This sober news should have prompted front-page headlines in the *New York Times* and *Washington Post*. But insofar as I know, apart from the lone report by Bloomberg.com, the U.S. media was strangely silent on the issue. Once again, the U.S. press failed to do its job.

A war with Iran would likely spin out of control and put the U.S. on a collision course with Russia and China, both of which are heavily invested in the country. China's surging economy depends on Iranian gas and oil. Moreover, China has become Washington's chief creditor — the result of Bush's unbridled deficit spending and the offshoring of U.S. industry. For its part, Russia still has a potent nuclear force, and one that is aimed at the United States. Madness, indeed. The truth is that Iran ought to be a U.S. friend and ally — not our foe.

NIE Exonerates Iran

As I write, the latest National Intelligence Estimate (NIE) was released on December 3, 2007, representing the collective judgement of all sixteen U.S. intelligence agencies.[75] It concluded that Iran abandoned all work on nuclear weapons in 2003, which — notice — coincides with the date of the Iranian peace offer already discussed. This strongly suggests that the Iranian offer was serious, not just posturing. Obviously, the timely release of the NIE dealt the neocons a temporary setback. In one fell swoop the U.S. intelligence community repudiated the Bush administration's main argument for bombing Iran's nuclear sites.

This may indicate that the U.S. power elite is deeply divided about Bush and is having second thoughts about U.S. military involvement in the Persian Gulf. At the very least, there appears to be growing dissatisfaction with Bush's style of U.S. imperialism. While this is good news and has slowed the drift toward a wider war, we should remember that the entire region, from Lebanon to Pakistan, remains a powder keg. The tense standoff is certain to continue as long as the White House belligerently spurns Tehran's peace overtures while maintaining U.S. occupation forces in Iraq and Afghanistan — on Iran's borders. The construction of numerous U.S. military bases inside Iraq, and a gigantic new U.S. embassy in Baghdad, which has been described as a self-contained fortress, surely indicates that the neocons have no plans for US withdrawal from the region. Does the U.S. leadership actually believe it can gain control over Iran's immense oil reserves? Will the U.S. go to war at the behest of Israel — again?

Need I remind the reader the disastrous quagmires in Iraq and Afghanistan, the looming crisis with Iran, the slumping U.S. dollar and economy, not to mention the skyrocketing price of gas at the pump, all resulted from the pivotal activities of September 11 and its mysterious white plane?

Endnotes

1. Clinton announced the new sanctions against Iran in a policy speech delivered in late April 1995 to the World Jewish Congress; Otis Pike, "Clinton gives impression Iran Policy is all politics," *Oregonian*, May 3, 1995.

2. Jane Perlez and Steve Levine, "U.S. Oilmen Chafing at Curbs on Iran," *New York Times*, August 9, 1998; also see S. Rob Sobhani, "President Clinton's Iran Option," *Caspian Crossroads Magazine*, Number 1, Winter 1995.

3. Ahmed Rashid, *Taliban*, Yale University Press, New Haven, 2000, p. 162.

4. Kenneth Pollack, *The Persian Puzzle*, Random House, New York, 2004, p. 343.

5. Michael Isikoff and Mark Hosenball, "Terror Watch: Haliburton's Deal with Iran," *Newsweek*, February 16, 2005.

6. Kenneth Pollack, op. cit., p. 40.

7. Highly recommended is Stephen Kinzer's, *All the Shah's Men*, John Wiley and Sons, Hoboken, 2003.

8. Ahmed Rashid, op. cit., p. 162.

9. Bin Laden enjoyed considerable influence in Saudi Arabia after the defeat of the Soviets in Afghanistan, due to his involvement with the Afghani resistance. However, a rupture with the royal family occurred after Saddam's 1990 invasion of Kuwait, when the Saudi king declined bin Laden's offer to employ Islamic fighters to repel the Iraqi army. Instead, the Saudi leader admitted U.S. military forces, which enraged bin Laden because the presence of foreign troops in the country was viewed as a defilement of the holy sites. Although bin Laden was placed under house arrest for a time, later he reportedly struck a deal with the Saudi government which allowed him to leave the country with most of his fortune, and to maintain contacts so long as he promised not to attack the royal family. For several years Bin Laden operated out of a base in Kartoum, Sudan, before moving to Afghanistan in June 1996. The amicable deal with the Saudi government would explain why bin Laden admitted Saudi intelligence chief Prince Turki to his hospital room in Dubai, just weeks before the 9/11 attack. Nafeez Mossadeq Ahmed, *The War on Truth*, Olive Bramch Press, Massachussetts, 2005, pp. 12-13.

10. Ahmed Rashid, op. cit., p. 74.

11. Kenneth Pollack, op. cit., p. 346; also see Stephen Zunes and Richard Falk, *Tinderbox*, Common Courage Press, Monroe, Maine, 2003, pp. 135-152.

12. Gareth Porter, "Burnt Offering," *The American Prospect*, May 21,2006.

13. Though some think it was bound for Hezbollah, in Lebanon.

14. Jimmy Carter, *Palestine: Peace, Not Apartheid*, Simon and Schuster, New York, 2006.

15. A dissection of the failed U.S. peace process is beyond the scope of this discussion. But see Stephen Zunes and Richard Falk, op. cit., pp. 119-135.

16. For a detailed discussion and sources, see Mark Gaffney, *Dimona: The Third Temple?* Amana Books, Brattleboro, 1989, p. 26.

17. "Sharon Moves to Center Stage," Report on Israeli Settlements in the Occupied Territories, Foundation for Middle East Peace, Vol. 11, No. 2, March-April 2001, p. 1.

18. Ze'ev Schiff and Ehud Ya'ari, *Israel's Lebanon War*, Simon and Schuster, New York, 1984, pp. 97-101.

19. For a discussion of the Kahan Commission's findings see Ze'ev Schiff and Ehud

Ya'ari, op. cit., p. 283.

20. Ellen Seigel, "After Nineteen Years: Sabra and Shatilla Remembered," *Middle East Policy*, December 2001. The Congressman was Charlie Wilson. See George Crile, *Charlie Wilson's War*, Atlantic Monthly Press, New York, 2003.

21. George W. Ball, *Error and Betrayal in Lebanon*, Foundation for Middle East Peace, 1984, p. 55.

22. Jewish Voice for Peace, December 8, 2004, posted at http://www.jewishvoiceforpeace.org/press/releases/release120804.html; also see Stephen Zunes, Richard Falk, op. cit., p. 109.

23. This is no exaggeration. In December 1987, a strongly worded anti-terrorism resolution came before the United Nations General Assembly. It condemned terrorism in the strongest terms and called upon governments to cooperate to put an end to it. Not surprisingly, the resolution passed by a near-unanimous vote. Only one country, Honduras, abstained, and only two others voted against it: the U.S. and Israel.

But why would the U.S., the land of the free and the home of the brave, reject a UN resolution that condemned terrorism? At first blush, the U.S. vote makes absolutely no sense.

The answer is that the UN resolution also included a paragraph which affirmed the fundamental right of people living under racist and colonial regimes, or foreign military occupation, to resist their oppressors, with the assistance of other states. In the 1980s President Reagan praised the Mujahedeen as "freedom fighters" for resisting the Soviet occupation of Afghanistan. Reagan even compared them to the founding fathers. But the U.S. was not prepared to afford the same right of self-defense to Palestinians resisting Israel's military occupation of the Arab West Bank. See Noam Chomsky, "The New War Against Terror," a talk recorded at the Technology and Cultural Forum at MIT, October 18, 2001, at http://www.chomsky.info/talks/20011018.htm.

24. For a thorough discussion and sources see Stephen Zunes and Richard Falk, op. cit., pp. 24-32.

25. A detailed look at PM Barak's "generous offer" shows that it was anything but. See John J. Mearsheimer and Stephen M. Walt, *The Israel Lobby*, Farrar, Straus, and Giroux, New York, 2007, pp. 103-107; also see Jimmy Carter's analysis in Jimmy Carter, op. cit., pp. 147-154.

26. For the text of the peace offer go to http://www.al-bab.com/arab/docs/league/peace02.htm.

27. John H. Richardson, "The secret history of the impending war with Iran that the White House doesn't want you to know." *Esquire*, November 2007.

28. Ibid.

29. Ibid.

30. Ibid.

31. Ibid.

32. Ibid.

33. U.S. Department of State, International Information Programs, "Bush Praises Powell's Message of 'Hope and Peace' to Mideast," April 18, 2002.

34. Glenn Kessler, "Scowcroft is Critical of Bush," *Washington Post*, October 16, 2004.

35. Ray McGovern, "Attacking Iran for Israel," www.InformationClearinghouse.info,

October 31, 2007.

36. John J. Mearsheimer and Stephen M. Walt, op. cit., pp. 204-228.

37. Jeffrey Steinberg, "In your guts, you know he's nuts," *Executive Intelligence Review*, August 18, 2006.

38. The quote is from Ron Suskind, *Price of Loyalty: George W. Bush, the White House, and the Education of Paul O'Neill*, Simon and Schuster, New York, 2004, p. 71.

39. Seymour Hersh, "The Syrian Bet," *The New Yorker*, July 28, 2003; also see. Seymour Hersh, *Chain of Command*, Harper Collins, New York, 2004, pp. 333-341.

40. Seymour Hersh, *Chain of Command*, p. 336.

41. Ibid.

42. Ibid., pp. 333-341.

43. John H. Richardson, op.cit.

44. Gareth Porter, "Burnt Offering," *The American Prospect*, May 21, 2006. Posted at http://www.prospect.org/cs/articles?articleId=11539.

45. Mearsheimer and Walt, op. cit., p. 293: "... the [Israel] lobby has struck up a close relationship with ... Pahlavi.... He is believed to have had personal meetings with both Sharon and [former Israeli PM Benjamin] Netanyahu, and he has extensive contacts with pro-Israel groups and individuals in the U.S.... Seemingly unaware that Pahlavi ... has little legitimacy in his homeland, pro-Israel groups have promoted his cause. In return, he makes it clear that if he were to come to power in Iran, he would make sure that his country has friendly relations with Israel."

46. Israel Shahak, *Open Secrets*, Pluto Press, London, 1997, pp. 54-61.

47. The concerns were valid. By 2004 Iran had perfected the Sahab-3B missile, which has a range of 2,000 km. This means that all of Israel is now within range of missile attack by Iran. In recent years, Iran also equipped the Sahab with an improved guidance system that employs global positioning. This improved the Sahab-3B's accuracy from 1-3 kilometers to 30-50 meters — a vast improvement. The days of the inaccurate Scud are gone forever. The trajectory of the Sahab-3B can also be altered in flight, making the missile difficult to take out with ABM systems. Moreover, the Sahab is fired from mobile launchers, which are extremely difficult to defend against. All of which means that if the U.S. and/or Israel attacks Iran's nuclear sites, the Iranians can respond by targeting Israel's Dimona nuclear complex, located in the Negev desert, possibly causing a Chernobyl type situation. Old reactors like the one at Dimona are dirty time-bombs waiting to go off. The destruction of the Dimona reactor would probably render large parts of Israel, perhaps the entire country, uninhabitable for thousands of years. Israel could escalate by nuking Iran. But the damage to Israel would already be done, and would be so great that Israel could never recover. The cradle of three religions would resemble the region around Chernobyl, i.e., a nuclear wasteland, poisoned by plutonium and a family of other highly radioactive nuclear by-products. Clearly, Israel was very foolish to develop nuclear weapons in the 1960s. The primary source for this note is www.globalsecurity.org

48. Kenneth Pollack, op. cit., pp. 255-265.

49. Mansour Farhang, "A Triangle of Realpolitik" *The Nation*, March 17, 2003.

50. Jonathan Wright, "Israeli Calls for 'Regime Change' in Iran, Syria"," Reuters, April 28, 2003, posted at http://www.reuters.com/newsArticle.jhtml?type=topNews&storyID=2643315.

51. Transcript, Vice President Cheney on Inauguration day: Don Imus interviews the

candidate he once poked fun on *Imus on MSNBC*, January 20, 2005. Posted at http://www.msnbc.msn.com/id/6847999/.

52. Brian Knowlton, "Nuclear-armed Iran risks 'World War III', Bush says," *International Herald Tribune*, October 17, 2007.

53. Uzi Mahnaimi and Sarah Baxter, "Revealed: Israel plans nuclear strike on Iran," *Sunday Times* (London), January 7, 2007.

54. "El Baradei denounces bomb Iran rhetoric," PressTV, September 8, 2007. posted at http://www.presstv.ir/detail.aspx?id=22255&sectionid=351020104.

55. Baruch Kimmerling, "Splitting paths," *Ha'aretz*, September 10, 2005. Posted at http://www.haaretz.com/hasen/pages/SHArt.jhtml?itemNo=632615.

56. For a thoroughgoing history of Israel's nuclear weapons program see my book, *Dimona: The Third Temple? The Story Behind the Vanunu Revelation*, Amana Books, Brattleboro, VT, 1989.

57. Graham Paterson, "Alan Greenspan claims Iraq war was really for oil," *Sunday Times* (London), September 16, 2007; Alan Greenspan, *The Age of Turbulence: Adventures in a New World*, Penguin, New York, 2007, p. 463.

58. Frank Rich, "And Now: 'Operation Iraqi Looting,'" *New York Times*, April 27, 2003. Also see Eleanor Robson, "The Collection Lies in Ruins, Objects from a Long Rich Past in Smithereens," *Guardian* (U.K.), April 14, 2003.

59. Robert Scheer, "It's U.S. Policy that's 'Untidy,'" *Los Angeles Times*, April 15, 2003.

60. Pratap Chatterjee and Oula Al Farawati, "To the Victors Go the Spoils of War: British Peroleum, Shell, and Chevron Win Iraqi Oil Contracts," CorpWatch.org, August 8, 2003; also see Rick Kelly, "Bush grants permanent legal immunity to U.S. corporations looting Iraqi oil," World Socialist Website, August 19, 2003.

61. Andrew E. Kramer, "Iraq, With U.S. Support, Voids a Russian Oil Contract," *New York Times*, November 4, 2007.

62. This is the view of James Petras and I see no reason to doubt it. James Petras, *The Power of Israel in the United States*, Clarity Press, Atlanta, 2006. p. 21.

63. Seymour Hersh, *The Price of Power: Kissinger in the Nixon White House*, Summit Books, 1983, pp. 216-222.

64. The plan was developed by STRATFOR, which claims to be a privately-owned intelligence agency; Aslam Khan, "U.S. plans to merge Iraq, Jordan after war," Center for Research on Globalization, September 29, 2002, posted at http://www.globalresearch.ca/articles/KHA209A.html.

65. Akiva Eldar, "Perles of wisdom for the Feithful," *Ha'aretz*, October 2, 2002.

66. In 1975, then-Secretary of State Henry Kissinger signed a memorandum of understanding (MoU) with Israel obligating the U.S. to ensure the security of Israel's oil reserves and energy supply in times of crisis. The U.S. also agreed to maintain a strategic oil reserve for Israel, even if it should entail domestic shortages. The estimated cost of the reserve to the U.S. taxpayer in 2002 dollars: $3 billion. The MoU is quietly renewed every five years.

67. Julie Stahl, "Israel, Jordan May Talk about Reviving Iraqi Oil Pipeline," CNS News. com, April 9, 2003.

68. Yahya Sadowski, "No war for Whose Oil?" *Le Monde Diplomatique*, April 2003.

69. George Tenet, *At the Center of the Storm. My Years at the CIA*, HarperCollins, New York, 2007, pp. 387, 426, 430.

70. The neocons also made the foolish mistake of hitching their star to Ahmed Chalabi, from the prominent Chalabi family of Iraq, who was to become the next prime minister. But Chalabi was a poor choice: a convicted embezzler and one of the least trusted men in Iraq.

71. Jo Freeman, "On the Fourth Anniversary of the Iraq Invasion Left and Right Agree: Get Out Now," Senior Web Women.com, March 2007, posted at http://www.senior-women.com/articles/freeman/articlesFreemanIraqFourth.html.

72. My research is still posted at http://www.informationclearinghouse.info/article8558.htm.

73. Tony Capaccio, "Navy Lacks Plan to Defend Against 'Sizzler' Missile," Bloomberg. com, March 23, 2007, posted at http://www.bloomberg.com/apps/news?pid=20601070 &sid=a5LkaU0wj714&refer=home#.

74. Ibid.

75. Ray Locker and Richard Willing, "U.S.: Iran Halted Nuke Work in 2003," *USA Today*, December 3, 2007.

— Conclusion —

What Is To Be Done?

The high likelihood that the World Trade Center was brought down with explosives on 9/11 is a staggering thought because of what this portends. But, given the evidence I have presented, it is one we must face squarely. This evidence leads us through a process of cold logic to the unthinkable. The shocking likelihood that Americans were involved in the mass murder of their fellow Americans poses a monstrous dilemma. How does one begin to wrap one's thoughts around something so diabolical? As humans we naturally resist such thoughts, which leave us shaken and speechless. Nonetheless, if we care about our families and our nation we must summon the courage to follow the trail of evidence, no matter where it leads. The likelihood that explosives were used can only mean that the events of 9/11 were planned down to the smallest detail. Difficult as this may be to accept, such a conclusion is inescapable.

Obviously, the likelihood that al Qaeda was responsible for planting the explosives is so remote as to be essentially zero, since foreign terrorists could never have gained access to the buildings for the time necessary to systematically plant the bombs. This can only mean that Americans were complicit in the attack. We must conclude that we are dealing with internal enemies who are every bit as ruthless and violent as al Qaeda is reputed to be. In fact, they are even more dangerous because their true identity has not yet been exposed. They live among us, a faceless adversary, operating in the shadows, under cover of national security jargon and black budgets. They also benefit from the witting or unwitting support of respected institutions, including the corporate media. Truth is anathema to their agenda.

If this unnerving and paranoid vision sounds familiar, it should. The nightmare I am describing did not originate with this writer but with George Orwell some 60 years ago. He was arguably the most important English writer of his generation, a smart and soulful fellow who had no patience for the inflationary hubris of the Western democracies. Orwell strongly opposed Soviet-style Communism, but he took no comfort in the self-proclaimed superiority of the West, because he saw through the rhetoric and correctly perceived that the same totalitarian tendencies that in those days afflicted Communism were also present in capitalism. Orwell worried more about the affinities than about the differences. He made it his business to shred the West's self-adulation with an uncompromising in-your-face style that, with hindsight, was prophetic. Orwell foresaw that East and West would one day converge, and, well, look around. He was largely correct.

The world we live in is increasingly the world he described. What is George H.W. Bush's New World Order if not a page out of *1984*? What is "Old Europe," Rumsfeld's slur upon France and Germany if not a textbook example of "Newspeak"? Recall, both nations aroused the ire of the neocons by opposing G.W. Bush's invasion of Iraq. The phrase "Old Europe" could have been lifted straight out of Orwell's dystopian novel, which was (and remains) so politically subversive that many governments have banned the book. Ironically, even as Orwell labored on his grim masterpiece, U.S. President Harry Truman was bringing the Central Intelligence Agency into existence. Although not widely known, it is relevant to this discussion that Truman lived to regret affixing his name to that perverse piece of legislation, i.e., the 1947 National Security Act.

His disclaimer, in the form of a letter, appeared on the op-ed page of the *Washington Post* exactly one month, to the day, after the murder of President John F. Kennedy in Dallas.[1] In his letter Truman warned that America's position as a free and open society was in danger as a result of the way the CIA had been functioning. Truman's letter appeared in an early edition of the Post but was promptly yanked — *it did not appear in later editions.*

Intense pressure was brought to bear on the editors to remove it. The fact that the U.S. president who fathered the CIA lived to regret his decision was of historic importance, and remains so. But, insofar as I am aware, there was no further mention of Truman's letter in the U.S. press. None of Truman's biographers mention it, for example.[2] I would wager that not one American in ten thousand is aware that Truman changed his mind about the CIA. Even as Truman's letter disappeared down an Orwellian memory hole, a very different public perception of the intelligence community was taking hold in America, with the CIA's active encouragement.

I refer to our collective infatuation with James Bond, the hard-loving British MI-6 agent with a license to kill, who always manages to land on his feet while saving the western world from real or imagined enemies. Every year or two, Hollywood cranks out another film in the sexed-up action series, perpetuating the glamorous mystique of 007. Politicians are presented as corrupt, and even engage in treachery. But it never fails, we can always count on the selfless intelligence agent to make the proper decision in the epic battle of right versus wrong. The message is romanticized and none too subtle. Even though phony, masses of us have internalized it, and many of us have no doubt come to believe it on some level.

In the real world, meanwhile, the ghost of Orwell stalks us. In his riveting 2006 testimony before the House Armed Services Committee, Lt. Col. Anthony Shaffer actually invoked the specter of Orwell as he recounted his own experience, and described how the weight of the Defense Intelligence Agency came down upon his head after he attempted to do his duty, by informing the 9/11 Commission about Mohamed Atta and Able Danger.[3] Do we dare to connect these dots?

In the opinion of this writer, we will continue to be haunted by Orwell until we shed our collective amnesia. I would argue that 9/11 was not a bolt out of the blue, but a logical development of Truman's monster. This is what happens when you create a vast intelligence community outside the framework of the Constitution. The idea that this same security establishment, including the U.S. military, were defeated on 9/11 by a ragtag bunch of jihadists using cell phones is absurd. The security "failures" were not failures at all, but merely appear that way to naive and uninformed Americans, the vast majority of whom know absolutely nothing about the CIA's long sponsorship of state terrorism and its equally-long history of staging covert operations.

I have already touched on this, but let us now consider the issue in broader historical terms. Although U.S. support for international terrorism is too vast a subject to summarize in a few words, certainly it has included the arming and training of Islamic fundamentalists before and during the Soviet occupation of Afghanistan, and, subsequently, the unapologetic use of al Qaeda mercenaries in the Balkans for the purpose of dismembering Yugoslavia. During the Bosnian war, the U.S. actively supported Muslim forces in their fight against the Serbs, and even allowed bin Laden's fighters to be airlifted into the region.[4]

In Kosovo the U.S. provided assistance to another bin Laden ally, the Kosovo Liberation Army, an extremist group with a known history of terrorism and links to the drug trade.[5] In the U.S. press they were portrayed as freedom fighters. The same pattern unfolded in Chechnya, which just happens to lie astride an oil pipeline strategically vital to Russia. No surprise that in 1999 the Russian Defense Minister publicly accused the U.S. of trying to weaken Russia by aiding the Chechen rebels.[6] The charge was probably correct. The Chechen rebel leaders reportedly trained at CIA-sponsored camps in Afghanistan and Pakistan. No doubt they also received generous U.S. arms and funding.[7] The CIA denied any involvement, but this should not surprise us. The CIA's longstanding policy in such cases is always to deny any involvement.

To be sure, Russian leaders also have blood on their hands. False flag operations are not the invention of the U.S. intelligence community. Early in 2000 the *Observer* (London) published photographic evidence linking the FSB, i.e., the Russian security service, to a series of widely reported bombings in Mother Russia. The bombings occurred in September 1999 and were originally attributed to Chechen rebels.[8] Two of the huge bombs went off in Moscow and killed some 300 innocent people. A third attack was averted by a stroke of dumb luck, when local police happened to catch FSB agents red-handed in the act of planting a bomb in the basement of a Moscow apartment that housed about 250 tenants. The live bomb was made of Hexagen, the same kind of explosive used in the previous blasts.

The evidence looked incriminating. Yet, the next day the agents were released when the FSB intervened in the case, announcing that its men had merely been conducting a practice drill. Does this sound familiar? The known facts in the case suggest that the Russian security establishment is not averse to staging covert false flag attacks of its own, though, so far, not on the grandiose scale of 9/11. But surely its motivation is the same. In this case Russian President Putin used the alleged terrorist attacks as justification to intervene militarily in the Caucasus. It would appear that the Russian people are no different from Americans. Like us, they are unenthusiastic about foreign military adventures and must be frightened into supporting them by the threat of "foreign terrorism." East or West, it is the same bogeyman.

Operation Gladio

The unpleasant truth is that U.S. intelligence agencies have a long and sordid history of collaborating with criminal, drug and terrorist elements. The pattern is worldwide and dates to at least World War II, when the U.S. Office of Naval Intelligence struck a deal with convicted drug boss Lucky Luciano, then incarcerated in a U.S. prison. Luciano was granted clemency and deported (along with many others of his ilk) to

Sicily to assist in the patriotic war against the Nazis.[9] Although Mussolini had nearly eliminated the Mafia, with U.S. support it thereafter staged a dramatic comeback.

After the conclusion of the war there was a curious realignment. Quite abruptly, the CIA ceased support for the communist partisans, who had fought bravely against the Nazis. Suddenly, the CIA began to collaborate with the former enemy: the Italian fascists!

The reason for the switch was to prevent a numerically superior united front of socialists and Communists from winning the Italian elections of 1948.[10] The CIA effort succeeded through a well-organized campaign of bribery, blackmail, character assassination, street thuggery, and murder. Thus began a pattern of social mayhem that would afflict Italian politics for nearly half a century. The CIA's cozy relationship with the Mafia also came home to America in the ready availability of Mafia-peddled narcotics on the streets of American cities. What this means, of course, is that we have sacrificed several generations of our own children upon the alter of national security — a false god, I would argue.

The facts in the Italian case were kept secret for many years, but finally became known in August 1990, thanks to the investigative work of a courageous Italian judge, Felice Casson, who found the proof, i.e., official documents, in the secret archives of the Italian government.[11] Casson turned over this evidence to a parliamentary commission, which then demanded an explanation from Italian Prime Minister Giulio Andreotti. The very next day Andreotti appeared before the commission and admitted that a clandestine security network had been operating inside Italy since World War II, run by NATO through the American CIA and British MI-6. The name of the rogue network was Operation Gladio. The word means "sword" in Italian and is the root of the word "gladiator."

The announcement touched off a political earthquake in Italy, as the nation came to grips with the shocking news that U.S. intelligence agencies had interfered in Italian democracy over a period of decades. Although many Italian officials denied any knowledge of Gladio, the Italian President Francesco Cossiga confirmed its existence, and even acknowledged that he personally helped launch the operation after World War II. Gladio had existed wholly outside the legal framework of constitutional government, with no accountability whatsoever, and had participated in extensive criminal activity. This included numerous mass bombings, kidnappings, and assassinations in Italy over many years, as well as the full spectrum of dirty tricks — the goal being to strike terror into the population and, thereby, to weaken the left-wing political parties. No fewer than 139 secret weapons caches were eventually uncovered in the country, buried in forests, meadows, even in churches and cemeteries.

The Italian case was not a fluke. In the fall of 1990 the scandal spread throughout Europe, as the full extent of the CIA network dribbled out.[12] A series of disclosures revealed that after World War II, the American CIA and British MI-6 had secretly organized a network similar to Gladio in every nation of western Europe. They were known as the "stay behind armies," and their purpose was to form the nucleus of a resistance movement in the event of a Soviet invasion of the continent. The paramilitary forces numbered in the thousands. Armed and trained by the CIA and MI-6, they were comprised mostly of conservatives and Catholics, but also included extremist groups, various right-wing elements and even, as we have seen, criminals involved in the drug trade. In Germany they included former members of the Nazi SS. Although the secret networks in each country were separately organized, NATO remained in overall control.

Some have since defended Gladio as honorable, but the fact is that the feared Soviet invasion never materialized, and the paramilitary forces were in many cases put to *other* uses. They are known to have participated in coup d'états in Greece and Turkey, as well as attempted coups in Italy and in France. In the latter case, the CIA strongly opposed French President Charles de Gaulle's decision to grant independence to the French colony of Algeria. The matter came to a head in 1958, when the CIA joined with reactionary elements of the French army in attempts to assassinate de Gaulle and overthrow his government. Outraged by this obvious infringement of French sovereignty, de Gaulle later pulled France out of NATO. Although the U.S. media never informed Americans about the actual reason, this explains why the U.S. military was forced to relocate NATO headquarters from Paris to Brussels, Belgium at the time.[13]

In November 1990, the European Union passed a strongly worded resolution condemning the U.S. for subverting European democracy. But of course, NATO denied any involvement, and only a handful of articles about Gladio have ever appeared in the U.S. press.[14] To the best of my knowledge, it has never been covered on U.S. television. As it happened, the Gladio scandal erupted in Europe on the day following Saddam Hussein's fateful invasion of Kuwait. Moreover, the further revelations about Gladio in the fall of 1990 coincided with the run-up to the first Gulf war.

At the time, U.S. media moguls surely reached a private understanding with the G.H.W. Bush White House, and agreed to scrub all mention of the scandal from the U.S. news. There was probably concern, for good reason, that the truth would undermine U.S. war planning, which was then picking up steam. The case is yet another shameful example of how the corporate media have kept the truth from the American people. No wonder that the average American has no awareness of the violent role that U.S. intelligence agencies have played in undermining democratic institutions around the world.

The facts surrounding Gladio decisively refute critics who charge that any sub-group of plotters within the U.S. government would never have been able to keep an extensive operation like 9/11 secret. Here in the case of Gladio was a much vaster conspiracy, one involving thousands of agents in different nations, yet it was kept secret from the people of Europe for 40 years, and remains largely unknown to Americans even to this day. Incidentally, the same pattern of criminal activity was repeated in South America during Operation Condor, which involved right-wing elements in Argentina, Chile, Paraguay, Brazil, and Uruguay.[15]

The Viet Nam War is yet another case. I would be remiss if I did not mention it, because, on a scale of terror, all of the above pales by comparison. Even today, no convincing reason has ever been given for the massive U.S. assault on Southeast Asia that started in the mid 1950s (by one estimate even before the conclusion of World War II[16]) and continued until 1975.[17] During this time, the U.S. dropped more tonnage of bombs on Southeast Asia than in all previous wars combined. Yet the final terms of the 1973 peace settlement were virtually the same as the agreement under discussion in Paris in the fall of 1968. The war would likely have ended at *that* time but for the treasonous subterfuge of Richard Nixon and Henry Kissinger. But that is another story.[18]

During the additional years of pointless warfare, the U.S. visited a holocaust upon the region. In the 1968 presidential campaign Nixon had promised an early (and honorable) conclusion to the war, but instead he escalated it in an attempt to bully North Viet Nam into surrendering. The only certain path to U.S. victory was to invade North Viet Nam and capture Hanoi. This was well within the reach of the U.S. military, but was off the table because it might have produced a nuclear confrontation with China and the U.S.S.R.[19] Such was the dilemma that U.S. war planners faced in Viet Nam. Nor have things changed in this respect. Given the renewal of the Cold War, we face the same dilemma today in the Persian Gulf, since a wider war with Iran would very likely escalate out of control, leading to the use of nuclear weapons.

Nixon's alternative to total victory was a massive escalation: the bombing of the Ho Chi Minh trail. But this never had a serious chance of bringing North Viet Nam to its knees. The carpet bombing of Laos and Cambodia, which Nixon and Kissinger kept secret from the U.S. Congress and the nation for three years, succeeded only in slaughtering an estimated 900,000-plus Laotians and Cambodians, mostly innocent farmers and villagers. By various estimates, another 2-3 million Vietnamese also died in the war. But no one knows the actual figure, because the U.S. military only kept track of U.S. fatalities. (Incidentally, the same policy is currently in effect in Iraq.)

But Viet Nam was not only a genocidal war, it was also a case of ecocide, i.e., a war against the earth. The U.S. military gets credit for destroying tens of thousands of square miles of precious tropical rain forest through carpet bombing and the use of chemical defoliants, whose toxic effects still plague the region — and U.S. veterans. I must emphasize: This litany of horrors is relevant to my topic of 9/11, because the Viet Nam debacle started as yet another CIA covert operation.[20] In fact, the CIA ran the war for many years, until President Johnson in 1965 ordered the major escalation after the Gulf of Tonkin incident, which, as we now also know, was itself a phony attack staged by the U.S. military and blamed on North Viet Nam.[21]

Even after Johnson escalated the war, CIA involvement continued on a high level. The agency's program of targeted assassinations, Operation Phoenix, gets credit for liquidating some 35,000 Vietnamese. Evidently the CIA compiled a list of names (based on who knows what?) and then went out and started killing people. The CIA also assisted in the overthrow of Cambodia's Prince Sihanouk in March 1970. This was followed by a U.S. invasion of Cambodia, plunging that country into a bloody civil war that culminated in the Pol Pot reign of terror.[22] For years, Sihanouk had pursued a policy of neutrality, but this was unacceptable to U.S. leaders fixated on the Cold War.

Have we Americans deceived ourselves about the source of terror? Do we have the courage to look in the mirror? Is it reasonable, any longer, to imagine that what happened in Europe, in South America and in Southeast Asia cannot also happen here at home? Francesco Cossiga, the former Italian president thinks it already has.

In November 2007, Cossiga told Italy's largest newspaper, *Corriere Della Sera,* that it is common knowledge among the European security agencies that 9/11 was an inside job — staged by the CIA with the assistance of the Israeli Mossad.[23] His bold assertion no doubt carried considerable weight with Europeans due to Cossiga's reputation as a political realist. As I have noted, he was personally involved in Gladio over many years. Several Google searches, however, failed to locate any mention of his explosive statement in the mainstream U.S. media. Evidently, the news lock-down in America continues.

During my recent trip to Washington D.C., to interview Ms. McNerney, I heard virtually the same story from the taxi driver who took me to the airport. It was an engaging conversation. He was a native of Kenya, site of the 1998 U.S. embassy bombing by al Qaeda. Although presently a U.S. citizen, the driver had maintained his African roots. He spoke perfect English, and, although he was not college-educated, I found him much better informed about world affairs than the average American. When our conversation turned to Bush and the war on terrorism, he matter-of-factly told me that in Kenya it is taken for granted that 9/11 was an inside job staged by elements of the U.S. military and intelligence community.

When Kenyan taxi drivers and former Italian heads of state are in agreement, should we not listen? What if they are speaking truth? If our leaders played any role in this heinous crime, they are no better than terrorists themselves, and if we fail to bring them to justice, we will probably inherit a future more horrible than we can imagine. Unpunished criminality among high officials can only lead to more of the same. In 1971, General Telford Taylor, who after World War II served as chief prosecuting counsel of Nazi war criminals at the Nuremberg trials, stated that if the principles established at Nuremberg were ever applied in the case of Viet Nam, a number of U.S. leaders and military men would swing from the gallows.[24]

As we know, of course, there was no such accounting, and, many years later, when the time came to select an individual of unimpeachable character to head up the 9/11 Commission, whom did G.W. Bush pick as his first choice? Why, none other than Henry Kissinger, the man most responsible, after Nixon, for the slaughter of millions in Southeast Asia. The deafening silence that this aroused suggests that America learned absolutely nothing from the Viet Nam experience. Why should we be surprised that history is repeating itself in Iraq and Afghanistan?

What will it be the next time? A nuclear strike on an American city? A mass attack with a chemical weapon or some human-engineered disease? Either way, the "terrorism" will be blamed on the scapegoat of the hour. Today of course this is Iran — the surest path to regional or even global thermonuclear war. If we care about our children, our communities, and our nation, we must face the facts. The unpleasant truth is that our nation and the world will never be secure until the conspirators who staged the 9/11 attack are brought to justice.

Toward that end, we must insist that Congress immediately launch a new and truly independent 9/11 investigation, one that is non-partisan, adequately funded, and empowered with the authority to subpoena witnesses and evidence. We need indictments. We also need clemency for whistleblowers, to encourage individuals with information to come forward.

We can draw strength from the knowledge that the events of 9/11, bad as they were, might have been even worse. It would appear that the plot against America fell short of complete "success." Had Flight 93 smashed into the Capitol building, with huge additional loss of life, including senior members of the House and Senate, the plotters might have achieved their ultimate objective: the suspension of the U.S. Constitution. In which case, we might today be living under martial law.

If we have the courage to face the frightening truth that our nation has descended into a swamp of corruption and evil, then perhaps it is not too late to salvage a future for ourselves and our children. If we fail, the events of 9/11 are likely to be repeated, but on a larger scale.

So long as freedom lives, we can choose to be the masters of our fate. In the coming days, let us choose well.

Endnotes

1. The following is an excerpt from former President Harry Truman's letter. It appeared on the op/ed page of the *Washington Post*, December 22, 1963:

> I think it has become necessary to take another look at the purpose and operations of our Central Intelligence Agency — CIA....

> For some time I have been disturbed by the way the CIA has been diverted from its original assignment. It has become an operational and at times a policy-making arm of the government. This has led to trouble and may have compounded our difficulties in several explosive areas....

> We have grown up as a nation, respected for our free institutions and for our ability to maintain a free and open society. There is something about the way the CIA has been functioning that is casting a shadow over our historic position and I feel that we need to correct it.

The letter was datelined Independence, Missouri, December 21. Incidentally, the National Security Act of 1947 was drafted by Clark Clifford, a Democrat, no doubt with considerable input from Wall Street.

2. This is according to Martin Schotz, who has been researching the matter since 1966. W. Martin Schotz, *History Will Not Absolve Us: Orwellian Control, Public Denial, and the Murder of John F. Kennedy*, Kurtz, Ulmer and DeLucia Press, Brookline, MA, 1996,

appendix VIII, p. 237.

3. Prepared statement of Anthony A. Shaffer, Lt. Col., U.S. Army Reserve, Senior Intelligence Officer, before the House Armed Services Committee, Wednesday February 15, 2006, full transcript posted at http://www.fas.org/irp/congress/2006_hr/021506shaffer.pdf.

4. Michel Chussudovsky, *America's War on Terrorism*, Global Research, Canada, 2005, pp. 41-42.

5. Ibid., p. 43-44.

6. "Russia accuses U.S. over Chechnya," *BBC News*, November 12, 1999.

7. Levon Sevunts, "Who's calling the shots? Chechen conflict finds Islamic roots in Afghanistan and Pakistan," *Gazette* (Montreal), Number 23, October 26, 1999.

8. John Sweeney, "Take Care, Tony, that man has blood in his hands," *Observer* (U.K.), March 12, 2000. Also see Helen Womack, "Russian agents 'blew up Moscow flats,'" *Independent* (U.K.), January 6, 2000.

9. Alexander Cockburn and Jeffrey St Clair, *Whiteout: The CIA, Drugs, and the Press*, New York, Verso, 1998, pp.115-141.

10. Wlliam Blum, *Killing Hope: U.S. Military and CIA Interventions Since World War* II, Common Courage Press, Monroe, ME, 1995, pp, 27-34.

11. Daniele Ganser, *NATO's Secret Armies. Operation Gladio and Terrorism in Western Europe*, Frank Cass, London, 2005.

12. Ibid.

13. Ibid.

14. My special thanks to Daniele Ganser for providing the following list of articles about operation Gladio in the U.S. press. You will notice that nothing has appeared in print since 1993. Clare Pedrick, "CIA organized secret army in Western Europe. Paramilitary Force created to resists Soviet Occupation," *Washington Post*, November 14, 1990; Steve Coll, "Everybody in Italy wants change. Talk is of revolution, but bombings raise question: At what price?" *Washington Post*, August 8, 1993; Clyde Haberman, "Italy discloses its web of Cold War Guerrillas," *New York Times*, November 16, 1990; George Black, "The Cold War's Devils were on both sides. The Soviets professed regret for past blood spilled. The West has as much to be sorry for," *Los Angeles Times*, November 29, 1990; No author specified, "Resistance trained at U.S. base. European network secretly prepared," *San Diego Union Tribune*, November 16, 1990; Daniel Singe, "The Gladiators," *The Nation*, December 10, 1990; Jonathan Kwitny, "The CIA's Secret Armies in Europe," *The Nation*, April 6, 1992.

15. Christopher Hitchens, *The Trial of Henry Kissinger*, Verso, New York, 2001, pp. 68-75.

16. L. Fletcher Prouty, *JFK: The CIA, Vietnam, and the Plot to Assassinate John F. Kennedy*, Birch Lane Press, New York, 1992, see chapter seven.

17. The official reason for U.S. involvement was the Dulles brothers' theory of falling dominos. The theory held that if South Viet Nam went Communist, the rest of Southeast Asia would soon follow. The theory is undermined by a number of facts. At the time, both Cambodia and Laos were committed to a policy of neutrality, a policy which Cambodian Prince Sihanouk actually succeeded in maintaining for many years, despite the fierce war in neighboring Viet Nam, intense pressure by the CIA, and intrusions by both the U.S. and the North Vietnamese into his territory. As for the Communist Khmer Rouge: the group was a minor insurgent group, with no chance of threatening Sihanouk's

rule, that is, until Nixon and Kissinger vastly escalated the U.S. bombing campaign in 1969 in an attempt to win the war. The U.S. dropped more ordnance on rural Cambodia than in all of World War II, essentially destroying the country. This and the CIA-supported coup in 1970 that toppled Sihanouk became a self-fulfilling prophecy. It was only after the fabric of Cambodian society had been destroyed that the Khmer Rouge gained in strength.

Moreover, the CIA's characterization of the Laotian Pathet Lao as a communist guerilla group simply because they were committed to land reform is dubious. The Pathet Lao described themselves as ultra-nationalist, not Communist. For a discussion of the domino theory see Noam Chomsky, *The Chomsky Reader*, Pantheon Books, New York, 1987, pp. 227-255. Also see William Blum, *Killing Hope*, Common Courage Press, Monroe, Maine, 1995, see chapters 20 and 21.

18. Christopher Hitchens, op. cit., see chapter 1.

19. I was convinced by Fletcher Prouty's analysis. Fletcher Prouty, op. cit., pp. 239-241.

20. Ibid. See also James W. Douglass, *JFK and the Unspeakable: Why He Died and Why It Matters*, Orbis Books, Maryknoll, NY, 2008.

21. If former CIA agent Ray McGovern is correct, many of us have failed to comprehend the actual role of the CIA. In his 2006 book, *Nemesis: The Last Days of the American Republic*, Japan scholar Chalmers Johnson presented the standard view that the CIA serves the wishes of the president. However, according to McGovern, at the time of the Gulf of Tonkin incident, the CIA actually deceived President Johnson by allowing allowing Johnson to believe that the USS *Maddox* had come under attack by North Viet Nam, even though the intelligence indicated otherwise. Who, then, was the CIA serving if not the president? Given that the Viet Nam War was a pointless exercise that benefitted no one apart from a small group of Wall Street bankers and industrialists, perhaps Mike Ruppert and Fletcher Prouty are correct that the CIA was created to serve these narrow interests. I, for one, was shocked to learn that most of the early CIA directors were Wall Street lawyers, not military specialists; also see Ray McGovern, "CIA, Iran and the Gulf of Tonkin," Consortiumnews,com, January 12, 2008, posted at http://www.consortium-news.com/2008/011108a.html.

22. Seymour Hersh presents plenty of evidence for the CIA's involvement in Cambodia in *The Price of Power*, though he also seems not to have realized the implications. Seymour Hersh, *The Price of Power*, Summit Books, New York, 1983, see chapter 15. Also see William Blum, op. cit., chapters 20 and 21.

23. Paul Joseph Watson, "Ex-Italian President: Intel Agencies Know 9/11 An Inside Job. Man who set up Operation Gladio tells Italy's largest newspaper attacks were run by CIA, Mossad," Prison Planet.com, December 4, 2007.

24. Christopher Hitchens, op. cit, p. 25.

— Epilogue —

Apparently, More Official Lies
NIST Releases WTC-7 Report — Finally

On August 21, 2008 the National Institute of Standards and Technology (NIST) unveiled its long-awaited report on the collapse of WTC-7. The announcement was made by NIST's lead investigator, Dr. Shyam Sunder, during a press conference at NIST headquarters in Gaithersburg, Maryland. The report can be downloaded from the NIST website.[1]

After studying the collapse of WTC-7 for five years, NIST scientists came to the surprising conclusion that ordinary office fires caused an entirely new phenomenon in the history of structural design. According to Dr. Sunder, the collapse of Building Seven was due to thermal expansion of lateral steel beams. This somehow occurred at temperatures of only 570°F and caused the floor beams to detach from one of the building's main core columns (#79), leaving the column unsupported. It then buckled, triggering what Dr. Sunder referred to as a "progressive collapse."

In a press statement Sunder reviewed some of NIST's key findings, then fielded questions.[2]

He acknowledged that the nearby collapse of WTC-1 caused only minor damage to WTC-7, which was unrelated to its collapse. Sunder also acknowledged that the substantial amount of diesel fuel stored in the lower section of WTC-7 was not a factor.

These latter admissions were startling, because this ruled out two of the main arguments previously advanced by FEMA in 2002, and by Sunder himself, for the strange collapse of WTC-7 at 5:20 P.M. on the afternoon of September 11——arguments that saw wide circulation, in part, because of a much-cited article in *Popular Mechanics* magazine.

Sunder mentioned that NIST examined alternative collapse scenarios, including the use of explosives, but ruled out incendiary devices because, according to Sunder, their use would have produced loud explosions that would have been heard throughout the neighborhood. Sunder claimed there were no such reports. However, NIST has also previously admitted that it failed to test for telltale residues of explosives.

Immediately following the NIST press conference, Architects and Engineers for 9/11 Truth staged a press conference of their own. Architect Richard Gage, a former quality-control administrator for Underwriter Labs named Kevin Ryan, Kamal Obeid and Michael Donly, both structural engineers, and Anthony Szamboti, a mechanical engineer, all took strong issue with NIST's proposed collapse model. They pointed out that for numerous reasons NIST faced a formidable challenge trying to explain the collapse of WTC-7 as the result of ordinary office fires.

Here are some of their salient points:

1. During a meeting of the NIST advisory committee, NIST scientists admitted that the fuel loading in WTC-7 was similar to that of the nearby twin towers. This means that, on average, the offices in WTC-7 had only enough fuel (i.e., carpets, desks, office dividers, etc.) to support a fire for about 20 minutes.

What is more, the steel columns in WTC-7 were protected with foam insulation rated to give at least 3 hours of fire protection. The steel beams in the floors had similar protection rated for 2 hours. How then did a 20-minute office fire cause thermal expansion and the catastrophic collapse claimed by NIST?

2. The pre-collapse photos and videos of WTC-7 do not support NIST's claim that the fires were extensive. On the contrary, the videos/photos strongly suggest that the fires were rather minor and were limited to a few floors.

3. NIST acknowledged in its 2005 report that WTC-1 and WTC-2 survived the plane impacts, despite serious structural damage, and would have stood indefinitely, despite the fires, but for the fact that the impacts jarred loose the SFRM foam and wallboard insulation. This allegedly exposed the steel columns and floor trusses to the fires.

Yet, in the case of WTC-7 there was no plane crash, hence, no violent impact to jar loose the insulation. For this reason all of the insulation in WTC-7 was 100% intact. The steel in the building was fully protected throughout and, therefore, would have been unaffected by ordinary office fires lasting no more than about 20 minutes. Thus, the fires had nothing to do with the total, symmetrical and near-free-fall collapse of this 47-story steel skyscraper.

4. Nor do existing videos of the WTC-7 collapse on 9/11 support NIST's collapse model. As Gage and the independent structural engineers pointed out, a progressive collapse means that failing columns will, in turn, pull over other nearby columns. This implies a gradual and asymmetric process, starting at the point of initiation, which then spreads throughout the structure. Yet, the videos clearly show that the collapse of WTC-7 happened everywhere all at once. The collapse was total, symmetric, and occurred at nearly free-fall speed.

Also, a fire-caused collapse would have followed the path of least resistance, that is, would have occurred in a random and haphazard manner. Yet, the video evidence clearly shows that WTC-7 did just the opposite. As it collapsed it followed the path of greatest resistance. The steel framework of the building, comprising 40,000 tons of inter-connected structural columns and beams, literally fell through itself into its own footprint, and did so as if there were no resistance whatsoever.

Gage and the independent engineers insisted that to explain this, many columns had to fail simultaneously. This strongly suggested that the collapse was, in fact, a controlled demolition.

Numerous eyewitness accounts and a considerable amount of physical evidence also supports this conclusion. Multiple witnesses reported seeing molten steel in the wreckage. Witnesses also reported the subsequent removal of huge lumps of slag from the bottom of the pile. Several different investigations found tiny spheres of iron in the dust. Moreover, thermal imaging from above conducted by NASA five days after 9/11 recorded surface temperatures of 1,376°F. No doubt, temperatures under the pile were much higher. All of this evidence confirms that something melted steel in WTC-7. Yet ordinary office fires obviously could not do this. Taken together, the evidence points to the use of high-temperature explosives.

5. Gage also disputed NIST's assertion that there were no reports of explosions. In his statement Gage identified numerous witnesses who heard explosions before WTC-7 collapsed. Some even

reported hearing a countdown. Ryan also pointed out that incendiary thermite and thermate explosions are not nearly as loud as blasts caused by more common explosives, such as C-4 and RDX.

6. The panelists announced the discovery of yet another chemical residue, namely, 1,3-diphenylpropane, which the Environmental Protection Agency (EPA) found in the WTC dust in great abundance. Its presence evidently puzzled EPA scientists, who had never seen it before. As it turns out, 1,3-diphenylpropane is the signature chemical residue for an especially explosive sol-gel form of nano-thermite, which can be applied to a steel surface like spray paint.

Ryan followed with another no less stunning disclosure. He claimed that nano-thermites were developed in the late 1990s by U.S. government scientists at the Lawrence Livermore National Laboratory. Moreover, highly placed individuals at NIST were also involved in the research. According to Ryan, these incendiary explosives were even tested at the NIST laboratories, for which reason NIST cannot plead ignorance.[3]

7. Finally, NIST admits that it had very few steel samples from WTC-7 to study because most of the steel had already been hauled away by the time NIST launched its investigation. So how did NIST scientists conduct their study? On what did they base their conclusions? Once again, it appears that NIST relied heavily on computer modeling.

In short, NIST's claim that the collapse of WTC-7 was caused by an ordinary office fire is extremely dubious — about as improbable as a chimpanzee scaling Mt. Everest. But the panelists acknowledged that it will take some time to analyze NIST's voluminous report. Gage and Ryan promised a detailed response by September 15, 2008.[4]

Endnotes

1. At http://www.nist.gov/public_affairs/r...wtc082108.html.

2. At http://wtc.nist.gov/media/opening_remarks_082108.html.

3. For more information see Kevin Ryan, "The Top Ten Connections Between NIST and Nano-Thermites," July 2008, posted at http://www.journalof911studies.com/.

4. The response will be posted at http://www.ae911truth.org/.

— Afterword —

You All Just Haven't Talked About It

By John Farmer

In mid-2006, I began a research project on 9/11, designed to allay my own personal concerns after becoming aware of Operations Mongoose[1] and Northwoods[2] developed by our own military-intelligence network, and advocating staged civilian attacks on United States citizens for the purpose of provoking a military conflict with Cuba in the 1960s. Although these plans were rejected by President John Kennedy at the time, it did concern me that anyone in our own government would seriously entertain such a plan.

In light of the events of September 11, 2001, which bear a striking similarity in concept to those earlier plans, I opted to focus on the events at the Pentagon on that day. It seemed to me that if the military-intelligence community were involved somehow, then that attack would have to be very controlled, to limit the damage and casualties to the nation's command-and-control facilities and personnel.

I am a process control engineer with a working knowledge of measurement systems. Prior to returning to college in the early '90s to study mathematics, I had spent 12 years in law enforcement, and then more in operations management while I attended college. I thus have extensive experience working with witnesses and security surveillance systems, which has served me well in this project. Moreover, due to my engineering and mathematics background, I set a high standard for any conclusions regarding the evidence set being considered. Before I consider an aspect of the event to be "historical," it must be supported by empirical (objective) data and backed up by non-empirical (subjective) data.

Regarding the Pentagon attack, most of the eyewitness statements are either ambiguous or tainted by the effects of time, and the empirical data is extremely limited. The flight recorder data released by the National Transportation Safety Board has significant irregularities at the end-of-flight,[3] the Federal Bureau of Investigation is refusing to release the information in their possession (videos and photographs), and the Federal Aviation Administration has been reluctant to release the air traffic control recordings and radar data for the Washington, D.C. area for that date. This is an issue of a Federal Court Complaint that is currently pending, which readers are welcome to examine for details.[4]

In early-2007, I was able to obtain the VHS tape sent to Scott Bingham by the FBI as a result of his Federal Court Complaint, which represents the security system video from a Citgo service station confiscated by them on September 11, 2001.[5] The Citgo station (also known as the Barracks K) is located on South Joyce Road, between the Navy Annex (to the west) and the Pentagon (slightly north of east), at the intersection with Columbia Pike. To the north of the station is Arlington National Cemetery, and an elevated section of I-395 is to the south.

According to the overwhelming majority of eyewitnesses, American Airlines Flight 77 (AAL 77) flew down from the south side of the Navy Annex (on Columbia Pike), passed within a few hundred feet of the Citgo station at between 100-150 feet above ground level (agl), then struck the tops of five light poles along Route 27 at Columbia Pike, and impacted the Pentagon at an approximate heading of 60 degrees from north. This path corresponds to the damage pattern observed within the Pentagon.

After receiving the VHS tape, I took it to an independent video firm here in Memphis, TN to have it evaluated and reproduced in DVD format. The original VHS was then shipped back to Bingham along with a DVD copy for his use. At that time, no significant issues with the VHS tape (symptoms of alteration) were found by either me[6] or the technician processing it. The security video consists of seven multiplexed camera frames captured on a single VHS tape such that all seven are visible at once.[7] The image is split into four quadrants, with three cameras (two cash registers and north-west pump bay) occupying a single quadrant each and the remaining one split into four additional quadrants.

Of these smaller quadrants, three are occupied by camera footage (south-east pump bay, the south entrance and sales floor area), with the other filled with a composite of the complete multiplexed image. This final quadrant appears to have at one time been occupied by an additional exterior camera, most likely the one on the south-west corner facing the ice machine (labeled "ICE"). Each of these camera views is refreshed according to multiplexer sequence in a set order of nine steps. Most refresh once every nine steps, while a few refresh twice. Since the frame rate of the video is 30 frames per second, this means that most of the cameras are refreshed at a rate of 3.33 frames per second. This frame rate for each camera will become critical as I continue the discussion.

I went to such lengths to obtain the best copy of the video available was due to a mathematical model and 3D study of the flight path in the vicinity of the Citgo done by me suggested that AAL 77 should have cast a rather significant shadow on the ground as it passed by the station to the south-east. Since the position of the sun is known, the range of possibilities is easily determined. In reviewing the YouTube version of the video, I ad determined that there was a high probability (80%) that camera number 5 (south-east pumps) would have captured a portion of that shadow. Unfortunately, due to the small size of the camera view on the video and the poor quality of the YouTube version, I could not locate the shadow. On the copy received from Bingham, the shadow was located in the area predicted at 09:40:35 (video time), confirming the 60-degree heading flight path discussed earlier.

Over the months ahead, I continued evaluating the video, especially the five seconds following the first appearance of the shadow. I examined every flash of light or other optical event fully, until I was satisfied with the source of each.

One such flash is seen in camera number 3 from a car as it begins to pull away at 09:40:38. With the known location of the sun (113 degrees azimuth, 32 degrees altitude) and a little trigonometry, it is relatively easy to demonstrate what is happening: the bumper or back window is passing through a point where the incidence angle is exactly right between the sun and the camera to reflect sunlight into it. This can be confirmed by watching other cars passing through the same area before and after this time, and seeing the same flash of light from them.

Another event is a dimming of light observed in camera number 7 at 09:40:39. A careful study of the way the window is shaped reveals that there is an area where the camera is in line with the impact point at the Pentagon through the end of the bay window located on that side of the station. After the flash of the fireball is glimpsed in camera number 5, camera number 7 responds to that event with an auto-iris adjustment.

As in this case, most such anomalies could be associated with real-world events, with the exception of one.

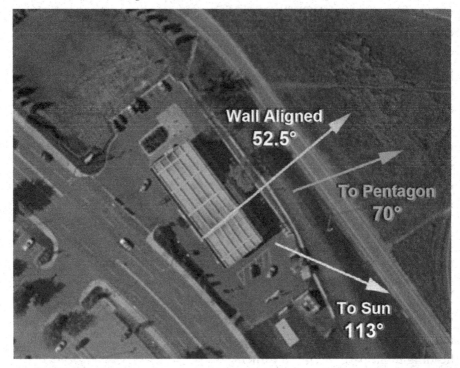

At 09:40:37, in camera number 2 (south entrance), a light begins to appear on the rough concrete wall to the left of the entrance door. This is a shadowed area which immediately rules out light from the Pentagon fireball. If that were the light source (a diffuse source), then it would illuminate the entire area under the canopy, not just a spot on a concrete wall. Moreover, the gas pumps are a very reflective white metallic surface which would have much more readily shown signs of the fireball light than a rough concrete wall, and there is no evidence of that at all. This particular camera is one of the few that refreshes twice in the multiplexer sequence. So it captures a frame, and then 1/30th of a second later captures another. Then it must sequence through 7 frames before refreshing again. This is fortunate, since the first captured frame gives for that instant a definitive clue to the origin of the source.

The point of impact at the Pentagon relative to the Citgo was located 70 degrees from north. The wall upon which the light is cast is perpendicular to the south-east wall which is aligned 52.5 degrees from north. This is significant, since in the very first frame, the light is shining over the top of the corner of that wall, which is slightly raised from the roof line. Based upon photographs and measurements I took on a trip to the location in April of 2007, the light is originating from a point to the left (less than 52.5 degrees from north) and approximately 3 degrees upward relative to horizontal. In simpler terms, the light source is airborne at a relatively low altitude and at least 17-18 degrees north of the impact area!

This lighting effect can be observed associated with a car pulling away and turning on the same camera at 09:41:45. As the car turns, sunlight strikes it and is reflected onto the wall directly above the south entrance door. This illustrates on a smaller scale the most likely source of the lighting effect under discussion. The light is consistent with sunlight reflecting off of a highly reflective airborne surface, but the altitude would have to be extremely low in an area north-east of the station.

The Citgo is at roughly 50 feet elevation and the spot on the wall in the first frame is around 10 feet above that. Using that as a starting point, with the 3 degree angle elevation, at the distance to Route 27 on a straight-line (1500 feet), the source would be at an altitude of 140 feet. The elevation at this point is approximately 35 feet, so the source would be just above 100 feet agl.

Further, this line-of-sight does not cross the flight path of AAL 77! Since light on the wall is relatively contained and localized, the light source would have to be reasonably close to the station. Quite frankly, none of this made sense to me with the information available at the time.

Visible on the video are a number of individuals outside the station at the time of the event who should have had a good view of what happened, so I began searching for any statements in the public domain from any of them. An Italian researcher (who wishes to remain off the record) alerted me to the work of a group called the Citizen Investigation Team (CIT).[8] CIT had gone to the area and interviewed a number of individuals, among them Defense Protective Services (DPS) SGT William Lagasse, who is seen on camera number 3 fueling his car. SGT Lagasse asserts that he saw the plane pass by the north-west canopy, corresponding to a flight path that would account for a reflective body in the right path to explain the lighting observed on the wall.

SGT Lagasse, however, describes the plane as doing a yaw maneuver that significantly changed its alignment. He asserts that the jet wash from the plane knocked him into his car as it passed to his left. Then he states that it approached the Pentagon at another angle consistent with the actual flight path of AAL 77. In other words, when he first saw it, he was looking at the right side of it, and then at the end he was looking at the left side of it (as he would have a plane passing the south side of the station where the shadow is visible on the ground). So his account is inconclusive.

Another of the CIT witnesses was DPS SGT Chadwick Brooks. SGT Brooks was parked across Joyce Road from the station in a parking lot. He asserts that his car was parked in a northerly orientation and that he saw the plane fly past the north side of the station exactly as described by SGT Lagasse. However, he gave a 2001 audio interview wherein he asserted that he observed the plane clip the light poles along the flight path south of the station.[9] There is an oddity in his earlier statement which may help explain this inconsistency. He asserts that he is watching a plane to his left: "I just happened to just look up to my left up in the air and just seen a plane." Yet he feels intense vibration and noise coming from behind his vehicle: "A few seconds shortly after that I heard a, what seemed to be a tractor-trailer or something coming behind me, well felt like it was coming behind me, and I looked again but this time I looked and I didn't see a truck." If the orientation of his vehicle is as he claims, then that would be consistent with the southern approach.

Unexplained is the plane he is watching at the same time, which he does not associate with the noise because after looking behind, "I looked to my left and low and behold I noticed that the plane was just going awfully low." When he gets out of his vehicle that is when he sees the, "very awful sight because, at the very end the plane literally just full throttle and to this day I don't know if I was able to watch it or not, but just to be frozen in time like that, and to see that plane literally just clip the lamp poles."

When SGT Brooks and SGT Lagasse's accounts are taken objectively, they both seem to be describing two different plane approaches simultaneously.[10] One is consistent with the southern path (Lagasse's yaw and Brook's vibration) and the other with a northern approach. If SGT Brooks 2001 account is taken literally, then he was hearing a plane pass behind him while watching another plane to his left. This scenario simply did not make sense, since the only other airplane known to be in the area was a C-130 from Andrews AFB that did not arrive in the vicinity until at least a minute later. The closest approach it made was to the west of the Navy Annex, where it veered away to the west. This plane was never lower than 2200 feet according to the 84 RADES radar data, confirmed by an amateur video which captured its turn.[11]

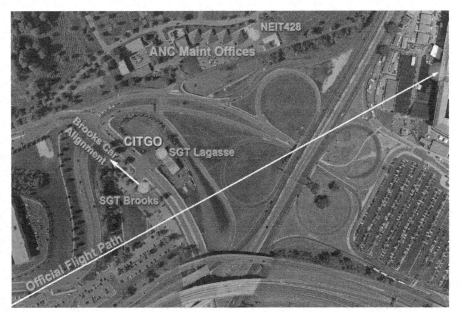

There was one public domain eyewitness statement that I hoped would perhaps shed some light on the situation. A *Pittsburgh Post-Gazette* article[12] dated 12/20/2001 reported that the Army Center for Military History (CMH) was conducting a historical project to record as many eyewitness accounts as possible for historical purposes. Among these were interviews with Arlington National Cemetery (ANC) employees who were located to the north of the Citgo station. Among these, one reported "a mysterious second plane was circling the area when the first one attacked the Pentagon." In late 2007, I filed a Freedom of Information Request for a number of the interviews conducted by CMH.

Across Columbia Pike from the station are the ANC maintenance offices and shops. A number of ANC employees were eyewitnesses to the event from this area, and those I have seen thus far describe AAL 77's fate and the C-130 approach later. At the far corner of this area, closest to the Pentagon, is a warehouse facility. This is an important location, because it is almost directly in the line of sight for the light source that had puzzled me for over a year. If any people could have seen anything to explain it, they would be located there. On May 21, 2008, I received the CMH statements from the employees located there, collected in April 2002. Among them was an interview (NEIT 428), which includes the following:[13]

Well, when we came out of the warehouse we heard this boom, you know, this big explosion. And we, all we could see was the smoke and the heat. We could feel the heat. And it was so intense that after that happened, we looked up in the sky and there was another plane. So, you know, so we panicked. So we started running, you know. So I just dropped on the ground. The plane was so low we were thinking it was going to do the same thing, but the plane made a turn and went in the opposite direction.

My first impression was that this must surely be the C-130 known to arrive in the area a minute or so later. However, the altitude of that plane was relatively high, and it seemed unusual that they would duck for cover in response to it.[14] The interviewer fortunately asked a follow-up question regarding the altitude. Answer: "It was low enough that it could touch the building, the warehouse. It was close."

The witness continues asserting that it was close enough to see the pilot through the window and that it looked like a large commercial plane. The full interview is 17 pages and worth a complete reading, eg.,

All I know is it was a big plane. It was a big plane and I could see the pilot. It was just so quick. So I'm assuming that it was one of our planes because it didn't go into the building. It just made a turn, you know.

The witnesses at the ANC claim the plane turned back to the left towards the Washington, D.C. area. Mark Gaffney[15] and "Pinnacle" have documented a plane that approached the White House from the Washington Monument area, which was photographed by Linda Brookhart as it turned over the White House towards the Capitol Building. Further, Peter Jennings reported a plane over the White House at 09:41, 2 ½ minutes after the Pentagon event official time of 09:38. So is the plane witnessed by the Citgo and ANC witnesses the same plane? Without more definitive evidence regarding the direction the plane left the area, it is difficult to say.

There are also a number of ambiguous statements by people who seem to have associated the plane over D.C. with the Pentagon attack. "My Team Leader came in to say as he was coming in to the building, he saw a 757 flying in a peculiar location roughly over the Mall. (We now know that was the 757 that hit the Pentagon as it did circle downtown DC, supposedly looking for a target, possibly the Whitehouse [*sic*] which is not as easy to pick out from the air as the Capitol or the Pentagon, before heading west again, then turning east for its final run at the Pentagon.)"[16]

With witness statements like these, it is clear that the 911 Commission failed in its job to fully explain to the American public exactly what happened at the Pentagon on September 11, 2001. As the ANC employee put it, "… a whole lot of people out here seen what I seen, but you all just haven't talked about it."

Endnotes

1. At http://en.wikipedia.org/wiki/Cuban_Project.
2. At http://en.wikipedia.org/wiki/Operation_Northwoods.
3. At http://aal77.com/ntsb/Final%20Analysis%20of%20NTSB%20Fight%2Data%20 Recorder%20Freedom%20of%20Inform.pdf.
4. At At http://aal77.com/foia_complaint/08cv02051_complaint.pdf.
5. At http://www.flight77.info/.
6. At http://aal77.com/citgo/citgo_video_overview.pdf.
7. At http://aal77.com/citgo/citgo.wmv.
8. At http://www.thepentacon.com/.
9. At http://memory.loc.gov/service/afc/afc2001015/sr/sr335a01.mp3.
10. At http://aal77.com/citgo/Citgo%20Update.pdf. My article also discusses testimony of another witness that I deem less reliable.
11. At http://aal77.com/movies/pentagon.i395.smoke.c130.mov.
12. At http://archive.southcoasttoday.com/daily/12-01/12-20-01/a02wn018.htm.
13. At http://aal77.com/cmh_foia/neit428.pdf.
14. The witness confirmed that "… the military plane came afterwards," see http://www. thepentacon.com/northsideflyover.htm.
15. Mark Gaffney, "The 9/11 Mystery Plane," at http://www.jimmarrs.com/news. php?recordnumber=453.
16. At http://forums.techguy.org/random-discussion/72752-hunt-boeing.html.

Appendix

DEPARTMENT OF THE AIR FORCE
WASHINGTON, DC

Office of the Secretary

RECEIVED IN PASADENA

NOV - 8 2006

CONGRESSMAN ADAM B. SCHIFF

November 8, 2006

The Honorable Adam B. Schiff
United States Representative
35 S. Raymond Avenue, Suite 205
Pasadena CA 91105

Dear Mr. Schiff

This is in reply to your inquiry on behalf of   regarding his request for
information relating to an unidentified aircraft that may have been in restricted airspace near the
White House on September 11, 2001, between the hours of 9:30-10:30 a.m.

Air Force officials have no knowledge of the aircraft in question. We suggest
follow-up with his request for information through the Federal Aviation Administration.

We trust this information is helpful.

Sincerely

Karen L. Cook

KAREN L. COOK, Lt Col, USAF
Deputy Chief, Congressional Inquiry Division
Office of Legislative Liaison

NOV-08-2006 08:12AM   FAX:Pentagon   ID:CONG. ADAM SCHIFF   PAGE:001 R=94%

Letter to Congressman Adam Schiff (D-CA) from the US Air Force denying any knowledge
of the E-4B fly-over of the White House on 9/11.

U.S. Department
of Transportation
**Federal Aviation
Administration**

Assistant Administrator for Regions
and Center Operations
800 Independence Ave., SW.
Washington, DC 20591

MAY 2 4 2007

The Honorable Adam B. Schiff
Member, United States House
of Representatives
87 North Raymond Avenue, Suite 800
Pasadena, CA 91103

Dear Congressman Schiff:

Thank you for your letter of May 2, 2007 to the Federal Aviation Administration (FAA) on behalf of your constituent, ███████████████████ made a Freedom of Information Act (FOIA) request to the FAA on June 19, 2006 for records identifying an aircraft seen flying over the White House on September 11, 2001 and for records showing an aircraft flying over the White House on that date. On February 6, 2007 the FAA answered the FOIA request with a "no records" response.

On February 9, 2007 ████████████ an administrative appeal of the "no records" determination. My office is currently processing ███████ FOIA appeal; and I will respond directly to him as required by the agency's FOIA regulations.

Sincerely,

Ruth Leverenz
Assistant Administrator for Regions
and Center Operations

Enclosure
Transmitted Correspondence

cc: Washington Office

Letter to Congressman Adam Schiff (D-CA) from the FAA refusing his FOIA request for information about the E-4B fly-over, on the basis of "no records."

301

DEPARTMENT OF HOMELAND SECURITY
UNITED STATES SECRET SERVICE
WASHINGTON, D.C. 20223

Freedom of Information and Privacy Acts Branch
245 Murray Drive
Building 410
Washington, D.C. 20223

MAY 1 5

File Number: 20070158

Dear Requester:

Reference is made to your Freedom of Information/Privacy Acts request originally received by the United States Secret Service on February 27, 2007, for information pertaining to records of the observation by Secret Service personnel of an aircraft flying near the White House or circling above it on September 11, 2001, between 9:30am and 10:00am.

A review of the Secret Service's systems of records indicated that there are no records or documents pertaining to your request in Secret Service files. Enclosed is a copy of your original request.

If you disagree with our determination, you have the right of administrative appeal within 35 days by writing to Freedom of Information Appeal, Deputy Director, U. S. Secret Service, 245 Murray Drive, Building 410, Washington, D.C. 20223. If you choose to file an administrative appeal, please explain the basis of your appeal and reference the case number listed above.

Sincerely,

Kathy J. Lyerly
Special Agent In Charge
Freedom of Information &
Privacy Acts Officer

Enclosure: Copy of Original Request

Letter to "Pinnacle" from the Secret Service denying his FOIA request for information about the E-4B fly-over, on the basis of "no records."

302

**U.S. Department
of Transportation
Federal Aviation
Administration**

Memorandum

Subject: **INFORMATION**: Partial Transcript;   Date: September 20, 2001
Aircraft Accident; AAL77; Washington,
DC; September 11, 2001

From: Support Specialist, Washington ATCT   Reply to
Attn. of:

To: Aircraft Accident File ZDC-ARTCC-212

This transcription covers the Washington National Tower TYSON
Departure Control Position for the time period from September 11,
2001, 1325 UTC to September 11, 2001, 1348 UTC.

Agencies Making Transmissions   Abbreviations

Washington Tower TYSON/FLUKY Position   TYSON
Baltimore Approach Control   BWI
Andrews Tower   ADW
ZDC Linden Sector   LND
USAF/SWORD31   SWORD31
CACTUS85   AWE85
USAF/BOBCAT14   BCAT14
USAF/BOBCAT17   BCAT17
COLGAN5981   CJC5981

I hereby certify that the following is a true transcription of
the recorded conversations pertaining to the subject aircraft
accident involving AAL77:

Robert F. Smoak

FAA Document from 9/11 released on June 11, 2008. Notice the reference to a USAF plane
identified by its call sign SWORD31.

303

Original 9/16/01
TR

Washington National Tower
TYSON Departure Sector
9/11/01

Timeline of Events For:

WORD31	H/B742/R	ADW DEPARTURE
BOBCT14	T2/P	DOVER DEPARTURE
BOBCT17	T2/P	DOVER DEPARTURE
GOFER06	T/C130/I	ADW DEPARTURE

13:23:57   **WORD31** released off of Andrews.

13:27:06   **WORD31** issued maintain 3000.

13:27:57   **WORD31** issued maintain 4000.

13:29:39   **GOFER06** released off Andrews.

13:30:07   **WORD31** issued maintain 15000.

13:30:38   **WORD31** issued heading 190.

13:31:31   **BOBCT14** issued heading 210, maintain FL230.

13:32:05   **WORD31** issued heading 360.

13:32:16   **BOBCT17** issued heading 210, maintaining 17000.

13:32:47   **BOBCT17** requested direct Linden VOR.

13:33:45   Dulles Approach advised TYSON of a fast moving primary target currently 10 west of DCA.

13:34:14   **BOBCT17** told direct LDN denied, maintain FL210.

13:34:32   **BOBCT17** reissued heading 210, maintain FL210.

13:34:33   **GOFER06** told radar contact, maintain 3000.

13:34:56   **BOBCT17** reissued heading 210, maintain FL210.

13:35:04   **BOBCT14** issued heading 245, vector for MOL VOR.

13:35:11   **BOBCT14** issued frequency change to ZDC MOL sector.

13:35:14   **GOFER06** issued maintain 4000.

13:35:30   **WORD31** issued join J149 and resume own navigation.

13:35:40   **WORD31** issued maintain 17000 and contact Dulles Departure.

13:36:16   **GOFER06** issued traffic, eleven o'clock, 5 miles northbound, fast moving, type and altitude unknown.

13:36:22   **GOFER06** advises traffic in sight at twelve o'clock.

FAA timeline document from 9/11 released on June 11, 2008. The top entry indicates that WORD31 was released for departure from Andrews AFB at 9:23:57 A.M. EDT (13:23:57 universal time). GOFER06 was released for take off at 9:29:39 A.M. (13:29:39 universal time).

Appendix

13:36:26	TYSON asked **GOFER06** the unknown aircraft type.
13:36:29	**GOFER06** advised it looked like a B757.
13:36:30	TYSON asked **GOFER06** what is the estimated altitude of the traffic.
13:36:34	**GOFER06** responded with "low altitude".
13:36:51	**GOFER06** states the traffic is still in a descent and rolling out northeast bound.
13:37:09	**GOFER06** instructed to turn right and follow the aircraft.
13:37:13	**GOFER06** instructed to turn right heading 080, in order to follow the aircraft.
13:38:00	**GOFER06** advised aircraft was down just northwest of DCA.
13:38:09	**GOFER06** instructed to maintain 2000.
13:38:26	**GOFER06** advised aircraft crashed into the Pentagon.
13:38:47	**GOFER06** instructed to fly heading 270 and maintain 3000.
13:38:52	**GOFER06** requested to circle the Pentagon on the turn to heading 270.
13:39:00	TYSON approved the request.
13:39:08	**GOFER06** advised to move to the west on heading 270.
13:39:16	**GOFER06** acknowledged and states aircraft impacted the west side of the Pentagon.
13:39:53	**BOBCT17** issued heading 260.
13:40:40	**GOFER06** instructed to maintain 11000 and heading 330.

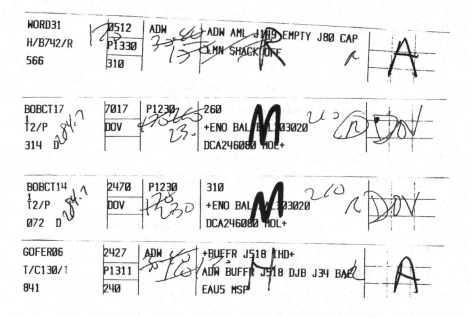

Flight progress strips from 9/11 released by the FAA on June 11, 2008. The top strip indicates that WORD31 (previously identified as SWORD31) was a Boeing 747-200 (B742) and departed from Andrews AFB (ADW) bound for Offutt AFB (OFF). The bottom strip refers to the C-130 departure (call sign: GOFER06).

mus$2 H(		B	↓	N/P			✓ 1402
PG/ H		V		⚓	2 N ADW ·· W32		1355
VEN 22 G3				LV			1359
LT RP2 H		B					1349
VENUS77 H/B747/I 365	0310 2124 P1345 330	ADW	ADW OFF RH VFR/25				1345
VM306 BE20/G 795	4761 P1330 150 140	NSF IK	+DAILY V33 V286 STEIN+ NSF DAILY V33 HCM NGU 125.65 HD HA		✓ N 1339		
GOFER06 T/C130/I 841	2427 P1311 240	ADW IL	+BUFFR J518 IHD+ ADW BUFFR J518 DJB J34 BAE XY EAU5 MSP		v N v 1333 U		
N9302N PH2		B	T4	VKX			1332
N9302E H 10CE		V	TO	DCA			1332
N9302N PA28		YR2	WVKX			1328	

Flight progress strips from 9/11 released by the FAA on July 25, 2008. The 5th strip from the top tells us that VENUS77, a Boeing 747, took off from Andrews AFB (ADW) at 9:45 A.M. EDT (13:45 universal time) bound for Offutt AFB (OFF). The type of plane and destination strongly suggest that this was also an E-4B. Notice the change in its M3 transponder code, from 2124 to 0310. The 4th strip from the bottom refers to the C-130, which left Andrews AFB at 9:33 A.M. EDT (13:33 universal time). This is a close fit with the RADES radar data.

307

ADW TRACON 09/11/01 9m						

VM306	4/61	NSF	+DAILY V33 V286 STEIN+			
BE20/G	P1330		NSF DAILY V33 HCM NGU			
795	150					

ADW TRACON 09/11/01 9m

ADW TRACON 09/11/01 9m

TROUT99	5632	KADW	+POLLA V312 OOD J42 RBV+			
H/C135/Q	P1110		KADW POLLA V312 OOD•••LHBP			
538	290		OICAO HUL/N0461F330 CAR•••		1108	

| *N3042M* | | | | | | |
| *P4l2* | | *V* | *11* | *120.75* | *1120* | *—* |

WORD31	56/2	A1114	IFR *30*	*LF*		
B/B742/1	TR1XY					*1128*
512	UCA		ADW ONAOC RTS/ALTS MA•••			

| *N34565* | | | | | | |
| *C177* | | *V* | *25* | *CGS* | *1131* | |

VM444	2125	NSF	+POLLA V312 PALEO V44 SIE+			
BE20/G	P1120		NSF PALEO V44 SIE J121 HTO			
960	210		GON		1141	

VV691	5613	NSF	+POLLA V312 PALEO V44 SIE+			
GLF3/G	P1050		NSF PALEO V44 SIE•••GON			
678	290		OFRC		1044	

Flight progress strips from 9/11 released by the FAA on July 25, 2008. The 4th strip from the bottom indicates that WORD31, a Boeing 747-200, arrived at Andrews AFB (ADW) at 7:28 A.M. EDT (11:28 universal time) on the morning of September 11, 2001. Here, the acronym NAOC tells us that this USAF plane was an E-4B.

VVTP1	5526	ADW	ADW OTT V33 WHINO NHK		*N*
T38/P	P1250		*7R 050 30*		
284	30		*348.725*		*1251*
VVTP 12	*0305*		*20*		
T38		*V*		*CI*	*I* *12 51*
	N 329 68				
N99510	*0307*		*15 ↑25*	*58*	*R 18.2*
C172	*35*	*V*			
VENUS22	461/	ADW	ADW FLUKY DCA246 PAUKI MOL		
T/GLF3/R	P1300		V290 NATTS LWB		
879	160		ODU+45 LWB AD		
N 7NF		*V*	*14*		*1320*
N 9302N	*0306*	*V*	*29*	*RC*	*I* *1323*
P4 28					
WORD31	0512	ADW	ADW AML J149 EMPTY J80 CAP		
H/B742/R	P1330		LMN SHACK OFF		
566	310				*1325*
VV7N309	5676	NSF	+CSN V140 MOL+		
BE20/I	P1330		NSF CSN J48 ODF DOB MGE		
620	200				
GOFER06	242/	ADW	+BUFFR J518 IHD+		
T/C130/I	P1311		ADW BUFFR J518 DJB J34 BAE		
841	240		EAU5 MSP		*1330*

Flight progress strips from 9/11 released by the FAA on July 25, 2008. The 3rd strip from the bottom indicates that WORD31, which we have identified as an E-4B, took off from Andrews AFB (ADW) bound for Offutt AFB (OFF) at 9:25 A.M. EDT (13:25 universal time). This is a close fit with the RADES radar data indicating that the plane left at 9:26 A.M. EDT. The bottom strip indicates that the C-130 (GOFER06) took off at 9:30 A.M.. EDT (13:30 universal time).

BULLY1	4631	ADW	+DAILY V33 COLIN+			
3/F16/R	P1200		DCNG6---ADW WHINO***R5314		12 34	
057	160		O PHELPS MOA CONCURRENT***			
VVIP12	5335	A1231	IFR K30 20	*LO*	*I*	
T38/P	NHK				12 35	
431	011		ADW ⊕0 0+15			
Skyfox Helo			*V* 8	⊕		1139
DECEE50	7046	ADW	+FLUKY DCA246 PAUKI MOL+			
B/C141/E	P1500		ADW FLUKY PAUKI MOL***HAR			
398	200		O AIR REFUELING WITH SL***			
MUSO4 H1			*B*	*ADW*		*1414*
VEN22 GLF5			*30 V*	*LV*		*1347*
MUS2 H1			*B*	*ADW*		*1413*
BULLY2	5302	A1407	IFR	*RtB*		*1418*
F16/R	OTT					
252	ADW		ADW			
VENUS77	2124	ADW	ADW OFF			
H/B747/1	P1345					
365	330					
N12501 C172	0304		*V*	2.5 *FDK* ⊠	(*125.65*)	*1239*

Flight progress strips from 9/11 released by the FAA on July 25, 2008. The 2nd strip from the bottom tells us that VENUS77 was a Boeing 747 and flew from Andrews AFB (ADW) to Offutt AFB (OFF).

Index

Symbols